An Introduction to
Rural Settlement Planning

An Introduction to
Rural Settlement Planning

PAUL J. CLOKE

METHUEN
London and New York

First published in 1983 by
Methuen & Co. Ltd
11 New Fetter Lane, London EC4P 4EE

Published in the USA by
Methuen & Co.
in association with Methuen, Inc.
733 Third Avenue, New York, NY 10017

Printed in Great Britain at the University Press, Cambridge.

British Library Cataloguing in Publication Data

Cloke, Paul J.
  An introduction to rural settlement planning.
  1. Regional planning—Great Britain
  I. Title
  711'.58   HT166
  ISBN 0–416–73800–1 Pbk

Library of Congress Cataloging in Publication Data

Cloke, Paul J.
  An introduction to rural settlement planning.
  Bibliography: p.
  Includes index.
  1. Rural development—Great Britain.
  2. Regional planning—Great Britain. I. Title.
  HN400.C6C57 1983   307'.14'0941   82–20859
  ISBN 0–416–73800–1 (pbk.)

Contents

List of figures

List of tables

Acknowledgements

The author and publishers would like to thank the following for their kind permission to reproduce copyright material:

Pergamon Press Ltd for figures 1.1 and 8.3
The Editor of *Regional Studies* and Cambridge University Press for figure 2.1
Norfolk County Council for figure 2.2
Her Majesty's Stationery Office (Crown Copyright reserved) for figure 2.3
The Association of County Councils for figures 2.4 and 8.1
Geo Abstracts Ltd for figures 2.6 and 11.3
Architectural Press Ltd for figure 2.7
Edward Arnold (Publishers) Ltd for figures 3.2 and 3.3
Macmillan, London and Basingstoke, for figure 3.4
Methuen & Co. Ltd for figure 3.5
Lincolnshire County Council for figure 5.1
Exeter City Council for figure 5.2
Andrew Blowers for figure 5.3
Gwent County Council for figures 6.1 and 6.6
Northumberland County Council for figure 6.2
Cumbria County Council for figure 6.3
Devon County Council for figures 6.5 and 11.1
I.M. Gilder and B.P. McLaughlin for figure 7.2
Berkshire County Council for figure 7.3
David & Charles (Holdings) Ltd for figure 8.2
George Allen & Unwin (Publishers) Ltd for figures 9.1 and 9.2
Martin Robertson & Co. Ltd for figure 9.3
Department of the Environment (Crown Copyright reserved) for figure 9.4
Huntingdon District Council for figure 10.1
Buckinghamshire County Council for figures 10.2 and 10.3
South Herefordshire District Council for figure 10.4
East Hertfordshire District Council for figure 10.5
Caradon District Council for figure 11.2
Geo Abstracts Ltd for figure 11.3
South Pembrokeshire District Council for figure 11.4
Wates Ltd, Builders and Contractors, for figure 11.5
H. Butcher, I. Cole and A. Glen for figure 12.1

Preface

This book has arisen from the teaching of rural geography and planning to undergraduates and postgraduates in Lampeter. Attempts to emphasize the applied nature of rural geographical study have encountered several problems stemming from the use of far-flung and multi-disciplinary source material, the analysis and integration of which has only gradually evolved into the body of more widely relevant information which is presented here. This evolutionary process has been greatly assisted by the participants in the 'Problems of the Modern Countryside' and 'Applied Rural Geography' courses at Lampeter, and many of the ideas in this book are the product of healthily disrespectful discussion which has occurred within these courses. To all such participants I offer my thanks.

The logistics of book-writing are closely related to the technical expertise and assistance offered by many individuals whose contribution far exceeds the call of duty. In this context I am indebted to the Lampeter powerhouse of Maureen Hunwicks and Margaret Jones, whose unenviable task it has been to type the manuscript and give spelling lessons; Trevor Harris, whose carto-graphic and photographic skills are evident; and Connie Gdula and John Griffiths. I have also benefited from the rarified intellectual atmosphere sponsored by the *Young Turks* especially Dave and Noreen Kay, Rob Young, Mick Griffiths, Chris Park (now sadly departed to the frozen North), Gareth Edwards and Ali and Nicki Donald. In addition I should also thank Alan Rogers and Ken Willis for their most useful comments on the manuscript.

1981 has been an auspicious year in the Cloke household, with the birth of Elizabeth Joy, the completion of this book, and the richly deserved success of Tottenham Hotspur's long awaited FA Cup victory. Throughout these personal peaks, and the troughs which have separated them, the overwhelming patience and support of my wife, Viv, has been a crucial factor. Apart from the practical help she has given at every stage of the preparation of this book, her understanding during periods of recluse study has been a real blessing, and for her mere thanks are totally inadequate.

P.J.C.
Lampeter, December 1981

Guide to reading

In its attempt to present a comprehensive and detailed analysis of rural settlement planning, this book has inevitably assumed a scale that will appear daunting to some of its potential readers. Moreover, it claims to be an *introduction* to this subject area (and therefore includes basic information vital for an introductory understanding) while at the same time presenting specific and sometimes intricate debate on particular aspects of rural areas and the planning process. This dual role also indicates that some parts of the book offer material that might be more or less useful to the individual reader depending on his or her requirements and approach. For these reasons some readers might welcome a skeleton for the book so that particular levels and areas of material become more easily accessible.

A basic description of what has been happening in rural areas since 1947 is provided by chapters 2, 5.3 and 12. Similar background material on the British planning system can be gleaned from chapter 4 (in terms of legislation) and chapter 8 (which gives detail of how planning operates in the rural context). For readers wishing to build on existing knowledge of these matters, several more detailed themes may be pursued in the book, including:

1 A review of *published plans* covering rural areas (chapters 5, pp. 89–102, and 6, pp. 144–63, cover county-level plans, and chapter 10 looks at the local level);
2 Discussion of *how these plans came about* (particularly chapter 3, and chapters 4, pp. 79–85, and 7, pp. 191–6);
3 The *implemenation* of rural settlement planning (chapters 8, pp. 201–23, and 9);
4 The *outcomes* of rural settlement planning (chapters 7 and 11 and chapters 5, pp. 102–13, and 10, pp. 286–9);
5 The *evaluation of policy and generation of alternatives* (chapters 7 and 12).

The book as a whole attempts to provide a structured and comprehensive treatment of the main themes connected with rural settlement planning. It has been carefully ordered to provide a *background* of socio-economic trends, prevailing theories and government legislation (chapters 1–4), followed by an account of *county-level* rural settlement planning (chapters 5–7). Only then does it delve into the detailed workings of rural resource allocation (chapters 8–11), and finally offers some thoughts on the future of rural communities and planning needs. At each stage, specific referencing offers the reader the opportunity to pursue individual issues, but the aim has been to maintain overall continuity and structure.

ONE

Introduction

Rural planning has come of age. For too long, it has been branded the 'poor relation' of the more favoured urban aspects of town and country planning, which have been allowed to dominate the morale and image (both internal and external) of the rural branch of planning. It is certainly true that planning attention in the latter half of this century has been focused upon matters of urban blight, deprivation and renewal, while the social and economic problems of the countryside have received only half-hearted and unconsolidated consideration. It is equally important that the campaign for an equitable share of planning resources for rural environments should not be permitted to lapse into an acceptance of the current imbalanced state. However, the time has come to discard the use of this underemphasis as the major focus for rural planning, and to develop new cynosures which are more in keeping with the progressive and seminal needs of modern-day countryside problems.

Discernible progress has been achieved in rural planning over the last half century, as is witnessed by the excellent reviews successively assembled by Green (1971), Woodruffe (1976), Davidson and Wibberley (1977) and Gilg (1978). Equivalent summaries have been slower to materialize outside Britain, a notable exception being Lassey's (1977) treatise on countryside planning in North America. What emerges from this accumulation of information is that rural planning has been gradually transformed from a young art in the 1940s and 1950s into a developing political, social and economic science in the 1980s. Thirty years of land-use planning in the countryside, marked by the three distinct stages of the development plans, their reviews, and, more latterly, the structure plans, have proffered a wealth of experience in how and how not to impose management techniques on the allocation of rural resources. Concomitantly, there has been an upsurge of interest in rural planning both on the part of the general public and within the planning and education professions. An increased level of media exposure has led to a heightened awareness of rural problems, and 'rural' courses in geography, planning and other related disciplines are proving to be extremely popular in universities and polytechnics.

Within this overall development of rural planning, the specific study and practice of rural settlement planning has loomed large. During the post-war period, the planning of villages and towns in countryside areas has been subjected to a range of administrative, methodological, technical and political pressures and problems, the interaction of which has moulded rural settlement planning into its current state. Indeed, there is at present a lively debate amongst planning professionals and academics concerning the whole future of rural settlement planning. The whole political question of what management mechanisms are required to deal best with problems of the dying village at one extreme, and the booming suburban town at the other, is both current and pressing.

An illustration of the evolving nature of rural settlement planning may be gained from a contrast of orthodox and heterodox presentations of the planning system as seen in countryside areas. Figure 1.1 can perhaps be seen to represent a view of the system from the inside looking out. The adoption of a systems approach to planning, pioneered by McLoughlin (1969) and Chadwick (1971) has generated a series of standardized and generally accepted stages of the planning process, progressing from social goals, information retrieval and problem-analysis via various forms of plan-making to policy implementation and finally reality. Batty's (1979) version (figure 1.1) expresses planning as a cyclic process of science and design but essentially marks the current tide-mark of the orthodox modelling of planning by stages. Rural settlement planning has, until recently, been characterized by a loose adherence to this rather traditional genre.

Figure 1.1 The orthodox view of planning (inside looking out)

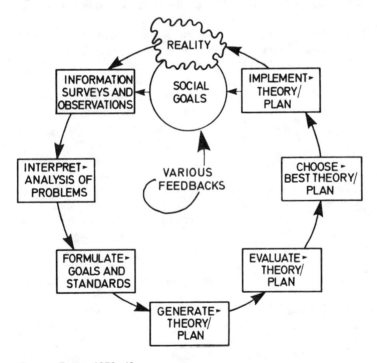

Source: Batty, 1979, 42

By contrast, a more heterodox view of the planning system is suggested in figure 1.2 which highlights more accurately the specific areas of guidance, influence and decision-making which shape rural settlement planning as it actually happens. The model is not designed to be a sceptical rejection of the orthodox *per se*, but rather a realignment from emphasis on stages to emphasis on causal factors, sparked by a view from outside of the rural planning system looking in. This would appear to be an equally valid approach with which to isolate the fundamental issues of rural settlement planning. The model is also useful because it can be applied both to the formal planning process and to wider systems of resource allocation and decision-making from which rural outcomes emerge. Figure 1.2 suggests a scheme of three *overt* and easily recognizable stages. These are linked by two *obscure* stages about which less is known but which fashion the following overt stages in the system.

Figure 1.2 The heterodox view of planning (outside looking in)

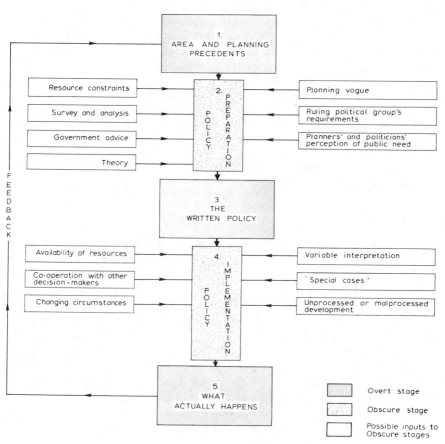

Area and planning precedents

The starting point for the generation of settlement planning policy in rural Britain has tended to be an assessment of previous policy, areal strategy and resource allocation, rather than the more utopian ideal of formulating social goals. Planning pragmatism will usually dictate that many entrenched policy dicta are to some extent honoured in successive plan considerations. At the local scale, this might mean that outstanding residential planning permissions will be the first input into the decision as to where additional housing will be permitted within a new plan period. Very few such permissions have been revoked in order to give new policy emphases a clean sheet to work from. On a more strategic level, those rural centres where growth in services and facilities has been encouraged during a previous regime are likely to receive continued development on the basis of the life-style opportunities already nurtured within these specific locations.

To recognize this transfer of commitment from one plan period to another is not necessarily to condone it as a basis for addressing contemporary rural problems through the allocation of resources. Indeed, it does appear that an acceptance of this 'trend' or 'inertia' planning is not only hindering the adoption of more radical policy solutions but is also ensuring that these less conventional approaches to problem solving will become increasingly difficult and expensive to transpose onto the deeply rooted established system of distribution. For example, a persistent strategy of concentrating services and facilities into rural growth centres will endow the alternative option of dispersing resources amongst the lower levels of the settlement hierarchy with an ever more extravagant image in the eyes of decision-makers and the agents of policy implementation. It may well be that rural settlement planning will only become more successful by allowing a clear statement of social goals to override all previous considerations, but it is important to note that at present these precedents do exist, are recognizable, and form an important limiting factor on subsequent policy preparation.

Policy preparation

The actual preparation of rural settlement planning policy consists of the interplay between several different variables. Of these, some are measurable and explicitly acknowledged in the resulting written policy, but others are intangible and act as covert influences on subsequent events. Some of these variables are listed in figure 1.2. For example, a major restricting factor on the scope with which alternative policies may be considered is the availability of financial resources for positive planning initiatives. All too often in the post-war period, planners have been compelled to resort to negative planning techniques and strategies of contraction simply because more positive policy options were barred by lack of finance at local, county and national levels. In this climate, planning alternatives are usually discussed in a framework of resource reallocation rather than resource increase.

Given this monetary straight-jacket, other tangible inputs to planning policy may be recognized. Survey and analysis techniques are of obvious importance to an assessment of trends and requirements in the area concerned. In the past, these surveys were preoccupied with demographic forecasts of in-migration or depopulation but more recently the housing, employment, transport and service requirements of existing populations have become increasingly emphasized, as has the need for public participation. In addition the influence of government advice (either by legislation or recommendation) is a crucial and definitive source of guidance in the policy presentation stage, while the impact of socio-economic, spatial or political theory is also relevant although less easy to monitor.

Alongside these easily recognizable factors, several surreptitious forces are also at work. For example, planners are often influenced by a certain vogue or strategic fashion in their assessment of alternative policy options. This may be partially underpinned by current government advice or theoretical leanings, but the diffusion of ideas from conferences and meetings is also important in the establishment of broadly favoured planning concepts. Another causal factor in the emergence of a particular policy direction is the political dogma (or at least the leanings) of the group controlling the planning and other committees of local authorities. This group can dictate the take-up rate of any permissive legislation from central government, and can also impose its own stamp on the overall planning strategy emanating from the policy preparation process. Finally, there is the question of how the various needs of rural areas are perceived and evaluated by both politicians and planners. Pocock and Hudson (1978, 134) stress that 'planners as a social group possess environmental images that may differ from those whom they seek to influence or those who are affected by resource allocation'. The different images of rural need perceived by these three groups are yet other elements in the policy-preparation equation.

The written policy

The result of these various interactions during policy preparation is some form of documented statement of policy in different degrees of detail. The written policy acts as a fulcrum for the rural settlement planning process. It serves as a forum for agreement between conflicting political and professional elements who held opposing views during the preparatory planning manoeuvres. In effect, such 'agreement' is largely equivalent to the reasonings of the dominant political and administrative parties. The draft written policy allows for feedback on a 'finished' policy from individuals and groups within society, and the adopted statement is designed to give the public a clear and reasoned account of the nature and justification of policy decisions. Also pivoting on the written policy are the opportunities for a clear interpretation of agreed policy as documented in the official planning reports – an interpretation that will be used by prospective developers as well as planners – and the possibility for the ministry concerned to ensure that individual planning areas do not stray too far from the prescribed rulings of central government.

With all these roles to play, the importance of policy statements should not be underrated, but at the same time it should be remembered that the content of the written policy is totally dependent on the machinations of the plan preparation stage. Furthermore the nature of planning policy will be manipulated and altered during the implementation stage and so while the written policy statement is a useful indicator of the broad characteristics of planning programmes, it is the individual planning decision at ground level which will most accurately reflect the success achieved by rural settlement planning in the fulfilment of its objectives. Culpability for the fact that written policy and actual decisions often exhibit signs of generic breakdown may be attributed to the process of policy implementation.

Policy implementation

The implementation of agreed rural settlement policy is the most clouded area of the planning process. Several explanations may be advanced as to why policy and action are often different, and some of these are reproduced in figure 1.2. For example, the inability to translate policy to ground-level decisions may be due to a restricted availability or even absence of particular resources in the right place at the right time. The idea of resources here should be viewed in its widest context so as to include such items as suitable parcels of land, manpower and developers who are sympathetic to planning objectives, as well as the more obvious financial considerations. Further complications arise from the fact that these resources are rarely under the immediate control of the planners themselves, meaning that policy implementation is consequent on the degree of co-operation achieved by planning authorities with other local authority departments (e.g. housing and education), national resource authorities (e.g. water and electricity), national public corporations (such as the Post Office) and the entire gamut of private sector individuals, groups and corporations who are concerned with the provision of life-style requirements in rural areas. Such co-operation is a complex logistic and (more important) political operation, particularly in a rural context where circumstances are continually changing and flexible planning approaches are required to serve these dynamic needs. Thus planners are faced with the difficult duality of requiring both rigid long-term proposals to ensure the concurrence of resource allocation by different organizations, and flexible short-term policies which are able to accommodate the changing nature of the settlements and communities which are to be planned. Policy implementation is easily hindered by this dilemma.

Other factors are also at work in the implementation process. For example, there will be considerable variation in the interpretation of written policy statements according to the motives of the interpreter. The translation of often abstract policy wording into active meaning will be different between planner and politician, economist and conservationist, developer and protester. Any such variation is extenuated in the numerous 'special cases' requiring decisions by planners. Certain applications may not conform with established policy but will receive the backing of planning authorities as 'one-off' developments in special circumstances. The special case phenomenon can equally be used to prevent the progress of an application which might otherwise have been allowed. Special cases will often form a platform for the exertion of localized political influence in either a negative or positive direction.

The implementation of planning policy should certainly not be symbolized as a tangled web of intrigue and corruption. Indeed, the majority of decisions involving implementation are processed in a straightforward and clearly defined manner. However, rural areas do display evidence of planning action which has deviated from written policy, and whether this is caused by administrative, perceptive or resource factors, it is the end result by which rural settlement planning is judged. Vagaries of implementation clearly shape the end result of planning activity in rural settlements.

What actually happens

The obscurity of how written policy becomes implemented is followed by the most visible element of rural settlement planning, that is the outworkings of planning decisions as they actually occur in settlements. Analysis of this stage involves not only a critical appraisal of changes induced by positive planning action, but also a recognition that negative decisions, or failure to enact planning powers at all, will also produce recognizable results in the socio-economic affairs and land-use structure of rural settlements. Monitoring of both positive and negative planning results is constantly being fed back into the system so that established policy can be adapted in the light of changing conditions or ineffectiveness of the policy response to specific problems. However, the monitoring process is conditional on an ability to enunciate the undesirable qualities of current planning systems – an art which has not been easily cultivated by rural commentators over the years.

This view of the planning process tends to highlight influential factors in the formation and implementation of policy rather than adopting the more traditional concentration on a step-by-step approach to an understanding of what planners do. This redirection of our scrutiny of planning can be applied to any type of environment, but is particularly relevant to rural areas because of four essential characteristics:

1 Rural areas are often governed by a stable political structure which is able to apply steady and long-term pressure for certain trends in widespread or localized planning action;
2 The paucity of financial resources in rural areas severely curtails experimentation with, and adoption of, planning approaches which are radical in character and which divert policy away from financial expediency;
3 Rural areas do not command the manpower services within planning departments which would allow an equivalent breadth of approach to that found in urban areas. This deficiency restricts the opportunities for thorough surveying, analysis and monitoring of planning areas while

conversely raising the likelihood that unconforming special cases will slip through the planning net;

4   Given the nature and size of rural settlements, any particular planning action has a significant marginal effect on existing circumstances. What would be considered small-scale development (or non-development) in urban areas constitutes a very important additional factor at rural settlement scale. As a consequence, inefficiencies in plan preparation or implementation are perhaps more noticeable in rural areas.

In view of these distinctive characteristics, it is important that rural settlement planning be analysed as a political process as well as a technical and professional science. This book attempts to fulfil this analytical need. It traces the theoretical and legislative foundation of rural settlement planning, assesses those policies which have been adopted at various times since the 1940s, and considers the everyday formative processes which, along with the commitment to various technical trends, have moulded rural settlement planning into its current posture. As a whole, the book attempts to provide a basis for a vital appreciation of the political planning system and its related mechanisms and techniques which are fundamental to rural settlement planning.

The author makes no apology for concentrating much of this book on the British context, since this is the environment most familiar to him and it ranks among the most highly developed rural planning systems which are available for study. Much can be learned, however, from innovative traits in rural settlement planning in other countries, and examples from these sources are included where significant. The author also readily admits that the book is written from the standpoint of a geographer. There are obvious inherent disadvantages in compiling a book of this nature from a position outside the planning system under review. To counter this, however, the geographer is able to take advantage of a certain detachment from the in-house dogma and political innuendo to which one is constantly susceptible within the planning system. Clearly, the planner and the applied rural geographer are in effect working towards the same end of analysing and improving rural settlement policies so that they may better serve the needs of rural people. If this book is able to clarify those aspects of rural settlement planning which are currently undervalued and often misunderstood then it will have served some purpose.

TWO

Change in rural settlements

Definitions

Rural settlements

It is traditional for authors concerned with rural matters to begin their deliberations with one of two opposing attitudes towards the specifications of their subject matter. One faction will argue that an unambiguous and representative definition of rural areas is denied by their internal complexity and their external similarity with adjacent communities, settlements and even land uses. As a consequence, any attempt at such a definition is seen to be steeped in futility and sterility. The alternative view is that rural definition (whatever its shortcomings) is a necessary first step in the understanding of the various differences and similarities between urban and rural areas. This debate has been fully aired elsewhere (Cloke and Park, 1983) but three salient points emerge:

1   Rural settlements *per se* should be distinguished from the concept of open countryside, because the processes which shape and develop the built and unbuilt rural environments are nowadays often very different (Wibberley, 1978);

2   No population parameter can by itself adequately represent the threshold between rural and other settlements. Moss (1978, 101) bravely attempts to pinpoint this size factor by suggesting that 'settlements falling between 200 and 5000 people are considered most likely to be villages', but has to admit that it is often the exceptions to this range which catch the eye of academics and planners;

3   Any broad definition of rural settlements should concern itself with the function and character of the settlements concerned. Thornburn's (1971, 2) view of a village as 'any place which most residents think of as a village' is important in this context as it links the visual and functional aspects of rural settlement with a concomitant view of rural people.

Thus, although it is a relatively easy process to specify what is *not* a rural settlement (Philip *et al.*, 1978) it is much more difficult to provide a positive and rigid definition of what a rural settlement is. This book deals with a range of settlement types and sizes which may be classed as 'lower order' in function (possibly ranging from 10,000 population downwards) and which demonstrate a strong relationship between buildings and extensive landscape resulting in their being perceived as rural by most of their residents. The 'rural' character may be established by the way in which a settlement engenders a style of life which is characterized by a cohesive identity based on respect for the environmental and behavioural qualities of living as part of an extensive landscape. Obviously this rural character comes in varying degrees and may be almost non-existent particularly in areas at the urban fringe (Giggs, 1970; Thomas, 1970; 1972).

Interpretation of these general guidelines for rural settlements has many difficulties. Figure 2.1 outlines a statistically derived index of rurality as applied to England and Wales in 1971, and from this simple distribution the interpretative difficulties are apparent. First of all, the index is based on census data recorded at the rural district level, reflecting the fact that central government has laid down preconceived boundaries between rural and urban districts in its selection of administrative areas. Despite the fact that the 1974 local government reorganization created new districts in Britain which often cut across traditionally conceived urban–rural delimitations, it is still true that many governments will only recognize a settlement as rural if it lies within a rural administrative area. Piatier and Madec (1977) highlight the paradoxical nature of these artificial boundaries, in that in France all communes with more than 2000 inhabitants round the main towns are considered urban, yet if this definition were applied to West Germany or the Netherlands the 'country' classification would disappear altogether. In Britain, even with the new ubiquitous districts, we often fall into the trap of labelling certain counties as 'rural' and others as 'non-rural', whereas these images merely reflect a superficial aggregation of varying degrees of rurality distributed throughout most British counties.

A different version of the same trap is to brand a particular county as being a particular type of rural area (e.g. Devon as a remote rural area, or Essex as a pressured rural area), whereas it is clear from figure 2.1 that considerable internal variation of rurality occurs within county boundaries. The lack of uniformity displayed by rural settlements is further emphasized by the variety of settlement patterns to be found in rural environments. For example, Powys County Council (1977, para. 4.06) stress the nature of this pattern in rural Wales:

> There are relatively few large villages in Powys; settlement in the rural area has, in the main, been by way of hamlet and the single house and farmstead . . . it differs from the predominant pattern of settlement in many parts of rural England where villages tend to be larger and more compact . . . it is frequently impossible to draw a line around a settlement and say what constitutes 'the village'.

Clearly the implications of settlement pattern type for selecting suitable planning policies are enormous. For example, a village envelope plan might be considered in a system of nucleated settlements, but would be inappropriate in many areas of Powys. Therefore although it is useful to delimit what is meant by rural settlement, it is clear that individual settlements and settlement systems should not be artificially combined as homogeneous phenomena. As

Figure 2.1 An index of rurality, 1971

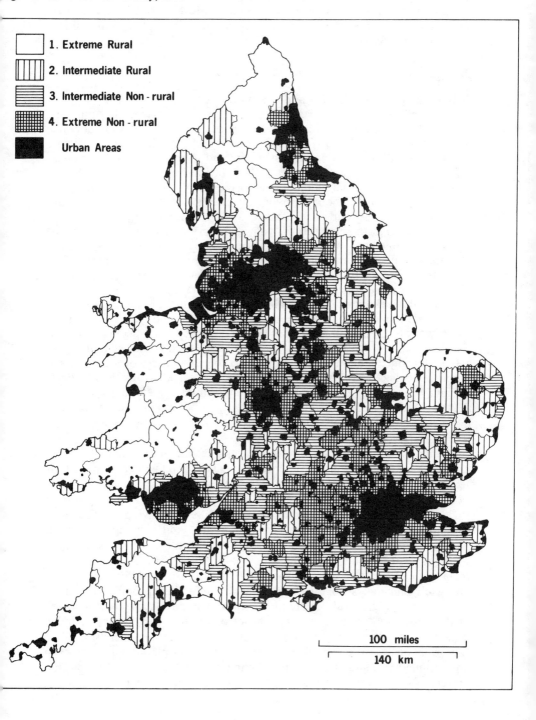

1. Extreme Rural
2. Intermediate Rural
3. Intermediate Non - rural
4. Extreme Non - rural
   Urban Areas

100 miles
140 km

the Countryside Review Committee (1976, 2) stresses, 'generalizations about the countryside . . . are unlikely to be useful. Most regions have their own particular requirements, and one must be cautious in applying unmodified, broad national objectives'.

Planning

Definitions of planning also abound elsewhere (e.g. Faludi, 1970; Keeble, 1969; Ratcliffe, 1974; Roberts, 1974). It is generally agreed that planning involves the allocation of scarce resources of both a social and economic nature. Eversley (1973) differentiates between the *economic planner* who allocates capital for housing, infrastructure and so on and the *social planner* who allocates land, capital, employment opportunities, educational and other social services with the intention of altering the distribution of real incomes. In effect, this division of labour is clouded by the time-scale within which various planning activities occur. For instance, we can recognize the *development control* planner who is concerned with the everyday allocation of land, the *structure* planner who takes a long-term view of a particular area, and a *strategic* planner who adopts a broad perspective of the living standards, life-styles and other needs of a population, and devises policies which achieve set objectives in these spheres. In rural settlement planning we are used to the activities of development control and structure planning, but have been effec-tively denied anything more than the nominal services of strategic planners whose work is often compromised in favour of short-term expediency. Thus if we are to agree with Friedmann (1966) and Rose (1974) that planning is an activity by which man in society endeavours to gain mastery over himself and shapes his collective future through conscious reasoned effort, then strategic planning should be granted far greater emphasis in rural areas than is presently the case. As it is, rural settlement planning in practice has thus far resembled a more restricted and short-term allocation of resources than Rose's rather idealistic approach.

Planning also takes place at varying scales of operation. Hall's (1974, 6) broad view that 'planning as a general activity is the making of an orderly sequence of action that will lead to the achievement of a stated goal or goals' can be contrasted with the neighbourhood-level role visualized by Hancock (1978, 315) who sees planning as 'a principal means of resolving conflicts, with community and special interest groups, about land use and settlement patterns'. Criticizing the idealistic approach to the achievement of broad-scale social goals, he argues that 'any attempt to design a future utopia would replace one obsolete model with another, which in turn would become rapidly obsolete'. The analysis of rural settlement planning in this book attempts to encompass both the local and broader levels of planning action, whether taken in the basic area of development control or in the quest for target living standards as pursued by strategic and structure planning exercises. Also, following the lead of Gilg (1978, 17, 18) the concept of planners as those 'who are occupied in planning by implementing or invoking the legislation and powers of their own particular organization and country' is largely adopted here, although it is equally recognized that the actions of a wide body of decision-makers and resource allocators serve to constrain the behaviour of 'planners' so defined.

Brief mention should also be made of the spectrum of opinion which has been expressed as to the degree to which rural problem analysis and policy prescription should be separate from equivalent urban processes. For example, Kyllingstad (1975) argues that policies developed for urban milieux create more problems than they solve in the countryside, while Lefaver (1978, 7) explicitly states that

> Planning for rural areas demands a new framework and tools quite different from those used in urban planning. Present planning policies assume that rural areas are no more than a part of the urban fringe. With this bias, public officials often attempt to solve rural problems with tools designed for urban areas. . . . Planners must understand that rural issues need to be defined in their own context and that the policy tools used to solve those issues must come from the rural perspective.

Clearly, there has been a considerable element of separatism on the part of rural planning in post-war Britain, and the adoption of rural and urban categories by planners has tended to condition their assumptions and approach to an area. Cornish and Cornish (1975) demonstrate that the structure plan for the area defined as *urban* Teesside embodied a potentially radical growth zone philosophy while the *rural* county draft structure plan for adjacent North Yorkshire conformed to a more traditionally conservative rationale. If this separatism has thus far been principally a perceptive factor brought about by a combination of circumstance and attitude, there are strong proponents for its continuation for the good of rural areas. A recent report by the National Association of Local Councils (1979, para. 6) regards 'the ingrained belief that rural problems are now the same as urban problems but set in a rural context' as a major contributory factor in the decline of rural areas. This view represents more than just an interest group displaying its natural bias towards localized government and planning responses to socio-economic problems. A national perspective towards service provision, for example, does discriminate against rural areas:

> the economic factors behind a service are judged on a national basis and the service is withdrawn if it is 'too costly' regardless of the fact that the items contributing to the cost are different, or at least of a different scale of effect in rural areas. This attitude has resulted in the withdrawal of rural services such as trains, buses and now schools 'which are not paying their way'. (National Association of Local Councils, 1979, para. 6)

On the other hand, it would be foolish to ignore the ever-present links between rural and urban areas (Buttel and Flinn, 1977). Many researchers (e.g. Bailey, 1975; Moseley, 1980) have developed the theme that the causal factors of rural and urban problems display many similarities, particularly in connection with the workings of national and international agencies in both the private and public sectors. It has been shown that the rural–urban distinction is becoming increasingly blurred (Cloke and Griffiths, 1980) and the erosion of a specific rural identity has led to considerable ambiguity and bewilderment over the nature and purpose of rural settlements. Furthermore, this erosion is likely to continue in many societies, for as Halpern (1967, 2) points out 'one of the characteristics of the modern political state appears to be the attempt to eliminate the distinctions between urban and rural life'. Indeed, the rural–urban relationship is inextricably linked with regional and political ideology. Sigurdson (1976) has shown that both India and China are challenging the traditionally exclusive linkages between urbanization and modernization (thus securing a future for a separate rural identity). By contrast, Eastern European nations regard the process of urbanization as 'deruralization' or the *demolition* of rural identity (Prochownikowa, 1975), with socialist activity being harnessed to put an end to differences between town and country in countries such as Poland (Bajan, 1976).

So far as Britain is concerned, the pursuance of structure planning at county level has ensured some recognition of rural–urban interaction. However, strategic advice from central government has tended to treat rural environments as a separate phenomenon whilst government legislation has been across the board, generally promoting the use of urban-scale planning devices whatever the area concerned. In effect we have a hotchpotch of attitudes towards the status of rural settlement planning and so when isolating the planning process as applied to different areas it is axiomatic to remain constantly aware of the essential interrelationship between town and country.

Why plan?

A growing minority of academics, particularly those such as archaeologists who take an historically confined view of settlement patterns, have begun to reopen the question of whether rural settlements should be planned at all. It is argued (e.g. Austin, 1979) that at various points in the past local communities achieved a high degree of self-sufficiency in their affairs and participated in the construction of villages which are so highly prized by present day conservationists. In addition, various anachronistic parts of the rural settlement pattern have bowed to economic forces, become disused, and are only recognizable today as 'deserted villages' (Roberts, 1977). Given the positive establishment of environmentally pleasing settlements and the flexibility in coping with fluctuations in the settlement pattern in an 'unplanned' society, would it not be better to allow rural settlements to evolve 'naturally' rather than attempting to intervene by establishing more formal and widespread methods of planning?

These views and the questions they pose represent an indictment of rural settlement planning and its non-achievement of physical, social and economic objectives in the countryside. Obviously, 'natural' forces do to some extent take their course in the rural areas of today despite our system of planning intervention. Conventional wisdom dictates that the rapid and widespread changes in the mobility and economic dependence of rural people has meant that resource allocation has to take place at an aggregate level. This means that formerly self-sufficient communities now have to share in large-scale communal resources such as hospitals, schools, social services and so on. What conventional wisdom fails to point out is that this allocation of aggregated resources is itself a source of problems for rural people, hence the idealistic wish to return to unplanned community self-sufficiency.

One of the most important innovations in rural planning in recent years has been the marked increase in the awareness demonstrated by various levels of government about problems associated with the planning system and its response to rural change. Perhaps most significant was the establishment of the Countryside Review Committee in 1974 whose task was to examine the current state of the countryside; to assess the effects of existing planning policies; to consider changes in planning policy and practice; and to make recommendations for enactment by central government. The committee's publication *Rural Communities* (1977) justifies the planning and subsidy of rural settlements and communities on the grounds that the continuation of living rural communities is necessary for three purposes:

1   To maintain and develop the production of domestic food and timber;
2   To conserve natural beauty and amenity;
3   To make available to everyone the aesthetic and recreational opportunities presented by rural areas.

To the Countryside Review Committee (1977, 5) 'these aims justify spending on the upkeep of rural communities, quite apart from the short term need to support them *for the welfare of their present residents or those who wish to live in them*' (author's italics). Thus this important document re-emphasizes a long-term role for vital rural communities supported by society as a whole. However the shorter-term purpose of planning of rural settlements is also important even though the committee offer it as a throw away to their three major justifications. This 'welfare opportunity' significance of rural communities was highlighted by the British representative to the Vienna meeting of European planning ministers under the auspices of the Council of Europe, who is reported to have stressed that

> Certain aspects of the pattern of rural living need to be safeguarded as an alternative to the urban pattern of living. The main objective of a rural planning policy must be based not only on economic criteria but on criteria which cannot be assessed in financial terms, based on man's needs in his traditional cultural context. (*Planning*, 1978, 4)

With these short-term and long-term aims it is clear that rural settlement planning has an important role to play in the shaping of the future countryside. Whether it can adequately perform that role will largely depend on the resources at planners' disposal and the way in which these resources are utilized given the current vagaries of policy formation and implementation. These themes are given more detailed attention throughout the book.

Change – past and present

The inability to provide adequate definitions of what rural settlements are and how they are planned may partially be explained by the constant dynamism taking place in the countryside and the resultant fluctuations both in the nature of settlements and communities and in their demands of the planning system. At one time, little was known of these changes, but the work of the Countryside Review Committee along with reports from the Association of County Councils (1979), the Association of District Councils (1978) and the National Association of Local Councils (1979) have done much to provide a clearer view of rural change.

An historical perspective

For a full understanding of changes taking place in today's rural settlements it is important to view current changes in the context of preceding events and conditions. Cherry (1978, 10) argues strongly for a conceptual framework within which rural problems and policy responses can be seen in the same perspective. In this context he cites an equivalent explanatory framework for the contemporary urban scene which may be viewed as stages of capitalist development:

> industrial capitalism created the nineteenth century city and particular kinds of economic and social orders acquired territorial significance; post-industrial capitalism has continued to feed on the city, for example in the exploitation of land values. The economic and social structure is now manifest in distinctive spatial patterns, changing over time with emergent areas of advantage and disadvantage.

The recognition of the *context* of social, economic and environmental problems is useful, for often that very context represents a seedbed of policy solutions to these problems. Therefore Cherry attempts to establish a conceptual framework for rural change, based on the progressive substitution of dominant social and economic orders:

> Over a number of centuries the feudal order was replaced by an agrarian capitalist order. Over the last 100 years we have seen how the enfeeblement of agrarian capitalism produced the twentieth-century problems to which planning in its widest sense has reacted: land, poverty, insecurity of jobs, housing squalor, community disadvantage and restriction of opportunity. In the last 30 years new forms of conflict have arisen, and others have sharpened as one dominant value system has challenged another: the urbanite earmarks rural land for recreation, urban water needs takes over rural farm land for reservoirs, the city dweller moves into rural housing. (Cherry, 1976, 265)

Cherry's conceptualization ossifies the historical development of rural settlements and communities. The original rural settlement consisted of a community of farmers engaged in husbandry (and sometimes mining or fishing) around the stable base of groups of cottages and barns. The community was self-sufficient and socially self-reliant under the protection of the manorial lord. Bonham-Carter (1976, 27) traces the metamorphosis from these mutual support communities in which every rural dweller owned his own land through the great enclosure movements between 1760 and 1820 to a 'free-for-all system underpinned by a race of landless labourers, who survived on starvation wages plus parish assistance'. This foundation of change was further developed during the clearance movements and the industrial and agrarian revolutions which prompted the steady outmigration of rural workers into the towns and cities. Village communities proved to be persistent survivors in this climate of outward movement and indeed as late as 1851 more than half the population of England and Wales lived and worked in rural areas. However the depopulation process dominated rural areas until the 1930s, leading to a situation whereby a pattern of rural settlements built around a labour-intensive form of agriculture became anachronistic and often superfluous to the modern agricultural economy. Thus, although few settlements have physically disappeared since medieval times, the communities within them have shrunk and have lost their fundamental *raison d'être*.

The post-war period has seen an overall reversal of these trends, with the proportion of the population of England and Wales living in rural areas increasing from 18.7 per cent in 1951 to 21.7 per cent in 1971. This apparent repopulation of rural areas has resulted from various population groups who have been able to combine rural living with a dependence on the urban economy, either by commuting, retirement or second-home ownership. Within this overall pattern of growth, a marked spatial differentiation has occurred. Areas close to urban centres have borne the brunt of commuter growth, but Woodruffe (1976) shows that almost a third of all rural districts continued to lose population between 1951 and 1971, these being mainly but not exclusively the remote upland areas.

Recent changes

The recent report, *Rural Deprivation*, produced by the Association of County Councils (1979), the research on which it was based (Norfolk C C, 1979), and most important of all the results of the 1981 Census, all give firm evidence of the trends of rural change outlined above. The first two sources, using 1971 Census information, suggest a national average pattern of population growth of 5.7 per cent, and conclude that, despite this overall increase, five so-called 'rural' counties have experienced a *decrease* in population over this decade. Depopulation, then, continued to be a problem in a significant number of rural areas at the 1971 data point, a trend supported by other researchers, for example Dunn (1976, 40) who notes that

> this reduction in attractiveness of rural areas as a residential environment will inevitably be felt most in the more isolated districts, where provision of public utilities and other communal services will be restricted to key settlements, and existing facilities such as surviving rural public transport services, and mobile or static retail services, will be withdrawn.

By contrast, this 1971 evidence also established several 'rural' counties as the recipients of above-average growth of population. Whereas areas of declining population appeared to be a relatively small and localized part of the rural

scene, the more widespread trend was one of a redistribution of urban population into the rural areas. The implications of this in-migration for the provision
of life-style opportunities in rural areas appeared to be aggravated by the
increasing numbers of retirement age population who were gravitating
towards the rural areas (figure 2.2). With a 16 per cent average increase in
retired population over the whole of Britain, it was evident that many rural
areas were experiencing rates of increase substantially above this average level,
and the aggregate county-level figures presented here are likely to ignore
localized pockets of more highly concentrated retired population. To some
extent, the areas of low growth in populations of retired age corresponded with
those areas which suffered negative or low overall population growth rates,
thereby confirming the importance of retirement movements to many rural
areas. Conversely, retirement increases are low on the fringes of major urban
areas where population growth has been sustained by in-migration of
commuters, and in the less popular and less accessible remoter rural areas such
as Mid and West Wales.

Analysis of 1981 Census evidence by Champion (1981) demonstrates a
tendency towards stronger rural growth over the latest intercensal period
although most growth seems to have occurred in the early part of the decade.
Using a detailed socio-economic classification of districts in Britain (Webber
and Craig, 1978) he isolates the population change taking place within 'rural
districts' in regional groupings (table 2.1), and these statistics clearly show a
uniform pattern of growth across Britain between 1971 and 1981. Although
Wales and the North grew less quickly, even these areas far exceeded the
national average of 0.3 per cent. Table 2.1 also highlights the difference
between irregular and wide-ranging population-change patterns between 1961
and 1971, and the conformity of growth over the following decade.

Table 2.1   Population change in rural local authorities, 1961–81, by region

Region	Number of districts	1981 population 000s	Percentage population change		
			1961–71	*1971–81*	*Difference*
Scotland	24	998	– 1.9	9.6	11.5
Wales	13	583	0.6	6.8	6.2
North	6	276	1.0	4.3	3.3
Yorkshire & Humberside	7	453	10.4	12.0	1.6
East Midlands	8	560	9.2	10.1	0.9
South West	20	1,368	10.3	11.0	0.7
West Midlands	8	427	7.7	8.1	0.4
East Anglia	12	1,035	14.5	12.9	– 1.6
South East	4	357	21.1	12.1	– 9.0
All rural districts	102	6,056	7.5	10.2	2.7
Great Britain	458	54,129	5.3	0.3	– 5.0

Source: Champion, 1981, 20

Figure 2.2 Percentage change in population of retirement age in county rural areas, 1961–71

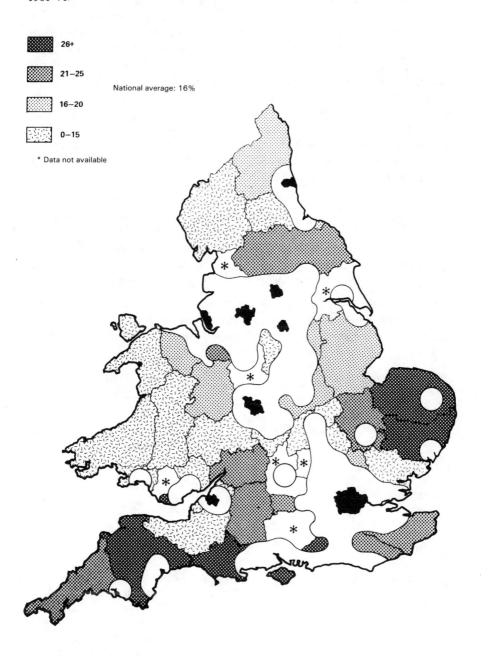

26+

21–25

National average: 16%

16–20

0–15

* Data not available

Source: Norfolk CC, 1979, 14

Further enlightenment of recent rural population trends is available from Champion's breakdown of census data into that pertaining to five rural clusters (table 2.2) which differentiate between remote districts in Scotland and Wales, less remote areas in west and east England, and least remote districts in peri-urban locations. This analysis suggests a marked revival in remoter rural areas (Clusters 7 and 10), a broad continuity of growth in west and east England (Clusters 8 and 9), although the rate fell slightly in East Anglia and the South-East, and a failure by peri-urban districts (Cluster 2) to maintain previous growth levels. These results are shown spatially in figure 2.3. Champion's explanation of these trends is twofold. The impressive revival in Scottish rural areas is linked with growth associated with North Sea oil developments, but the resurgences in the North and in Wales are less easily accounted for. He suggests (1981, 22) that:

> they may reflect the geographical extension of the processes which have produced at least two decades of rapid growth in the rural parts of less peripheral regions. The discovery that regional variations in rural growth rates were relatively small in 1971–81, coupled with the similarities found in the annual trends of population in different types of rural area, suggest that population change in these areas is influenced by a common set of factors.

Some of these 'common factors' are discussed below, but it is important to note that the pattern of *settlements* in rural areas has changed much less over the years than has the pattern of population. While the movement of

Table 2.2   Population change in rural local authorities, 1961–81, by cluster type

Cluster	Number of districts	1981 population 000s	Percentage population change		
			1961–71	*1971–81*	*Difference*
7 Rural Wales and Scottish Islands	16	645	– 0.2	7.0	7.2
8 Rural, mainly West	32	2,009	7.2	8.8	1.6
9 Rural, mainly East	31	2,411	15.0	12.7	– 2.3
10 Rural, mainly Scotland	23	911	– 1.9	9.3	11.1
Sub-total	102	6,056	7.5	10.2	2.7
2 Rural growth areas	31	2,872	22.0	8.6	– 13.4
Total	133	8,928	11.8	9.7	– 2.1

Source: Champion, 1981, 21

Figure 2.3 Rural Britain by socio-economic cluster

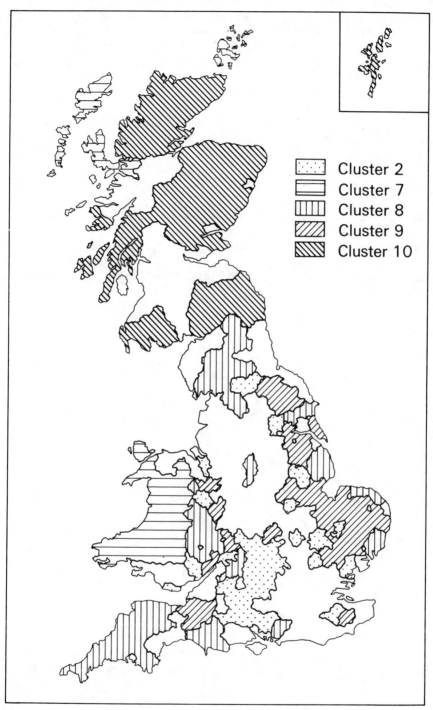

Cluster 2
Cluster 7
Cluster 8
Cluster 9
Cluster 10

Source: Champion, 1981, 21

people has ebbed and flowed, settlements have remained relatively static. An analysis of the existing structure of rural settlements in Britain (Norfolk C C, 1979) reveals that most rural people live in relatively small settlements and that most of these settlements are situated at some distance from urban centres. In other words, the recent rural resurgence has not as yet resulted in a new breed of rural settlements of substantial size and within close proximity to centres of urban employment. Figure 2.4 illustrates the large number of small settlements in the non-metropolitan counties of England and Wales. Over 9000 settlements have populations below 1000, and of these, four-fifths have fewer than 500 population. The Association of County Councils (1979) estimate that three-and-a-quarter million people live in settlements with fewer than 1000 population. This figure represents 10 per cent of the total population of the non-metropolitan counties.

In addition, it appears from figure 2.4 that many people living in small rural settlements suffer more from remoteness than do those living in larger settlements. All in all, about four million people live in settlements which are situated more than 10 miles (16 km) away from an urban centre of 20,000, and nearly half of these rural residents live in settlements of under 2000 population.

Figure 2.4 Number, size and remoteness of rural settlements in non-metropolitan counties of England and Wales

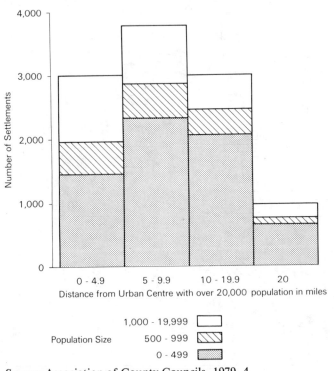

Source: Association of County Councils, 1979, 4

The changes taking place in rural areas are complex and interconnected. Although a repopulation appears to be taking place in many areas, it is clear that problems generic to small remote settlements continue to be important and to require planning action. Given these rather complicated spatial manifestations of change, our understanding of rural trends is perhaps best enhanced by a view of the systematic forces which are sponsoring change in rural settlements.

Agents of change

No clear-cut and distinctive boundaries exist between the various forces which have prompted changes in rural settlements and communities. Change has come from a series of interrelated factors imposed on a sparsely populated settlement structure. This has created an impetus for change which is greater than the combined influence of the individual components. Nevertheless five broad agents of change may be isolated which contribute to the overall processes of dynamism in rural settlements, and to these is added the factor of *inertia* which has perhaps prevented positive changes and indirectly promoted somewhat more harmful trends.

Decline in traditional labour forces

A fundamental instigating process in rural change has been the wholesale decline in traditional forms of rural employment. This trend has been well documented (Ministry of Agriculture, Fisheries and Food, 1967; Chisholm and Oeppen, 1973) and is so established a phenomenon that Kotter (1962) was able to describe it as an inevitable process in the development of a civilized economy. In 1750, 75 per cent of Britain's population was employed on the land. By 1801, census material reveals that this proportion had decreased to less than 50 per cent and by 1951 a mere 20 per cent of the population was employed in agriculture. Today the figure has fallen to around 2 per cent although another 8 per cent are employed in ancillary and support trades mainly based in urban locations. Farming, however, has never been the only source of employment for the rural labour force. The primary employment in farming, forestry and quarrying was traditionally balanced by a profusion of secondary small craft and consumer industries, and in fact it was this industrial element of the rural economy which was first to suffer from technical development (in this case the development of urban-based industry in the Midlands and the North). Bonham-Carter (1976, 28) paints a vivid image of rural craft industry 'flickering out like the flame of a dying candle all through the nineteenth century'.

The concomitant decrease in agricultural labour requirements was brought about by the increased efficiency of agriculture. The establishment of an oil-dependent, mechanized and intensive system of farming which took advantage of the improvements offered by artificial feedstuffs and fertilizers meant that the labour input to agricultural processes steadily dwindled. Alongside this shrinkage of jobs, the life-style of agricultural workers was characterized by low wages, long working hours, an isolated and basic way of life, and a general lack of prospects. These push factors combined to present the conditions from which rural workers could contemplate moving from their countryside location, but as Gasson (1973) suggests, the *opportunity* for out-migration hinged on the pull factors of urban employment, aspirations and living standards. Hodge and Whitby (1982) go so far as to suggest that rural labour problems are at the *core* of depopulation from rural areas.

The loss of primary and secondary rural jobs has been a continual backcloth to rural change right up to the present day. In Britain the employment shrinkage has decelerated from an annual outflow of some 4 per cent in the 1960s, although it has been recorded that 6000 farmworkers left agriculture between 1975 and 1976 (Ministry of Agriculture, Fisheries and Food, 1977). Those farmworkers that remain are often poorly paid, and continue to be one of the main centres of poverty in rural areas (Winyard, 1978). Rural job loss and consequent out-migration should not be considered as a purely British phenomenon. Rodgers (1970) gives graphic account of similar processes in the Mezzogiorno region of Italy, and elsewhere in Europe the complicating factor of structural reform of agriculture has artificially generated rural–urban migration flows (see the work of Bryant (1974) and Clout (1975) in France, and Mayhew (1971) in West Germany). Clearly the replacement of the old agricultural economy with some new economic base is one major task for planners involved with rural settlements and communities.

Mobility and energy

Rural settlements and communities have traditionally been isolated from higher-order urban centres, and have therefore been reasonably self-sufficient. Over the last century this isolation has gradually been overcome with the development of transport systems based on roads, railways and canals. This framework of transportation paved the way for technological improvement and rises in income levels which allowed many rural dwellers to buy personal mobility in the form of private cars or use of public transport, and it is this rise in mobility which has had widespread ramifications in the spatial aspects of social and economic components of rural life.

The importance of the private car in rural areas is stressed by Moseley (1979) who points out both the overall rise in car ownership (0.25 cars/person in 1975 and a forecast 0.44 cars/person in the year 2000) and the propensity towards higher-than-average rates of car ownership in rural areas where even low income families make car ownership a major priority for marginal disposable income. These increases in mobility have facilitated easy movement between rural settlements and urban centres giving access to jobs and services in urban locations. The journey to urban work has maintained the viability of many rural settlements whose accessibility to urban areas has presented them with the new role of commuter settlement. Accessibility to urban services and facilities has also broken down village self-sufficiency. The National

Association of Local Councils (1979, para. 13) stresses that the freedom of choice available to mobile consumers of services

> means that the providers of services can expect that a large part of their 'trade' will be able to come to them: they can therefore plan their outlets on the assumption that it is no longer necessary to provide them within close reach of all the users.

Increasing personal mobility has also promoted increased tourist and recreation movement into the countryside, which has presented economic opportunities to some rural communities in high-quality environmental areas. However, other less beneficial processes have been exacerbated by high rates of car ownership. For example, as car usage has increased, the level and frequency of public bus and train services have declined, and Mitchell (1976) establishes a causal link between these two trends. Two sectors of the population are discriminated against by these changes in mobility patterns. First, it is still the case that 25–30 per cent of British households do not own a car and that perhaps 75 per cent of rural people do not have access to a car at all times during the day (Moseley *et al.*, 1977). These non-mobile elements are thus thrown back on a declining public transport service. Second, there are now many remoter (and not so remote) rural areas where there is little or no access to public transport, and so non-mobile groups in these settlements are being subjected to the loss of home-based services without the counterbalance of available access to centralized services. Again, it should be stressed that these mobility trends are also occurring elsewhere in the western world. Clawson (1966) and Hodge (1966) provided early indications of growth and decline trends caused by changing mobility in small settlements in the United States, and Lewan (1969) shows how mobility has brought about the urbanization of rural areas in Sweden. These patterns are duplicated wherever the motor car has dictated spatial distributions of living and working for rural residents.

The reliance on private mobility is in many ways an unstable basis for the future planning of rural settlements. Such mobility (along with industrial and urban growth as a whole) is dependent on inexpensive energy, and now that we are beginning to realize that energy may well become an expensive commodity, the possible ramifications of the withdrawal of easy mobility should be investigated. One scenario is outlined by Warren (1980, 183):

> As fuel becomes expensive, high density patterns of living will become unworkable. It will become uneconomic to shift goods and people to and fro . . . the farming industry will be faced with rapidly rising prices for fuel and fertilizers and will have no alternative but to reduce specialization and reduce the use of machinery. This in turn means that more people, probably many more people, will be needed on the land. Yet more people will be needed to provide back-up services: shops, small industries and so on, for the new workers. In place of a drift to the cities there will be a movement of people, ideas and talent from the cities to the countryside.

This effect of expensive energy is perhaps overstated here. One more cynical alternative would be to envisage a countryside where only the most affluent could afford the necessary personal mobility to exist on urban-based facilities, however expensive. Certainly the oil crisis thus far has not produced as marked and widespread a decrease in commuting practices as might have been expected. However it is clear that the factors of mobility and energy will continue to inflict change in the countryside, and rural settlement planners are forced to pay particular attention to the effects of these factors on the future state of rural communities.

Resource rationalization

Another cause of rural change is the process whereby rural facilities, services and opportunities have tended to gravitate up the settlement hierarchy away from small rural settlements and towards the larger clientele offered in more sizeable villages and towns. A recent survey of service provision in seven counties in the south-west of England (Standing Conference of Rural Community Councils, 1978) uncovered an alarming pattern of service decline in rural areas. Table 2.3 summarizes the results for four counties and demonstrates the sweeping decline of basic services and facilities in rural settlements. Even where rates of decrease are low, evidence from the report suggests that a minimum level of provision has been reached whereby services have already been concentrated into the larger settlements. The overwhelming message from the report is that smaller villages are taking the brunt of closures, and that many now exist on an extremely limited range of services. For example, almost half of the population of West Dorset live in villages of less than 500 inhabitants, yet of these villages:

87 per cent have no doctor's surgery
75 per cent have no school
68 per cent have no garage
61 per cent have no public house
50 per cent have no sub post office
30 per cent have no shop

Patterns such as these are duplicated in villages across Britain.

The rationalization of resources is partly a 'natural' and partly a 'planned' process. The natural element stems from the operation of the market system,

Table 2.3   Services losses from rural settlements in four counties, 1972–7 (in percentages)

County	Shop	Sub post office	Primary school	Chemist	Doctor's surgery
Avon	– 6	– 4.5	– 4	– 4.5	– 14
Gloucestershire	– 13	– 8	– 2.5	0	– 3
Wiltshire	– 13	– 8	– 9	– 14	– 2
Somerset	– 5	– 2.5	– 1	0	– 5

Source: Standing Conference of Rural Community Councils, 1978

although it is clear that managers of private-sector services are in effect *planning* a contraction of services into larger settlements. Current trends in the organization, marketing and pricing of any particular service or facility have progressed towards the economies of scale to be gained from one large outlet serving a wide geographical area and a sizeable clientele. This dictum is also true of public-sector services where education and health services have been rationalized into larger and often urban-based units. The centralization of various rural resources in a planned or semi-planned manner gives rise to two areas of perpetuated decline. First, the loss of rural opportunities is a contributory factor in out-migration from rural settlements. As depopulation occurs, population thresholds within a settlement or group of settlements decline and therefore there is an increased propensity for further service losses. Second, the recognition of declining opportunities in rural areas has prompted a certain type of planning response, centring on the concentration of housing, infrastructure and employment developments in key centres or settlements where population thresholds are sufficiently high to support a range of services. In 1957, Saville recognized that most rural settlements appeared to be too small to act as effective nuclei for rural living in the future. This trend of thought was developed by Green (1966) who argued for the progressive redistribution of rural settlements into viable units. Thus it is that resource rationalization has been engrained in planning thought over the past two decades. As Ayton (1976, 68) confesses in the Norfolk context:

> Services for the scattered population are costly to provide and maintain and, with limited resources, it appears that effective provision can only be made on the basis of selective and co-ordinated investment, both public and private. . . . With the large number and wide scatter of small villages the need for selectivity in relation to village development policies is even greater.

This combination of falling population thresholds, the vogue for centralized marketing and the adoption of resource rationalization by various levels and aspects of the planning system serve as both the cause and effect of many of the changes taking place in rural settlements. Furthermore, the recognition that these factors are both causes and effects of other trends suggests a downward spiral of rural living standards in small settlements if resource rationalization is allowed to continue.

Environmental quality

If resource rationalization can be seen to promote and be promoted by out-migration, the counterbalancing in-migratory trends must also be accounted for. It can be seen from the marked increases in rural population totals that ex-urban areas have (for one reason or another) proved attractive to previously urban residents. One major explanatory factor in these increases is the sheer volume of suburban overspill into the immediately adjacent but administratively rural areas. These movements are largely but not exclusively promoted by 'suburban' magnetism rather than any particular desire to live in a rural area. However, rural in-migration can also be seen to be connected with a positive wish on the part of some people to participate in what they see as a distinct *rural* life-style, and to live in a *rural* environment, even if this decision entails long commuter journeys to urban employment.

Several studies have been carried out in Britain to ascertain the reasons why migrants are attracted to rural settlements. The outcome of this research is the recognition of a pattern of complex and interrelated circumstances, desires and needs, which suggests that the motives for in-migration are by no means clear-cut. As a starting point, the demand for rural housing can be seen to stem from multifarious sources. Scott-Miller (1976) isolates ten basic categories (table 2.4) of which in-migration from urban areas only constitutes part of the total demand. Obviously in some areas the influence of commuters, or retired people seeking homes in rural settlements is very strong. Studies of particular concentrations of these groups; for example in the Hertfordshire commuterland (Pahl, 1965) and the Peak District (where both commuting and retirement trends are strong (Penfold, 1974), have proved the existence of the phenomenon. However the reasons for these population movements are less clear. Table 2.5 shows the stated motives for moving to a village, as reported by three studies in different areas. Two important conclusions emerge: first that even when respondents are not led towards a certain type of answer by the format of the question asked of them, it is seemingly very difficult to isolate explicit reasons for the desire to live in a rural settlement; and second that although a broad component of rural environmental quality pervades the responses in all three areas, the perceived reasons for recent in-migration show marked variation in each survey which could be due to spatial or technical causes.

In light of this complexity we can give generalized account to these trends, but are less able to explain the specific weightings of individual but interacting variables which occur in varying degrees in different locations. Clearly there are many rural areas which are dominated by the inflow of commuter populations. Equally apparent are those scenic, coastal or in other ways attractive

Table 2.4   Sources of demand for rural housing

1	Those wishing to live in a village and to commute to work
2	Those who have obtained local employment
3	Those wishing to retire to a village
4	Those changing houses because of age, health or changes in circumstances
5	Those having to leave service accommodation for any reason
6	Those couples who are newly married where one or both parties are native and wish to set up home there
7	Those established family units without separate homes
8	Those living in caravans, overcrowded homes or unfit housing
9	Those who are homeless
10	Those wishing to acquire holiday homes

Source: Scott-Miller, 1976

Table 2.5 Reasons for moving to villages (in percentages)

Hampshire		East Anglia		Worcestershire*		
More natural	8					
More peaceful	55					
Community life better	27	Easy to get to know people	47			
More privacy	7	Can keep yourself to yourself	37			
Countryside beautiful/ enjoyable/	21	Leisure activities	17			
Countryside healthier/ cleaner	22	Better surroundings to bring up children	64	Countryside/health	5	11
		Cheap to live	22	Convenient house	24	56
				Husband/wife born in village	11	5
				Husband/wife's family in village	13	7
				Change of job	34	21
				Retirement	8	2

Source: Hampshire CC and Mass Observations Ltd (1966); Emerson and Compton, 1968; Radford, 1970

* Two surveys were undertaken in this case.

rural settlements where retired people settle in significant numbers and where some houses are used as holiday homes or second homes. Some of these movements may be explained by urban push factors, which in America signify an escape from dirt, violence and racial or religious tension, and in Britain tend more towards the repellent effect of stress, overcrowding and the cost of land and housing. It is also reasonably well proven that rural areas exert a pull factor, to which the *perceived* nature of rural landscapes, communities, lifestyles and to some extent the traditional status that rural living affords, all contribute. However it is also the case that the price and suitability of housing in those settlements which are less in vogue and therefore less expensive in terms of property, also makes a significant impact on in-migration trends in pressured rural areas (Dunn *et al.*, 1981).

Land use and landownership

The changing natures of land use and landownership have played a considerable formative role in the shape and dimensions of rural settlement change. Best (1981) has given full analysis of a wide range of significant land-use issues, ranging from the importance of the increasing size of farm units to the dimensions of rural land loss. The exact proportions and therefore importance of rural-to-urban land-use change in Britain has been hotly contested. For example, in the report of a conference on this issue Best (1978, 13) considers that 'there is no real land problem in Britain at the moment. Most of the problem is simply in the mind; it is not out there on the ground'. The opposite view is taken by Coleman (1978, 32) who contends that 'while there are 50 km^2 of derelict land in London, we should not take a single additional hectare of farmland in the surrounding countryside and while there is still urban fringe to be infilled, we should not take a single hectare from the truly rural area'.

Whatever view is adopted in this debate, it is clear that land-use changes are important to an understanding of changes in rural settlements. Moss (1978, 122) uncovers the roots of this relationship:

> Landownership patterns in the countryside have . . . become less expansive in the more remote areas of Britain and increasingly fragmented towards the urban fringe and metropolitan areas . . . pressure to divide the countryside into increasingly smaller parcels is at its greatest in urban land around large villages, inhabited by commuters or attractive to tourists or both.

The last century has seen the breakdown of estate systems and their accompanying squirearchies – the very factors which in many cases were the historical establishers of the villages and hamlets which constitute the major proportion of current rural settlement patterns. Davidson and Wibberley (1977) stress the selective nature of land released for settlement expansion. In favoured rural areas, the rapid take up of agricultural land has led to the fragmentation and often dereliction of farmland surrounding rural settlements. In unfavoured areas, where agricultural land is of lower quality, there is a paradoxical absence of demand for expanding rural settlements. This partially accounts for the marked disparity of population densities between rural settlements in highland areas (30.6 ha/1000 p) and lowland areas (37.1 ha/1000 p) (Best and Rogers, 1973).

Selectivity also occurs at the local scale. The form of development displayed by a rural settlement located in a zone of urbanization pressure will vary greatly according to the pattern and attitude of landownership. Some farmers have been willing to release large areas of land for housing development, channelling their profits into land in a less-pressured location. Others have ensured the availability of a steady flow of small plots of land, often one field at a time, so that the capital gained can be used in support of their existing farming enterprise in the rural fringe. A third group have resisted the forces of prospective profit or political pressure, refusing to allow any of their land to be converted for settlement purposes. The haphazard distribution of these landowner attitudes has had a marked impact on whether pressured rural settlements have been allowed to grow or not, as land availability has encouraged planners to permit growth in these locations.

Inertia

In discussing the agents of change in rural settlements it is important to emphasize those elements which have stood in the way of possible beneficial changes, and thus indirectly have promoted many of the more problematic trends in rural communities. Burrell (1979) labels these factors as *inertia*, and outlines main areas where this phenomenon has been influential:

1 *Urban attitudes*: urban people responding to the pull factors of the countryside tend to perceive rural settlements and communities as they were, rather than within the present-day context. As a result, their attitudes often differ markedly from those of established rural residents, leading to social difficulties of integration in commuter settlements;

2 *Rural attitudes*: longstanding rural residents also tend to display conservative and 'old-fashioned' attitudes towards change in rural settlements. Any form of planning (whether of growth or no-growth) may be viewed with suspicion and met with an unwillingness to enter into participation or co-operation. This inactivity may relinquish community leadership and initiative to newcomer groups;

3 *Planning responses*: because of the priority given to urban problems in post-war Britain, the planning system has been tardy in its response to rural problems. Even now, a form of inertia has prevented planners from discarding urban planning frameworks and fully adapting to small-scale rural situations. This trend is manifest in the application of rigid urban-based regulations, particularly in matters of highways, building lines and space indicators to rural settlements where local circumstances are often ill-suited to the 'standard' planning response;

4 *Departmentalism*: the administrative subdivisions into individual government and public-authority departments, each with its own responsibility, have created an inertia stemming from an unwillingness on the part of one

administrative section to take an active interest in other departments' plans or problems unless these directly impinge on their own work. The separate strategies and budgets of each department are carefully guarded, and thus co-operation is hindered;

5 *Discussion not action*: Burrell also identifies an inertia of 'high hopes', by which the mere discussion and rationalization of rural problems is seen, particularly by planning committee members, as a major achievement. These high hopes are symbolized by the propensity for discussion to lead to further discussion (perhaps in the form of establishing a working party) rather than deciding on *action* to alleviate problems.

The existence of these various forms of inertia has in many cases forfeited the opportunity for positive planning action to allow a more sympathetic and sensitive accommodation of rural changes taking local factors into consideration. Inertia of planning response and action may have accumulated through the constant lack of resources which has prevented positive planning in many rural settlements.. However, attitudes of inertia have continued to prevail among planners and planned and it is these attitudes which have detrimentally influenced rural problems.

Resulting rural conditions

These various planned and unplanned agents of change interact in many different ways to produce varying conditions in rural settlements and communities. It is, however, possible to formalize certain systematic results of rural change which are present to a greater or lesser extent in rural settlements depending on their location, size and character, and which represent problems for planners to solve. It should be recognized from the beginning that 'it is not automatic that we can, or are ever capable, of resisting these changes' (Peregrine, 1979, 16). These rural conditions are summarized briefly here, as it is necessary to understand the problems before analysing their solutions.

Depopulation

A recent review of the causes of rural depopulation (Department of the Environment, 1977, 113) suggests that 'the increased expectations and demands of the rural population and the greater penetration of information concerning the better amenities and opportunities, either real or apparent, of urban living' have both sustained the process of depopulation, and indeed have complicated the causal factors promoting this movement of people out of rural areas. These causal elements are neatly summarized by Wallace and Drudy (1975) in their 'vicious circle' of depopulation (figure 2.5). Given that a lack of rural employment is one of the main causes of population decline, they describe the subsequent decrease of population which itself results in a lowering of service thresholds. As fewer services are demanded, service levels will eventually contract thus diminishing the economic attractiveness of the area, which in turn pre-empts further employment opportunities being offered. This

Figure 2.5 Vicious circle of depopulation

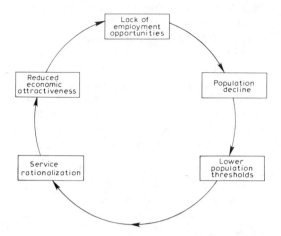

Source: After Wallace and Drudy, 1975

gloomy prognosis faces planners in many remoter rural areas.

Much has been written elsewhere concerning the process and ramifications of rural depopulation (e.g. Commins, 1978; Dunn, 1976; Lowenthal and Comitas, 1962; Mitchell, 1950). However, two factors should be stressed here. First, because the process has continued for so long, some commentators have become almost blasé about the acute and crippling effects that depopulation has on the morale and life-style of residual communities. Important elements of these communities are disappearing and are not being replaced. For instance, the Countryside Review Committee (1977) emphasizes the declining numbers of people of working age and the drastic social and economic imbalance that results. Elsewhere, the loss of younger age-groups is highlighted (House, 1965), building up a picture of an over-representation of ageing members of the remaining community. Class structures are also overturned:

> the balance of class structure will be tipped towards those people who can meet the financial requirements connected with second home ownership or long-distance commuting, and also towards those people who do not have the required affluence or personal mobility (or indeed the inclination) to move out of the remoter rural areas once they are established there. (Cloke, 1979, 21)

The second factor about which some misunderstanding has developed concerns the continuing presence of depopulation as the major social ill in many communities. For example, the Government Interdepartmental Group report on rural depopulation (HM Treasury, 1976, 2) is optimistic that 'there are some reasons for thinking that things may be changing and that the problems of these (remote) areas, or at least some of them, will be less serious in the future'. This conclusion is based on the widespread population increases in rural areas over the last two decades, and on the reduction of out-migration trends in some remote rural areas over the same period. However, this loss of momentum was almost certainly due at least in part to high levels of national unemployment which have assuaged the movement of rural people to urban work, so these trends should not be viewed as a problem solved. Indeed a brief review of survey reports by county council structure plan teams and of corroborative research from academic sources is sufficient to convince us that depopulation remains a major planning problem, even when some replacement occurs through selective in-migration. McCleery (1979, 10), using the Scottish context, demonstrates the complexity of the processes involved:

> A region may be experiencing net population gain but within that region the more sparsely populated areas are more than likely to be losing out to the areas of established growth. Traditionally, the Highlands have lost to the Central Belt and although this trend has recently been reversed, the Western Highlands continue to lose out to the Eastern Highlands.

Moreover, Drudy (1978) has demonstrated that depopulation is also occurring in prosperous agricultural regions as well as marginal ones. The strength of this evidence suggests that the selective out-migration of people from many different types of rural area should continue of be placed in the forefront of rural planning attention.

Social polarization

The major paradox of rural change in post-war Britain has been the widespread repopulation of rural settlements with a new dormitory role for commuters. Some settlements have thus been physically revitalized but often torn as under socially. Furthermore the socio-economic benefits to be gained from population increases have to be set against the reduction in environmental value caused by estate-type developments in more traditional village architectural settings. Newby (1979) notes the stark contrast that has arisen between the affluent, ex-urban, middle-class newcomer and the established rural population who are tied to the settlement or its immediate area by their low-paid employment, by old age, and by a lack of resources or desire to promote a move to an urban area.

> The former group lives in the countryside mostly by conscious choice (and this includes the majority of farmers and landowners) and has the resources to overcome the problems of distance and access to essential services. The latter group, by contrast, has become increasingly trapped by a lack of access to alternative employment, housing and the full range of amenities which the remainder of the population takes for granted. (Newby, 1979, 273)

This process 'of social polarization encompasses both pressing social problems for the established village resident, and several snares for the planner who is faced with addressing these problems. First, the most common perception of rural living conditions is that of considerable material improvement since 1947. In that the basic needs for living such as food, clothing, housing and education have undergone significant increases in overall standards, this optimistic perception is correct, but these absolute improvements mask a very definite relative deterioration in opportunities in terms of services, facilities and jobs. The danger is that this relative poverty is being submerged by the urbanite invasion of rural England, and may disappear from view as the term 'rural' increasingly takes on the middle class attributes of affluence and security. Indeed with this social invisibility of the less affluent rural population groups, public attention is becoming increasingly centred on the internal issues of the more monied newcomer populations; hence the trend towards environmentalism (Lowe, 1975; 1977).

Further problems occur in the housing markets of settlements with significant numbers of newcomers, in that the allocation of public and private sector housing within rural settlements has largely influenced the social composition of the community. In effect, housing may be viewed as a mechanism of social control, either conscious or unconscious (Rogers, 1976) and of social segregation in the physical layout of a village. Segregation increasingly occurs between the newcomer residents occupying new and improved housing at one end of a village, and the established 'local' people trapped within the council estate at the other. With the rising demand for rural housing, planners have spurned the opportunity to allow the building of significant increases to the housing stock so as to release the pressure imposed on rents and prices of village accommodation. Rather, there has been a tendency towards strict control of new building, again often based on the 'environmental' or 'conservation' ethic (Haines, 1973), and where a settlement is scheduled for no-growth it immediately becomes residentially desirable, property prices increase, and it eventually becomes *gentrified*. A similar phenomenon has been recorded in the urban 'villages' of London by Hamnett and Williams (1979; 1980).

Social polarization is also expressed in other forms. Studies by Ambrose (1974) and Pahl (1965a; 1966) have demonstrated that middle-class newcomers have tended to maintain most of their social contacts outside the settlement in which they live and so integration with the established residents has been slow, if attempted at all. Thorns (1968) contrasts this pattern of social linkage with the village-orientated contact patterns of farmworker families. Social activities present a microcosmic view of this polarization 'with the traditional organizations and events which revolve around church and pub in rural communities being shunned by many newcomers in favour of more middle-class pastimes such as the badminton club and the drama group' (Cloke, 1979, 18).

Finally, social selectivity has resulted in problems of servicing rural settlements. Large and sudden inflows of population into small villages place great strain on the educational and sewage-disposal building programmes for rural areas. Furthermore, the services demanded by the middle class are often of a specialist nature, such as the delicatessen and the coiffeur, rather than the providers of the more basic needs of local residents. Lastly, a selective in-migration of retirement-age population can easily overburden social and medical services in rural areas. All these social and economic strains are placed on rural settlements through selective in-migratory movements, and the reconciliation of these imbalances presents a mammoth task for rural settlement planners.

Political influence

Our awareness of the chief actors in local rural policy-making and of its main processes has been greatly enhanced by a recent study of the way in which land-ownership serves as a power resource in the political system (Newby *et al.*, 1978; Rose *et al.*, 1978; 1979). Taking an East Anglian case study, Newby and his colleagues disclose that in fact the influence of landowners has declined in the national, and to a lesser extent the local planning arenas, but that this influence remains as an important factor in the planning of rural areas. Although the national scale leverage enjoyed by the farming fraternity has been widely recognized (Self and Storing, 1962), the local level activities of this powerful group have been less well-advertised, which leads to some speculation as to the virtual autonomy of decision-making which must have been enjoyed in some areas before the occurrence of a decline in power, as highlighted by the East Anglian study.

Even with a diminished power base following local government reorganization in 1974, it is clear that 'in rural areas such as East Anglia, landowners are not simply well represented on local councils but are consistently able to define key issues in ways which tend to further their sectional interests to the detriment of working-class groups' (Rose *et al.*, 1978, 15). An analysis of the make-up of Suffolk County Council showed the influential 'gatekeeper' positions (Pettigrew, 1972) controlled by the landed section of the rural community:

> The council chairman and vice-chairman, and the chairman of the Planning, Education, Social Services, Finance and Policy Committees were not only drawn exclusively from among the ranks of farmers and landowners; five of them had been educated at Eton and came from families whose names had been familiar in the government of the county for centuries. (Rose *et al.*, 1978, 19)

With this foundation, landowning classes have been able to translate their own interests and ideologies into 'the public interest' thus often unwittingly pursuing their own objectives to the detriment of less powerful sections of the rural community. For instance, Newby and his colleagues report an almost fanatical obsession with the maintenance of low rates in Suffolk, which has resulted in limited local resources and therefore low spending on education and social services. Whereas ruling groups would argue that low rates are in the 'public interest', this strategy does, of course, discriminate against less affluent residents who can afford neither to send their children to fee-paying schools nor to subscribe to private medical systems.

Perhaps the policy area which is most affected by landowner influence, not only in East Anglia but wherever the ethic raises its head, is that of a strict conservation of the countryside. Conservation ideology tends to favour both urbanite recreationalists who seek to gain or maintain aesthetic value in the countryside, and rural landed classes who at present own and enjoy the countryside, although there is a marked tendency for the latter group to take active steps to discourage the former who are seen as 'spoilers' of a conserved rural idyll. However conservation policies can have a number of ramifications on other socio-economic decisions made in rural areas. They can prevent development of industry and 'mass-produced' (and therefore inexpensive) housing, which coincidentally would also counteract an influx of ex-urban, working-class (and possibly Labour voting) people into the rural areas. They can lead to rigid restrictions on the type of house permitted, favouring the environmentally pleasing but very expensive type of property, and can be the direct cause of a shortage of low-cost housing which in turn drives working-class residents either to out-migration to towns or to the paternalistic bonds of tied housing. The exclusion of industrial development maintains agriculture as the priority rural industry, and maintains low wages through a lack of competition for labour.

The only real challenge to this power base comes from the adjunct of new middle-class rural residents, rather than from the political organization of working-class or 'non-conservative' elements. The new adventitious village populations represent an articulate and often affluent group who have made incursions into the political arena, particularly at the very local level. Far from showing an awareness of problems suffered by the rural poor, these newcomer groups are also often dominated by environmental ideals which prompt them to support the denial of new housing developments which might spoil the rural character which they have specifically migrated to. Rather, these groups tend to be preoccupied with opposition to developments in modern agricultural systems which are seen as destroyers of traditional landscapes. Davidson and Wibberley (1977) suggest that these adventitious political groups have access to only limited means of action, but even if they were to usurp some of the influence enjoyed by landowning classes, it would still be the rural poor who are disadvantaged by rural political structures.

Rural deprivation

A vast number of words have been devoted to the subject of rural deprivation (e.g. Runciman, 1972; Shaw, 1979; Walker, 1978; Association of County Councils, 1979; Connor, 1980; Knox and Cottam, 1981; McLaughlin, 1981) to the extent that the term, and the concept, are fast becoming hackneyed in the consideration of rural problems. Only a very brief review of salient issues is attempted here in order to isolate the major policy requirements desired of rural settlement planners wishing to tackle the individual problems which in combination constitute the overall deprivation state.

First it should be stressed that rural deprivation is not a new phenomenon. At all times during the history of the countryside there have been some individuals and groups who have been privileged, while others have been underprivileged. The exposure of rural deprivation has suffered because of its often invisible nature. Warrington (1978) stresses that high unemployment, poverty, poor living conditions, social stress and isolation in small and scattered rural communities remain hidden 'out of sight, out of mind' compared with the immediacy and scale of similar afflictions in urban environments. Moreover, the concept of deprivation *per se* is a tricky one to grasp with any confidence. Wibberley (1978, 5) questions:

> Should we be mainly concerned about absolute poverty or deprivation, that is, an absence of some or all of the necessities of life? Even this absolute situation is hard to identify and measure because of the shadowy distinction between absolute and conventional necessities.

Clearly the answer is that both poverty and deprivation are the concern of the rural planner, bearing in mind that it is the *combination* of individual problems which serve both to limit the range of opportunities open to rural residents and in some cases to deny opportunities altogether. Deprivation exists in three broad categories which (as with depopulation processes) when linked together can be viewed as a cyclical and self-sustaining process (figure 2.6).

Household deprivation

This category includes several background criteria which dictate the ability of individuals or families to make use of those opportunities that are available in rural areas. The major constraint in this context is a paucity of income, and it is clear that there are many low-income groups, including farmworkers, economically inactive, unemployed and retired people, who find themselves

Figure 2.6 The rural deprivation cycle

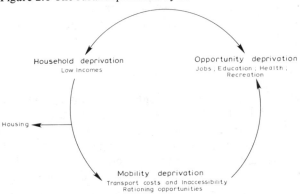

Source: Shaw, 1979, 184

located in rural settlements. Once there, these groups find it difficult to escape. Thomas and Winyard (1979) demonstrate how a combination of direct taxation and rigid welfare state benefits have channelled rural low-income families into a poverty trap which makes no allowance for the cost of journeys to urban work. Income deprivation is directly linked to rural housing problems (Dunn *et al.*, 1981), whereby low-income families have found it increasingly difficult to secure adequate accommodation in their local rural area. The rented sector has declined because of the outworkings of various Rent Acts, the tied-cottage issue, and the low priority given to rural council housing. In addition, owner-occupation has been hit by steeply rising prices created by an urban demand for rural housing. Planners, when criticized for their straight-jacketing of housing markets through strict development control, point out (not without some justification) that the housing market is not a closed system but rather is subject to strong external pressures which can negate the fulfilment of local and regional housing objectives. For example the high demand from households wishing to obtain housing in Hertfordshire has been seen by the County Council (1979) to have two major effects:

1 House prices are inflated beyond the means of local households wishing to stay in the county;
2 The building industry has been encouraged to develop land in excess of that required for local housing needs and of a type which is inconsistent with those needs.

The combined effect of these income and housing factors has been to discriminate against the low-income families who wish to remain in rural settlements.

Opportunity deprivation

Against this background of discriminatory factors serving to force established rural residents into centres of better household opportunities, several other elements of rural life are fast disappearing from rural settlements. Together, these may be described as opportunity deprivation. For instance, rural settlements have failed to reclaim the employment opportunities which were lost with the decline in agricultural jobs. Even with the introduction of small manufacturing firms and expansion of the service sector, employment prospects in rural areas remain severely limited with resulting high levels of unemployment, dim prospects for school leavers, low female activity rates and a mismatch between the jobs that are available and the characteristics of the unemployed workforce. These trends are exacerbated by economic recession which reduces the likelihood of new employers being attracted to rural locations, so the choice for many rural dwellers is to remain unemployed, accept the costs and strains of a long journey to work, or move to locations where work opportunities do exist.

The opportunities presented by local provision of services and facilities in rural settlements are also declining. In the private sector, a number of studies (e.g. Harman, 1978) have highlighted the demise of local village shops and their accompanying sub post offices. Even where shops and services remain in villages, the rural resident pays a higher price for food than his/her urban counterpart, and generally incurs additional expenses in the achievement of the standards of services which are available to urban people. In the public sector, resource rationalization and the high *per capita* costs of servicing a scattered and small scale rural population have again induced opportunity deprivation. The trend has been for the village school, the doctor's surgery and the local post office to be withdrawn in favour of concentrations of junior and secondary education, and three or four-doctor health centres in the larger towns. These vanishing acts again present the rural resident with the choice of incurring additional costs for access to centralized services, or uprooting themselves to a place where opportunities are more plentiful.

Mobility deprivation

The third element of overall deprivation concerns those groups within rural society who may be classed as non-mobile and who are therefore discriminated against by the withdrawal of opportunities from rural settlements Research by Moseley (1979) and others has established that non-mobile elements include the elderly, young children, teenagers, mothers left in the home, the infirm and the low-paid, all of whom do not own or have access to a car. With the decline in public transport services in rural areas, this collective majority of the rural population find it difficult to adapt to any incidence of opportunity deprivation. As a consequence, yet another choice has to be made by the disadvantaged groups: meet the additional costs of access to centralized facilities (if access is available); go without the missing opportunities (although this is almost impossible with such elements as health services), or migrate.

The combined effect of household, opportunity and mobility deprivation is to isolate particular groups within rural communities and present them with complex and sometimes insurmountable difficulties in obtaining the basic needs for survival in their established place of residence. Moreover these effects of deprivation are cumulative. The Association of County Councils (1979, 2) analyses this multiplicity:

> children from low income families in poor rural housing, suffering from the added disadvantage of limited educational provision and inaccessible further education facilities, are not likely to acquire the skills necessary to obtain employment offering the opportunity of a higher standard of living for their own families.

Clearly, rural deprivation presents planners with urgent and difficult social problems to resolve.

A timely article by Moseley (1980) has established two characteristics of rural deprivation which should be noted here as a postscript to the consideration of that form of deprivation to be found specifically in rural settlements. Moseley stresses that rural deprivation and urban deprivation are but localized expressions of problems which are essentially aspatial – a point emphasized by McLaughlin's (1981, 32) comment that 'it is people who have problems not places *per se*'. Naturally, this assertion does not deny that rural areas have distinct characteristics of which three stand out:

1 Their pleasant environment (which attracts those released willingly or unwillingly from employment);
2 Their spaced-out geographical nature (which leads to accessibility problems and high costs in providing public services);
3 Their local political ideology (which favours the market, the volunteer and self-reliance rather than public provision).

However, none of these three characteristics actually causes deprivation, and indeed most of the decisions which underlie rural deprivation are taken *outside* rural areas by national and international agencies.

The second point is that the study of rural deprivation has focused almost entirely on the *consumers* of deprivation, not the *producers*. Much more attention should be directed towards the institutions which allocate scarce resources – that is, the factors that actually dictate rural life chances. In short, it would seem that an understanding of rural deprivation may not be best achieved either by focusing upon the rural deprived, or indeed by focusing on rural regions at all.

Settlement categorization

The interaction of various agents of rural change to produce trends of rationalization, polarization, political manipulation and deprivation occurs at differing speeds and intensities according to the specific conditions prevailing in individual settlements. There is a great temptation to aggregate these sets of circumstances into generic classifications of rural settlements so that acceptable and workable planning strategies may be established for each settlement category. At a general level, this procedure does little harm and indeed acts as a clarification mechanism for describing changes and conditions in rural areas. For example, the Countryside Review Committee (1977) outlines three rural categories:

1 *Remote areas* with declining population, employment opportunities and service provision;
2 *Dormitory areas* where rapid in-migration of urbanites puts pressure on resource provision and social cohesion;
3 *Leisure–retirement areas* where an ageing population can overwhelm social and medical services, and where tourism and recreation also bring specific problems.

This classification, although internally heterogeneous, does at least begin to crystallize the important character-forming processes in rural settlements.

A somewhat different approach is taken by Moss (1978; 1979), who defines three types of village according to the manner in which the administrative system of rural planning has responded to the socio-economic needs of rural communities:

1 *Advantaged villages* with adequate population, government investment,

employment and accessibility opportunities to create a stable social and economic base for rural living;

2 *Disadvantaged villages* with inadequate population to support essential services and facilities, but with sufficient accessibility to share the opportunities in adjacent settlements;

3 *Deprived villages* with declining population and lacking in employment and service opportunities but unable to share other facilities due to remoteness or inaccessibility.

Moss's prognosis is that advantaged villages will continue to grow carrying many disadvantaged villages along with them, while deprived villages are doomed unless injected with considerable financial investment particularly in the provision of employment opportunities. He views these trends of growth and decline as cyclic and self-sustaining processes (figure 2.7) in which deprived rural settlements become progressively deprived and advantaged villages, once embarked upon the growth trend cannot escape the prospect of further growth. Moreover it is clear from figure 2.7 that the essential sustaining factor in both cyclic models is that of planning strategy. The point of ultimate feedback (emphasized in the diagram) in each case is the policy of centralized investment in selected key areas of least need, to the detriment both of the selected locations (by the disappearance of traditional village characteristics caused by uncontrolled growth) and of smaller settlements where investment is least possible yet most needed.

Two immediate issues emerge from this thoughtful yet polemic model of deterministic rural change. First, the model suffers from endemic difficulties of over-generalization. This in itself is not a cause for criticism since only by embellishment of homogeneity can the fundamental contextual problems be clearly isolated. However, as subsequent chapters will show, the planning of rural settlements has been over-endowed with the notion of grouping settlements into broad categories and making crucial resource allocation decisions on the basis of those categories. Only more recently have we come to realize that individual settlements and their communities display discrete and often egocentric problems which require localized planning action rather than the broad-brush categorized approach. Thus to label all deprived villages as doomed, and all advantaged villages as healthy would be to fly in the face of the need for localized planning action. What is important is to understand the mechanisms through which disadvantaged and deprived villages have overcome their individual problems and to offer these mechanisms as a starting point for the planning of other individual settlements suffering a similar malaise.

The second resultant issue is central to the analysis of rural settlement planning as a problem-solving process. The model embodies the rising tide of recent criticism which has been levelled at rural planning on the basis that far from solving problems in village communities, the planning process has actually exacerbated those problems in the majority of rural settlements. That is, by pursuing policies of selected growth, rural settlement planning has induced problems of deprivation and polarization, particularly in small

Figure 2.7 Cyclic models of village growth and decline

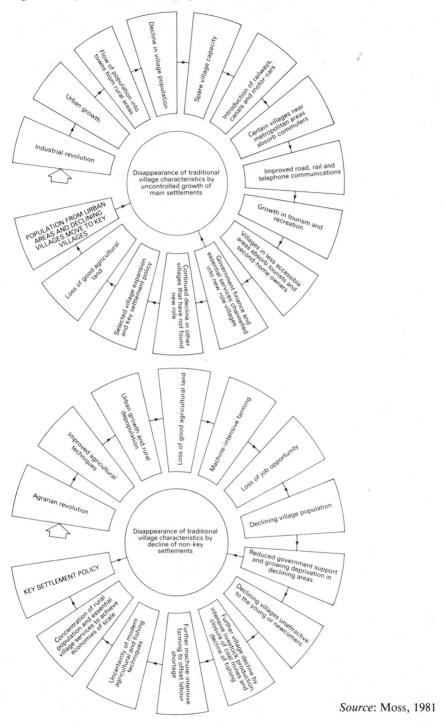

Source: Moss, 1981

non-key settlements, but also in the favoured growth settlements themselves. The validity of this assertion should be analysed in the light of rural conditions prior to the initiation of planning in rural settlements, restrictions imposed on planners by scarce resources, government advice, lack of policy-making and policy-reviewing experience, and the progressive alterations made to the rural settlement planning ethos during successive temporal stages of planning, as well as in comparison with the variously prescribed alternative policy frameworks for rural settlement planning.

THREE

Theory and rural settlement planning

A taxonomy of contextual theoretical options

Gunnar Olsson (1974, 16) draws attention to the complex problems which have been encountered in the use of familiar social science theories as a basis for social, economic and regional planning. He concludes that

> if we continue along the methodological and manipulative path we have been following thus far, then we run the risk of increasing those social, economic and regional inequalities, which the planning initially was designed to decrease; our good-natured attempts to rectify current injustices will be self-defeating, not because some vicious bureaucrat designed them that way, but because we have failed to understand the deep structure of social research and action.

Although these reactions are founded on regional planning experience in Sweden, they also serve as a cogent summary of the relationship between theory and rural settlement planning, in which descriptive social science has often been translated literally and with few modifications into prescriptive social engineering. This chapter sets out to describe the theoretical alternatives open to settlement planners in rural areas, and to pinpoint those elements of theory which have exerted a formative influence on rural settlement planning, particularly in Britain. Analysis of the theoretical underpinnings of settlement policy is an extremely important task; first because if a narrow, blinkered view of available theory has been adopted in planning then due emphasis to ignored theoretical issues may aid the explanation of the shortcomings of planning in practice; and, second, because any search for replacement policies for rural settlements will inevitably begin with the rejection of some (if not all) of the theoretical constructs on which present policy is based.

No discrete and homogeneous categories exist between theoretical sources. In many ways, for example, political theory is inexorably interlinked with social and economic dicta and dogma. However, for the purposes of outlining theoretical options, a series of notional headings is used, based largely on the existing terminology created by theorists. These notional categories serve not as an attempt to exhaust every possible theoretical pathway but rather as a simple multiple-choice listing against which to check the progress of rural settlement planning which has so often been directed by 'instinct' and implicit action rather than explicit acceptance of particular theoretical stances.

Political theory

A fundamental dichotomy between *rationality* and *ideology* has served to engender a rather schizophrenic attitude towards political theory in rural settlement planning. Glass (1959) has shown for planning in general that rationality has been adopted both as a pointer to an objective and value-free image of the real world, and as a logical and positive basis for policy prescription. Rather than suffering the 'biases' inherent in the idealized states sought after by political action, rationality has been seen to pursue standardized goals such as 'the public interest' in an objective and apolitical manner. Therefore planners have sought to present an air of independent and detached professionalism by furthering this rational approach. Indeed, several authors (e.g. Friedmann, 1966; Simon *et al.*,) have defined planning as a purely rational exercise, in which social action based on value-free truths leaves little room for ideology.

The presentation of planners as rationally objective professionals has opened the door for the adoption of crucial controlling influences which have moulded rural settlement planning into its current form. For example, Simmie (1974) clearly shows that the economics of planning, with its utilitarian foundations, has opted for the normative element in rational planning which has resulted in the maximization of interests, the search for optimum economic solutions, and (as a consequence) the rejection of the socially necessary but irrational or sub-optimum alternatives. The very strong predominance of economic criteria over other circumstances in rural settlement planning stems largely from this overemphasis on the rationality of the planning process.

Despite the favour shown by planners to the rational approaches to planning, the inevitability of ideological influence in planning processes is apparent. The idea that a 'true' understanding of society can be translated into social action dates back to Hegel, Feuerbach and Marx. However, this 'truth' is in fact based on the requirements of specific groups and can only be discovered 'by uncovering the special interests served by ideologies and exposing how they served the particular interests of their authors' (Simmie, 1974, 160). Therefore the logical and rational steps taken within a normative planning framework are subject to the ideologies of planners themselves and to those of their political masters. At a national scale in Britain, markedly different ideological stances from both ends of the political spectrum have been received in alternate doses, as the balance of political power has changed. As a result, the interpretations of social reality and the resultant need for social action have also swung with the political pendulum. Results of this ideological instability have filtered down to rural settlement planning, which has been bounded by the financial and policy dogma constraints of successive governments. In urban planning, the popular images of the market-based, economically-oriented and hard-line policies of right-wing ideology followed by the interventionist, socially-oriented and soft-line tendencies of the left have generally held true to form. However, the rural environment has proved to be less of a platform for ideological reforming zeal, being at the bottom of the pecking order for priority social action, despite the fact that the right-wing power base in Britain is traditionally conceived as stemming from the conservatism of the countryside. Even so, a programme for the nationalization of small shops (so that village shops could be operated as a social service to rural people), widespread subsidy of other rural services, national government sponsorship of worker co-operatives as a solution to rural employment problems, public-sector housing to be given total priority over the private sector, substantially increased minimum wages for agricultural workers, and so on would immediately be classed as ideological and find more support from the left than from the right.

Ideology in rural settlement planning has perhaps been more visible at the local level. The political make-up of county and district councils and their committees has had a marked influence on the policy-making and policy-implementation techniques prescribed for different rural areas. Differentiation occurs not only in policy-making, but in the levels of subsidy afforded, for example, to public transport services, peripatetic social services and experimental projects aimed at solving particular social problems. While all rural settlement policies appear to have been restricted by the rationality of minimization of exchequer costs, it is clear that in some counties, the effects of this rationality have been exacerbated by the ideological stringencies imposed by the desire to maintain a low level of rates, or to prevent settlement growth for conservation reasons (as uncovered by Newby *et al.* (1978) in Suffolk). It is fair to say that we have yet to see a widespread incidence of left-wing ideology encased in localized policies for rural settlements, and this lack of experience has led to the linking of resource concentration policies with right-wing dogma, and resource dispersal policies with that of the left-wing. The inevitable inference here is that a shift of political power in rural areas would herald a new approach to the spatial allocation of rural resources. This theme is discussed further in chapter 4 where the evidence of recommendations and advice from various shades of government suggests that the ideological links with concentration and dispersal policies are not proven. However, rural settlement planning will differ according to the political nature of central and local government, even though the planning process itself is viewed by its actors in a more rational and objectively apolitical light.

Planning theory

Theory connected with the planning process is closely tied up with the political options briefly reviewed above. Cherry (1974, 83) stresses that

> the development of planning thought has not been shaped in a vacuum. Nor will it; it will continue to be fashioned by a context of political and social attitudes. The scope and content of our planning system, its objectives and methods will reflect our style of democracy and its assumptions.

Theoretical options may be discussed in terms of planning *ethos* and planning *method*. At its most basic level planning can be seen to deal with three sectors of economy and society (Broadbent, 1979):

1 *Private firms*: producers, distributors, banks and other financial institutions;
2 *Public agencies*: corporations and government, of which planning is a part;
3 *Households*: and the social groups and community organizations to which households belong.

The way in which planning is able to influence and modify the actions and interactions of these sectors will thus have direct consequences on the availability of finance and resources, the demand and supply of land for development, the deprivation experienced by various social groups and the overall levels of wages, profits and public spending. Moreover, the influence of planning in Britain is hampered by the rift between the statutory and non-statutory operative modes. Statutory plans such as development and structure plans are the result of the configuration of vast levels of planning effort and resources, and are subject to public consultation during their preparation. However, there is very little power to implement them. Non-statutory plans, on the other hand, often slip by unnoticed by the public yet are the source of huge financial investments in housing, infrastructure and so on. We are therefore faced with an apparently mismatched situation whereby the bulk of planning time and effort is expended on a negative response to socio-economic problems while the more positive non-statutory strategies are given only secondary consideration.

Given this discord between effort and finance within planning, it is not surprising that the fundamental distinctions between the three main sectors of economy and society often remain irreconcilable. After all, each sector has its own ambitions:

> The private sector produces saleable goods and services in the market. The public sector's main role is to provide social goods and services out of taxation and to keep the economy stable. It also provides grants, and goods and services which are used by the private sector – 'planning for production'. The general public provides the labour force and consumes the goods produced by the other two sectors. (Broadbent, 1979, 20)

The public sector has grown steadily in recent years to the extent that, according to national income and accounts data, it now controls over 60 per cent of the gross national product. In many ways, the public sector has established a broad level of guidance over the national economy, and more specific controls in various areas where the private sector is excluded by law from challenging public agencies. Nevertheless, the private sector retains considerable powers of policy- and decision-making, and as a consequence the losers in the triumvirate struggle outlined by Broadbent are those sections of the general public whose life-style requirements do not attain the minimum standards operated by either the private or the public sectors. Planning ethos options for the global reconciliation of the demands of the three sectors represent variations of emphasis between the public and private sectors:

1 *Withdrawal*, with planning playing a less interventionist role, allowing conflicts to be resolved within the market place;

2   *Private-sector support*, with planning intervening only to support the private-sector needs of industry, developers and landowners;
3   *Intervention*, with planning centred on the direct provision of social facilities and opportunities by the public sector, and recognizing the need to replace private-sector roles with public effort in some or all cases.

Rural settlement planning in Britain represents a mixed bag of these three options. Although based on support of the private sector in industry, commerce, retailing, housing and so on, several roles of opportunity supply to rural residents (e.g. most education, health, infrastructural and social services) are performed by local authorities. However this apparent intervention by the public sector is far from comprehensive and very often perpetrates trends of withdrawal similar to those consequent on private sector supply of opportunities. Therefore many rural residents perceive planning as a process which has 'allowed' the allocation of resources to be governed by economic criteria either in the private sector market place or the public sector meeting place. Thus, despite appearances, rural settlement planning has seen few beneficial consequences of the positive intervention option except in those larger centres which would have been favoured by open market economic conditions anyway. There is, however, a very strong case to be made for the adoption of a much higher degree of planning intervention in rural settlements. The notion of social conflicts being resolved within the private sector disregards the peculiar characteristics of rural areas: namely that they consist of small settlements and scattered populations at low densities. Thus the thresholds normally required by private-sector service agencies are often difficult or impossible to achieve in these rural conditions, leading to the inevitable conclusion that if the future of rural communities is to be maintained, the job of providing the basic necessities for living will increasingly be required of public-sector agencies following an interventionist strategy. The alternative, when painted at its blackest, is one of gentrified rural communities containing only those whose affluence allows them access to retrenched urban-based opportunities provided by the private sector.

In terms of planning method a series of theories which are relevant to rural settlement planning may be recognized, largely stemming from the socio-political and epistemological theories of Popper (1963; 1968; 1969; 1972):

1   *Verificationalism* represents a set of methods designed to prepare an adequate information base for rational decision-making. The requirements of this approach are summarized by Camhis (1979) as:
   1   A general set of values expressed as goals and objectives;
   2   Generation and examination of all alternatives open for achieving the goals;
   3   Prediction of the consequences of each alternative;
   4   Comparison of the consequences in relation to agreed goals and objectives;
   5   Selection of the alternative which best corresponds with goals and objectives.
   Inherent in this approach is the need to verify (either by intellectual

rationalism or by the evidence of empiricism) the hypotheses which are inevitably raised by statements of 'alternatives', 'consequences' and 'goals and objectives'. Friedmann and Hudson (1974) outline several criticisms of verificationalism. First, the planning system usually deals with uncertainties and cannot therefore provide accurate and relevant data for use in the prediction of the consequences of planning action. Second, this approach takes little heed of the community welfare function; that is the calculation of trade-offs among a community's preferences for different objectives. Finally, with current levels of bureaucracy there is a further problem of minimizing administrative friction following the taking of decisions. To decide on a course of action is not necessarily to ensure that this action is carried out. Despite these criticisms, verificationalism has continued to form the perceived ideal method for rural settlement planning, even though its adoption has been implicit rather than explicit;

2 *Incrementalism* is a form of planning which both describes how planners make decisions and presents a normative model of how these decisions should be made. In essence, incrementalism is the science of 'muddling through' which takes the exact opposite path to verificationalism. The view of planning as a series of interrelated and controlled stages is rejected in favour of piecemeal planning in short-term increments rather than pursuing long-term objectives. In addition, the idea of evaluating all possibilities to find the best match with desired aims and objectives is dis-regarded in favour of a more pragmatic evaluation of available resources and the likelihood of a decision being accepted by political and administra-tive authorities. Thus incrementalism is problem-orientated rather than goal-orientated and is bound by the existing order of society. These qualities give the approach a conservative nature because the most powerful interest groups in society are able to control the decisions which are made. To some, incremental planning equals realism. To others it prevents the adoption of longer-term and more radical policy solutions to planning problems. Evidence of incrementalism in rural settlement planning may be noted throughout this book;

3 *Falsificationism* is an approach based on 'learning by mistakes'. Rather than offering proof of what *is* happening in the environment to be planned, it is envisaged that a continuous sequence of self-criticism will lead to recognition of planning errors and result in a clear picture of what *is not* happening. Falsificationism has received considerable support, for example from Wilson (1969, 7) whose methodological leanings are 'concerned with hypotheses, theories and models which are in principle *falsifiable*, and that the scientist should seek to test by seeking to falsify'. However it is subject to the same genre of criticism as incurred by verifi-cationalism in that dogmatic rejection of facts or truths is also dependent on the quality of information available to the planner. At first sight, falsificationism as an approach has little to offer rural settlement planning which appears to be some years behind its urban counterpart in the development of *positive* techniques and therefore has little need of the

more negative aspirations of falsificationism. However, recent years have witnessed an increasing interest in this form of planning theory, simply because traditional wisdom in favour of resource concentration in rural areas has formed a *self*-verifying process in which every individual implementation of concentration policy reaffirms the need for continued concentration in the future. Consequently, a falsificationalist backlash has been directed at these conventional verifications of rural settlement planning policy (see chapter 7).

Social theory

There is a very strong link between social theory and planning. Bailey (1975, 145) stresses that 'every social theory, whether implicit or not, has attached to it a view of man as planner and planned for, which are part of the basis on which we assess that theory's ability and validity'. Once again, theorists have assembled a range of theory (e.g. Grabow and Haskin, 1973; Horton, 1970; Pinker, 1971) from which rural settlement planning attitudes may be formed. Bailey (1975) outlines four categories:

1 *Positivist theory* stands at the scientific extreme of the socio-theoretical spectrum and entertains the notion that planning is the deterministic and quantitative science of prediction and control. Positivism therefore reflects a series of causes and effects in society. Original causes such as physical circumstances or inborn predispositions determine human behaviour; human behaviour results in distinct forms of social structure; social structures may be manipulated by the planning process. The individual is thus viewed as a pre-determined and highly controlled being;

2 *Social–structural theory* uses the scientific model to explain human behaviour and other social phenomena according to the nature of prevailing social institutional structures and values. Consequently, an analysis of misfits or deviants from these rigid roles laid down for the individual in society will identify those parts of the structure where stress occurs, and planning action can be channelled towards these problem areas. Once again the individual is seen to be trapped in a rigid social structure which he or she can do little to alter;

3 *Interpretative theory* rejects the preceding deterministic models which can only explain broadly described categories of behaviour, and which deny the importance of individual choice and freedom as inputs into social problems. Instead, it offers a view of society where behaviour, attitude and relationships may be explained by individual and group interpretation of environment and community (as expressed through freedom of choice) as well as by conformity to pre-established social structures.

4 *Conflict theory* adopts a stance in which power is the ultimate agent in the structuring of society. Using this perspective the individual has potential for freedom of choice yet this potential is repressed by power-bearing authorities and their representatives who control the allocation of resources and opportunities in society. Inherent in the adoption of conflict

theory by planners is the desire to break down conflicts through direct action for social change.

The applicability of this body of social theory to rural settlement planning is historically marginal but is nevertheless of crucial importance to the future of rural areas. There has been no explicit adoption of a particular theoretical position by rural planners, although their implicit leanings towards the interpretative maximization of personal freedom has led to a general favouring of non-intervention policies in rural areas. A simple justification for not restricting the activities of the private sector, or for refusing to allocate public-sector resources to the solution of a particular problem in rural settlements is to emphasize that to do so would negate the freedom of choice for some individuals. In fact, the opposite is often true, whereby a failure to act *reduces* opportunity for particular groups of rural residents. Therefore the tacit adoption of the interpretative position may represent a further influence on the direction taken thus far by rural settlement planning. More recently, rural problems have been increasingly viewed as symptoms of wider structural inequalities, and renewed emphasis is thus being placed on more radical socio-structural theories of planning in the rural environment. The future importance of socio-structural and conflict theories to rural planners is stressed repeatedly below (particularly in chapter 12).

Economic theory

The relationship between economics and planning is a complex interaction of national- and local-scale variables involving many political overtones (Willis, 1980). In most western countries, the accepted economic format has been the free market economy in which the functions of government are minimized while social well-being is ensured through the pursuit of self-interest within a freely operating market system. However, it has become increasingly clear from the work of welfare economists (e.g. Nath, 1973) both that the free market economy is full of imperfections – e.g.

1 The world is not one of universal competition;
2 Many natural monopolies exist;
3 Externalities (social costs) exist;
4 Pronounced income inequalities exist

– and that these phenomena present a strong case for government intervention to act in cases of inequality. The justification for intervention is traditionally measured in terms of the Pareto function which describes an efficient situation as one where no welfare benefits can be added to an individual or group without some other individual or group losing out. However, Whitby and Willis (1978) point out the difficulties presented by factors underlying the Pareto function, and thus question the basis on which government intervention has been attempted in the past.

The general issue of an optimum degree of public-sector intervention on a private-sector market is beyond the scope of this book. However, Turner and

Collis (1977) neatly summarize the range of strategic options which are theoretically available to planners. The two extremes of this range are indicative of the continuum between them:

1 *Traditional Stalinist economy* was used in the Soviet Union between 1928 and the mid 1950s and was adopted by Eastern European satellite states in the late 1940s. It represents the closest practicable facsimile of a fully state-administered, centrally directed socialist economy which demonstrated a rigid centralization of power, a partial decentralization of administration and an extreme use of a welfare economics system.

2 *Traditional French economy* as practiced in France, which influenced planning in many other EEC countries (including Britain in the 1960s and early 1980s), represents the most proximate example of a state-guided but market-directed private enterprise economy to be seen in recent years.

It is important to note that the British planning relationship with economics has been oriented towards the free-market category of theoretical economic options. Planning policy decisions have thus been constrained by this framework of interaction with economics in that planning has aimed to control the free-market economy rather than to create new economic systems based on the welfare edict. Thus rural settlement planning has been restricted by indirect rather than direct policy measures and by a lack of problem-solving options.

Contextual theory and rural settlement planning: a reprise

It is most unlikely that the various theoretical options outlined above have ever been explicitly discussed or evaluated by rural settlement planners in their formulation of policies. However, rural settlement planning in Britain *has* been directly influenced by these theoretical matters which have in effect marked the operational boundaries within which planners are constrained to work. In the same way that a blind person can negotiate a length of pavement by locating the spatial boundaries of pavement and wall with a white stick, rural settlement planning has fumbled its way along a theoretically constrained path with a series of movements within the edges of practicality and politico-economic structure. This pathway can be seen in figure 3.1, which offers a summary of the theoretical categories open to a hypothetically unfettered planning system, and a breakdown both of the primary and secondary theoretical routes adopted by rural settlement planning and of the theoretical options which may be regarded as residual to the past and current requirements of rural planning.

By matching theoretical options with the broad tenor of post-war rural settlement planning in Britain a clear distinction may be discerned between pertinent and residual theoretical descriptions. A primary routeway can be seen linking the themes of respect for individual freedom of choice and support for private-sector dominance (in both economic and planning ethos terms). Although an attempt has been made to present planning as a rational, apolitical process, there are distinct and strong secondary leanings towards a

Figure 3.1 Primary and secondary pathways for contextual rural settlement planning theory

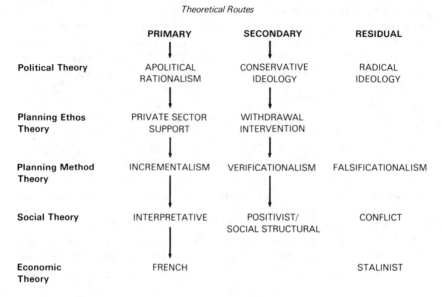

Theoretical Routes

	PRIMARY	SECONDARY	RESIDUAL
Political Theory	APOLITICAL RATIONALISM	CONSERVATIVE IDEOLOGY	RADICAL IDEOLOGY
Planning Ethos Theory	PRIVATE SECTOR SUPPORT	WITHDRAWAL INTERVENTION	
Planning Method Theory	INCREMENTALISM	VERIFICATIONALISM	FALSIFICATIONALISM
Social Theory	INTERPRETATIVE	POSITIVIST/ SOCIAL STRUCTURAL	CONFLICT
Economic Theory	FRENCH		STALINIST

conservative ideology in the planning of rural areas, which support the primary economic, social and political options favouring the free operation of market forces. Even the instances of intervention by public sector agencies have been constrained by economic and sometimes ideological factors from performing a positive role of opportunity supply in small rural settlements. Indeed the only seemingly discordant note in the identifiable theoretical context of rural settlement planning is that of the adopted planning method of incrementalism. Although the public image of rationalism can be seen to be founded on a strongly conservative political ideology, the verificationalist techniques which would be expected to accompany a rationalist political theory have been linked with the rather piecemeal and incremental planning methods which have dominated rural settlement planning in Britain. However, the factors of conservatism and incrementalism may, in fact, be happily combined in the notion of *pragmatism*, and it is this concept which best describes the theoretical context for rural settlement planning which will be shown (see chapter 4) to be a series of reactions to events and trends in the countryside. This pattern of pragmatism occurs in both private- and public-sector planning and it aligns closely with the original assertion that although contextual theory may be subsequently recognized within rural settlement planning, it is clear that at the time of plan- and policy-making, these generalized theoretical aspects acted as an implicit set of guidelines rather than a consciously selected routeway.

Figure 3.1 is also interesting from the point of view of those theoretical options which have played no part in British rural settlement planning. It hardly comes as a surprise to note that these residual theoretical routeways also conform to a recognizable pattern. What has been lacking is a more radical and socialist theoretical framework which would encourage the positive intervention of public-sector resources to alleviate the conflicts of powerful and powerless in rural communities. It should not be inferred from this string of unused theoretical options that a more positive interventionist policy will necessarily be radically left-wing, or that a new falsificationalist approach would necessarily reject all current policy mechanisms. Indeed, a recent review has noted the similarity of policies emerging from vastly different ideological backgrounds:

> *A gauche* of the political spectrum, the inevitability of eliminating social, economic and cultural differences between town and countryside by rationalizing rural settlement patterns has been strongly argued by Marx, Engels and Lenin. *A droit*, the free market political theorists would appear to support a non-interventionist policy of decision-making in the market place which would manifest a similar trend of scale-orientated selectivity in the rural settlement pattern. (Cloke, 1980, 98)

Between these two extremes, followers of the more liberal approaches to geography and planning (D.M. Smith, 1977) have argued for an incremental approach to the supply of welfare opportunities to rural residents. Clearly, at any point on the ideological continuum, rural settlement planning could be made more positive and interventionalist *given greater resources* (particularly financial). In some ways, the question of whether intervention should be directly by the public sector or by indirect subsidies to private-sector agencies is immaterial to the central issue of the need for opportunities to be provided whatever the means.

Therefore, the residual options in figure 3.1 should be regarded as individual alternatives rather than an all-embracing package. If rural settlement planning is discovered to be constrained by the theoretical routeway within which it has been compelled (largely by external factors) to operate, then these residuals offer significant theoretical changes of approach which might be evaluated for more thoughtful and explicit adoption by planners and their political overseers.

Formative theories I: a hierarchical settlement pattern

Within this framework of contextual theoretical constraints, the details of policy trends in rural settlement planning have been directly influenced by a number of locational and economic theories and concepts. If contextual theory has been an implicit restraint on the development of rural settlement planning, these more specific epistemological contributions may be described as formative. In many cases their input has been more explicit and recognizable in the various policies and plans which have been produced. The importance of formative theory in the explanation of rural planning trends is considerable. The post-war era in which the initial modelling of vogue policies was taking place was coincident with a period of intense co-operation and integration between geography as a discipline and planning as a profession. As a consequence, the theoretical matters of interest to geographers were automatically given exposure during planning deliberations so that rural settlement planning at that time reflected the geographical awareness of the need to base planning policies on proven theoretical considerations. In addition, with the wish to justify their selected policies, planners tended to isolate those particular tenets of spatial and economic theory which best suited the resource concentration strategies which were generally adopted in the 1950s and early 1960s. The paradox here is that the same theoretical evidence has been used both in the establishment of early rural settlement policy and in its retrospective and independent justification during subsequent analyses. It is therefore difficult to adumbrate with any precision the extent to which theory has been incorporated at the outset or accrued during the progress of rural settlement planning.

The first set of theories of relevance to the planned management of rural settlements concerns both the assumption that rural settlements occur as part of a hierarchical pattern, and the ensuing planning objective that the operation of this hierarchy should be upheld by supporting nodal points within it. The original work on central places carried out by Christaller (translated Baskin, 1966) and built on by Lösch (1938–9) and Berry and Garrison (1958) has been fully reviewed elsewhere, for example the historical account by Dawson (1969) and the methodological treatise of Beavon (1977). Theoretical postulations of a hexagonal service area surrounding each settlement have allowed the recognition of nested hierarchies of settlements within which settlements are ranked according to population size and levels of service provision. Chapman (1979) relates a three-stage process in the spatial evolution of a theoretical central-place system (figure 3.2):

1   The starting point is an even distribution of small central places (*hamlets*) which provide common levels of services and serve equally spaced hinterland areas which are determined by the threshold population required to support the services offered by the hamlet;

2   A number of larger settlements (*villages*) develop to serve a wider range of service functions, and these villages absorb the market areas of existing

Figure 3.2 Evolution of a theoretical central-place system

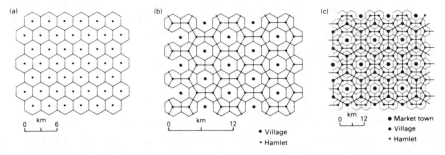

Source: Chapman, 1979, 249

hamlets in such a way that the regular lattice of central places is retained. The villages are more widely spaced than the hamlets because their services are used less often and so require higher population thresholds and exert longer ranges then the smaller service settlements;

3   The third stage occurs with the superimposition of larger settlements with even greater levels of service provision (*towns*). Christaller identified seven rankings of settlement in his original study.

As well as this spatial arrangement of settlements, a hierarchical arrangement may also be noted in the relationship between the size of settlements and the frequency with which they occur in the landscape. Figure 3.3 shows Chapman's (1979) simple example of a three-level hierarchy which corresponds to the three-stage spatial sequence described above. Assuming an island of 900 population, the thresholds of settlement functions will decline with settlement size (a), the occurrence of each settlement type is determined by the number of threshold populations which can be supported by the total population (one town, three villages and nine hamlets in (b)), and since the higher-order central place will perform all lower-order functions, the occurrence of central places will be one town, two villages and six hamlets in (c), resulting in a nested hierarchy of settlements according to size and function.

This apparently simple explanation of the differential distribution of settlements in rural areas proved most attractive to rural geographers and planners in the formative years of the 1940s and 1950s. Dickinson's (1942) research in East Anglia highlighted the concept of a nucleated rural settlement which functioned as a service centre for the surrounding tributary area. Smailes's (1944) attempts to delimit the hinterland areas or 'urban fields' of central places in England and Wales extended the practical application of central place theories in the understanding of current settlement issues. This general recognition of the relationships between service centres and their hinterlands

Figure 3.3 A three-tier central-place hierarchy

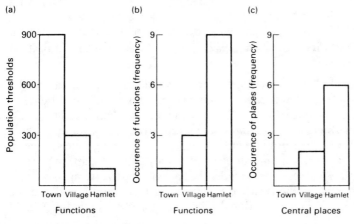

Source: Chapman, 1979, 250

was influential in the decision to adopt policies of planned promotion of rural service centres during the development-plan stages. However, the principal early attempt to test the central-place model in rural environments was carried out by Bracey who undertook extensive and detailed surveys in Wiltshire (1952) and Somerset (1953) and then tested his results in a wider investigation (1956) taking in the six counties of Somerset, Dorset, Wiltshire, Oxfordshire, Berkshire and Hampshire. His work is detailed in these specific reports and elsewhere (Bracey, 1958; 1970) but in summary the research found substantial support for the central-place model in the rural areas of southern England.

Perhaps most important among the results achieved by Bracey was the uncovering of the phenomenon which he termed the *English central village* (Bracey, 1962). Noticing that 'one village of 600 people has a couple of general shops and no other services whilst another, of similar size a few miles away, possesses ten or a dozen shops, a doctor, chemist and solicitor' (p. 169), he built up a generalized picture of the type of village which has a higher level of services than would be expected for its population size, and which appears to operate these services for the people of neighbouring settlements as well as for its own residents. These central villages were categorized into first-order (twenty shops or more), second-order (ten to nineteen shops) and third-order (five to nine shops) and their spheres of influence were defined according to the range and extent of mobile services based in the central village but serving smaller villages in the rural hinterland. Bracey's confirmation of central-place tendencies has since been corroborated, by Brush in America (Brush, 1953; Brush and Bracey, 1955) and by Whitelaw (1962) and Fookes (1974) in New Zealand.

The importance of central-place theory, and these various attempts to translate the theory into practice should not be underestimated as a guiding influence on early rural settlement planning policy. The seemingly 'proven' fact that natural centres exist within settlement hierarchies was incorporated in the policy decisions contained within development plans and their reviews, and indeed, Bracey's own work was used as a direct input to the Wiltshire County Council Plan (1953). Two statements, one contemporary with Bracey's work, and one forming part of a more modern review serve to re-emphasize the magnetism of central-place theory to the rural settlement planning process. First, Lipman (1952, 212–13) describes the impact of Bracey-type studies:

> For the physical planner, the importance of studies of this kind is equally obvious; indeed, it is significant that much recent research in this field has been conducted as part of the surveys preliminary to planning. This holds good whether the task is to analyse the social structure of an area like a County or to plan the future layout of a town, in the light of the services it performs for the surrounding countryside. Analysis of the pattern of rural settlement and service centres provides the background to attempts to determine what should be the future distribution of rural population and the provision of social and educational facilities and other public services in rural areas.

Thus at the time when research findings on central villages were being produced, the importance of these results were clearly recognized by planners and administrators. In more retrospective mood, a recent study of the theoretical influences of key settlement policies suggests that:

> At the time of the Development Plans, planners perceived a logical progression from the identification of existing rural centres to the continuing support of these centres as the focus for investment in rural areas. In effect, many planners were attempting to build up certain key settlements into the ideal central-village model whereby additional service provision in one central location would benefit a wide rural hinterland. The early Development Plans' emphasis on existing central places thus not only set the pattern for trend planning in rural areas, but also had some considerable bearing on the introduction of key settlement policies which stress the importance of a centre's ability to service its surrounding area. (Cloke, 1979, 42–3)

The concept of a hierarchical settlement pattern containing 'natural' service centres which, if supported by the planning process, will continue to serve hinterland rural areas has thus been instilled in British rural settlement planning policy. It has supported the case for selective resource allocation and has even been utilized as a model on which to base entirely new settlement patterns such as those on the Dutch polders (Thijsse, 1968; Van Hulten, 1969). However, just as the basic assumptions of the central-place model have been subject to criticism stemming both from empirical investigation (e.g. O'Farrell, 1970) and from a rejection of the neo-classical economic underpinnings of the theory (Broadbent, 1977), so its specific function as a prop to selective resource-allocation policies in rural areas has been opposed on a number of grounds. First, the inbuilt supposition that rural environments are homogeneous and therefore that patterns of central places will be equally applicable to pressured and remote rural areas is a non-starter in an era of social planning where the needs of residents in individual settlements are far more relevant than all-embracing and universalist generalizations suitable for all rural locations and circumstances. Chapman (1979, 262) argues that 'clustered settlement patterns often reflect uneven population distributions which violate the assumptions, but not the principles of central-place theory' but it is certainly true that differences in settlement pattern type do rather mock the central-place interpretation that planned service centres can perform the same role regardless of the type of area in which they are located. This conclusion is supported by Johnston (1966, 549) who stresses that 'village size and degree of nucleation of settlement are more important than total population or number of villages in determining the distribution of the elements of social provision'. A second criticism arises from central-place theory's reliance on consumers travelling to the nearest available provision of a particular good or service. There is now widespread empirical evidence (Martin, 1976) to suggest that journeys to opportunities and services in rural areas are by no means as simple as this. On the one hand, intervening small central places are often ignored by rural consumers from hinterland areas in favour of a multiple-use visit to even larger settlements with wider ranges of opportunities in different spheres. On the other hand, the apparently haphazard use of individual village services also confounds traditional edicts of consumer behaviour. There is extensive incidence of small villages contributing an opportunity or service which is unique to its surrounding area. Martin (1976, 80) maintains that

> For these 'unique' functions, a village will have a much wider catchment area than its own residents, and people in adjoining villages, instead of going to progressively higher-order and, probably, more distant centres for specialist services may turn to neighbouring villages; to one for electrical goods, to another for furniture, to a third for shoe repairs and so on.

This type of pattern has also been recorded in the United States (Hahn, 1970) and certainly will be familiar to residents with experience of remoter areas such as the author's in Mid Wales. As a consequence, the central-place notion of 'natural' service centres may constitute a revision of the existing order of rural behaviour rather than a supporting of linkages which are inherent in the ordering of rural settlements.

The third criticism levelled at central-place theories in a rural context concerns the temporal changes in central-place relationships. Several authors have attempted to account for such changes. Semple and Golledge (1970) found that the distinction of central places on the central Prairies of Canada has tended toward a more uniform pattern over time, whereas Berry *et al.* (1962) found an under-representation of hamlets in the south-western Iowa settlement pattern which they attributed to the gradual disappearance of these small-scale settlements due to the increased accessibility offered by rising car ownership. It is not only the hamlet-scale settlements which have declined. Clawson (1966; 1968) notes the disappearance of American small towns which 'as their business volume declines . . . will be less able to offer services that will attract farmers, who will gradually go to larger towns at farther distances' (1966, 287). Two contrasting interpretations may be linked with this appreciation of change in the rural settlement hierarchy. Traditionally the decline of small rural settlements has been associated with the planned support of successful, or potentially successful central places. Hodge (1966), in America, records the detection of some surviving small-scale centres serving purely local needs and a few large-scale centres with higher-order facilities to service wider areas of the rural hinterland. Rural planning has attempted to mirror these 'automatic' trends (Clout, 1972) by selecting a small number of centres as locations for continued investment and subjecting other settlements to no-growth or even decline. An alternative view of changes to the rural settlement hierarchy would be to maintain a flexible approach to the needs of individual villages. Rather than imposing an over-rigid and stereotyped system of selectivity, the needs of local people could be better catered for by different types of planning strategy in different areas; thus allowing sensitivity to particular problems. As Martin (1976, 81) argues: 'There is a strong feeling that there is too much change in rural areas and the planner should take care not to compound the situation by proposing policies which ignore existing patterns of rural life'. The extent to which planners have been able (or willing) to adopt a flexible approach has been significantly influenced by their treatment of changes in service thresholds, and this theoretical issue will be dealt with separately.

Formative theories II: changing thresholds

The early adherence to central-place theorizations of rural settlement hierarchies guided planners to an affinity with, and often dependence on the establishment of threshold figures for vital rural facilities. Traditionally, a threshold has been viewed as a static indicator of the minimum population required to support a particular service or facility and much of the early thinking in rural settlement planning revolved around analyses of service thresholds. For example, the rural settlement policy for Norfolk at the development-plan review stage was greatly influenced by the supposed level of population needed to support commercial and public services. Green (1966) uses data from the 1961 Census of Distribution (table 3.1) to stress the breakdown of village self-sufficiency and increasing centralization of service outlets. Subsequently, specific research in rural Norfolk generated roughly comparable figures for commercial services (Green and Ayton, 1967) and in addition spelt out threshold populations for public services such as the home nurse (5000), primary school (5000), three-doctor medical practice (6000), health visitor (8000) and secondary school (10,000).

The importance of these thresholds to resultant planning policy is clear. Green and Ayton (1967, 4) conclude

> If it is accepted that methods of retailing are changing in favour of larger catchment populations, that some degree of competition is desirable, and that a chemist is a necessity, the minimum population to support an acceptable range of retail shopping may be 8000 or even more. From this it appears that most community services need between 5000 and 8000 people to support them.

Table 3.1 Service thresholds formulated for East Anglia

	Census of Distribution (rural East Anglia)	Norfolk County Council (rural Norfolk)
Grocer	325	300
Butcher	2840	2000
Baker	2515	3000
Draper	1070	2500
Household goods	2170	2500
Chemist	4150	4000

Source: Green, 1966; Green and Ayton, 1967

Once these figures had been firmly planted in the planning psyche, several almost automatic policy ramifications emerged. First, there was a sentiment that thresholds would inevitably continue to rise just as they had done historically, despite the fact that past threshold increases were undeniably interlinked with radical changes in mobility and administrative organization which were not certain to be repeated in future years. Second, the magnitude of an aggregate threshold population for what were considered vital rural services spawned an inevitable planning response of rigid concentration of resources and investment; this being the only practicable answer to a situation of high and rising service thresholds. Third, the declining numerical importance of agricultural employment was seen to lead inevitably to a desire on the part of rural populations to concentrate for convenient access to levels of services in accord with rising urban-scale expectations. These perceived inevitabilities may be summarized in a clear statement of what rural settlement planners viewed as 'the obvious':

> The greater the concentration of population the easier it would be to support local facilities. . . . The difference between concentration and dispersal in the countryside can be summarized as convenience for the dependants or convenience for the farm worker and farmer. It seems reasonable that the agricultural worker should accept the longer journey, the farmer the inconvenience of not having his labour (what is left of it) so readily available, that the women and children may have the benefit of more convenient living facilities and the other advantages that go with greater numbers; a wider choice of friends and a greater variety of social organizations. (Green, 1966, 31)

This reasoning behind resource concentration policy now appears very dated in its emphasis on the social advantages of larger rural settlements while ignoring the social problems to be faced by the remaining small settlements and the residents who because of poverty or job location are trapped within them. However, it does indicate the preoccupation of rural settlement planning in the 1950s and 1960s with the provision of *services* in rural areas. It is almost as if a solution to the servicing problem would result in the rectification of all other rural imbalances, and consequently the priority given to service provision led to a distinct underemphasis on other socio-economic problems in rural settlements at that time. The future of rural settlements was seen in black and white. Concentration was the agent with which 'to improve rural living standards and to save the countryside from death by diminution'; the dispersal alternative would lead to 'the continued gradual decline of rural facilities and the growing reliance of many small, and socially and economically unviable communities, on urban facilities many miles away' (Green, 1966, 34).

In many ways the Norfolk planners were trendsetters in their outspoken linking of threshold theory with the need to concentrate resources into larger rural settlements. However, chapter 5 reveals that this emphasis on the difficulties of servicing rural areas became a common feature amongst the planning policies published by rural counties in the 1960s and early 1970s.

Therefore although the Norfolk work has been most widely publicized, the underlying theoretical influence can be traced in many other parts of Britain. It is difficult to substantiate the exact role of threshold theories either as reasons for policy formulation or as subsequent justifications for policy born out of economic expediency. Clearly, the rather simplistic threshold notion can no longer be used as a central cog in rural resource location decisions. Significantly it is the current county planning officer of Norfolk County Council who has published an exposé of the real-world fallacies of thresholds. As part of the preparation for the Draft Structure Plan for Norfolk, a study was made of the threshold concept as applied to village food shops (Shaw, 1976a). Assumptions of village shops all offering a similar range of goods; catchment areas identical with administrative areas; identical shopping behaviour by all rural residents; and identical motives and attitudes on the part of all shopkeepers, are found to be untenable in practice, yet it is this type of assumption around which threshold theory is built. Shaw notes that:

> Inhabitants of parishes without shops may well use the shop in a neighbouring village, while the extent to which local inhabitants provide support for a shop will depend on their income levels and patterns of behaviour. . . . Also while it is generally assumed that thresholds relate closely to the limits of economic viability, this ignores the possibility that shopkeepers may not be fundamentally concerned with achieving fixed profit margins. (1976, 73)

Thus the idea that thresholds will demonstrate how shops and other services will respond to changes in village populations cannot be adhered to in reality. Not only are thresholds of economic viability rising as the attitudes and activities of consumers and suppliers change (meaning that a settlement might cross a threshold without a change in its population size), but it is also the case that the threshold at which a service is withdrawn from a settlement is likely to be different from that at which the same service might be introduced. Thus factors of risk and inertia dictate that a declining village is likely to lose its shop at a much lower population threshold than that at which a growing village will gain a similar shop. This generalization forms the foundation for a growing body of threshold theory relating to the staging of planned growth in settlements (Jackson and Nolan, 1971; 1973; Malisz, 1969). The Norfolk study does isolate a threshold band around 250 to 300 population at which a village is likely (90 per cent probability) to lose its last remaining foodshop, but the general conclusion is that 'the concept of a theoretical catchment population is a theoretical simplification for planning purposes and as such is of strictly limited value' (Shaw, 1976a, 79).

The value of thresholds to current rural settlement planning is further limited if we appreciate that this essentially *economic* indicator is but one element in the complex equation of rural life which also includes non-economic and often unquantifiable factors which are ignored by pure economic analysis. For example, if rural settlement planning were to be based on *social thresholds*, that is the number of services and facilities needed to support the rural population in a fixed location, then the goals and objectives of planning policy would be very different from those seen in post-war Britain. Of course, total emphasis on social thresholds ignores the *economic 'reality'* of limited resources and would therefore be disowned by practising planners, yet the economic practicality of this argument merely serves to highlight how *social 'realities'* have been equally ignored whilst economic thresholds have been accepted by the planning process. Thus although threshold conceptual-izations were a formative influence in early rural settlement policies, the more recent turn towards flexible strategic policies and detailed local-scale plans have largely diminished their importance.

Formative theories III: economies of scale

Although the direct influence of service thresholds has diminished in recent years, rural settlement planning remains firmly founded on a number of *a priori* economic reasonings which tend to exert similar policy magnetism to that preferred earlier by threshold analysis. These reasonings have been restated recently by Ayton (1980):
1 Small villages cannot individually support education, health and commer-cial services which require 'support' populations of thousands;
2 Public-sector service options are constrained by limited and diminishing resources;
3 Private-sector services and some public-sector services (such as gas) will not be provided where they are unprofitable, and rural areas often fall in this category;
4 Mobile services incur high running costs and offer a low quality of service.
The policy direction suggested by these sentiments is once again that rural planning should identify selected foci for 'fixed-point' services (although the planning process may only marginally influence their location).

The underlying theme in these economic statements is that of economies of scale suggesting, for instance, that the building of one big school or health centre is usually economically more acceptable than the building of several smaller schools or health centres, or that several small retail outlets with scattered clientele are less viable than one or two larger shops with all their cus-tomers within easy reach. Economies of scale are usually defined in terms of the classical theory of the firm. Most units of population demonstrate a U–shaped long-run average cost curve, and will therefore incur economies or diseconomies if they do not operate at the lowest point on that curve. Figure 3.4 demonstrates examples of these curves presented by Toyne (1974) in relation to housing, *per capita* rate fund expenditure and social and welfare services. Rural areas are traditionally viewed as being located on the down-ward slope of the curve with the consequent assumption that the provision of services and facilities at ever increasing scales will result in a closer position to the trough of the long-run average cost estimation. Quite simply, rural areas have been endowed with an economic philosophy of the bigger (and therefore the more concentrated) the better.

There have been several attempts to test this philosophy in practice. The

Figure 3.4 Scale effects on service costings

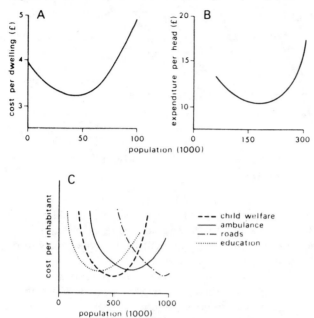

Source: Toyne, 1974, 58

most often-quoted evidence comes from Gupta and Hutton (1968) in their study of economies of scale in local government services. Measuring economies and diseconomies at varying levels of local authority, they found clear diseconomies at the rural district council scale, particularly in the provision of housing. These conclusions are broadly matched by other sources (e.g. HM Treasury, 1976; Yorkshire and Humberside Economic Planning Board, 1976) which display evidence of the relatively high cost of providing public services in rural areas with scattered settlements and populations. However, the justification of resource concentration in rural settlement planning on scale-economy grounds requires a clear demonstration that such economies exist between different scales of *rural* settlement rather than between the rural and urban extremes. Despite the inherent problems of definition, a clear relationship has been shown between rising population size and falling per capita costs for the provision of single fixed services in rural settlements. For example, Gilder (1979, 245), in the first stage of a broader study of rural planning policy alternatives in the Bury St Edmunds area, suggests that 'there are substantial internal economies of scale for both primary education and sewage disposal when average costs are analysed'. This conclusion is worthy of note as later in his report Gilder progresses to a heavily critical view of resource concentration policies in his study area, but at this earlier stage is happy to concur with previous findings (e.g. Cumming, 1971; Hibbs, 1975; Riew, 1966; Townend, 1960) of scale economies for single services.

Figure 3.5 Aggregate long-run cost curve for three services

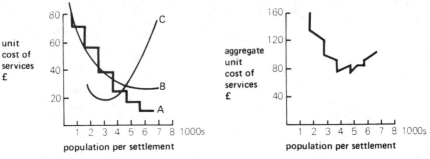

Source: Whitby and Willis, 1978, 234

The relevance of single service economies to rural settlement planning is limited because rural settlements embody a range of facilities and activities, and policies of planned concentration of investment have to take account of this multiplicity. As a consequence, the testing of scale economies has progressed to the combination of single service cost functions into an aggregate long-run cost curve for a chosen assemblage of services. Once again the trough of this aggregate curve would represent the optimum scale for service provision in rural settlements. Whitby and Willis (1978) present a hypothetical example in which three services A, B and C are deemed necessary to a settlement (figure 3.5). Service A can only be provided in discrete units and is therefore represented by a stepped curve, service B offers economies of scale throughout the range of settlement populations, and service C very quickly incurs diseconomies over a similar range. A combination of these three individual curves produces a stepped aggregate function with clearly defined threshold points, and although this example is a gross simplification of real-world conditions, it contains the essence of various attempts to produce aggregate functions for case study rural settlements. Methodological difficulties abound in this process, particularly in the standardization of the quality of various services throughout a range of settlement sizes, and in the isolation of the particular mix of services deemed necessary for rural settlements. Thus, the measurement of aggregate cost functions are often dependent on the social and political assumptions underlying data collection and analysis. For example Whitby and Willis (1978, 235) stress that

> If decisions as to the level and quality of provision are taken centrally there is considerable danger of over-provision. Such over-provision might be regarded as a cost inherent in running an equitable social system, but there would be grounds for questioning how much regrouping of rural settlements its existence would justify.

Given these differences in methodological approach, it is hardly surprising that varying results have been achieved in the aggregate analysis of economies of scale in rural settlements. Such analyses have usually been performed as part of a wider economic appraisal of alternative settlement strategies, and these are reviewed in chapter 7, but on a general level, the studies by Warford (1969) and Norfolk County Council (1976) support the notion of investment concentration on the grounds of scale economy, while Gilder's (1979) important study comes to the opposite conclusion. Despite finding evidence of substantial internal economies of scale in education and sewage disposal costs at one point in time, the translation of these costs to individual case-study settlements in Gilder's analysis causes other factors (such as demographic differences, distance effects, varying capital charges and varying standards of service) to be included in the overall calculation. These extraneous variables were found to create a higher degree of cost variation than that caused by economies of scale, and so the traditionally valued assumption of 'bigger is better' was overwhelmed by other elements of service provision which had previously been underemphasized. His conclusion is clearly stated (p. 263):

> No economies of scale in the establishment or running of these (schools and sewage disposal) facilities are sufficient to outweigh the lower marginal costs of utilizing spare capacity in rural fixed services, even if the overall unit running cost remain higher.

Although the methods employed by Gilder to reach this conclusion may be criticized (see chapter 7), his rejection of the benighted credence given to the universal applicability of theoretical economies of scale in rural settlement planning accords with a rising tide of social and economic challenge to the very basis of rural selection policies. Despite the fact that this dissention from conventional thinking has yet to be supported by thorough and broad-scale research results, it is certainly the case that the 'gut reaction' in planning that economic theory will unswervingly favour resource concentration in rural areas should no longer be viewed as infallible, particularly if the social costs of rural living are to be included in the overall economic appraisal of settlement policies.

Formative theories IV: growth centres

A series of ideological and conceptual notions concerning growth centres represent a further theoretical influence on rural settlement planning. Much has already been written on this subject, so comment here will be restricted to a brief resumé of findings detailed elsewhere (Cloke, 1979; Moseley, 1973; 1973a; 1974). The ideological stimulus to a small scale rural growth village with sufficient services and facilities to satisfy both the needs of its residents and those of its hinterland population has been traced back to two dominant personalities of the inter-war and immediate post-war period. First, Harold Peake (1916–18; 1922) provided the idealistic vision of how rural settlements might be organized in such a way that basic service thresholds could be overcome.

> We must have larger and more compact villages, real village communities suited to modern conditions, not small towns with their streets and slums,

but well-designed compact villages, containing sufficient inhabitants to make commercial life possible. (Peake, 1916–18, 245)

Peake estimated that the minimum population for such a compact village would be around 1200, with possible expansion to 2000, and furthermore:

All the everyday requirements of health, education and recreation . . . would be found within the village itself, while the population would be sufficient to command reasonable transport facilities to the neighbouring town, where they could satisfy their rarer needs. (Peake, 1922, 232)

Here, then, we have a blueprint for the building up of rural resources in selected ideal villages, and this was adopted and implemented by the second innovating personality, Henry Morris, who as Chief Education Officer for Cambridgeshire (1922–54) was responsible for the notion and introduction of village colleges, which were to be centralized secondary schools by day, and centres for adult education and social gatherings outside school hours. Village colleges were designed for use by residents of hinterland settlements as well as those of the villages in which they were located, and this idea of a centralized focal point serving smaller surrounding villages was a forerunner to a broadened key settlement concept (Needham, 1942). Twenty village colleges were built, more than half of these being located in Cambridgeshire.

The conceptualization of growth centres is complementary to the ideological stance represented by Morris and Peake. Relationships between selected service centres and their hinterlands are described in analogue by the growth-pole model. For example, the inherent contradiction between selected key settlements acting contiguously as both *provider for* and *retarder of* small hinterland settlements has been tackled by adopting those parts of growth-pole theory which illustrate two opposing forces governing the movement of economic prosperity.

1 *Backwash* forces (Myrdal, 1957; Hirschmann, 1958) where central nodes attract factors of production from their surrounding areas, have been used as a model for pressured rural areas where economic and population overspill need to be controlled and channelled into suitable reception centres;

2 *Spread* forces, which describe the transmission of economic prosperity from centre to periphery, have been used to model the remoter rural situation.

Thus at a superficial level, growth-pole theory presents a firm justification for the concentration of development into selected service centres in both pressured and remote rural areas. However, the implementation of backwash and spread effects has been problematic in rural settlement planning. A growth centre's ability to attract factors of production from its hinterland by way of backwash forces has not been seriously questioned by commentators of rural planning. Development-control processes, strictly implemented, have been used to supplement the market forces which dictate a centripetal bias in the centre–hinterland relationship. However, the centrifugal spread of development to the periphery has been more difficult to achieve. Lucey and

Kaldor (1969) in Ireland and Moseley (1973a) in East Anglia have shown that the spread effects of rural growth centres are only applicable in limited circumstances. Thus, although there would appear to be no theoretical reason why small-scale growth centres cannot spread small-scale benefits to their peripheries (particularly if they are of sufficient size to attract entrepreneurs who will use local labour and suppliers), in practice it would seem that settlements of less than about 13,000 population do not exert traditional growth-centre spread effects. It is significant that most rural service centres fall below this population threshold.

Different levels of success in the implementation of spread and backwash mechanisms in rural areas have led to spatial variation in the success with which growth centre theory has been applied to rural settlement planning. In pressured rural areas where demand for development is strong, backwash effects have been achieved by planning restrictions on growth in non-selected settlements and incentives for growth inside the chosen growth points. Moreover, by definition, rural areas in these locations are themselves within the shadow of larger urban centres and so receive spread benefits from this source. It is in the remoter rural areas that the applicability of growth centre theory is diminished. In these areas it is difficult on both social policy and practicality grounds to deny growth to any settlement merely because it is not one of the chosen growth centres. Furthermore the number of selected centres is crucial, as a surplus would spread growth too thinly while a deficit would exclude many peripheral areas from any spread benefits emanating from growth centres.

Perhaps the most important element in the achievement of growth-centre attitudes in rural areas is that of exactly *how* hinterland settlements will benefit from a centralization of resources in growth centres. In order to counteract the criticism that selected centre policies are egocentrically important for the settlements concerned but are damaging for those settlements which will not receive localized growth, the exact mechanism for the transfer of benefits or opportunities from centre to hinterland must be isolated and implemented. The only mechanism which fits this description in rural areas is that of accessibility. In a situation of perfect accessibility between hinterland and centre, the resources established in the growth centre would be available to residents of outlying villages and so a spread effect of a kind would exist. However, the problems of markedly imperfect accessibility outlined in chapter 2 represent a denial of these opportunities to many groups of rural residents; hence the breakdown of the spread effect. Therefore, although we might sympathize with the sentiment expressed by many planners that it is difficult to conceive of any other settlement theory that offers the problem-solving capabilities seen in the growth centre concept as applied in higher-order settlements, it should also be admitted that there is no real evidence that growth-centre theories (and the policies which have been influenced by them) have achieved their desired spread objectives at the rural scale.

A note on conservationism and environmentalism

> More then ever before British people are aware of their heritage. . . . The glories of our royal palaces and great houses, the splendours of our cathedrals and larger churches, the modest charm of the village church, the old manor house and rectory, the sweep of downland or the rugged moors, the fragrance of an English garden or the heady exhilaration of cliffs and coastline – these are just some of the assaults on the senses which we categorize as our heritage. (Cormack, 1978, 10)

Although this type of sentiment should not be graced with the title of theory, no account of formative influences on the post-war progress of rural settlement planning would be complete without some brief mention of the importance of conservationist and environmentalist attitudes on the part of rural planners and some of the rural planned. Newby (1979) notes that the tendency to idealize (and therefore to protect) rural life has a long history connected with the literary tradition of pastoral poetry and art which has stressed both the relationship between nature and civilization and the conflict between urban life and rural life. There has been a gradual process of the pastoral and the picturesque being taken as literal descriptions of rural life by urban dwellers, particularly those sectors of the middle class who are 'professional rather than entrepreneurial, liberal, possessed of a social conscience, faintly intellectual and artistic in their pursuits, sensitive, knowledgeable about natural history but mostly ignorant about agriculture' (Newby, 1979, 18). These population groups have not only been instrumental in the embodiment of conservationist ideals in county and national political policy, but have also formed the bulk of newcomer populations in pressured rural settlements, thus adding a conservation element to local attitudes and politics.

Allison (1975) distinguishes between two types of conservationist attitude:
1 *Genuine conservationism* which is the sincere holding of either want-regarding or ideal-regarding conservationist principles (often seen in nationally based amenity groups);
2 *Superficial conservationism* where privately oriented opposition to particular developments is hidden behind a set of conservation principles (often seen in local groups who wish to shunt development elsewhere).

In effect, both types have made an impact on post-war rural settlement planning. Chapter 4 demonstrates how advice from central government has consistently stressed the need to conserve high-quality rural settlementscapes and indeed how permissive legislation has been passed to allow such measures to be enacted at local level. Some credit for these trends may be attributed to genuine conservationist attitudes expressed either by pressure groups or by individual politicians and civil servants. However, the actual initiative to adopt these conservation opportunities at the local level comes from varied sources, including those of superficial conservationism. Development plans, drawn up at county level have continually emphasized the importance of preventing the spoilation of established settlements by excessive growth. In addition, policies of restricting isolated buildings in the countryside have served to reinforce the conservationist ideal in many areas of Britain.

The balance between restrictive and liberal conservation policies in rural settlement planning has been discussed by Haines (1973, 97) who concludes that 'much of the blanket conservation of today is based on a theory that it is better the conserve everything rather than to risk destroying something that might be valued later'. It is this philosophy which has underpinned the policies of restricting growth in small environmentally attractive villages in Britain. However, this planning philosophy conflicts with popular public demands based on the premise that 'people prefer to live in communities slightly smaller than the ones in which they currently reside' and that 'the smaller community . . . appeals to the romantic nature of most urbanites as a "better" place in which to live and rear a family' (O'Riordan, 1976, 127). The duality between the popular wish to conserve rural settlements and the popular wish to live in rural settlements has usually been arbitrated in favour of the former, and this inherent bias in rural settlement planning has been directly responsible for the trends of gentrification and geriatrification of villages whereby opportunities for living in small rural settlements are becoming increasingly restricted for less favoured groups in society.

Thus, although conservationism and environmentalism have not been formalised as *explicit* theoretical inputs to rural settlement planning, the *implicit* philosophy demonstrated by plans and planners in the rural environment has largely adopted conservationist ideals as a basis for resource allocation within the rural settlement hierarchy.

Conclusion

Theoretical inputs to rural settlement planning should be viewed from at least two levels. The major influence on policy making in Britain (including the planning of rural settlements) is the overall socio-economic system in which particular outcomes are tempered not only by government policy-making requirements, but also by the financial decisions arrived at, for example, by large-scale multi-national companies (Dicken and Lloyd, 1976; Hood and Young, 1976) and by other institutions of economic and social formation such as the International Monetary Fund. Even extreme socialist systems are subject to financial and resource constraints (note the payment in gold for purchases of grain by the USSR). It is often overlooked, however, that political theory and action is constrained by the socio-economic structures imposed by these sources, and the interaction of these socio-economic and political meso-structures produces a very narrow theoretical pathway for pedestrian activity by those lower-level decision-makers that are more visible to the public. Therefore a fuller understanding of the options open to rural settlement planning might be gained by regarding *contextual* theories as dominant in the shaping of policy-making and implementation at ground level. Within these narrow contextual boundaries, relatively minor decisions are taken at the micro-level in order to allocate available resources within a pre-established socio-economic system. Although such decisions do not appear minor to those rural people affected by them, they are nevertheless directly limited by the meso-scale context. Thus the *formative* theoretical inputs at this second level, although important *per se*, should be viewed within the overall contextual framework.

Most theoretical investigations of rural settlement planning have concentrated on formative theories. From the brief review above it is clear that definite links can be drawn between various formative theories and the course taken by post-war rural settlement planning. However, two factors temper the importance of these links. First, there is a strong suspicion that formative theories have been used as retrospective justification for policies which were founded on economic and administrative expediency. Second, decisions actually being taken by various resource allocators often appear to pay little heed to theoretical considerations. These doubts concerning the importance and validity of formative theory merely serve to reinforce the viewpoint that it is contextual theory that will become increasingly important in the understanding of rural settlement planning. Moseley (1980a, 38) amplifies this suggestion in noting that:

> the urban researchers' paradigm seems to have shifted from a census/questionnaire basis to one resting on more fundamental questions about the distribution of power and the workings of society's allocative mechanisms. This paradigm needs expression in the rural context.

Therefore the study and analysis of theory in rural settlement planning should first be directed towards the taxonomy of contextual theoretical options, and only with this uncovering of the effects of meso-scale theory can the localized importance of the previously dominant formative theories be substantiated.

FOUR

Central government legislation and advice

Why is it important?

Most commentators on the affairs of planning pay lip service to the importance of central government legislation and advice. Traditionally, the details
and innuendoes of various acts, reports and advice notes have attracted discussion 'because they were there' and because a chronological description of
these tangible manifestations of government thinking offers an ideal framework within which to present detailed analysis of a particular part of the
planning process. More recently, a more critical and evaluative approach has
been adopted towards the historical development of centralized planning dicta
(notably by Hall *et al.*, 1973) and it has become increasingly important to enunciate the reasons and aspirations which underlie the attention given to legal and
permissive expressions of government policy.

Three major justifications may be proposed in the context of rural settlement planning. The major one is that legislation and advice from central
government have formed the basis for strategic planning in Britain. Therefore
any attempt to trace the temporal and spatial incidence of rural problems and
to evaluate the various strata of policies which have been introduced by way of
response to these problems requires a familiarity with, and understanding of,
the institutional constraints within which rural settlement planning performs.
Whereas parliamentary and ministerial activity is by no means the only
institutional constraint, it does represent a combined judicial and permissive
framework which often forms the skeleton of the political and professional
planning processes. A second motive for analysis of legislation and advice
from government concerns the manner in which the United Kingdom is often
portrayed as the pinnacle of legislative excellence in planning. McAuslan
(1979, 2) complains of a somewhat uncritical acceptance both home and
abroad of the legal aspects of British planning. Conventionally, planning
legislation is viewed as a neutral vehicle for the exercise of power, exhibiting no
inherent bias towards particular ideologies or philosophies which might influence that exercise of power. However he argues that:

> the law relating to land-use planning . . . lacks objectivity and neutrality so
> that far from being the 'golden metewand' of planning with all other aspects
> in a state of disarray, the law, in administration and official interpretation
> (via circulars and ministerial decisions as much as by cases decided in
> courts), is itself a major contributory factor to the current disarray of
> planning.

Again, an understanding of the subjectivity and ideological biases of planning law is of considerable potential benefit to the student or practitioner of rural settlement planning.

The third justification for an examination of government involvement in planning relates to the manner in which laws and advice acknowledge the rural–urban relationship. The 1932 Town and Country Planning Act is often viewed as a breakthrough for rural areas because it represents the first occasion when 'country' planning is officially acknowledged in planning legislation. However, in many ways the inclusion of rural nomenclature in generalized planning Acts of Parliament is misleading. Cherry (1978, 4) points out that 'British post-war planning policies have been directed overwhelmingly towards the resolution of *urban* problems', with the result that rural areas have often lacked the machinery to tackle their real economic, social and environmental needs (Dower, 1975). This perceived urban bias in planning mechanisms has led to several popular images of planning in rural areas, notably that summarized by Philip *et al.* (1978, 17):

> Although the best practitioners would energetically deny it, rural planning has become an exercise in tidily urbanizing the countryside. Indeed, the profession which perpetuates some of the worst crimes prides itself on membership of the Royal *Town* Planning Institute.

These attitudes, though understandable in the face of what actually happens in many rural settlements, are unhelpful in the elucidation of those stages of the planning process which tend to operate to the detriment of (or at least in ignorance of) rural areas. If, for example, it is the institutional machinery of legislation and advice from government which underlies the urban domination of planning concepts and techniques, then the planning profession should be recognized as being constrained by those imposed structures, in which case accusations of urban bias against rural planners are ill-directed. In any case, there is now a strongly held view (Cloke and Griffiths, 1980) that any perceived dichotomy between rural and urban planning issues should be rejected in recognition of the common structural components underlying social problems wherever located. Proponents of such a view might well argue that planning legislation concentrates *too much* rather than too little on specifically rural phenomena. For these reasons and others connected with the tracing of theoretical inputs to government thinking and the analysis of motives underlying various phases of planning philosophy, a brief review and evaluation of the legislative background in Britain is an essential prerequisite for an understanding of rural settlement planning.

The early years

Planning legislation is rooted in the Public Health and Housing Acts of the nineteenth century which were designed to combat squalid housing conditions in urban areas (Ashworth, 1954). It is therefore not surprising that the main tenor of government activity in the early years of planning up to 1947 (see table

4.1) was dominated by the needs and practical experiences of *urban* administration. The first legislation directed towards 'town planning' came in 1909 enabling local authorities to prepare 'schemes' for controlling the future development of housing areas. Any such scheme was to be vetted by the Local Government Board, and this clause along with problems of compensation payments, a downturn in housing estate development and the onset of war resulted in a mere three schemes being undertaken. A revision of this Act appeared in 1919, which, among other things, allocated powers and subsidies to local authorities for the building of public housing; this sparked a nation-wide growth of council house estates (Bowley, 1945) including some in rural centres.

Legislation to separate town planning from housing (1925) and to introduce county councils into the planning hierarchy (1929) followed, but the traditional starting point for rural planning came in 1932 with the first Town and Country Planning Act. This rather perfunctory Act, although again dominated by urban concerns, allowed local authorities to produce a planning scheme for those rural areas which were being developed or which were under threat of development. The Act's aims were dominated by motives of protecting existing rural amenity and of preserving buildings and places with inherent interest or natural beauty, although as each scheme required the consent of 75 per cent of landowners concerned, many of these motives were ignored in order to achieve an acceptable compromise between landowner and land-user. Substantial claims have been made on the Act's behalf. For instance, Wheeler (1977, 3) argues that:

it led to surveys of the current situation and assessments of local needs for housing and economic development; it encouraged the formation of opinion favourable to a planning approach both in the public mind and

Table 4.1 Government activity in the early years of planning

1909	Housing, Town Planning, etc. Act
1919	Housing, Town Planning Act
1925	Town Planning Act
1929	Local Government Act
1932	Town and Country Planning Act
1935	Restriction of Ribbon Development Act
1940	Barlow Report
1942	Scott Report
1942	Uthwatt Report
1943	The Minister of Town and Country Planning Act
1943	Town and Country Planning (Interim Development) Act
1944	Town and Country Planning Act
1944	Education Act
1944	Rural Water Supplies and Sewerage Act
1947	Agriculture Act
1947	Nationalization of the electricity industry
1947	Town and Country Planning Act

within the civil service and local government machine; and it fostered the growth of professional planning expertise.

Perhaps these assertions are best evaluated by a review of schemes which were successfully introduced in rural areas. In many counties, such as Devon and Cornwall, the 1932 schemes amounted to little more than travelogues of scenery and amenity. Elsewhere, county schemes were at least able to highlight socio-economic problems in rural areas. Warwickshire Joint Planning Committee (1935), for example, recognized the difficulties of providing essential services where large-scale residential building had taken place in areas of the countryside regardless of the location of existing public facilities. Furthermore, Durham County Council (1932) in their scheme gave vent to the notion that village rationalization was an inevitable rejoinder to the trends of pit closures in mining areas. However in both these cases, no action was taken to establish planning responses to the problems which had been outlined. Only in Cambridgeshire (Joint Town Planning Committee, 1934) were planning scheme proposals implemented in rural areas. Building on the work of William Morris, whose concept of village colleges encompassed the provision of centralized community facilities for a rural hinterland, the Committee's consultant, W. R. Davidge, proposed a rudimentary hierarchy of service villages in the county, each boasting its own village college. This scheme, with the help of Morris as Chief Education Officer, was implemented in rural Cambridgeshire, although only four village colleges were completed before 1940.

The 1932 schemes, then, were very much a first approximation of rural planning. By 1942 only 5 per cent of the land surface of England was covered by an approved planning scheme, although 73 per cent was subject to schemes in preparation. Even in approved schemes, rates of policy implementation were minimal, and in the event the onset of war prevented further progress in this respect. Therefore, although the 1932 Act may be viewed as a harbinger of rural planning, its permissive rather than obligatory stance meant that rural areas were not subject to compulsory planning controls within the inter-war period during which substantial rural development was taking place. As it was, the problems of inappropriate development in rural areas were heightened by the 1935 Restriction of Ribbon Development Act which tended to broaden rather than constrain areas of acceptable growth.

A sense of future vision pervaded legislators immediately prior to and during the Second World War, and proposals for future planning concepts were dominant within the overall image of a land fit for heroes. In particular, three major reports were issued which represent a significant influence on and stimulus to post-war planning philosophy. The Barlow Commission was appointed in 1937 with terms of reference which embraced present and future geographical distributions of industrial populations in Britain; the social, economic and strategic disbenefits of urban industrial concentration; and remedial measures which might be taken to redress any current disadvantage. The commission reported in 1940 and, despite the fact that its findings have often been overlooked in the subsequent search for rural planning roots, it can be argued that the Barlow deliberations formed the source of wartime planning philosophy from which ensuing reports by Scott and Uthwatt gleaned their nourishment. Hall *et al.* (1973) describe the Barlow Report as the essential basis of the post-war planning system in Britain, and from an *urban* viewpoint the reasons for this accolade are distinct. Barlow's proposals for new towns and comprehensive controls over industrial location were adopted in post-war legislation and directed urban planners towards particular emphases in the 1950s and 1960s. The importance of Barlow to *rural* planning is more subtle but equally important. For example, the report's backing for a comprehensive land-use planning system led to the Town and Country Planning Act of 1947 from which issued the development-plan stage of rural settlement planning. In addition a less immediate policy influence has been outlined by Newby (1980). Barlow insisted that the growth of large urban centres such as London should be restricted so that population and employment growth could be redirected to the more disadvantaged areas. An important spin-off from this redistribution of resources was that urban take-up of rural land in the South-East and the Midlands would be reduced, resulting in the salvation of threatened countryside. Newby (1980, 229–30) therefore suggests that 'in this way a humane desire to improve the distribution of industrial development and improved living standards in the urban centres was combined with a fairly rigid preservationist approach to the countryside'. Essentially, the Barlow report ensured that rural areas would be viewed as zones of preservation and that the character of these zones would be perceived as mystically 'natural countryside' which would benefit neither from serious study nor from positive planning.

The Scott Report of 1942 was overtly directed towards planning in the rural environment, and its importance may be judged by the large-scale acceptance and implementation of its policy recommendations in the post-war period. Gilg (1978) isolates five major rural planning issues which were discussed in the report –

1　The lack of overall planning direction;
2　The lack of industry and commerce in the countryside;
3　The poor state of agriculture;
4　The poor state of village social life and the need to preserve village amenities while at the same time making them accessible;
5　The lack of overall planning control

– and highlights the importance of the report's findings by pointing out that four of these five issues 'have mostly been tackled by post-war planning policies in an effective manner' (p. 353). However, the Scott Report's major impact on rural planning was to reiterate Barlow's recommendations for the containment of urban growth, and by so doing to reinforce the philosophical convention that agriculture should be the dominant land-user and resource-developer in rural areas. This presumption against residential and industrial development in the countryside probably stems from the Committee's vice-chairman, Sir Laurence Dudley Stamp, whose geographical stature and authority were able to overcome the minority viewpoint (led by Professor Stanley Dennison) that rural land should be assessed in terms of its value to the community under various types of usage. The result, as succinctly stated by Newby (1980, 231) was that a 'general presumption of a rural *status quo* has . . . been incorporated into planning practice'. Although the Scott Report's deliberations were never explicitly adopted by planning legislation, they nevertheless underwrote the generally accepted tenor of rural preservation which has pervaded rural settlement planning since the 1940s.

The third wartime report emanated from a committee chaired by Lord Justice Uthwatt. One direct result of a presumption against housing growth in rural areas was that many landowners would be prevented from accruing profit by selling their land for development, whilst in the privileged locations where development was to be permitted, landowners would receive undue profit due to the scarcity value of rural land for non-agricultural growth. The Uthwatt Report of 1942 dealt with the questions of *compensation* payments in the first of these cases, and *betterment* taxation in the second. A form of nationalization of undeveloped land was suggested as a solution to these problems. More specifically, it was the development rights to such land that would be acquired by the state, with the actual land to be purchased if and when required for urban expansion. These ideas were the subject of considerable political controversy, and although a Central Land Board was set up in 1947 with the task of accumulating land for development, it lasted only 6 years before falling foul of the same political and financial obstacles that subsequently defeated both the 1967 Land Commission and the 1976 Community Land Act. Had Uthwatt's recommendations become as central to the conventional wisdom of rural settlement planning as have those of Barlow and Scott, the techniques and achievements attributable to post-war rural planners might have been markedly different from those we recognize today.

The time-period between these reports and their commonly acclaimed antecedent, the 1947 Town and Country Planning Act, saw the introduction of a series of legislative measures which had an important (if unsung) role to play in the development of rural settlement policy. In a series of planning Acts, a separate Minister was established to secure consistency and continuity in national land-use and development policies (1943); land for which no planning scheme had been agreed was brought under interim development control (1943); and an element of innovative positive planning (including compulsory purchase of land) was introduced for badly utilized or blighted land, some of which was located on the rural-urban fringe (1944). A parallel series of events initiated some important decisions on rural resource location. The 1944 Education Act required local authorities to plan for the expansion or contraction of the number of schools in their area; the 1944 Rural Water Supplies and Sewerage Act enabled basic provision of water services to rural areas; and the nationalization of the electricity industry in 1947 led to extensive electrification in countryside areas. All of these measures led to the consideration of how local authorities might optimize the usefulness of investment in various services, and one important result of this deliberation was the establishment of resource *concentration* as a cost-effective and pragmatic model for the allocation of investment in rural areas. This trend to some extent pre-judged the rural planning strategies adopted within the framework of the 1947 Town and Country Planning Act.

The 1947 planning system

The planning system embodied in the 1947 Town and Country Planning Act has been described as 'the most comprehensive and radical framework for the control of land use in the world' (Ratcliffe, 1974, 77). By placing responsibility for planning in the hands of county and county borough councils, the Act reduced the number of participant planning authorities in England and Wales from 1441 to 145. Each county authority was required to carry out a survey in its area, and to prepare and submit a development plan to the Minister demonstrating how the land within its administration would be used over a 20-year time period. Development plans were to be submitted by 1951, and were to be revised every 5 years (although this schedule proved impossible for most authorities). The comprehensive nature of development plans was supported by the introduction of the *planning permission* mechanism whereby landowners were required to seek the permission of the local planning authority before any material land-use alteration could be carried out. In this way, local authorities were given strong powers both to plan for a controlled allocation of development and to enforce individual decisions made as part of the overall plan.

The 1947 Act owes a great deal to the philosophies recommended by the wartime reports of Barlow, Scott and Uthwatt. Presumptions of status quo or minimal growth for rural areas were supported by the designation of rural white land, where agriculture was to remain sacrosanct. Furthermore, the arguments for overall planning direction and control contained within the Scott report were heeded in the Act's administrative strategy, while the requirement for planning permission before any development was allowed to proceed owed much to the deliberations of the Uthwatt Committee (Cullingworth, 1979). Thus, although not explicitly acknowledged, the wartime philosophical precedents were largely followed in the 1947 legislation. The practical application of this accepted philosophy was more clearly established in a series of circulars and regulations from the Ministry of Town and Country Planning which were intended to clarify the detailed requirements of a development plan. *Circular 40* (1948) advised that pre-plan surveying in rural areas should be concentrated on the social and economic functions of the larger settlements. Indeed, many counties slavishly followed this advice and restricted themselves to a cataloguing of the educational, health, retail and social services which were provided in nodal locations. On the other hand, a settlement's capacity for residential development was given little attention at this stage. The role of agriculture was also made abundantly clear. The circular (Section III) states:

> For predominantly rural areas, it should be sufficient at this stage to make a broad appreciation, against the agricultural background (since agriculture is the basis of the whole rural economy and the dominant user of rural land)

of the existing pattern of communities, and their social and economic function in relation to the surrounding area.

Circular 59 (1948) gave details of how planning authorities should illustrate the locations of centres for social, educational and health services on their statutory county maps. These centres were to be indicated by a series of circles, divided into quadrants, each demonstrating that a certain service existed or was planned for that centre. Quickly dubbed 'hot cross buns', these notations were seen to represent a logo for growth in the rural settlement concerned, and as such attracted widespread controversy both from residents who feared that future growth would impair the quality of their environment and community, and from those who perceived the lack of future development to indicate a decline in village vitality. In fact, the early development plans encompassed a wide variation in the number and types of settlements covered by this notation. However, the 'hot cross bun' now stands as an historical but precursive indication of the ensuing polarization of views concerning the concentration and dispersal of resources in rural areas.

In 1950 the Ministry issued an advice note on the *Siting of New Houses in Country Districts*, and two major philosophical themes were reaffirmed in this document. First, it was acknowledged that the economic provision of services in rural areas could only be achieved by the selection of certain settlements for expansion. In the most extreme economic circumstances this type of policy was seen to suggest that in some non-selected settlements planners would be forced 'to demolish and clear the village and resettle the inhabitants in new centres, where employment, houses and services can be provided' (Section I). This strongly worded advice, together with policy precedents established under the 1932 planning schemes, represented a blueprint for rural settlement planning which was difficult for planners either to ignore or to diverge from in their attempts to allocate resources in rural areas. The second theme dealt with by the advice note was a strong presumption against the building of dwellings outside of established rural settlements, unless these dwellings were required for the specific needs of various sections of the agricultural labour force.

Planning authorities received little further advice between the preparation of the first round of development plans and the submission of their reviews. The next major piece of government advice was issued in *Circular 42* (1955) from the new Ministry of Housing and Local Government, which encouraged the authorities to establish green belts in order to restrict the sprawl of built-up areas. A spin-off from this advice was that rural settlements trapped within these restrictive zones were denied further expansion, thus effectively establishing a new breed of rural settlement policy for those settlements located within green belts.

Towards the end of the period dominated by the 1947 Act, government advice to planning authorities reflected some of the changes which were imminent. An amendment to the development-plan regulations in 1965 discontinued the use of 'hot cross bun' notations and in 1967 *Circular 72*, otherwise known as *Planning Bulletin 8* (Ministry of Housing and Local Government, 1967) stressed the need for an overall county policy framework for village development and for a co-ordinated programme for public investment. It presented planning authorities with a formal model for the formulation of rural settlement policy and the preparation of individual settlement plans. Although the Bulletin was cased in rather vague and generalized terms, it laid the foundations for detailed local planning of individual settlements in rural areas and thus represents a turning point in the advice from central government to planning authorities. Whereas early circulars contained rigid and broad-scale policy directives, the emphasis now reflected a more flexible regional policy within which the planning of individual villages assumed a far greater importance.

An analysis of the plans produced within this period and of what actually happened in rural settlements under their jurisdiction is attempted in chapter 5. However this review of legislation and advice does permit several broad conclusions to be reached concerning the nature and emphases of the 1947 planning system. The Working Party on Rural Settlement Policies (1979) notes that the development-plan system was built around a framework of good housekeeping in rural areas. Three major constraints are recognized which reflect the physical land-use orientation of the 1947 Act and its ensuing advisory circulars:

1   The existing pattern of public investment in services and likely future expenditure;
2   The need to safeguard higher-quality agricultural land;
3   The desirability of locating new development on land of low landscape and ecological value.

The dominant nature of these constraints led to a period of rural planning which operated through negative powers of control to ensure that the seemingly changeless countryside and its way of life were protected. Social planning was not provided for by the available legislation and so a planning system born of the liberal and progressive political aims of redressing social injustice was in fact instrumental in overlooking social issues in favour of a rigid and bureaucratic approach to resource allocation. The emphasis on rigid negative control also led to a high number of appeals against planning refusals, which overloaded and slowed down the entire planning process. With the benefit of hindsight, these shortcomings can be seen to lead inexorably to significant and considerable problems both for rural planners and (more importantly) the rural planned. These problems are explored in chapter 5.

The 1968 planning system

A growing dissatisfaction with the old-style development plans was highlighted by the deliberations of the Planning Advisory Group (1965) whose official status as part of the Ministry of Housing and Local Government did not prevent a series of recommendations in favour of a radical restructuring of the nature and administration of planning in Britain. The Town and Country Planning Acts of 1968 (for England and Wales) and 1969 (for Scotland) accepted these recommendations as the basis of a new system of planning which was put into operation by the 1971 Town and Country Planning Act (amended in 1972). In essence, the previous development plans were replaced by a dual-scale system of statutory planning. At the broader level, structure plans were to be submitted by English county councils for the approval of the Secretary of State for Environment, who was the head of the new government department set up in 1970 to oversee planning affairs in the widest sense. The Welsh county councils and Scottish regional councils submitted their plans to the Secretaries of State for their respective countries. These structure plans were to form a written statement (supported by necessary diagrammatic material) in which the proposals and policies for large-scale change over a wide area were outlined within a flexible and adaptive framework. Matters for consideration in the structure plans included:

1 An analysis of the socio-economic and environmental characteristics of the area;
2 An appraisal of existing planning policies for the area;
3 A recognition of any existing commitments to be accounted for in the future planning of the area;
4 A recognition of mutual interest and influence with adjoining areas;
5 An examination of the main planning issues in the countryside;
6 An indication of the aims underlying strategic policies;
7 A formulation of policies to achieve these aims;
8 An examination of the organization and administration required to implement these policies.

Normally the structure plan would also include more detailed proposals and policies for particular topics (outlined in table 4.2) although it is noticeable here that rural settlements were to be studied piecemeal under these various subject headings rather than as a topic in their own right.

These overall strategic proposals formed a framework within which detailed small-scale planning could be carried out using *local plans*, which following the Local Government Act of 1972, were to be initiated and implemented by the new district councils who were also given charge of day-to-day development control procedures. Local plans were to consist of a written statement and a formal map which in combination would detail any proposals for the development and other use of land within the plan's area. Four main tasks were required of the local plans:

1 To comply with the overall strategic aims of the structure plan concerned;
2 To provide a detailed basis for local development control;
3 To highlight local planning issues for public debate and participation;
4 To act as a basis for the co-ordination of development.

Table 4.2   Topics for individual attention in structure plans

Population	Industry	Education
Employment	Commerce	Social and community services
Resources	Transportation	Recreation and leisure
Housing	Shopping	Conservation
Utility services	Minerals	

One of the underlying aims of local plans was to provide a forum for positive planning at the local scale. There was an optimism that local planning authorities could use local plans as a set of guidelines which could be followed by land and property developers so as to achieve a form of development which would be in keeping with the wider social and economic aims of the strategic policies contained within the structure plans. This role of local co-ordination was strengthened by the fact that local authorities were not required to gain the Secretary of State's approval for local plans. Thus a process of continuous review and reassessment by the local authorities themselves was expected to prevent local plans from becoming out of date.

The 1968 planning system heralded several other innovations from its 1947 counterpart. Structure plans were not to be tied to a rigid agenda of presentation and review. Rather, they were to be subjected to a continuous review process, and indeed the generalized and often vague form in which strategic policies were cased allowed the concept of continual shifts of policy to cater for the dynamism of wider social and economic trends at a regional or national scale. Although this inherent flexibility presented problems for the long-term allocation of fixed resources, provision was made within the structure-plan process for the co-ordination of resource-allocation decisions between various local authority departments and between local authorities and other decision-takers within the plan area. In addition, the 1968 system formalized the role of public participation in the planning process. Following the 1967 Skeffington Report, the Town and Country Planning Acts of 1968 and 1971 required that opportunities be given for representations and objections from members of the public at the 'proposals' and 'draft' stages of both structure plans and local plans. Although the effectiveness of participation has been widely questioned (Sewell and Coppock, 1977) its inclusion in the statutory process of planning affords yet another example of the changes towards 'accountable flexibility' and 'social awareness' which the 1968 system was designed to achieve.

Legislative measures contained within the various acts were supplemented by a series of circulars containing informal advice from government on more detailed aspects of the new planning system. Of particular relevance to rural settlement planning are *Circulars 10* (1970) and *102* (1972) from the Department of the Environment, which allowed for the release of additional building land in rural settlements located in specially controlled zones such as green belts and Areas of Outstanding Natural Beauty, and thus gave a strong indication that the pressures for development in such settlements were becoming irresistible. This trend of land release was mirrored in *Circular 122* (1973), which outlined new guidelines for development control in rural settlements. It suggested (Section I) that:

> Some villages have reached the limit of their natural growth. But a good deal of housing land can be found by infilling of villages, and by further modest expansion, including expansion outside (but not divorced from) village envelopes, where this is consistent with community capacity.

In effect, this advice to local planners again indicates that pressures for development in many peri-urban settlements had created conditions which could no longer be catered for by previously rigid zoning policies in village plans, and that local flexibility was allowable in these cases. Very often it has been this form of unsung yet influential advice which has actually dictated the shape of village planning at the local scale, and the role of this advice deserves fuller attention than is possible here (Working Party on Rural Settlement Policies, 1979). Nevertheless, the recognition of rapidly changing trends in rural areas by central government acts as an important complement to their establishment of a new planning system with the flexibility to cope with social and economic dynamism.

The rural settlement policies contained within structure plans and local plans are given specific attention in chapters 6 and 10. However, it is again possible, and indeed important, to establish some preliminary generalizations arising from the legislative and advisory role of government in establishing the 1968 planning system. Although immediate success in overcoming the short-falls of development plans would be an unrealistic expectation of the structure-plan system, it has nevertheless been the case that significant problems have arisen in the operation of post-1968 planning which may be traced back to the initial establishment of a two-tier flexible planning process. One such difficulty 'is raised by Leach and Moore (1979) who describe some of the tensions which arise from the division of planning powers between county and district authorities. This shared function, where the county has strategic and large-scale development control powers and the district has powers of medium- and small-scale development control takes on an interdependent nature whereby one authority is inevitably affected by actions of the other. Interaction of this nature has led to conflict in certain areas over certain issues, and often constitutes an even more potent recipe for delay than the much criticized development-plan process. Thus the 1968 system is criticized because of its tardiness in responding to change.

Hall (1979, 384–5) develops this critical appraisal in three directions. First, the new system is viewed as too weak and ambiguous:

> Many question whether structure plans can be effective when the real action lies with district councils as local agents of development control and as housing authorities. They wonder what will happen when district councils . . . engage in conflict with big brother in county hall.

Second, the system is too theoretical and academic to be understood by large sections of the community. Largely because prevailing legislation has dictated that structure plans are cased in vague and diagrammatic terms, the actual content of policies and strategies appears to be several stages removed from the actual life-style requirements of the population. Third, the 1968 system appears to have increased the input of manpower and other resources into planning, but has produced no apparent concomitant increase in output. These three criticisms may become less important over time, as county–district interactions become calmer, education and participation programmes bring about a more favourable public image for planning, and the positive achievements (such as they are) of structure planning become more visible. However, these issues are pertinent at this stage of structure-plan history and indicate at the very least, that the new system has encountered several teething troubles which might explain why rural structure-plan policies have been less successful than expected.

Perhaps a more fundamental criticism of the 1968 system concerns its treatment of the rural–urban relationship. Newby (1980, 240) sees the structure-plan system as offering 'a means of transcending the divide between urban and rural areas'. Not only were structure plans seen as mechanisms for the implementation of positive resource development to replace the former negative controls of development planning, but the newly constituted districts, which combined many areas previously labelled 'rural' or 'urban' into more hierarchical settlement systems, were viewed as units within which the structural processes underlying both rural and urban problems could be attacked on a more united front. In fact, it appears that the envisaged change of approach to rural planning has been less evident than expected, with evidence from the Countryside Commission (1976) suggesting that the potential improvements in tackling rural problems have not been realized during the structure-plan era. These issues are further developed in chapter 6.

Government inputs to planning – a concluding note

This brief review of central government legislation and advice in the realm of town and country planning has highlighted many apparent changes in approach, starting with the early plans of the 1932 Act and progressing to the most recent structure-plan era. Undoubtedly, planning as a professional process has indeed benefited from the fundamental improvements attained as one system has been replaced by another. However, if we view these events as a backcloth to the development of rural settlement planning, it is less easy to acknowledge the steady progression of 'change-for-the-better' which might be attributed to the system as a whole.

The balance between negative and positive planning in rural areas has been firmly tilted in favour of the negative pole throughout the development of planning in Britain (figure 4.1). As a result of both the 1932 and 1947 Acts an early precedent was set in favour of urban domination in land-use planning. In these early years, planning was conceived as an *urban* problem, and this notion was exacerbated because of the need for immediate action in war-torn urban areas. Allied to this view of rural areas as an appendage of the urban mass, the philosophical dogma of the wartime Barlow and Scott Reports ensured that the dominance of agriculture in rural areas would be maintained through the preservation, or at least heavy-handed conservation, of the countryside. Thus the philosophy of preserving the *status quo* through no-growth or minimal growth policies in rural areas became ingrained in the planning system at the start of the 1947 era, and rural planning during this period was characterized by planning for control rather than any positive attempt to alleviate social problems in the countryside. Even though the 1968 system appeared to alter

Figure 4.1 The balance of positive and negative planning in rural areas

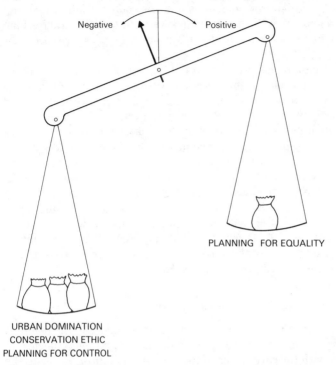

the planning process in such a way that positive social planning became more of a practicable proposition in rural areas, the changing process was not matched by a complementary change in the underlying philosophical assumptions of rural planning. With the established conservation ethic continuing to dominate, the opportunities for positive planning available within the scope of structure plans and local plans were nullified, and a propensity to indulge in negative control has tended to continue, particularly in view of the economic depression which has reduced the proportion of the public purse which is available for positive planning purposes.

Moseley (1980a, 5) offers further evidence that the balance of rural planning continues to be tilted in favour of rural conservation:

> The current government review of rural areas (undertaken, revealingly, by the *Countryside* Review Committee – not a 'rural areas' review committee) purports to be a total analysis of those areas' problems. But it is clear from the dominance of conservation, landscape, agricultural and recreational issues in their reports . . . that it is nothing of the sort.

This seemingly intransigent attitude from central government may be at least partially explained by the local political balance in rural areas. Although the squirearchal role of rural landowners in local politics has declined in some counties, its demise is by no means complete, and has in any case given way in the main to political involvement by new rural residents of the professional and managerial classes. In either case, both dominant political groups in rural areas are likely to support the ethic of the dominance of agriculture and the restriction of developmental growth in rural settlements. Therefore the views expressed by local politicians tend to mirror the accepted philosophy of a negative form of rural planning.

Sadly, the continuance of this negative ethic has not simply maintained a status quo in rural areas. In many cases a restriction on new housing development has led to an artificially high price tag being placed on a substantial proportion of the rural housing stock. As a consequence, housing opportunities in rural areas have been polarized towards those groups in society whose affluence allows them to purchase their rural experience and away from lower-income groups who are being squeezed out by the gentrification process. Similarly, opposition to new industrial development in rural areas has restricted rural economic growth and weakened the bargaining power of existing local labour. By maintaining a low-wage rural economy, the presumption against rural economic development has had similar results to those occurring in the housing sector. As Newby (1980, 242) clearly states, 'Strategic planning has therefore contained a strong element of planning for the interests of the better-off'. Thus, the results of negative planning policies have had regressive social implications, making the task of positive social planning in rural areas even more difficult than before.

The counterbalance to negative planning in rural areas is as yet rather weak, although potentially it could make a substantial impact. Even under current planning systems, experiments in the manipulation of legislation in order to attain selective social goals represent one important point of progress towards positive planning. Such experiments have largely relied on Section 52 agreements (which taken their name from Section 52 of the Town and Country Planning Act of 1968, enacted 1971). These have been used to attach conditions to planning permissions granted for residential development (Suddards, 1979). In the Lake District (Baynes, 1979; Clark, 1982; Shucksmith, 1981) Section 52 agreements have been used both to ensure that newly built properties would be sold to 'local people', and to make this condition binding in the event of resale. Although in this particular case problems have arisen because demand from outsiders has been concentrated on the existing housing stock, thus protracting the difficulties experienced by local people in entering the housing market, the utilization of informal agreements may be one method of moulding existing legislation to meet social requirements.

Another form of positive planning which is currently the subject of successful experimentation concerns the idea of comprehensive development programmes. Thorburn (reported in *The Planner*, 1980, 102) suggests that:

> we should be pursuing comprehensive rural development programmes involving housing, industry, schools, services, road improvements, or whatever else may be needed in a particular area by farmers and others. In other words, comprehensive programmes for particular areas rather than sectional programmes for the whole countryside.

Despite the agricultural slant to this comment, the idea behind it argues that a proper co-ordination of life-style requirements can, in itself, represent a form of positive planning. Certainly the comprehensive schemes backed by resources (e.g. in the Highlands and Islands and Mid Wales) appear capable of positive contributions to the easing of rural social problems, although where schemes in less-favoured areas merely rely on the usual level of local authority resources this level of attainment may be less easily reached. If structure plans can successfully achieve a greater degree of co-ordination between decision-makers then a starting point for positive planning action will have been reached.

The main stumbling block to a more positive form of planning in rural areas – the dominance of the conservation ethic – remains firmly ensconced in Britain. Even if planning methods and processes are modified in favour of a more direct attempt to overcome social inequalities, this underlying philosophy will continue to impede the development of problem-solving responses from planners in rural areas. Therefore, despite the valid criticisms of the various post-war planning systems, it would be less than just to attribute the failure to cope with social deprivation in rural areas to the ineptitude of professional planners who, after all, have been hamstrung by an established philosophical and methodological tradition. Nevertheless, even within the structural limitations imposed upon them, planners have arrived at differing strategic patterns of resource allocation in rural areas. Within this range of policies, some schemes have proved more successful than others, and these are analysed in the following three chapters.

FIVE

Development plans and their reviews

Development plans – the written policies

The development-plan policies for rural settlements represented in many ways a unique opportunity to create planning strategies than were unfettered by policy precedent. Indeed this first stage of the heterodox model of the planning process suggested in figure 1.2 was absent at this time apart from the rather feeble attempts to produce planning schemes under the 1932 Act. Thus, the various agents of policy preparation leading to the written development-plan policies played a peculiarly formative role during this era of planning history. The various factors involved in policy preparation have been detailed elsewhere (Cloke, 1979; Woodruffe, 1976) but their overall effects can be clearly traced. Indeed, given the weight of government advice in favour both of rural conservation and of the need to concentrate services and resources within the rural settlement pattern, it is hardly surprising that the first crop of development plans after the 1947 Act differed only in the degree of rationalization proposed rather than in the actual decision between concentration or dispersal of investment. Rural planners in this early period were encouraged by a simple logic:

> The greater the concentration of population the easier it would be to support local facilities, to support economically the water supply and sewerage schemes being installed as a matter of government policy, and to support public transport between rural settlements and the towns. (Green, 1966, 31)

Therefore, the combination of government policy trends and, to a lesser extent, concurrent geographical research on the relationships between central-place theory and rural settlements (for example Bracey's work (1962) on 'central villages') proved irresistable in the formulation of policies for rural areas. Three main categories of policy may be identified at this stage:

1 *Key settlement policies* in which a comprehensive concentration of housing, employment, services and facilities into selected centres is designed to maintain a level of rural investment in order to support both the key settlement and hinterland villages. This type of policy may be distinguished by an outward-looking view of how centralized resources can be used to serve the rest of the settlement pattern;

2 *Planned decline policies*, where a direct rationalization of the settlement pattern is pursued, including the termination of public support for

outmoded small villages, and the regrouping of population into larger centres;

3   *Village classification policies*, where settlements are categorized according to environmental quality and service capacity so that optimum use may be made of existing public investment by ensuring that new development will be channelled into larger villages. This type of policy is characterized by an inward-looking view of the planning of each individual settlement, and counties adopting this strategy tend to be those who accepted formal government advice without too much local innovation.

These categories of policy are not mutually exclusive, neither are they all-embracing, since policy modifications to account for green belts, national parks, AONBs and other special designations make significant contributions to the maze of small-scale policy variations already existing due to the individuality of presentation by each county. However the three category types do provide a yardstick against which various individual policies may be measured, and they do serve to concentrate our analysis on the *underlying* aims of rural settlement policy during this period. Was the overall objective to support the rural settlement pattern, or to rationalize it, or indeed merely to establish a convenient basis for the local-authority obligations of service provision? These questions should remain at the forefront of any analysis of what actually happened under the auspices of development-plan policies and of whether these policies fulfilled the objectives which underpinned them.

Key settlement policies

This type of policy during this period was mainly favoured by counties with problems associated with a high level of rurality rather than by more pressured counties whose policies were simply geared towards development control. The policies were diverse in both structure and detail. On the one hand, the Cambridgeshire policy (1954) established the general concept of *king villages* (which constituted the 'natural' centres for surrounding smaller villages and hamlets) and outlined a rather vague policy of favouring development in king villages with development elsewhere being treated on the merits of the individual case. Despite its lack of detail this policy does demonstrate an attempt to build up rural resources to support the existing pattern of settlements (Cambridgeshire CC, 1966). Similar policies were pursued in Hampshire (1955) and Cornwall (1956). At the other extreme of detailed presentation, the plan for Lindsey, Lincolnshire (1955) followed the standard practice of undertaking a survey of village facilities and using this information to create a hierarchy of service centres, each serving a stipulated hinterland. Figure 5.1 demonstrates the intricacy of the resultant pattern, with two tiers of rural centre underlying three grades of urban market node. On the surface, this pattern would appear to be the product of a concerted attempt at a coherent rural strategy, following the classic key settlement model of planning for centre–periphery relationships. However, a more detailed view of these seemingly comprehensive early policies demonstrates that strategic planning diagrams are often belied by the underlying processes of selection,

Figure 5.1 Proposed hierarchy of settlements for Lindsey, Lincolnshire, 1951

• Small village

○ Rural Service Centre serving small area with daily facilities

▲ Self contained village

△ Self contained village acting as Dormitory Settlement

□ Local Service Centre serving larger area with some weekly facilities

■ Small Market Town serving larger area with all weekly facilities

■ Other towns

▧ Large towns (County Boroughs)

Source: Lindsey, Lincolnshire CC, 1955

establishment and implementation of key settlement policies. For example, Wheeler (1977) points out that the selection of rural growth points was usually governed by:

1 The financial advantages of concentrating statutory facilities in one settlement;
2 The precedent of development in individual settlements (particularly relating to existence of spare sewerage capacity);
3 The 'accident' of pressure from adjacent urban areas.

Of the Lindsey plan, Wheeler (1977, 5) bemoans the fact that:

an elaborate distribution of satellite, central and development settlements is set forth, based almost entirely upon the existing distribution of settlements and of facilities within settlements, rather than upon any idea of a dynamic change in settlements.

Some evidence of a more dynamic view of rural settlement policy is shown by Somerset County Council (1958), whose development plan contained a four-fold classification of settlements:

1   Towns and main villages which act as local centres;
2   Settlements showing evidence of developing, and which from their position and circumstances might become main villages;
3   Settlements, which although not showing evidence of developing, could serve as local centres for areas not now enjoying good facilities;
4   Other settlements.

The isolation of potential rural growth centres in the Somerset plan does inject a temporal dimension which is lacking in the policies produced by many other counties. However, it is prudent to remember at this point that written plans are only indicators of what actually happens, and the policy of selecting potential rural centres will depend for its success on the measures taken to fulfil the recognized potential.

Other variations in key settlement-type policies of this period reflect the number of growth points selected, and the intended function of those settlements not selected for growth (the so-called non-key settlements). Key settlement policies were predominantly favoured by the more remote counties during this period, and thus there was a tendency to select large numbers of key settlements (often between fifty and one hundred) simply because the settlement patterns in these areas consisted of a large number of small villages. Several other reasons have been noted for the choice of so many growth centres in each county (Cloke, 1979). First, planners drawing up development plans had little previous experience of key settlement type policies and therefore had no basis for the accurate prediction of the effectiveness and dynamism of various sizes of rural centre. Thus, the selection of key settlements tended to be based on the threshold populations for various services which in turn led to an emphasis on the minimum size needed for key settlement status almost without regard to the numbers of settlements attaining that minimum size. Second, key settlement policies were something of a novelty at this stage. The selection of a key settlement has been likened to the touching of a talisman, after which planners could sit back and wait for a flood of applications for development. Underlying this simile once again is the need for planning *action* to support planning *designation*. When these factors of inexperience and novelty are added to the planners' wish for an even geographical distribution of key settlements and to the political pressure exerted on behalf of each settlement to gain 'key' status, it may be more readily understood why counties chose to over rather than under-subscribe in key settlement selection.

Attitudes to non-key settlements varied considerably. Some counties (among them Hampshire and Cambridgeshire) recognized that every application to develop in these locations required individual determination in the light of local circumstances. Elsewhere (for example in the 'other villages' categories of counties such as Somerset) a firm presumption against growth was established. Indeed, one of the hallmarks of early key settlement policies was that short-term population flows from small village to key settlement were to be encouraged as one answer to rural depopulation. Only in the longer term could non-key villages expect to receive a backwash of investment and perhaps prosperity. At the written policy level it appears that remoter counties took a rather more restrictive attitude towards development in non-key settlements in order to channel growth into their larger number of key settlements, while pressured areas were less strict in this respect. However, as will be seen later in this chapter, policy intentions and planned reality often differed with regard to permitting housing development in small villages.

Planned decline policies

The most extreme attitudes towards growth in small villages were adopted in an important subset of policies where the rural settlement rationalization process included a virtual shutdown of the smaller, poorly serviced villages in the hierarchy. Again, theoretical work on service thresholds was a significant factor in the promotion of this policy. The conclusions of contemporary planners like Ray Green (1966, 34) are clearly stated:

> There is a clear indication that any settlement of less than 5000 population is unlikely to be able to support a reasonably full range of facilities in the future . . . a population of 5000 might well be taken as a theoretical minimum for planning rural settlement in the future.

Figure 5.2 gives a theoretical impression of the rationalization process envisaged by Green in circumstances of rural deprivation and service loss, and it is evident that the 'discouragement' of new development is both more widespread and potentially more destructive than the centre–hinterland mutual support ambitions of the key settlement policies described above. However, it is equally clear that a rigidly imposed key settlement policy could easily lead (whether consciously or unconsciously on the part of planners) to a situation of planned decline, and consequently it is the *implementation* of resource concentration policies rather than their stated objectives which holds the key to policy interpretation and analysis. One major difference between the conventional key settlement policy and the planned decline policy concerns the latter's presumption against local need development in small villages as compared to the former's more lenient attitude in this respect.

The best-known example of a planned decline policy was initiated by Durham County Council (1954) where the dense network of ninteenth-century mining villages had been anachronized by twentieth-century pit closures and where a definite need was perceived:

> to create a more modern, efficient and compact settlement pattern appropriate to the needs of the twentieth century by concentrating new development in those settlements which have a more hopeful economic future and where, in the long run, better living conditions can be provided. (Atkinson, 1970, 439)

Figure 5.2 Green's model for planned concentration of settlement and facilities

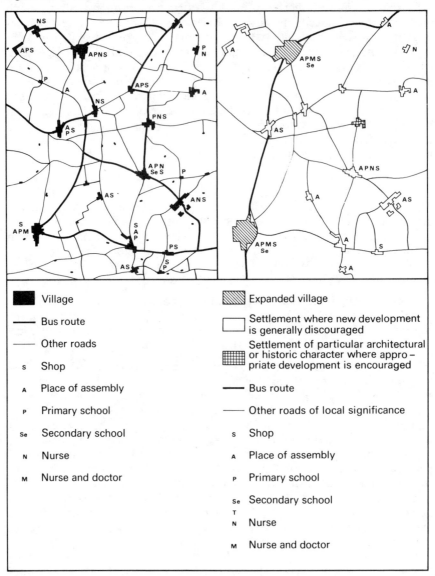

Source: Green, 1966, 33, 35

The Durham example has been fully described elsewhere (Barr, 1969; Blowers, 1972), but the four-fold classification produced in the development plan is worthy of detail.

A   Those settlements in which the investment of considerable further amounts of capital is envisaged because of an expected future regrouping of population, or because it is anticipated that the future natural increase in population will be retained (seventy settlements).

B   Those settlements in which it is believed that the population will remain at approximately the present level for many years to come. Sufficient capital should be invested in these communities to cater for approximately the present population (143 settlements).

C   Those settlements from which it is believed that there may be an outward movement of population. Sufficient capital should be invested to cater for the needs of a reduced population (thirty settlements).

D   Those settlements from which a considerable loss of population may be expected. No further investment of capital on any considerable scale should take place. This generally means that when the existing houses become uninhabitable they should be replaced elsewhere, and that any expenditure on facilities and services in these communities which would involve public money should be limited to conform to what appears to be the possible future life of existing property in the community (114 settlements).

Figure 5.3 shows the distribution of these categories. It is the D category (dubbed as 'decline', 'death' and 'destruction') which has attracted considerable controversy both inside and outside the county. In fact some of the smaller D villages, where pit closures had occurred and where residential dereliction was a problem, were bulldozed as a result of this policy and their sites were 'assimilated into the surrounding countryside'. In other larger D villages, major clearances of substandard housing stock took place, and these extreme forms of planned decline were heavily criticized for riding roughshod over local communities and for allowing physical planning to dominate the important considerations of social planning.

Two rejoinders place the Durham plan in its true context. First, it might be regarded as something of a special case in that the immediate problems which induced the policy of planned decline were directly concerned with the over-endowment of villages first created and then discarded by fluctuations in the coal-mining industry. These settlements overlaid the pre-existing agricultural network, and it was the poor standard of some of the pit-village housing stock which accelerated the financial decisions of spatial resource reallocation by local authorities. Similar problems were encountered in Cumberland (1955) where designation of D villages where 'development is unlikely to occur' raised less public outcry. Second, the Durham plan set out to achieve the type of rural settlement pattern coveted by many other planners in other rural areas. Certainly, the planning measures adopted elsewhere in order to achieve a rationalized settlement system were less direct and produced less immediate conflict than the Durham example, but nevertheless there is strong evidence to suggest that a relocation of population from small villages to larger, more easily serviced settlements constituted an objective which was close to the heart of many rural planners at this time. It could be said that conventional resource

Figure 5.3 The settlement pattern of County Durham, 1951

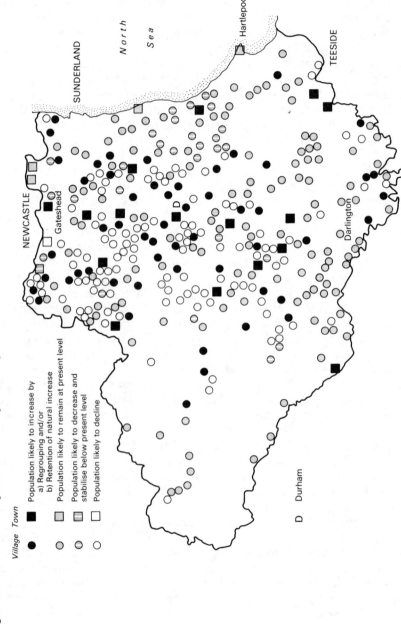

Village   Town

■ □ Population likely to increase by
        a) Regrouping and/or
        b) Retention of natural increase

■ ■ Population likely to remain at present level

● ● Population likely to decrease and
        stabilise below present level

○ ○ Population likely to decline

D   Durham

Source: Blowers, 1972, 146

concentration policies were designed to achieve the same ends as planned decline policies, only by way of more indirect and protracted planning inaction.

Village classification policies

A third category of rural settlement policy should be recognized as an integral part of rural development planning. In some counties (e.g. Gloucestershire, 1955; Hertfordshire, 1958; Wiltshire, 1959) the results of rural community surveys were used to produce settlement classifications which were regarded as ends in themselves rather than as stepping stones to more comprehensive settlement policies. In these counties the emphasis was on the ability of each individual settlement – both in terms of environmental criteria and of the presence or absence of various services and facilities (particularly spare sewerage capacity) – to to accommodate growth over the plan period. For example, Kent County Council's (1958) plan recognized a need to cater for those who wish to live in small rural communities, in so far as this demand could be satisfied without destroying the character of the villages concerned. The plan also stressed its wish to provide for local housing needs, emanating both from the agricultural workforce and from commuters to nearby urban employment. Thus even within its classification of those villages suggested for moderate expansion and those suggested for no expansion, the Kent policy did look favourably on small developments in any settlement provided that settlement was capable of accepting the development concerned.

The village classification type of policy proved attractive both to rural counties close to major urban areas, and to other counties whose development plan represented a holding operation while a more comprehensive and all-embracing strategy was formulated for initiation at the development-plan review stage. What is clear is that the three policy types described above are merely variations on a similar theme of resource concentration into the larger and better serviced rural settlements. Even in areas such as East Sussex (1953) and Nottinghamshire (1959) where the innovation of village clusters was discussed, the resultant policy rejected this discussion and was founded on the resource concentration ethic. Equally clear from this review of development-plan policies is that the major preoccupation of rural counties was with the difficulty of providing statutory *services* over a dispersed settlement pattern. Under these conditions of government advice on rural conservation current conceptualizations of settlement hierarchies and the dominance of servicing strategies, concentration policies for rural settlements inevitably flourished.

Development plans reviewed

The statutory reviews of development plans represented a significant opportunity for policy change in rural areas. Although there was a nominal obligation to publish reviews after 5 years of development planning, in practice they appeared much later than intended and were therefore more able to tackle the teething problems experienced in the original plans. These problems were manifold. The development plans took several years to prepare, and often suffered a further delay before being finally approved by central government. Thus it was not unusual for a decade to pass between the 1947 legislation and the approval of individual county plans. This institutional delay led to the plans being overtaken by rural events even before they were implemented in rural areas. Cambridgeshire County Council (1966, 1138) summarized their development-plan period in this manner:

> There had been changes in development trends not fully anticipated when the Plan was first prepared. . . . The most significant change had been an acceleration of the rate of population growth over the whole of the county. To a large extent this was attributed to factors outside the influence of the Plan policies.

Many other counties were similarly taken by surprise, particularly by the trend of increasing personal mobility which permitted greater levels of commuting and thereby created a new clientele for housing in rural areas. The development plans were prepared during a period in which new rural housing was mainly provided by local authorities rather than by private developers. However, in the late 1950s and early 1960s, demand from commuters and changes in government housing policy led to a more dominant role for the private developer in the construction of rural housing estates. As Woodruffe (1976) notes, this structural change in housing demand and supply necessitated a drastic rethink of county settlement policies in the development-plan reviews of the early and middle 1960s.

Development-plan reviews, then, should be seen as far less dependent on central government advice than their predecessors and more as a reflection both of the changing conditions in rural areas and of the more careful consideration devoted to rural problems by planners who were able to divert themselves from the initial priority given to urban environments. Indeed, the reviews themselves were preceded in many counties by a system of informal non-statutory plans which ensured that development control and revisions in county policy could keep pace with the rapidly changing situation.

The policies which emerged from these reviews are not easily categorized. In some counties such as Huntingdon (1959) and North Riding (1963), no change was thought necessary to existing rural policies. Elsewhere, the review stage produced the first rural policy to be adopted by a county. Lancashire (1962) conformed to this pattern and reacted to the influx of new population by a careful control of development in rural areas using a three-fold settlement classification:

A   Settlements suitable for substantial expansion;
B   Settlements suitable for smaller expansion;
C   Settlements where development is to be severely curtailed.

This change of emphasis from previously favoured service provision categories to residential development categories may be viewed as a hallmark of the development-plan review policies. However, concern with providing statutory services in rural areas continued to be an important consideration for county planners, with the relative importance attached to the themes of servicing and development differing according to the circumstances in individual counties. In most instances, both themes led to a similar policy structure, that is the concentration of resources into viable centres. For example, the Lancashire review (1962, 80–1) aimed to:

strengthen the rural economy, retain the local population, assimilate in suitable localities a judicious intake of urban population and/or suitable industry, provide new and improve existing public services, social facilities, housing and transport, and retain village character

and in order to do so recognized that:

it is economically impossible to take social facilities to every small village that requires them; neighbouring settlements must share centrally placed facilities. The aim is not self-sufficiency for every small settlement but an integrated rural community.

These guidelines demonstrate two features of the development-plan review period. First, they attempt to portray a comprehensive view of rural settlements and their requirements of the planning system. Second, they show that resource concentration policies were thought useful as an agent of *consolidation* in pressured rural areas as well as of *rationalization* in remote areas.

Devon (1964) also produced its first rural policy at this stage, and a strict key settlement policy emerged in the hope that rationalized service centres would stem the high level of rural depopulation occurring in the county. Both the Devon and Lancashire policies give evidence of the continuing importance of rural resource-concentration policies even in areas where planners had not rushed into pragmatic policy-making at the development-plan stage. Furthermore, key settlement policies were also adopted north of the border, as in Berwickshire (1972) where the development of a limited number of rural growth points was seen as the only realistic settlement policy alternative.

Despite the continuing overall trend of resource concentration, two important changes of policy detail occurred in the development-plan reviews. First, most counties revealed a prominent concern with the guidance and control of residential development. Second, selected rural service centres were overtly given a more comprehensive planning role which included housing and employment growth as well as service provision. In combination, these changes meant that the categories of 'key settlement' and 'village classification' policies (see pp. 89–97) tended to merge somewhat during this period, and even the policies of 'planned decline' became less distinct as attitudes towards non-key settlements became decreasingly polarized.

A good example of these modifications is provided by the Somerset (1964) review which can be compared with the development-plan policy quoted above. Both development control guidelines and a more comprehensive type of rural centre are indicated in a scheme of three settlement classes:

1   Villages intended as centres for social, education or health services. Favourable consideration to be given to satisfactory proposals for the development of these villages. The amount of development that will be permitted will depend on the character of the village, local physical features, accessibility and the need for economy in the use and provision of public services;

2   Centres considered suitable for more limited development in the form of infilling consistent with the established character of the village and with such essential public services as exist or can reasonably be anticipated;

3   Small villages and hamlets. Development is not precluded in these settlements. The local planning authority will give sympathetic consideration to development needed for the livelihood of any established rural community.

The relationship between rural centres and other settlements is important in the context of these policy reviews. Some commentators have suggested that review policies 'showed adjustment to the new facets of rural life, with fewer, larger and more consciously selected central villages, more widely spaced and having more extensive hinterlands, and a resulting simplification of the proposed hierarchy of settlement' (Wheeler, 1977, 6). In fact, rural policies did not radically alter the numbers of rural centres proposed, particularly in view of the fact that the 1961 Census followed immediately after the formulation of the initial development plans, and the next information platform for the assessment of policy performance did not materialize until the 1971 Census. Even where county authorities carried out their own detailed surveys, it was found that the delays in implementing the initial policy meant that the reviews came along too soon to allow a realistic reduction in the optimum number of rural centres needed for any particular area. The main exception to this retention of rural centres appeared in the Northumberland (1966) review where the Education Authority's decision to halve its support for rural primary schools led to a drastic reduction in the number of rural centres viewed as viable growth centres for planning purposes.

Even with a maintained level of rural centres, the settlement categories produced at this review stage ensured that a majority of rural settlements were zoned for only limited growth or less. For example, in addition to six urban development areas, East Suffolk (1965) nominated:

- Sixteen Category B settlements (comprehensive service, housing and employment centres);
- Thirty-eight Category C settlements (smaller key villages);
- Eighty-five Category D settlements (small villages with only limited development);
- Approximately 115 Category E settlements (other settlements with growth only for local needs).

In some cases these scales of development were given quantitative expressions of population growth estimates. Wiltshire (1970), for example, attached averages of 300, 125, 25 and 20 new dwellings over a 10-year period to the four settlement categories in the Salisbury sub-region. These estimates of population growth were often aided by a trend towards local planning within the county policy system through the production of a series of informal village plans and maps (e.g. Cornwall, 1969). Other counties (e.g. Northamptonshire, 1965) deliberately chose not to ascribe growth targets for settlement categories or individual settlements for fear of prejudicing the planners' control over the rate and type of development permitted in specific locations.

The onset of this greater consideration towards the needs and capabilities of individual settlements led to a noticeable change of approach towards the large numbers of villages not selected for growth within development plan policies. Although different counties adopted different tolerance levels towards development in smaller settlements, there was a general softening of the apparently ardent 'no-growth' attitudes of the initial development plans. Some small settlements (for example in the coastal area of Cumberland, 1964) were upgraded in review policies as a cyclic response to changing social trends (Woodruffe, 1976). Elsewhere, adverse public reaction to previous policy attitudes towards small settlements forced changes to policies of planned decline. In the Durham example, the review policy (1964) replaced the notorious category D with a seemingly less-harsh category of settlements in which new capital investment was to be limited to the social and other facilities needed for the life of the existing property. Again, some settlements were upgraded in order that small amounts of public investment could legitimately be channelled into these locations. However, any analysis of attitudes towards non-key settlements should be approached cautiously in that it is policy *implementation* and not policy *statements* which provides an acid test of planning intentions in this respect. There certainly have been cases where little difference can be detected between the operation of seemingly rigid development-plan policies and the apparently more flexible review policies.

One further important progression in the typology of rural settlement policies occurred in the review of the development plans. The introduction of green-belt legislation, leading to the imposition of severe restrictions on settlements within green-belt areas, represented a major external change which dictated the type of policy adopted in some local areas. Some counties (e.g. Hertfordshire, 1971; Surrey, 1972) became wholly engulfed within green-belt restrictions. Other areas such as Berkshire (1960), Essex (1965) and Kent (1972) were only partially affected, but in all these cases the adoption of green-belt zoning overruled all other rural planning considerations. There is also evidence that the green-belt policies in parts of counties such as Warwickshire (1966) may have been directly responsible for the adoption of key settlement policies in residual rural areas where development forced to leapfrog the green belt could be channelled into settlements capable of accepting such growth.

With the wealth of variation forthcoming from individual counties, and the widely differing dates of both the publication and the approval of review policies (indeed some policies have never officially been approved), it is difficult to establish a summary of attributes and trends which is all-embracing. Nevertheless, some factors are unequivocable. Review policies continued almost without exception down the established road of resource concentration, although some counties gave credence to the key settlement ideals of using centralized resources to support hinterland villages while others were more concerned with pragmatic considerations of either accommodating growth or rationalizing decline into centres which afforded reasonable service provision. It is also clear that review stage saw the adoption of a much more comprehensive role for selected rural centres. An increased demand for residential development in the countryside often necessitated the detailing of how much housing growth was acceptable in each selected settlement, and factors such as conservation, public transport and employment opportunity provision become increasingly apparent as part of the function of a selected rural centre. In addition, the trend towards greater consideration of the needs and capabilities of individual settlements to accommodate growth marked a significant step away from rigid settlement categorization and towards a more sympathetic appraisal of local conditions.

It is in the overall assessment of planning policy for groups of rural settlements that interpretations of the development-plan review period begin to differ. Woodruffe (1976, 37) is critical of the uncoordinated nature of planning policies:

> Whilst considerable attention has been paid in regional and urban planning to theoretical strategies and locations of growth, in rural planning there has been very little. Apart from proposals like the Hampshire rural centres and the key settlements of Devon, there is little evidence to show that authorities have considered spatial relationships for residential development.

Wheeler (1977, 9) on the other hand suggests a rather more cognizant role played by county planners:

> By the end of the 1960s Local Planning Authorities which had responsibility for rural areas had mostly evolved some system of hierarchy for their smaller settlements, and that they were using increasingly strong methods of persuasion to concentrate private as well as public investment in . . . 'selected villages'. They were thus coarsening the spatial network of rural settlement and eliminating the lower order components of the hierarchy.

The evidence of development-plan reviews is inconclusive in deciding between the images of a pragmatic and short-sighted planning strategy with no concept of the interrelationships of settlements, or a deliberate restructuring of the settlement pattern to rationalize anachronistic villages and hamlets. Once again it would be more reliable to base such judgements on implemented planning policies rather than written statements, as evidence of deliberate relocation of development from small to large settlements would suggest the latter interpretation while some sign of permitting development for local need (even in an era of 'natural' decline of rural facilities) would lend support to the former view. Thus, there is a need to consider what has actually been achieved in rural areas under development-plan policies and their reviews.

The achievements of rural development plans

> Blind acceptance of policy dogma, such as key settlements or short-term economy measures bringing with them long-term deprivation, without the background research into the effects of such policies, has landed the rural areas in a mess. (Darley, 1978, 299)

> Orthodox policies have worsened conditions in the remote villages, totally changed the character of small towns and larger villages, hastened the drift of the young from rural regions, and have been helpless to prevent the erosion of our landscapes. (Hancock, 1976, 520)

> The idea of putting all the services into one village to serve several surrounding ones offers a financially viable solution to this problem, and is therefore very attractive to administrators and planners. Unfortunately when one puts all the council house and old people's bungalow allocation for the area into one village, leaving the other villages to 'die naturally' (i.e. be taken over by the better off . . .) this destroys the natural balance of social groups. (MacGregor, 1976, 526)

The 1970s and early 1980s have been characterized by a dramatic reversal in the responses of various commentators to the rural settlement planning system which has been fostered during the development-plan era. From a previous position of benighted acceptance of resource concentration policies for rural areas, a bandwagon effect has occurred whereby a strongly critical stance has been adopted towards orthodox rural settlement planning practice. The three authors quoted here give illustration both to the ferocity and to the wider-ranging nature of this criticism, and indeed there would now appear to be a very strong body of opinion in favour of the introduction of significant changes to the policies established by the development plans. Various components of this debate are summarized here, with particular emphasis being placed on research evidence concerning *implemented* policies rather than further deductive discussion on material contained within written planning statements.

Acknowledged achievements

The anti-concentration lobby has now become so deeply institutionalized that it is difficult to discover anything other than a grudging acknowledgement of the benefits secured by the rural development-plan policies. However, there does appear to be some agreement on the beneficial effects of policies on physical land-use factors. The Working Party on Rural Settlement Policies (1979) points out that the restrictive policies of resource concentration adopted by the counties have usually prevented sporadic development in the countryside (a point also noted by Newby, 1979). By achieving some measure of compactness of residential development, the plans have also indirectly sponsored an increase in the provision of infrastructural services such as sewerage networks, piped water, electricity and telephone services, as witnessed in an area of West Suffolk by Gilder and McLaughlin (1978). These successes of physical planning should not be underrated. Indeed, the concentration/conservation ethic has to some extent succeeded in its objectives of limiting undue urbanization in the countryside, retaining small villages with high environmental quality, and pragmatism in the provision of statutory services.

The reports of surveys published by counties as part of their structure-plan preparation reflect this perceived success in physical planning terms, particularly in those areas where heavy urban pressure has received a restrictive policy response. For example, Bedfordshire (1976, 59) considers that its development-plan policy 'has been successful in conserving much that is worthwhile in village character' and uses this assessment to suggest that the broad principles of a village classification policy should be retained in the structure plan. Hertfordshire (1979), a county exerted to a very high level of urban pressure, appears equally satisfied with its rural policy. Four policy aims are outlined:

1   To limit rural development;
2   To sustain the rural community;
3   To co-ordinate facilities and services;
4   To conserve the rural environment.

The performance of the development-plan policy is reviewed against the yardstick of these aims. Generally, all four aims are considered to have been met, although the second aim of sustaining the rural community is assessed only in terms of housing and employment opportunities and it is admitted, for example, that while the provision of family housing has been adequate for local needs in villages, provision for small households has not. However, the general conclusion is that past and present rural settlement policies in Hertfordshire have generally been effective and successful in their own predominantly physical terms.

It would thus be erroneous to suppose that development-plan policies had been of no perceived benefit to rural areas. The Countryside Review Committee (1977) argue that the strength of the British planning system should not be undervalued, and it does appear that an undervaluation of the system's merits has resulted from the bandwagon of critical comment. However, a commonly used adage suggests that no system can be stronger than its weakest link, and in the case of rural settlement policies the weak link has been an overemphasis on physical planning to the detriment of social conditions in rural communities. This assessment is echoed by the Department of the Environment's research report on rural settlement policies (produced by Martin and Vorhees Associates in 1981), which reaches the general conclusion that 'key settlement policy has demonstrated greater effectiveness in tackling physical planning problems than socio-economic ones' (p. 199). An analysis of these socio-economic deficiencies may usefully be structured around an evaluation of the two classic aims and objectives of concentration policy (Cloke, 1980):

1   The concentration of residential and employment growth into selected centres in order that the optimum economic patterns of polarized service and infrastructure provision may be effected;

2   The use of these centralized facilities to improve or stabilize the opportunities or residents of hinterland settlements.

The degree to which these objectives have been met, and the cost to local communities of meeting them gives some indication of just how much has been achieved by rural development-plan policies.

The build-up of selected centres

It is commonly recognized that planning policies have led to definite improvements for the residents of key villages and their commuting hinterlands (McLaughlin, 1976; Woodruffe, 1976). Case studies of the key settlement policies in Devon and Warwickshire (Cloke, 1979) provided evidence that, by and large, residential and employment growth had been concentrated in the selected centres where services and infrastructure had been provided. The development of key settlements was seen to have ensured that at least a majority of rural residents in these areas now enjoy the standard of water, electricity and sewage-disposal facilities which they might expect if living in urban areas. Furthermore, the concentrated effort of house-building and establishment of industrial estates in key settlements have ensured that rural people have an apportunity to live and work within the rural milieu rather than migrating to higher-order urban centres. The provision of health centres and other public services together with the retention of a certain level of private-sector retail and service outlets have also created some degree of economic viability within the rural settlement pattern. Bearing in mind that the operation of a growth centre policy is a long-term process and that the Warwickshire and Devon policies reflect only 15 years of this type of planning, it was firmly concluded that the build-up of key settlements had added to the material progress of pressured rural areas and has acted as a stabilizing effect for facilities in remoter rural areas.

Recognition of these broad trends, however, tends to overshadow a greater diversity of achievement in establishing thriving growth centres in rural areas at the local level. A local-scale case study in the Okehampton area of Devon (Cloke, 1981), for example, demonstrates that, despite positive attempts to establish six key settlements as centres of housing and services, not one of them exhibits clear evidence of a stable and long-term pattern of population growth. Similar trends have been noted in the Caernarvonshire subject report on structure, policies and commitments (no date) which shows that settlements designed to act as regional sub-centres had in fact shown few signs of development.

Many of the problems with establishing viable centres stem from the procedures adopted for the selection of key settlements which were often arbitrary and usually either politically motivated or based on existing conditions rather than future considerations. There are clear signs that especially in remoter areas, too many settlements were selected for development and that resources were found to have been spread too thinly. (Lindsey County Council (1973, 16) admits this trend and gives evidence that:

In the period 1951–71 of the 91 settlements selected for development, 37 lost population, and 26 gained less than 100 people. It is evident that the choice of selected centres needs to be reviewed, and that a redistribution and reduction in the number of centres is required.

That selected centres have not reached their expected levels of development has also been partially due to an inability on the part of planners to stick to approved planning strategies in the day-to-day decisions which are the basic task of rural land-use control. This flexibility of implementation (discussed in greater detail in chapter 9) has been directly responsible for the under-development of rural centres in some counties. For example, Devon's key settlements accounted for 9 per cent of completed dwellings in the county between 1965 and 1975, while unselected settlements accounted for 12 per cent (table 5.1). A strictly imposed key settlement policy would have channelled a greater proportion of this rural growth into the selected centres. Similar problems of implementation (in this case concerned with co-operation between planners and resource agencies) were experienced in the provision of sewerage facilities for Devon's key settlements. In 1975, thirty-four out of sixty-six key settlements had inadequate sewerage systems or treatment plants and were thus subject to restrictions on further development (Devon CC, 1977).

Thus, although we can recognize a general pattern of benefits accruing from the build-up of selected centres, it is clear that this objective of rural-resource concentration policies has only been partially successful. Moreover, the growth of key settlements has usually been most efficient in areas which are themselves within range of urban centres and which therefore are set in a growth context. Less success has been achieved in the more remote and declining areas, where the selected centres are smaller and had no pre-existing impetus for growth. This imbalance is partially displaced by the problems arising from growth and environmental damage in more pressured selected centres, although socio-economic viability rather than settlementscape preservation has been by far the most difficult task in rural-resource centres. To this extent it can be said that remoter key settlements have been less well-served by rural policies than their pressured counterparts. These conclusions are mirrored to a large extent by the Martin and Vorhees report on rural settlement policies, which has this to say on the build-up of rural centres (1981, 198):

> The key settlements which function as central places are relatively few, and they are those which had a good range of facilities and were central places prior to designation. Again, key settlement policy has worked best when it has been reinforcing past trends. No cases were found where key settlement policy was able to reverse the trends and establish a new central village by injecting new community facilities.

Table 5.1 Dwelling completions in Devon, 1965–75

Settlement classification	Local authority sector		Private sector			Total	% of county total
	Number built	% of total for each group of settlements	Numbers built	% of total for each group of settlements		Total	% of county total
Sub-regional centres	10,940	36	19,860	64		30,800	47
Key inland towns	2,830	34	5,590	66		8,420	13
Coastal resorts	1,700	20	6,780	80		8,480	13
Sub-urban towns	500	15	2,830	85		3,330	5
Key settlements	1,250	21	4,760	79		6,010	9
Other settlements with agreed outline plans	280	10	2,540	90		2,820	4
Elsewhere	800	16	4,290	84		5,090	8
Devon total	18,300	28	46,650	72		64,950	100*

Source: Devon CC, 1977, 163

*Due to rounding this column actually sums to 99

Maintaining hinterland villages

Most of the criticism of resource concentration policies has revolved around the process which has been described as:

> discrimination against development in any hamlet or village other than a key village and perhaps one or two secondary villages. The result of this is often to speed up the process of concentration whereby the majority of population, employment opportunities, and services concentrate in ever larger settlements. (McLaughlin, 1976, 158)

Thus, rural residents living in or near the selected centres are perceived as receiving all the benefits, while those living in hinterland settlements are directly disadvantaged. Again, evidence may be drawn from the detailed study of key settlement policies in Devon and Warwickshire (Cloke, 1979) which shows that the operation of these policies has coincided with a general deterioration in employment, service and housing opportunities in small villages which is at least partly due to the planners' reluctance to allow even small-scale housing or employment development in non-selected villages. This reluctance has placed planners in the invidious position of having exacerbated rural housing problems in small settlements. Young families have been forced to leave their villages, not only because of competition from the retired and second-home markets, but also by the lack of new council dwellings. Consequently, the positive social consideration in slowing down depopulation and in conserving settlements where further growth would be environmentally damaging has been counteracted by the exacerbation of social problems in small villages.

The wealth of information collected by counties in their structure-plan reports of survey should have provided evidence with which to compare these research results. However, most counties, either by design or neglect, have failed to analyse rural trends on the basis of settlement categorizations adopted by the immediately preceding rural settlement policy. It is therefore unfortunate that the assessment of how previous policies have performed in the task of maintaining hinterland villages is rather sketchily carried out in most of this documentation. Indeed there is some evidence to suggest that some rural settlement policies have been *less* restrictive than at first feared. Table 5.1 showed that non-key settlements in Devon accommodated a higher proportion of new housing than did the key settlements during the period 1965–75. This trend is reflected in Kent where the report of survey (1976, 322) admits that:

> the amount of new development that has taken place in rural Kent over the last 30 years has been very substantial despite national, regional and local policies that it should be limited, and despite the fact that the rural economy needs fewer people to support it.

However, the unwillingness of county planners (with the exception of Devon and Norfolk) to analyse past trends in terms of planning categories tends to mask the specific ramifications of planning policy on non-key settlements. Table 5.2 shows Norfolk County Council's (1976) breakdown of population changes in various categories of village and offers evidence that 'those villages where most new development was felt to be appropriate in the County Council's Interim Statement Policy (1972) grew most during the 1960s and the 1970s' (Shaw, 1978, 78–9). Conversely it was the hinterland villages in Norfolk which experienced population decline between 1961 and 1975 although lower average occupancy rates prevented this pattern being repeated in the data for new housing development.

We are thus presented with something of a paradox in terms of the fate of hinterland villages. On the one hand, reductions in life-style opportunities in these locations are well-documented (see chapter 2), and find support from structure-plan surveys (witness the loss of primary schools in Devon's non-key settlements between 1961 and 1975 shown in table 5.3). These trends have led

Table 5.2 Population change in Norfolk villages, 1961–75

| | | Rate of population change | |
| | | --- | --- |
Village category	Number of villages	1961–71 % pa	1971–5 % pa
(i)	17	+ 0.7	+ 2.5
(ii)	67	+ 0.5	+ 2.2
(iii)	85	0	+ 0.6
(iv)	178	– 0.9	– 0.1
All villages	347	0	+ 1.2

Source: Shaw, 1978, 79

Table 5.3 Distribution of primary infants' schools, in Devon settlement types, 1961 and 1975

Settlement classification	1961		1975		Change 1961–75	
	Pupils	Schools	Pupils	Schools	Pupils	Schools
Sub-regional centres	33,800	136	46,800	165	13,000	29
Key inland towns	7,500	36	10,100	38	2,600	2
Coastal resorts	4,700	29	7,500	34	2,700	5
Sub-urban towns	1,700	10	2,600	9	900	– 1
Key settlements	5,900	67	8,900	71	3,000	4
Total	53,600	278	75,900	317	22,200	39
Elsewhere	8,900	179	9,600	139	700	– 40
Devon	62,500	457	85,500	456	22,900	1

Source: Devon CC, 1977, 164

Powys County Council (1977, para.3.36), for example, to doubt the ability of selected centres to support hinterland settlements:

> The degree to which the growth towns assist the extensive rural areas of the county which are not close to them is debatable. The establishment of growth towns was also thought to be a way of combating depopulation. However . . . decline continued in most areas more distant from these towns.

On the other hand in all but the most remote locations there remains an element of in-migration (particularly of the retired and the affluent) which, whether or not it is sufficient to counteract out-migration, changes the social structure of hinterland villages, and creates demand for housing in these locations (see table 5.1).

In pressured rural areas, the problems of selective in-migration of non-local population groups are more acute. Here, restrictive planning policies in small villages attract the gentrification process and prevent the building of dwellings for local need. Even where restrictions on housing growth are less strong, social polarization continues to occur. Gilder and McLaughlin's (1978) study of thirteen parishes in West Suffolk throws light on this point. Residential planning applications between 1965 and 1976 are analysed according to whether the villages concerned are classed as A (restricted), B (semi-restricted) and C (minor growth), and although the data in table 5.4 conform to the expectation of most approvals being channelled into category C villages, they do not suggest that category A and B settlements were unduly restricted.

Table 5.4   Residential planning applications in thirteen West Suffolk villages 1965–76

| Parish | Village category | Number of dwellings | | Refusals |
| | | Approvals | | |
		New dwellings	Conversions	
Chedburgh	C	141	0	208
Chevington	B	129	1	26
Cowlinge	A	22	5	27
Denston	A	5	2	6
Depden	A	14	3	38
Hargrave	B	39	2	39
Hawkedon	A	6	3	43
Lidgate	A	16	2	30
Ousden	B	29	1	58
Rede	A	10	1	2
Stansfield	A	10	2	7
Stradishall	A	16	4	27
Wickhambrook	C	166	3	234
Total		603	29	745

Source: Gilder and McLaughlin, 1978, 12

Indeed the study shows that only 20.7 per cent of applications in category A settlements and 9.8 per cent in category B were approved on the grounds of local need, and concludes that as a large proportion of development in non-selected (A and B) settlements was speculative and unrelated to local need, the rural settlement policy in this area has not been rigidly applied. Nevertheless, the authors stress that:

> Planning has little or no control over who actually buys residential property. As such the area has witnessed considerable changes in social structure of some villages with the resulting implications for housing service provision and community structure. (Gilder and McLaughlin, 1978, 48)

Two important points arise from the paradox outlined above. First, the development-planning system, whether strictly applied or not, is impotent to deal with problems of social polarization. Parsons (1980) in his study of rural gentrification concludes that social imbalance in rural settlements cannot be *directly* attributed to planning policies. Rather, the cause and effect process is *indirect* through the constraint of opportunities for developing low and medium-priced private housing as well as local authority housing in non-selected villages. He stresses that 'it would be naive to assume that gentrification would not exist if development control were not instituted through settlement classifications' (p. 20). Similarly, Herington and Evans (1979) dispel the popular myth that key settlement policies (at least in a pressured context) generate movements from non-key to key locations. Rather they found a reverse trend in the rural area around Leicester as rural residents move 'up market' from large settlements to smaller ones. Therefore, planning can influence but not direct population movements. A second important conclusion is that the current development planning system does not directly induce the loss of rural life-style opportunities. Shaw and Stockford (1979, 125) conclude that 'the number of village facilities such as schools, child health clinics and shops would continue to fall, regardless of the amount of development which was permitted in individual small settlements'. The message here is clearly one of the need to develop innovations in service provision rather than attempting to solve servicing problems through the manipulation of housing development through the planning system.

Therefore the role of rural settlement planning in maintaining opportunities for the residents of hinterland villages is a complex one. Two major criticisms of development-plan policies appear valid in the light of the evidence reviewed.

1 County-level plans have attempted to apply broad strategies to individual settlements. They have lacked what the Wye College reply (1980) to the Countryside Review Committee's Papers calls a 'sociological approach': that is by following an assumption that there is a standard type of rural community which behaves in a standard manner, the local scale variations of village or settlement area which call for different planning solutions are ignored. There is now reaction against this uniformity of policy, although the Working Party on Rural Settlement Policies (1979) insist that rural

communities should not be considered individually without taking wider account of strategic issues;

2   County-level plans have proved too inflexible to cope with changing circumstances. In some instances, counties have proved willing to amend established policies in an attempt to introduce a flexible approach. For example Northamptonshire (1977) revamped their settlement policy so that development could proceed in accordance with phased programmes in the key centres (table 5.5). However, the inherent inflexibility in rural settlement planning has largely ignored the scope for dispersal in the provision of suitable housing services and employment in hinterland villages. Here, though, the analysis of effects caused by development plans moves into an *indirect* rather than *direct* area, where rural needs appear to fall outside of the development-planning process.

Non-achievement outside the planning process

Much of the criticism of rural settlement policies enacted in the development-plan era concerns issues which are only indirectly addressed by a physically based planning system. Matters of providing rural employment, suitable housing for rural needs, sufficient services for non-mobile groups, and transport links between selected centre and hinterland may be viewed as outside the remit of planning powers. Indeed there is evidence to suggest that the loss of opportunities in these spheres would continue whether or not rural development-plan policies had been implemented. The Martin and Vorhees (1981) report, for example, admitted great difficulty in differentiating between social problems caused by key settlement policy and those exacerbated by the policy but caused by other factors. It suggests that 'since key settlement policy has been a fairly weak policy instrument, there are few social problems which can be attributed to it alone' (p. 200). It would, however, be false to excuse rural settlement planning of any culpability for these trends. Although not necessarily the cause of rural social problems, the planning process has to a large extent allowed them to develop, preferring to concentrate on more pragmatic and attainable targets such as village conservation and 'optimum' settlement patterns for statutory services. In this respect, rural settlement

Table 5.5   Northamptonshire change of categorization, 1972

Former	Amendment
Moderate growth villages	*Category B* – estate development is to be allowed on a programmed basis.
	Category C – development to be limited to infilling.
Limited growth villages	*Category D* – development to be limited to infilling.
	Category E – development limited to single dwellings only.

Source: Northamptonshire CC, 1977, para. 3.31

planning (or more specifically the legislation behind it) can with some justification be criticized for not incorporating specific solutions to those socio-economic problems.

It has now become clear that the key settlement-type policies established in development plans can at best act as framework strategies within which other, more positive planning developments are required. In fact, the reliance on restrictive rather than positive rural planning has ensured that vital stages in the development of key settlements and the spreading of their opportunities out to hinterland villages have remained external to present planning systems. To fulfil its true potential, the key settlement policy should be supplemented by positive policies to combat specific problems. Transport and peripatetic service links between key settlement and hinterland need a positive impetus from planning authorities. The establishment of suitable small-scale housing projects and workshop employment also demands policies of attraction rather than mere permission should any application arise. There have been isolated cases of such positive planning, but tough financial and administrative barriers prevented a co-ordinated approach to rural planning in this period. Small wonder that Ray Green (1971) was moved to declare that the 1950s and 1960s represented 20 years of wasted opportunity for positive rural planning.

Contemporary rural planning overseas

Analysis of rural settlement planning in Britain is often hampered by an insularity of approach which tends to ignore the progress made by rural planners elsewhere in the developed world. One method of assessing the relative merits of rural development plans in Britain is to compare their achievements with those of contemporary efforts elsewhere. Two contrasting comparisons are made here, reflecting the differences between *laissez-faire* and socialist approaches to government and planning.

Rural planning in the United States has been reviewed by Lassey (1977) who points out that despite a long history of urban planning, the preparation and implementation of rural plans has until recently been viewed as both unnecessary and inappropriate. For most of the development-plan period in Britain, concurrent trends of agricultural modernization, settlement-pattern rationalization, gentrification and increased recreational activity were taking place in the United States in an unplanned fashion, with the resulting not inconsiderable social, economic and physical impacts on the countryside being largely left to chance. So it was only in the latter part of the British development-plan stage that rural planning techniques were adopted in the United States. Even then, proponents of rural planning found it difficult to overcome both the poor perception of rural problems (as rural areas were so vast as to absorb urban pressures without visible scars), and the ingrained belief that individuals are better able to make decisions about land use than are government institutions. These barriers hampered the onset of rural planning and were only broken down because of concern over environmental (rather than socio-economic) deprivation and thus it was that rural planning has assumed an eco-bias: 'in the context of the current environmental and resource 'crisis', rural territory and its human-guidance system are crucial in maintaining a viable life-support system for the planet' (Lassey, 1977, x).

As the American rural planning system has evolved it has focused on the need for increasing economic viability and productivity in rural areas, and the need to achieve these goals has led to the establishment of a set of commonly recognized ground rules (table 5.6). Two major features of this list are important to this discussion. First, the comprehensive nature of the American approach has been coveted by many commentators (see chapter 12) who have been critical of the institutional fragmentation of British rural planning. Second, the American ideal of improved human welfare, which has traditionally revolved around the maximum welfare for those individuals who could effectively compete in the evolving economic system, has now progressed to the introduction of minimum economic and social levels in rural areas in order to reduce the imbalance between urban and rural standards of health care, housing, employment and so on. This recognition of differential deprivation might also be a pointer towards a useful future approach for social planning in British rural areas.

However, to take this interpretation of American rural planning at face value would be as meaningless as to analyse public pronouncements on the British planning system without testing the links between written policy and planning action. After all, the Department of the Environment has issued an equally impressive list of goals for British planning, but it is generally recognized that such objectives could not be implemented within the legislative machinery and resource allocation provided. Equally, Lassey (1977) in describing the implementation of American planning goals in rural Washington State reports a very limited achievement record. Given the difficulties of reviewing national-level rural planning in the United States with individual states varying widely in the degree of formalized planning for rural regions, Washington was selected because it was regarded as archetypal of many 'middle-ground' states. The state contains thirty-nine counties each with its own separate planning programme and each with an elected commissioner with responsibility for planning in rural areas. Planning enabling legislation

Table 5.6   Ground rules for American rural planning

1 Preservation of ecological integrity so as to provide a continuing supply of life-supporting resources
2 Development of efficient and appropriate land use
3 Creation of healthy living conditions through the construction of a suitable physical environment
4 Preservation of aesthetically pleasing environment
5 Creation of effective social, economic and government institutions
6 Improvement of human welfare
7 Development of physical structures and adapted landscapes of pleasing design
8 Adoption of a comprehensive viewpoint to include physical, biological and human factors in rural regions

Source: Based on Lassey, 1977

dictates that a comprehensive plan be developed for the orderly physical development of each county, and ensures that factors of land use, accessibility, conservation, recreation, services, housing and finance are all given consideration in the plan. However, the Planning Enabling Act does not allow for the inclusion of social planning functions, and these activities have to be introduced tangentially through the direction of elected commissioners who apply for state or federal support for social planning programmes.

It is therefore clear that the apparently 'comprehensive' approach to rural planning is, in fact, far from holistic. For example there are no methods of employment redirection or local authority housing allocations operational in this area. Furthermore, the implementation of written plans is dependent on the zoning mechanism whereby areas of land are zoned for specific use. This technique is a broader and less powerful planning tool than the British planning permission, as is shown by the absence of detailed planning *within* specific zones. Therefore with lower standards of planned local vernacular or visual amenity, successful achievement of broad zonings constitutes a lower standard of physical planning than in successfully implemented fine-mesh policies in Britain. Furthermore, the *laissez-faire* nature of the American approach has meant that there has been little or no attempt to pursue overall conceptual targets such as concentration of investment in order to service rural hinterlands or dispersal of resources on the grounds of community equity. Therefore, rural planning in Washington State takes the form of a holding operation against undue urban expansion, with positive forms of planning being confined to action on areas of environmental disaster rather than being directed towards remedial work on declining rural areas. On the basis of this evidence, these types of planning are well behind concurrent efforts in Britain in terms of legislation, administration and implementation, although the end result of planning in both areas may be similar if population decline and haphazard development are allowed to occur.

A rather different picture of rural planning has emerged from the socialist domination of government in eastern-block nations. Although information on rural planning activities in these areas has been rather sparse, a series of translated commentaries (Kovalev, 1968; 1972; Voskresensky, 1976) and a useful summary by Pallot (1977) have served to outline the development of a strong framework policy for rural settlements in the Soviet Union. Given a formative belief that a strong determining relationship exists between the social mode of production in rural areas and both the character of individual settlements, and the character of the overall settlement system, there has been a deliberate attempt in the Soviet Union to move away from the capitalist pattern of dispersed owner-occupied farmsteads towards the more socialist pattern of rural settlement concentration. The elimination of rural–urban differences has been central to the theoretical guidance offered by Marx, Engels and Lenin, and therefore planners in Soviet rural areas have been given the task of directing processes of resource concentration which would create an equality between rural and urban life. This strong theoretical influence in planning has not, however, been matched by any consensus on how the rural population should be concentrated into nucleated settlements. The degree of concentration which might be appropriate in varying conditions, the length of time over which the concentration process should operate, and the selection criteria for growth settlements, have all raised practical policy issues for which socialist theory offers little detailed advice.

The first major step towards the achievement of these rural planning objectives came in the Khruschev era with the proposal to rehouse the Soviet rural population in purpose-built towns ('agrotowns') connected to systems of collective farms. In theory, the agrotowns were to provide rural dwellers with a similar range of services and facilities to those enjoyed by their urban counterparts. These proposals were strengthened in 1959 with the requirement that each agricultural district should produce a long-term development plan, whose remit would include any proposals to restructure the rural settlement network. Although 80 per cent of districts had produced plans within a decade, the effective implementation of plans was hampered both by the lack of power over developments within the district and by the lack of financial backing for new approved developments. However, the plans were important in that they entertained a two-fold categorization of rural settlements into *perspektivnyi* (translated as 'perspective' settlements) which were to receive future growth, and *neperspektivnyi* ('non-perspective' settlements) which were either to be left to wither naturally or in some cases were directly disused and their population resettled elsewhere.

After the demise of Khruschev, these strong policies of concentration were closely scrutinized. Kovalev (1968) notes that the rationalized settlement pattern had led to a decrease in agricultural productivity caused by longer journeys to work for agricultural workers. It was also found that out-migrants from non-perspective settlements were bypassing the perspective settlements (which were designed as rural holding points) and moving directly to urban areas. Similarly, residents of perspective settlements exhibited a propensity to migrate to urban areas, and thus the theoretical ideal of nullifying rural-urban differences began to be questioned by Soviet researchers who believed that it was better to emphasize these differences in order to attract residents who preferred a rural way of life. These theoretical doubts in turn prompted a movement for a replacement of the perspective/non-perspective categorization by a settlement hierarchy based on 'degrees of perspectiveness' in which capital construction and maintenance were to be linked to the predicted lifespan of each setttlement.

Just as early rural planning in Britain was overtaken by rapid socio-economic changes in the countryside so the Soviet policies were similarly compromised during the 1960s by declining agricultural labour forces, diversification of rural occupational structures and greatly improved patterns or rural accessibility. The outcome of these changes was that policies of rural resource concentration overcame previous criticisms to arrive once more at the forefront of Soviet rural planning. However in the late 1960s, rural policies became characterized by the planning of settlement systems as one unit rather than individual villages. Thus the provision of employment, services and transport was planned hierarchically for groups of settlements allowing the identification of settlements which were either superfluous to the system or which could play a more important role in the operation of the system. In effect this change of policy emphasis resulted in a doubling of the designations of perspective settlements and a rather less ruthless attitude towards non-perspective settlements in some areas.

It is clear that the development-plan period in Britain was paralleled by strong planning policies for Soviet rural areas. However, Pallot (1977) emphasizes that the achievements of Soviet policies should not be over-estimated. She points out that many rural areas in the Soviet Union have never been the subject of demographic or social surveys and indeed that the selection of non-perspective settlements for liquidation is carried out in a most subjec-tive and unscientific manner. She also offers evidence that although an overall increase in settlement size has been achieved by these policies, little material improvement in the standard of living enjoyed by rural residents has resulted from settlement rationalization. It is important to remember the vast scale of the rural Soviet Union, in which any restructuring process achieving reason-able standards of living will inevitably be a long-term process. Nevertheless, the Soviet government have proved capable of working social and economic miracles in the past and so it might be surmised that the leadership has not as yet been sufficiently impressed by the relative gravity of rural settlement problems to devote sufficient resources to the replanning process.

There are strong parallels between Soviet and British rural planning in this period. In addition to the inability to attract sufficient central government resources for positive rural action, it can be seen that in both environments, the process of plan and policy formation has attempted to apply specifically urban solutions to problems which have peculiar outworkings in rural areas, and has been slow to recognize the special needs of small rural communities. Despite wide differences in contextual ideology, the fundamental attractiveness of resource concentration policies is evident in both cases as is the procrastination in proposing reasonable alternatives to existing strategies. Indeed, strong fundamental links may be traced between the draconian liquidation of small Soviet non-perspevctive settlements and Durham's D village proposals, and between Soviet policies of allowing villages to die naturally and most rural settlement policies in Britain. Apart from scale effects, the other major differ-entiating factor is the lack of gentrification trends in Russia which have tended to prop up anachronistic settlements in Britain, but clearly the underlying policies of settlement reorganization without accompanying programmes of socially oriented expenditure are strongly related in both cases.

The examples of the United States and the Soviet Union provide some com-parative evidence to suggest that rural planning in Britain was certainly no less developed than elsewhere in the developed world, and in some respects was in advance of rural policies elsewhere. Of particular importance to the British situation is the powerful tool of planning permissions which potentially allowed for strict local planning in conjunction with the wider strategic con-siderations of development plans. This strong backup to regional plans was not available elsewhere and the fact that so many parallels occurred between socio-economic and planning trends in Britain and those in the United States and the Soviet Union suggests that the potential of the 1947 planning system for positive planning in rural areas was underused as British rural planners succumbed to the pragmatism of concentration of investment. In fact, rural planners appear to have been mirroring 'natural' trends in their concentration policies rather than seeking to attack either the causes or symptoms of these trends. In this respect, rural planning in Britain at this time could be said to have performed a slightly better holding operation against the spread of urbanization than was managed elsewhere, but so far as positive social planning is concerned, planners made very little additional headway in solving rural problems than was achieved by their colleagues in other countries. A far greater level of social awareness was displayed in the rural areas of developed nations during the structure-plan era, and these changes in attitude and achievement are discussed in chapter 6.

SIX

Structure-plan policies

Contemporary rural planning attitudes

The preparation, formulation and implementation of structure plans has presented planners with an ideal opportunity to change the objectives and directions traditionally pursued by rural settlement planning. Early advisory notes from the Department of the Environment (such as *Note 7* (1973)) instructed local planning authorities to consider underlying social and economic issues when preparing structure plans, and although *Circulars 98* (1974) and *55* (1977) appeared to reduce governmental emphasis on social considerations, their importance was reiterated in *Circular 4* (1979, 18–19):

> In formulating their policy and general proposals, the authority should take account of existing social policies and the social impact of their policies, e.g. on different groups in the population. It should be explained in the reasoned justification how social considerations and policies have been taken into account in the formulation of the plan . . . Social considerations should be treated as an integral element of all topics. . . .

Given this latitude to include social issues in structure planning, and given the widespread publicity devoted to social problems in rural communities under previous planning regimes, it may be thought surprising that early analyses of rural policies in structure plans (e.g. Bracken and Hume, 1980; Derounian, 1979) indicated that the new rural settlement policies showed comparatively little change from those previously in operation. Derounian (1980) reports that eighteen out of the twenty-one structure plans which he studied were committed to a form of key settlement policy, that much criticized cornerstone of the development-plan era. Before giving detailed consideration to the evolution of rural settlement policies in the new structure plans, it is worth investigating the contemporary planning attitudes which formed the foundation for this apparent lack of expected redirection in rural settlement planning. It would be all too convenient to suggest that rural planners *en bloc* adopted a pragmatist approach to settlement policies in structure plans, yet the attitudes underlying these policy decisions are, in fact, far more complex than this simple analysis would indicate.

In 1981, the author and David Shaw (Cloke and Shaw, forthcoming) undertook a survey of county planning authorities, with the principal aim of cataloguing and checking the details of rural policies contained within structure plans (see pp. 144–63). A secondary objective was to test the prevailing attitudes in planning departments concerning major issues in rural settlement policies and plans. Thirty-five responses to this second survey were received from non-metropolitan counties, and although replies cannot be labelled as representing the attitude of the planning authority, their status as individuals' attitudes within the context of an authority's approach to rural planning make them a relevant contribution to our understanding of these matters. Indeed, the responses to this survey provide a fascinating insight into the varying approaches adopted both between and within county authorities, and belie any straightforward or simplistic taxonomies of rural planning in this era.

One major finding of the survey was that individuals within planning authorities are extremely well-informed about the problems associated with those key settlement type policies that have been adopted in various rural areas in Britain. The popular view of planners uncaringly continuing with problematic policies for rural areas is refuted by the depth of awareness demonstrated by respondents. Four main problem areas were most often isolated:

1   The assumption that dependent settlements will be able to benefit from the services provided by key settlements has been undermined by the decline in rural accessibility. Any 'benefits' are almost entirely related to the key settlements alone;

2   The existence of the key settlement concept has aided and abetted the process of rationalizing and concentrating rural services as well as lending the process respectability and dissuading the consideration of alternative policies. It has positively discouraged opportunities for beneficial forms of development (local employment, local housing need and so on) in non-selected villages;

3   Particularly in remoter rural areas, the scale of *new* public investment is small. This calls into question the 'benefits' of concentrating such investment as, given the limited amounts involved, it is difficult to view them as being a boost to local services. Much of this investment in any event is required to replace or expand facilities closed down elsewhere in the process of rationalization, which may be a false economy;

4   Planning authorities have limited control over the provision and disposition of facilities, so policies have not always had the desired effects.

Even within this broad appreciation of rural problems, however, one or two respondents thought that the key settlement policy had performed its function quite well (in the counties they represented) even though they recognized that some colleagues would argue that this success was achieved 'at the expense of rural character and environment'.

Some measure of agreement was also forthcoming in the indication of the genre of criterion which has proved the most influential in shaping the character of rural settlement policies prior to structure plans. Although such categorizations may only be loosely applied, most respondents regarded *economic* and *conservation* criteria as most influential, with the proviso that political manoeuvering is also important in the selection of rural settlements for growth. Only six (17.1 per cent) respondents indicated that *social* criteria had exerted a formative influence on rural policy during the development-plan period. More variation was apparent in the details of whether rural settlement policies in current structure plans are based on a realignment of these formative criteria. Twenty counties (57 per cent) suggested that a shift had taken place, a response which again refutes the suggestion of a direct carry-over of policy from development-plan to structure-plan stages. However, these policy redirections are not, as might have been anticipated, viewed as replacing economic and conservation criteria with social criteria. One-half of realigned policies (ten counties) were increasingly influenced by economic factors, one-quarter (five counties) by conservation factors, and only the remaining five by social factors. No correlation occurred between the direction of policy and the type of area concerned (broadly remote or pressured), though two main reasons were offered for the apparent rejection of increasing social input into policies. First, the socially oriented policy aspirations of some counties have been frustrated by resource deficiencies and so rural settlement policies represent an outcome of resource allocation decisions made elsewhere. Second, at least two counties regarded themselves as prevented from pursuing social problem solving policies by governmental advice. One respondent regretted that wider social criteria were not considered admissible in structure plans by the Department of the Environment, who were seen as having back-pedalled to a great extent from the advice given in *Structure Plans Note 7* (1973, 'Social Aspects of Development Plans'). An even more extreme case is provided by the North Yorkshire plan which as submitted offered a realignment of rural policy towards a greater degree of social planning, but which as modified by the Secretary of State continued its emphasis on economic and conservation criteria (see pp. 162–3).

Even though the broad categorization of formative criteria into economic, social, conservation and so on is open to misinterpretation at a detailed level, and cannot be viewed as a mutually exclusive matrix of influences on rural policy, it is clear from these responses that there has not been a widespread take-up of socially orientated rural policies in structure plans. In some counties, planners have attempted to make their policies more socially acceptable within an admitted domination of policy direction by economic and conservation considerations. Elsewhere, there has been no desire for greater social inputs for rural policy. Several respondents suggested that local opinion (at least as expressed by elected members and at public meetings) was largely in favour of limiting development in rural areas and conserving rural settlements, and that this opinion overrides the importance of any social problems which do exist within the rural environment. We should therefore expect that rural settlement policies within structure plans, far from being a homogeneous and easily described grouping, are in fact a complex and detailed set of variable responses to local as well as national pressures.

In a further attempt to ascertain broad trends in the new structure-plan policies the survey requested views on several notions connected with the concentration or dispersal of resources in rural areas. First, the degree of investment and resource concentration in the structure plan policies was ascertained with the following result:

1 Greater concentration than previously – ten counties;
2 Similar levels of concentration – fifteen counties;
3 Lesser degree of concentration than previously – seven counties;
4 No answer – three counties.

Counties who could give no direct response to this question were generally those where the urban development policies dominate. For example the Derbyshire structure-plan policy is one of concentrating development in a relatively small number of large developments in, or on the fringe of, existing urban areas. *Rural* development policy is seen as residual in nature and (as approved) random in location. However, it is significant that of the thirty-two positive answers, twenty-five counties were viewed as adopting similar or greater levels of resource concentration, and only seven admitted to the opposite path of some greater degree of resource dispersal.

When asked whether greater levels of dispersal of investment and resources throughout the rural settlement pattern constitute a desirable planning goal, the respondent planners offered a similarly mixed reaction:

1 Twenty county representatives rejected further resource dispersal as a desirable planning goal;
2 Twelve accepted the need for further dispersal;
3 Three fell between these polarized attitudes.

Superficially, these figures represent a clear majority in favour of the resource concentration concept with more than half of the respondents rejecting the idea of resource dispersal even in a hypothetical situation. Once again, however, the use of broad categorizations such as 'concentration' and 'dispersal' tends to gloss over important underlying details. Both are relative terms, and therefore a vote in favour of either as a desirable planning goal will stem from widely variable motives. Most of the responses opposed to further resource dispersal are founded on analyses of past experience in rural settlement. One respondent explained his opposition in this manner (personal communication):

> It still appears to us that if we had allowed a greater dispersal of development it would have done little to boost or maintain services in the smaller settlements because of the scale of development needed. Results from a recent survey of rural facilities have indicated a loss of services even in some communities that have experienced growth of housing and population. The end result of dispersal would simply be more people living further from a good range of services.

Policies of resource dispersal were similarly criticized on more theoretical grounds:

> [Dispersal policies] have the hidden danger that although they appear to benefit outlying areas more than do key settlement policies, they only increase accessibility to certain services, not to all. Thus they do little to maximize opportunities in the form of providing access to the 'outside

world'. They seem to be pointing us back in the direction of the 'self-sufficient' villages of the past which were of arguable merit then and are of doubtful value to the modern world.

Alternatively, a rejection of further resource dispersal in some cases stemmed from the view that sufficient dispersal had already occurred in that county. One county, for example, regarded that the selection of seventy-five villages for growth and service provision represented 'a fair dispersal of investment and resources', and that provided the housing needs of rural areas are being met, reasonable choice is provided, and access to services for those in rural hinterlands is maintained, then further dispersal is unnecessary. Most respondents registering opposition to further resource dispersal offered some combination of these arguments of past experience, theoretical analysis, and some measure of satisfaction with current policies.

Where resource dispersal was viewed as a desirable planning goal, the underlying reasoning was rather more uniform. This group of responses represented a strong rejection of past policies and the criteria on which they were based. One respondent noted that:

> economic criteria will nearly always point to concentration for greatest economic efficiency; unfortunately the service consumers in rural areas are generally not so conveniently concentrated. Their needs should be balanced in the equation, and the means of ensuring a greater dispersal of development sought.

This perceived need to devote additional attention to 'local needs' for housing, services and employment in all rural settlements was seen by some counties as a strong incentive for further dispersal of rural resources. In addition, the dispersal option found support on economic grounds (where the use of spare capacity in existing infrastructure can be maximized) and on conservation grounds (where further development in key settlements might radically change their environmental character). Full support of future resource dispersal was, however, tempered by an acknowledgement that the ramifications of such a policy are as yet unclear and can only be illuminated with the testing of practised alternative strategies. As it will be some time before the full utility of resource dispersal will be apparent, support for the concept among planners is largely given practical expression by 'seeing if dispersal policies are at least worth a try', rather than by a dramatic policy reversal from traditional techniques of resource concentration. Once again, however, semantic problems serve to cloud this issue. Whereas many respondent counties viewed resource dispersal in terms of the entire rural settlement pattern, some adopted a more restrictive definition whereby dispersal meant the promotion of employment and housing opportunities in *a wider number of key villages in declining areas*. This approach suggests a slightly wider dispersal within an overall pattern of concentration and may not therefore requite the social criticisms of traditional key settlement policies.

A cross-tabulation of trends of resource concentration between development-plan and structure-plan policies, and attitudes concerning resource dispersal as a desirable planning goal, is shown in table 6.1. This simple analysis isolates a group of respondents who may clearly be placed in the 'concentration' camp(!) with structure-plan policies based on higher levels of resource concentration, and with an overwhelming rejection of dispersal as a hypothetically sound concept. It should be noted, however, that in two cases policies of further concentration have been pursued despite support for further dispersion. Where similar or lower levels of resource concentration have been incorporated into rural structure-plan policies, opinion appears evenly divided as to whether further dispersal is an attractive planning objective. Once again these attitudes appear somewhat anomalous in that three respondents do not support further resource dispersal even though their structure-plan policies have in fact moved in this direction.

This rather rigid exercise in attitude matching highlights a number of important questions. First, there is no such thing as a dichotomous split between support for rural resource concentration and support for rural resource dispersal. Even if the semantic difficulty involved with these broad terms can be overcome, the attitudes uncovered by this survey are complex, multi-dimensional and localized, and do not easily lend themselves to simplistic categorization. Second, the allocation of rural resources (in so far as planners can exert any influence over this process) is seen as a means of achieving individual packages of planning goals and not as an end in itself. Table 6.2 summarizes some of the aims of rural settlement planning as suggested by the survey respondents. Even this sample of aims shows internal contradictions where planning effort in one authority is directed towards one particular objective to the detriment of other policy areas. The general approach may be summarized as seeking to equalize opportunities in terms of access to employment, shopping, educational, recreational and community facilities and housing choice as far as is economically possible and environmentally acceptable. However, even this broad generalization of policy aims will produce vast differences of planning outcome according to the different priorities allotted to different parts of the implementation process.

The third conclusion arising from this exercise is that the assessment of policy, even at county level, is difficult and can be misleading. Problems and opportunities differ sharply from one area to another within a county, and local opinion concerning these problems and opportunities varies even more widely. Therefore, the submission of a county-wide rural strategy should

Table 6.1   Cross-tabulation of policy trends and support for resource dispersal as a desirable planning goal

Degree of resource concentration in new policy	Is further resource dispersal desirable?		
	Yes	*No*	*Possibly*
Greater	2	8	0
Similar	7	7	1
Less	3	3	1
No answer	0	2	1

Table 6.2   Stated aims in the planning of rural settlements

1   To safeguard agricultural land, areas of attractive landscape and green belt
2   The continuance of a viable agricultural industry
3   The maintenance of a basic fabric of rural settlements and services
4   To conserve the form and character of settlements
5   To secure the retention of viable communities in rural settlements
6   To supply services at a price which reflects the cost of providing them
7   To minimize the need for new investment
8   Encouragement of 'self-help' provision of services, enterprises and accessibility schemes
9   Encouragement of local employment opportunities
10 To act as a co-ordinator between relevant agencies so that services and facilities do not occur in isolation
11 To provide for essential local housing needs by influencing the scale, rate and density of development
12 To seek to retain, and where possible improve, the range of community facilities available to people living in rural areas

necessarily be expected to be vague and non-commital. Too rigid a policy at county level would seem to restrict the opportunities for the local planning process to respond to localized problems.

The survey of planners' attitudes towards rural settlement policy did at least reveal one area of almost total consent. When asked which factors in practice prevent the adoption and implementation of otherwise desirable rural planning policies, three major elements were repeatedly stressed:

1   Paucity of administrative and financial resources;
2   Public opinion, which tends towards environmental protectionism and which appears unconvinced of the equity of diverting scarce resources to bolster 'uneconomic' settlements in rural areas;
3   Political opinion, particularly among resource agencies which have not yet accepted the need to provide solutions sensitive to the needs of local communities rather than to the aspirations of the agencies themselves.

Even were these restrictions to be lifted, many respondents expressed the opinion that resource dispersal policies would only become *feasible* if considerable rural population growth occurred so that essential facilities became viable, and only become *desirable* if rural settlements could become more self-sufficient in jobs. This situation may only occur with concurrent advances in communications and word and data processing which might result in greater decentralization of employment.

The attitudes uncovered by this survey, even though broad and generalized, appear to offer important lessons for planners and academics wishing to interpret structure-plan policies. Indeed, it might be suggested that an awareness of these attitudes is a vital prerequisite to the understanding of how rural policies evolved within structure plans, how trade-offs were made between planning objectives, resource availability and public opinion, and how local responses to parochial issues differed widely from authority to authority. The diversity of opinion expressed by the survey's respondents serves to underline the complexity and area-dependent nature of the formal plan-making process for rural areas.

Policy preparation

It was suggested in chapter 1 that the arrival of an approved planning policy in its written form was a function of two umbrella processes: namely taking heed of those policy precedents which are already established in the area concerned, and carrying out a detailed technical programme of policy preparation. In the context of structure plans these two broad processes represent a gross over-simplification of the range of tasks involved in producing a written policy (see figure 6.1), but a two-stage analysis like this does highlight the intrinsic

Figure 6.1 The structure-plan-making process

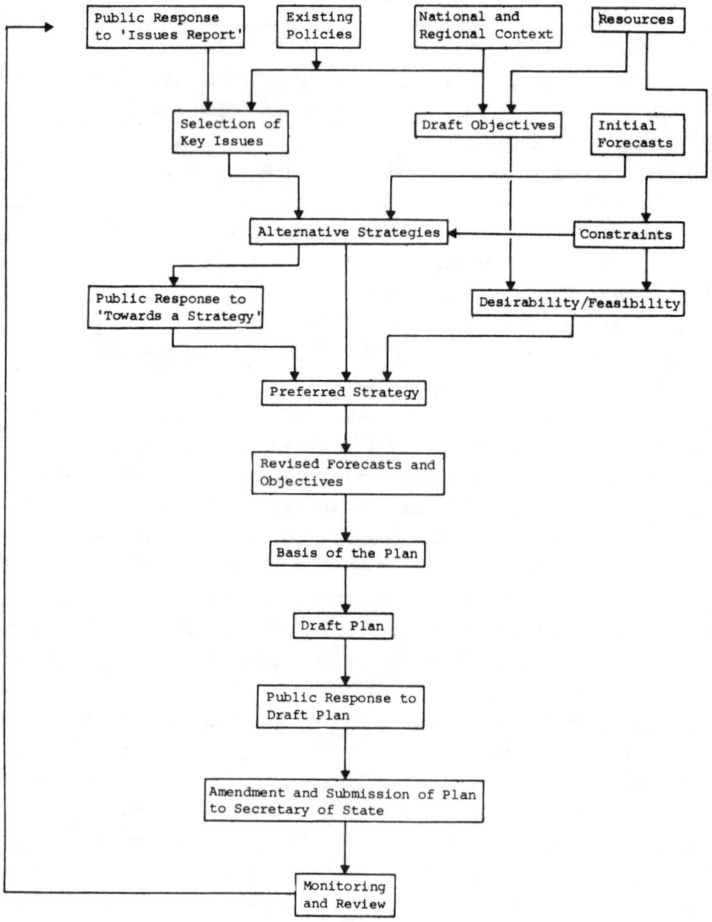

Source: Gwent CC, 1978, 248

importance of 'existing policies' which are often subsumed within the overall activity of plan preparation (as shown by the figure). A considerable depth of information is made available by county planning authorities regarding the premeditation of structure-plan policies. Section 6 of the 1971 Town and Country Planning Act requires each authority to make a detailed survey of all matters which affect the development and planning of its area. Certain matters are specifically earmarked for inclusion in this survey:

1 The principal physical and economic characteristics of the area;
2 Demographic size, composition and distribution;
3 Communications and transport systems in the area;
4 Relevant and overlapping features of neighbouring areas;
5 An estimate of how all these factors may be expected to change within the plan period.

The results of these deliberations have to be compiled and forwarded to the Secretary of State for Environment when the written statement of the structure plan is submitted. These *reports of survey* offer valuable evidence of the extent to which various factors are instrumental in shaping the final written policy statement, and some of this evidence is presented here under the broad but important headings of 'policy precedent' and 'detailed plan preparation'.

Area and planning precedents

A review of the reports of survey attached to county structure plans gives a clear indication of the importance of previous and existing policies as agents of the *status quo* in rural settlement planning. This revelation is predictable in view of the truism that planning is a medium to long-term procedure which cannot be given an instantaneous change of direction. Thus even if structure plan-makers wished to instigate radical alterations to rural settlement planning they would face a time-consuming 'roll-on' effect arising from previous decisions. There is, however, some suspicion that adherence to existing policies often transcends this resulting time-lag and represents more of an inbuilt inertia within decision-making processes in rural planning.

Both the roll-on and inertia influences are evident in the reports of survey. In some cases there is an explicit reference to previous documents as formative motivators for the retention of a particular type of policy. For example a study by Northumberland County Council (1969) which immediately preceded the structure-plan deliberations by that authority proposed a planned settlement hierarchy of main growth points, supporting growth points and consolidation points (figure 6.2). The justification for this proposal was largely accepted in the structure-plan system which supported rural resource concentration and isolated main and minor service centres. Indeed it would be surprising if the latter policy had done much more than update the former which had been the result of specific and detailed study. This process of minor adaptation of immediately previous rural settlement policies is common in non-metropolitan county structure plans. Bedfordshire County Council (1976, 59) is one of many

Figure 6.2 Northumberland's proposed settlement hierarchy

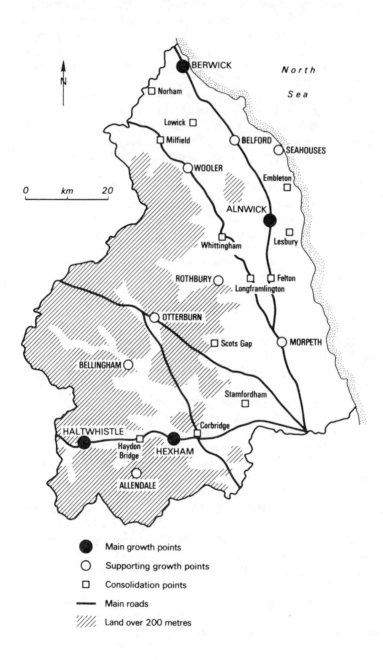

Source: Northumberland CC, 1969, 31

which considers that its previous village classification policy is worthy of further support:

> This policy has been successful in conserving much that is worthwhile in village character, although in many cases its effect has not been immediately apparent because of the scale of the commitments inherited from the 1950s. This settlement policy will require reassessment as the Structure Plan is developed, but the success of the policy and the ease with which it is understood, make it likely that the broad principles of a village classification policy could be retained.

Similarly the report of survey for Durham (1978, 12) 'recommends a continuation of the present policies of local planning authorities of concentrating the provision of opportunities upon the larger towns and villages which can act as centres for the surrounding area'.

This is not to suggest that county authorities have been blind to the faults of previous policies. Indeed most reports of survey are well aware of the malfunctions of existing strategies. Devon County Council (1977), for example, are quick to isolate the deficiencies of their development-plan key settlement policy, with the recognition that large scale expansion had taken place in some non-key settlements while the selected key settlements had not always been sufficiently strong foci to reverse existing trends of rural depopulation. Despite this awareness of policy failures, however, there has remained a strong tendency to follow the basic tenor of previous strategic decisions, and this form of trend planning may perhaps best be ascribed to individual mechanisms of the planning process.

One such mechanism is the granting of planning permissions for housing and other forms of development. In some cases (e.g. Gwent, 1978) the existence of land with planning permission constituted a major input into the assessment of the suitability of individual settlements for further development. This process can quickly become a self-fulfilling prophecy whereby if a settlement is selected for housing growth (and therefore receives planning permissions) under one policy regime, it is likely to be a prime contender for further development under the next, and so on. Elsewhere, existing planning permissions represent the bulk of new housing requirements over the structure-plan period. Kent County Council (1976, 374) reveal that:

> The extent of the housing stock available in villages, and of existing planning permissions, suggests that a much higher restraint on such development would be appropriate in the future; indeed, no new permissions are necessary in the short term except in particular local circumstances.

The stranglehold of existing planning permissions is a tight one. Permissions for housing can (if good reason is presented) be revoked and the planning authority's intention to use the land for housing purposes can thus be withdrawn. Compensation is liable to be paid to the person who would have benefited by the planning permission and, as Cheshire County Council (1977,

45) point out, 'the sum involved would normally be considerable, often result-ing in the need to reject this course of action outright'. A more likely alterna-tive for planners wishing to erase anachronistic decisions is to refuse to renew lapsed planning permissions or to 'de-allocate' land earmarked for housing but which has not yet received formal planning permission. In the latter case no compensation is payable, although resources could still be wasted if expenditure (e.g. on the provision of services) had already occurred on the basis of this allocation. Tampering with previous planning permissions has loomed large in the strategic thinking of several counties (e.g. Norfolk, 1977), but in general planning authorities have stepped back from the costly brink of revocation.

The patronage occurring between past and present rural settlement planning policies is wider than just the planning permission sector. Gwent County Council (1978) stresses that existing commitments for large housing develop-ments will have already imposed obligations on various development agencies to provide interrelated services such as schools. At a larger scale, the council (p. 225) clearly indicates that:

> Known commitments for major investment proposals in, for example, road construction, sewerage schemes, have been taken into account in preparing the plan in order to maximise the use of investment and minimise the necessity for new schemes.

If these specific commitments tend to restrict the scope for change within rural policies in structure plans, the public participation exercises (which often reinforce the conservationist or environmentalist ethics) tend to reinforce any inbuilt inertia in the planning system. The combined result of these various factors is to create a flourishing habitat for trend planning whereby the new structure-plan policies cannot shake off the shackles of previous rural policy decisions and (with few exceptions) at best represent modifications rather than wholesale redirections of former policy alignments.

Elements of plan preparation

The formal process of plan preparation is a curious mix of overt and covert influences. Reports of survey and related structure plan documentation are excellent sources of information for the overt factors of policy preparation but give very few hints as to the importance of other equally relevant but more obscure sources of formative influence suggested in figure 1.2. The layout and style of most reports of survey have adopted the model suggested by the initial development-plan manual guidelines which favoured a structured analysis according to a set of subject areas such as 'population', 'employment', 'housing' and so on. Table 6.3 shows a fairly typical set of chapter headings for a structure-plan report of survey, and nearly all plans have adopted this pattern of separate detailed analyses for individual facets of society and economy. This approach has been heavily criticized:

The technical methods available to planners have tended to reinforce the fragmentation of analysis into these component subjects, which reflects the fact that it is the linkages between different parts of the local economy that are least understood in current theory. This is why, for example, most plans do not adequately explore those crucial interrelationships in the local labour and housing markets that determine migration behaviour and the match between demographic and employment structure. (Barras, 1979, 21)

Similar objections may be raised from the point of view of rural settlement policies where the interaction of housing, employment, services and transport in one community or a group of communities is ill-considered within the rigid divisions of structure-plan analysis (this point is reinforced by Barras and Broadbent, 1979). In this way, the Northamptonshire report of survey shown in table 6.3 contains no 'rural survey' *per se* and answers the need for information on rural settlements with brief surveys of, for example, transport and employment in the 'rural west' and the 'rural east'. In general any specific analysis devoted to rural areas tends to deal with matters of environment, landscape and conservation. Thus the Buckinghamshire (1976) report of survey devotes a chapter to 'the rural environment' in which settlements and settlement pattern form only 10 per cent of the analysis. Some deviations from this norm do occur, for example with Oxfordshire's (1975) emphasis on 'countryside and villages', Gwent's (1978) specific study of 'settlement pattern' and Leicestershire's (1974) detailed chapter on 'rural settlements', but in general the treatment given to socio-economic problems in rural areas is fragmented and often of low priority.

Surveys provide the bulk of local information input for structure-plan policy-making and in almost every case, census material has been used as a backcloth to the specific data accumulated from survey sources. Table 6.4 lists the survey input to the Devon structure plan and gives some indication of the resources devoted to this part of the policy-making process. The importance of surveys as a formative influence on resulting rural settlement strategies is ultimately dependent on the reasons for seeking certain types of information and the application of data to particular purposes. In the rural context, these factors vary considerably from county to county. Perhaps the 'standard'

Table 6.3   Typical contents of county structure-plan report of survey

A	*Statutory framework and background*	C	*Other structural issues*
	1 Introduction		8 Housing
	2 Regional and local setting		9 Education
B	*Key issues*		10 Shopping
	3 Population		11 Public utilities
	4 Employment		12 Conservation and townscape
	5 Transportation		13 Countryside and recreation
	6 Finance		14 Minerals
	7 Implementation and monitoring	D	*Evolution of the plan*
			15 Evolution of the plan

Source: After Northamptonshire CC, 1977

Table 6.4   Surveys undertaken for the Devon Structure Plan

Survey	Date	Coverage
Household questionnaire survey	Dec 75 – Feb 76	Selected households in selected settlement throughout the county
Community facilities survey	Dec 75 – Feb 76	One form to each identifiable settlement in the county excluding those above key settlement classification
Employers' surveys	Nov 75 – Feb 76	1 Industrial and those services with industrial location; all firms with 100 + employees, plus, for the smaller establish ments, a minimum of 20 per cent from each employment group in each Employment Exchange Area where 1971 ER II recorded 50 + employees in that group; postal questionnaire followed by 10 per cent sample interview; 2 100 per cent postal questionnaire of 4 industrial estates: Sowton, Estover, Pottington and Dobles Lane (Holsworthy). NB 1 and 2 not mutually exclusive surveys; 3 Offices in Groups 26 & 29 that have sub-regional function (at least 50 per cent services provided outside 20-mile radius); postal questionnaire and 10 pre cent sample interview; 4 Survey of public sector by questionnaire; most bodies also interviewed
Shopping behaviour survey	Nov 75 – Feb 76	A random sample of shoppers interviewed in 43 of the largest shopping centres in Devon
Dual use of school facilities	March 76 – Sept 76	All schools and colleges in Devon

Related background studies
Towards 2001: The Future of the Plymouth Sub-Region, Cornwall and Devon CCs, 1975
Towards 2001: The Future of the Exeter Sub-Region, Devon CC, 1975
Plymouth and Environs Transportation Study, Cornwall and Devon CCs, and Plymouth City Council, 1976
Exeter and Area Transportation Study, Devon CC, 1977

Source: After Devon CC, 1977, 179

survey in rural areas has been to assess current position of fixed services and facilities in rural settlements. This information is then presented as part of a county-wide analysis or, in the case of counties including large rural components, as a separate report. Dorset County Council (1979), for example, has issued the results of a village facilities survey which is intended to highlight issues and options for public discussion (table 6.5). Basic level results such as these offer one level of debate as to what constitutes village viability in terms of service provision.

Other counties have geared their rural surveys towards more specific objectives. Derbyshire County Council's (1977) approach was to measure thirty-nine social indicators in rural parishes (or groups of parishes) and urban wards in an attempt to produce an index of 'social malaise', so that high score areas could receive priority attention from structure plan policies. However, as all areas with a total population of less than 1000 were excluded from the analysis, the degree to which this technique may be viewed as appropriate in isolating problem rural areas is open to question. In Gwent, surveys were undertaken to assess the suitability of each rural settlement for future development. Several criteria were considered:

1 Availability of community facilities, especially primary schools and shops;
2 Capacity of utility services, particularly spare main drainage capacity;
3 Historic and architectural quality of the village and its surrounding landscape;
4 Access to the main road network and centres of employment;
5 Quality of agricultural land, particularly where development would involve the loss of Grade 2 or 3 land;
6 Village form and topographical constraints, particularly availability of suitable areas for development, either within the village or on its periphery;
7 Existence of land with planning permission.

In effect, this type of procedure represents a more vigorous version of that adopted in some development plans, and this emotion of *déja vu* is strengthened by the fact that village selection was finally carried out on the basis of a presence or absence of spare sewerage capacity, shops, bus services, suitable access, primary school and significant existing undeveloped commitment (Gwent, 1978, Appendix I), a list which duplicates earlier selection procedures adopted for rural settlements.

A rather more sophisticated quantitative approach to settlement differentiation was adopted by Essex County Council (1978) which made use of potential surface analysis to select villages or clusters of villages where further investment into community facilities was in keeping with various strategic objectives reflecting conservation and growth strategies. The value of this exercise was thwarted, however, by overall strategic decisions, which overrode the smaller scale rural settlement policy deliberations. The report of survey, having outlined the use of potential surface analysis for village classification, has to admit that: 'The County strategy eventually rejected all further growth alternatives and adopted a pattern of development already committed subject to reservations about planned developments in the "wrong places" ' (p. 134).

Table 6.5   Facilities and settlement size in Dorset villages

Settlements			Percentage of settlements with							
Population 1977	Number	Percentage	Public hall	Post office	Public house	Food shop	Mains sewerage	Garage/filling station	Primary school	Surgery
0–49	53	18	4	6	11	4	9	2	0	0
50–99	67	23	31	18	20	15	18	12	7	0
100–49	29	10	66	62	48	34	28	17	10	10
150–99	36	12	83	72	64	67	44	36	25	11
200–49	16	5	94	75	68	75	56	50	31	6
250–499	49	17	100	94	84	86	73	63	51	33
500–999	22	8	100	100	100	100	100	95	91	50
1,000 +	21	7	100	100	100	100	100	95	100	90
Total	293*	100	60	55	51	48	43	36	30	18

Source: After Dorset CC, 1979, 18
*Includes information for the 12 towns as well as for the 281 villages covered by the Village Facilities Survey

This Essex example reinforces two fundamental issues raised elsewhere in this book. First, the development and evaluation of rural settlement policies within structure plans is dependent on and often overshadowed by the larger scale strategic decisions made at a county level. An overall 'no-growth' strategy, for example, dictates that a restrictive policy be adopted in rural areas. Second, the commitments and decisions made under previous policy regimes are highly influential in narrowing the scope for radical policy changes in rural areas.

Perhaps most typical of the survey/analysis/classification techniques adopted during structure-plan preparation stages is that exemplified by Leicestershire (1974) and Warwickshire (1973). Both methods reject population distribution patterns and infrastructural capacity as bases for rural settlement classification, preferring to adopt a multivariate analysis of settlement attributes. The Leicestershire approach was based on 'the varying significance of the *social role* [author's italics] of villages and small towns in providing services and facilities for a surrounding area of countryside' (p. 80) and revolved around the availability of social facilities, accessibility by public transport and (inevitably) existing housing commitments. Three functional levels were observed:

1 Settlements with a large range and number of facilities some of which are not closely related to the size of the village itself;
2 Settlements with a lesser range and number of facilities, although some providing more than would be expected from their population size;
3 Settlements with a limited range and number of facilities, and these categories correspond closely with the 'expansion', 'restraint' and 'local needs' classification in the resultant policy.

A similar approach was adopted in the case of Warwickshire. This technique is the subject of detailed review elsewhere (Cloke, 1979) but may briefly be described an an amalgam of 'development potential' (measured by fourteen variables representing various services or infrastructural attributes), 'land constraints' and 'existing commitments'. Quantitative expressions of these three criteria were aggregated into overall scores which influenced the selection of key settlements in the county, although the analysis as a whole was hampered by mathematical error and by the fact that the aggregate index for each settlement tended simply to reflect population size. Thus the biggest settlements automatically become key settlements.

It can be seen from the application of these various surveys that the information gained therein has been utilized to translate a deductive policy decision (i.e. to classify villages and to concentrate growth in some of them) into an inductive reality through a process of settlement selection. Survey materials as such should not then be viewed as influential in forming the policy, but rather as a means of colouring in a picture that is already sketched out. In the examples quoted above this preconceived use of survey information is often not spelt out. Elsewhere, however, surveys are deliberately delayed until specific policy decisions have been made. In the case of Salop (1977, 355) it is clearly stated that:

'main villages' constitute the key element in the proposed rural settlement policy. The Plan proposes that the service functions of these villages should be strengthened to help to mitigate the effects of a decline in services in the rural areas and to prevent further population loss.

The main villages were selected either as settlements already performing an important service function, or as centres where a wider range of services and facilities was to be promoted to support the more rural parts of the county. Following this set of decisions, further surveys were instigated in the form of a housing location appraisal which sought to:

1 Suggest the main villages in which large groups of houses should be allowed;
2 Identify those investment thresholds that should (and those that should not) be crossed over the structure plan period in order to permit new housing development

On the basis of these appraisals, some main villages were selected for housing development in addition to their service role.

Rural surveys have also been used at one stage further removed from the making of policy decisions. Hertfordshire's (1979) county-wide settlements study rural was undertaken after the submission of the county structure plan in order to 'test and examine the Structure Plan "villages policy" with a view to its amplification or amendment' (p. iii). Far from being just a monitoring exercise, this study gives detailed examination to the merits and demerits of two main types of rural settlement planning:

1 *Countywide policy* which was found to be simple to operate, and a good means of co-ordinating various aspects of village development, but blunt and unresponsive to the particular functions and characteristics of individual villages;
2 *Individual village policy* which was better able to respond to the discrete characteristics of individual settlements but represented an extremely complex method of defining village types and adequately reflecting the differences between them in strategic rural settlement policy.

It is this kind of detailed and unpreconditioned debate which might have been hoped for in structure-plan surveys of rural areas. Instead, such surveys have been used as a backcloth to broad trends within counties and as techniques to translate preconceived policy decisions into divisions for and against development in particular rural settlements. As such, much of the potential benefit to be gained from the vast surveying effort collectively undertaken by county authorities has been of little use to the progress of rural settlement planning outside of localized interests.

One notable exception to this trend of prejudged parochialism is to be found in the Cumbria report of survey (1976). Using a number of socio-economic indicators, a 'social profile' of community characteristics in the county, was produced. Five social types resulted (figure 6.3) incorporating urban local authority communities (1), urban peripheral communities (2), central urban and old settlement communities (3), agricultural communities (4), and rural residential and commuter communities (5), and although these were

Figure 6.3 Distribution of community characteristics in Cumbria

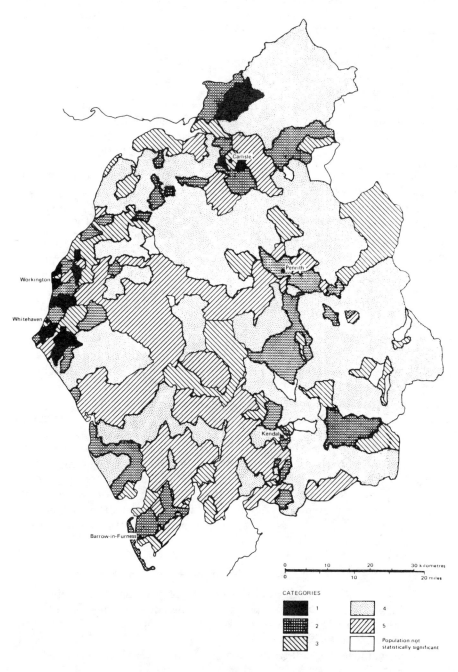

CATEGORIES

1

2

3

4

5

Population not
statistically significant

Source: After Cumbria CC and Lake District Planning Board, 1976, 46

necessarily generalized, they did provide a starting point for a detailed investigation of problems and policies in rural areas. This careful and far-sighted analysis resulted in the presentation of four themes for the future of rural planning in Cumbria:

1 A current trend theme;
2 A conservation theme;
3 An economic development theme;
4 A regenerative or remedial theme.

The first three are fairly standard options, but the fourth, which arises directly from the various surveys undertaken, is somewhat innovative within the formal statement of structure-plan alternatives. It assumes that parts of rural Cumbria need positive action to rejuvenate them (p. 152):

> The need for such rejuvenation might be based on general population decline, leading to the reduction of services and job opportunities, or social and economic need. . . . The implications would be similar – a need for policies which would contribute most to the achievement of the rejuvenation of community life or the enhancement of the environment.

Not surprisingly in view of this type of policy preparation, the example of Cumbria arises again later in this chapter as one of the few policies which deviates significantly from the normal pattern of rural settlement planning.

It may appear rather cynical to include *public participation* under the general heading of 'surveys' instead of isolating it as a process which constitutes a separate formative influence on resulting policies. Indeed, it would be erroneous to undervalue the efforts of county planning authorities to publicize various stages of their plan process and to invite participation in one way or another. Table 6.6 gives some impression of the lengths to which county planning teams (in this case Devon) have gone to attempt a realistic integration of public opinion into their structure plan. Evidence from the reports of survey, however, suggests that in broad terms public participation may often be viewed as yet another type of survey which serves to ratify or enlarge upon decisions which have already been made. It is beyond the scope of this book to provide the in-depth examination of participation found elsewhere (e.g. Sewell and Coppock, 1977; Muir and Paddison, 1981) but one or two examples suffice to demonstrate the difficulties faced by both planner and public in sharing decisions over formal rural settlement policy (these themes are reprised in chapter 8).

The problems of explaining possible future planning options for rural areas are outlined by Dyfed County Council (1978, para. 319):

> The process of generating alternative strategies was complex, involving the meshing together of various options into coherent groupings. A generation process was needed that was concise yet took full account of the various facets of the problems posed, and at the same time was capable of presenting in an understandable way the real planning issues which the Council and the public needed to decide.

Dyfed's response to these problems was a 'strategic choice' approach by which compatible combinations of policy choices were generated for public discussion. These packages of options were necessarily aggregated to make them 'more understandable to the public' (para. 3.13) and in fact the Dyfed public were finally presented with three broad themes:

A To encourage the dispersal of employment and housing throughout the rural areas on as broad a basis as possible to meet these needs;
B To encourage the concentration of new employment opportunities in the main towns of the county but also to encourage the dispersal of new housing throughout the rural area on as broad a basis as possible, involving a concurrent dispersal of transport investment;
C To encourage the concentration of employment and housing in the main towns with transport investment being directed mainly to these centres and major links between them.

Although 'each option was explained in detail in order that the reader could make a choice, and where relevant the main implications of the adoption of an option choice were explained' (para. 3.16), the usual problems of a low and badly sampled response were encountered. Nevertheless the variety of comments received both from the general public and from public and private sector agencies were considered by the Dyfed Planning Committee, who favoured theme A as the preferred option.

On the surface, the public participation exercise appears, in the case of Dyfed, to have aided the acceptance of a resource dispersal policy. In fact the preferred option is a trend progression from previous policies adopted in areas of the county, and may well have been the planners' choice prior to the participation process. Some doubt must be cast over the objectivity of such processes (and indeed has been cast by the planners who operate them). For example Gwent County Council (1978) outlined two alternative strategies, A (the concentration of new housing development) and B (its dispersal), for public scrutiny. The results were reported as follows (p. 266):

> There was support for both housing and settlement alternatives, some organizations preferring part of each strategy. A few bodies made their own suggestions since they disliked both strategies. Alternative A was favoured since it implied less consumption of agricultural land for urban development, a reduction of journey to work distances, and a safeguarding of the character of rural settlements. However, Alternative B was preferred by several organizations since it suggested more housing in the market towns. In addition, other organizations which disliked both of the housing and settlement strategies advocated the maintenance of small communities through selective redevelopment, improvement, and infilling.

In light of this expected and understandable lack of unified opinion, the power of the deliberating planning committee is widespread. Planners and politicians set the questions and planners and politicians interpret the answers, and so it cannot be surprising that public participation surveys tend to reinforce or at best modify existing preferences. Many counties have acknowledged these

Table 6.6 Devon Structure-Plan programme for public participation and publicity

Phase	Commencing date	Object of consultation	Provisional period		Nature of consultation/publicity
I	Early 1975	*Structure Plan* Announcement that work on the Structure Plan is to commence	2 months	A	Announcement (advertisement giving details of public participation proposed and broad timetable) in the press, press conference, radio/television coverage; poster campaign in selected public places and invitations to bodies to register their interest;
		Public comment on draft key issues, initially by Structure Plan Sub-Committee		B	Consultation with district councils (who will be asked to consult parishes)/government departments especially the Department of the Environment/ interested bodies/public including tear-off response strip in newspapers
II	October 1975 – February 1976	*Feasibility Studies* public discussion on selected alternative strategies	3 months each	A	(i) Invitation in the press for public comment/ representations; radio/television coverage after publication of 'popular' edition of the study – the 'discussion document'; (ii) District council consultation/visit to Council meetings, if invited
	June – July 1976	*Transportation Studies* Plymouth	2 months each	B	Generally as (i) and (ii) above
	June – July 1977	Exeter		B	
III	March 1977	*Structure Plan* Publication of report of survey	Information continously available		Press/radio/television coverage; distribution of publicity leaflet

IV	Spring/summer 1977		Structure Plan Publication of selected alternative strategies for the various parts of the County explaining their relationship	3 months		(i) Main exhibitions in Plymouth, Torbay, Exeter and Barnstaple; mobile exhibition starting at County Hall; subsequently two mobile exhibitions visiting some of the other major settlements; (ii) Press including advertisements/radio/television coverage/press conference; (iii) Public meetings related to exhibitions; (iv) Leaflets to be available in public places (e.g. local authority offices, libraries, gas and electricity offices) outlining main alternative/proposals with tear-off portion to comment; (v) Consultation with district councils; (vi) Consultations with other statutory bodies and groups of voluntary bodies plus offer in some cases of members and/or officers to attend their meetings
V	Autumn 1977	A	Structure Plan Publication of policies and proposals to be submitted to Secretary of State (draft structure plan)	2 months	A	(i) Final public participation stage; (ii) Consultations with district councils; (iii) Consultations with other statutory bodies and groups of voluntary bodies; (iv) Presentation to government departments; (v) Press/radio/television coverage/press conference
	Spring 1978	B	Publicity regarding any major changes arising out of consultations, and submission to plan	Prescribed period to be at least 6 weeks	B	Representations to Secretary of State

Source: After Devon CC, 1977, 178

shortcomings and recognize that, in the three-fold relationship between *feasibility*, *objective achievement* and *public comment*, some minimum degree of public tolerance is sufficient support for a preferred strategy if the other two criteria can be satisfied.

Resource constraints have loomed large in the background to discussion of preparatory surveys of one kind or another. Since neither investigative surveys nor public participation methods appear to be the sources of original preference for particular rural strategies then we might conclude that feasibility of policy alternatives may be uppermost in planners' minds when making crucial policy decisions. Certainly this is the opinion of many commentators such as Hughes (1980, 396) who claims that:

> the key settlement idea [is] still suspended like cigar smoke in the air of rural planning departments . . . [because] in the annual negotiations over rate support grant, each authority must marshall its arguments to advocate rural development against the competing claims of, say, inner urban areas. This advocacy role gives rise to policy formulation and poor as it may be, key settlement policy may be all that is available.

Circular 98 (1974) from the Department of the Environment requires county structure plans to assess whether the demands on financial resources controlled by government departments are in scale with what is likely to be forthcoming and whether demands on other resources are realistic. Consequently, most reports of survey include detailed considerations of the financial implications of policy-making. Cumbria County Council (1976) outlines five relevant areas of study:

1 *Capital expenditure by local authorities*, where housing, education, highways and transportation and social services predominate. Capital expenditure is normally financed at least in part by loan and so by controlling the level of borrowing approvals made available to local authorities, the government can control the level of capital investment on individual services;

2 *Revenue expenditure*, the cost of maintaining and operating local authority services. A growth in expenditure is often desirable or necessary to implement government policies, to improve levels of services or to adapt to changing population structure and distribution, but expenditure growth requires additional grants or rates income to balance the books;

3 *Rateable resources*, the rates collected within the area are supplemented by government through the rate support grant (the resources grant) in order to bring the rate yield up to a predetermined level. Thus if a county creates additional rateable value of its own, it will lose an equivalent sum from the resources grant. Moreover, government policy to reduce public spending can and has been implemented by reductions in this grant;

4 *Government grants*, which consist of a variety of capital and revenue support measures, such as the transport supplementary grant, housing subsidies and a 50 per cent Home Office reimbursement of police expenditure. The rate support grant is the dominant mechanism here, with the govern-

ment deciding on a total global rate support grant for the country as a whole on an annual basis. The formula for grant distribution within this total is subject to continuous adjustment so that funds can be redirected into areas of perceived 'high need'. This can lead to rural areas having to fight their case each year in direct competition with other areas with other problems;

5 *Private sector investment*, comprising a complex network of organizations which rely on profitability for their continuing function. Obviously housing developers and employers are integral decision-makers in rural settlement planning, but the levels of investment forthcoming from these sectors is very difficult to predict.

These financial resource issues inevitably impose severe restraints on the feasibility of structure-plan options. Although the plan is not itself a resource-allocation document and therefore the approval of a policy does not guarantee grant aid for particular projects, it is clear that county decision-makers have taken careful note of resource constraints. Cheshire County Council (1977, 139) admit that the bleak economic prospects, affecting not only the spending of Local Authorities, industry and commerce, but also the expectations of individuals, will condition the kind of structure plan and policies to be produced. This conditioning is re-emphasized by the uncertainty of out look which dominates economic and financial affairs. Some counties therefore express concern over high levels of population growth in their area which they cannot afford to service adequately. Elsewhere, a reduction in population levels is feared because the reduction in rateable income cannot be compensated by a *pro rata* reduction in services. Demographic forecasting is thus crucial to the financial argument and counties tend towards a conservative estimate of their thresholds of feasibility so that financial risk is minimized. As a consequence, low-growth policies are favoured. Similarly, the risk of adopting radically different policies which divert or increase capital or revenue expenditures has tended to be shunned in favour of the 'safer' option of continuing with current (and therefore perceived as manageable) patterns of resource distribution.

The allocation mechanisms of local government finance are constantly subject to fine tuning according to the ideological preferences of the government of the day. The 1980 local government legislation, however, introduced more radical changes to the manner in which central government's grants to local authorities are determined, and to central government's control over local authorities' capital expenditure. In essence the existing *needs* and *resources* elements of the rate support grant have been replaced by a single *block grant*. The significance of this change is stressed by Watts (1980, 29):

The new block grant is tapered in that above a certain level of expenditure, additional expenditure only attracts grant at a decreasing rate. This contrasts with the (previously) existing resources element of the rate support grant which, when paid, is paid at a constant rate of matching and is thus open ended to an authority, lowering its cost of spending by this rate and leading to substitution of public for private expenditure – a feature not likely to recommend itself to a Conservative government.

In other words, past a certain threshold level, the more is spent by local government, the less subsidy it receives from central government. This reinforcement of the ethic of reduced public sector spending has given counties further reason to opt for low-cost policies that are concerned with the allocation of *existing* rather than *new* resources. These economic policy trends exert considerable influence on the scope for change in rural settlement planning during the structure-plan era.

In addition to these overt influences during the policy preparation stage, it is suggested that several less easily recognized (or less readily admitted) factors also contribute to the final shape of rural policies within structure plans. Few references are made in published reports of survey to any adherence to planning vogue. Indeed each county tends to view its policy as a specific response to the problems and attitudes of its own area so that any suggestion of policy imitation would be anathema. However, the fact remains that the rural surveys in most structure plans take for granted that rural settlements should be classified and that growth should be concentrated at one level or another. No indication is given as to where this undiscussed policy dictate arises from and so it can only be surmised that alongside the explanations offered by trend planning and resource constraints that structure-plan teams have gained comfort from the fact that others are adopting similar strategies to their own – a process of 'safety in numbers' which reinforces the idea that certain types of policy remain in vogue. In addition, it should be recognized that the largely conservative or landowning ruling political groups in rural areas are best able to achieve their own objectives (based on their own perceptions of what is 'needed') by favouring rural policies that are oriented towards low costs and low growth, and which seek scale economies in establishing a local equilibrium. These more obsure policy influences are of real importance in rural areas despite the fact that structure-plan documentation gives little hint of their existence.

Rural settlement policies

The written rural policy settlements contained within structure plans are prone to misinterpretation. All too often in the past, bald policy statements have been taken by commentators at face value as rigidly applicable local legislation which will exert predictable trends on rural settlement patterns. In fact, the written policies should be considered more as statements of the ideal which are rarely reproduced exactly when subjected to a tortuous series of implementation procedures. Very often the planning intentions which are not spelt out in structure plans are as important to the outcome of rural settlement planning as those which are. Nevertheless the written policies do give some idea of what county authorities would prefer to happen in rural areas given reasonably predictable conditions, and such policies are therefore of interest both in terms of the temporal development of rural settlement planning, and as a broad guideline to the expected pattern of resource management in rural communities.

In order to avoid the type of interpretative misunderstandings which have previously dogged rural policy analysis, all non-metropolitan county planning authorities in England and Wales were contacted and invited to scrutinize and modify a series of observations concerning the rural settlement policies contained within the written statements of their individual structure plans. This procedure ensured that basic policy details could be cross-checked and, if necessary, altered. In addition the survey was able to present the authorities with an opportunity both to comment on various relevant factors and trends which were not detailed in the written statements and to offer more general and broad level descriptions of the rural settlement policies adopted. Following a very high level of response, the survey accumulated details of fifty-four plans, of which thirty-five had been approved by the Secretary of State, eighteen were at the submission stage and one was still in draft form (table 6.7). Scottish plans were not included in this analysis because of their separate and distinctive nature (Boyle, 1980; Fladmark, 1980; Wannop, 1980), although the need for a similar analysis in the Scottish context is clear.

From the previous analysis of the formative influences in policy preparation, and from previous studies of rural policies in structure plans (notably by Derounian, 1979), it might be expected that the overall pattern of policy would reflect an overwhelming continuation of the key settlement concept based on a need for economy and the conservation of environmentally endangered rural settlements. The results from the survey reveal a far more complex combination of policies. Even though structural factors within policy preparation have served to shape the general nature of policies for rural settlements, a considerable degree of variation exists between counties at the detailed policy level. This book allows insufficient scope for the cataloguing of policy minutiae for each individual county, which are in any case subject to constant modification and monitoring. Instead, the various strategies have been aggregated into a loose taxonomy based on the major perceived thrust of the policy (gained both from inspection of the relevant documentation and from the survey of county authorities). Inevitably some county policies are more easily categorized than others. The classifications used here, then, should be viewed as broad types of policy in which some policies are positioned in the 'grey area' between two classes. Nevertheless, six broad policy categories may be recognized (figure 6.4) and each represents a slightly different emphasis for rural settlement planning.

Concentration in market towns

A significant subset of three counties have chosen to concentrate housing, services and employment into market towns within rural areas and to discourage growth lower down the settlement hierarchy. In Cornwall (1980), the rural policy is considered in the context of the even distribution of some twenty

Table 6.7   Current structure plans for respondent county authorities

Avon	1980	S
Bedfordshire	1980	A
Central Berkshire	1980	A
East Berkshire	1980	A
West Berkshire	1979	A
Buckinghamshire	1980	A
Cambridgeshire	1980	A
Cheshire	1979	A
East Cleveland	1980	A
Cornwall	1980	S
Cumbria and Lake District	1980	S
Derbyshire	1980	A
Devon	1979	S
South-East Dorset	1978	S
Dorset (excluding SE)	1980	D
Durham	1978	S
Essex	1979	S
Gloucestershire	1980	S
Mid Hampshire	1980	A
North-East Hampshire	1980	A
South Hampshire	1977	A
Herefordshire	1976	A
Hertfordshire	1979	A
Humberside	1979	A
Kent	1980	A
Central and North Lancashire	1980	S
North-east Lancashire	1970	A
Leicestershire	1976	A
Norfolk	1980	A
Northamptonshire	1977	S
Northumberland	1980	A
Nottinghamshire	1980	A
Oxfordshire	1979	A
Salop	1980	A
Somerset	1980	S
Staffordshire	1978	A
Suffolk	1979	A
Surrey	1980	A
East Sussex	1978	A
Warwickshire	1975	A
North-east Wiltshire	1980	S
South Wiltshire	1979	S
West Wiltshire	1979	S
Worcestershire	1975	A
North Yorkshire	1980	A
Clwyd	1979	S
Mid Glamorgan	1978	S
South Glamorgan	1977	A
Gwent	1978	S
Gwynedd – Anglesey	1980	A
Caernarvonshire	1980	A
Dyffryn Conwy	1980	A
Merionnydd	1980	A
Powys	1979	S

D Draft   S Submitted   A Approved

Figure 6.4 Settlement-policy categories for respondent counties

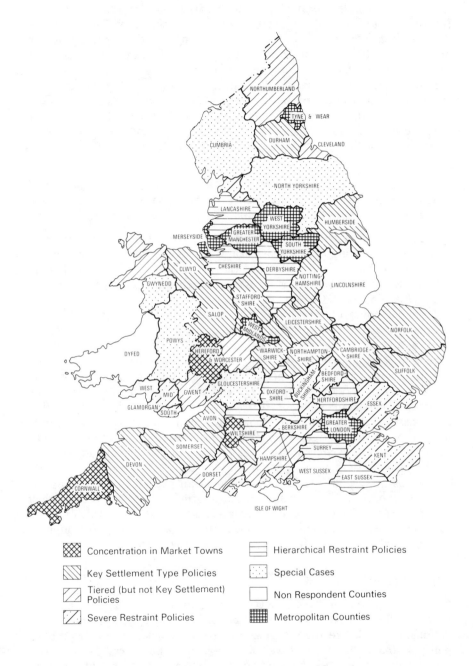

small- or medium-size towns across the county. As very few other rural settlements are more than 6 miles (4 km) distant from these towns it is considered that they are capable of providing for many of the housing and service needs of the whole rural population. On the surface, this preference for new development in market towns is supplemented by a flexible approach to new housing in smaller rural settlements. The plan identifies various attributes (e.g. sewage disposal facilities, shops, primary schooling, social and medical facilities, accessibility) which a village should possess or have access to before further substantial development should be accepted. However, it is the manner in which these attribute requirements are interpreted which will determine how much development takes place in Cornish rural settlements, and the county's presentation to the plan's Examination in Public (1980a, para. 11) submits that:

> all the criteria are important and that if, at a time of limited resources, they restrict growth to only a limited number of villages then this is preferable to the problems that would result from a relaxation of the criteria.

Underlying this restriction on 'substantial development' is a permissive approach to infilling (defined in para. 8 as 'developments of one or two dwellings') in anything up to 100 additional villages to cater for local needs. Again, the relevance of this tier of rural settlement planning depends upon the rigidity of implementation processes.

A similar policy of concentrating development in market towns has been adopted by Herefordshire (1976) although semantic warnings are apposite here, as two of the selected growth towns, Bromyard and Kington, have populations around 2000 and might therefore be considered as large villages and not towns. Each aims to service a large rural hinterland and may thus be fairly described as akin to the key settlement concept. In cases such as this, where one overall policy assumes differing ramifications according to the fluctuating size of the growth centres concerned, policy classifications cannot be mutually exclusive. The general intention of the broad strategy for the county, however, remains to concentrate development into specified market towns. A further example of this type of policy occurs in the West Wiltshire plan (1979a) where most villages are in relatively close proximity to one or more of the nine main towns of the area, which are seen to perform many of the functions which might otherwise be undertaken by selected key settlements. In this case a further twelve settlements were designated for limited residential development with residual villages restricted to local-needs growth only.

Key settlement type policies

County structure plans have been very wary in the use of the terms 'key settlement' or 'key village'. Vocal criticism of the concept, both locally and nationally, has led to the use of alternative nomenclature for this type of policy, so that although the survey of county authorities reveals that only four respondents actually use the 'key' notation, sixteen counties confirmed that they had adopted 'a form of key settlement policy'. Semantics apart, this grouping of policies represents the selection of certain rural settlements where comprehensive growth of housing, services and (usually) employment will be encouraged so as to serve the surrounding rural hinterland. A common corollary of this strategy is that growth in non-selected settlements is restricted to some degree. The arguments for adopting this type of policy are rehearsed and expanded in chapter 7, but most counties concerned recognize the trend as inevitable: 'The main issue concerning settlement policies has been how far to plan for concentrated development rather than continuing existing policies which have encouraged dispersal' (Cambridgeshire CC, 1980, 33). Cambridgeshire County Council also justify their policy according to four classic objectives which are to be found in most of the plans within this section:

1 To keep down the cost of providing essential public services;
2 To make it possible for more people to reach a fuller range of services than can be found in most small villages;
3 To keep down the need to travel, particularly commuting, and thereby keep travel costs and the use of energy to a minimum;
4 To conserve the character of the villages and the countryside and to minimize disturbance to agriculture.

The details of selected growth centres differ from county to county. Devon, for example, identifies three hierarchical levels of chosen centre (figure 6.5):

1 *Sub-regional centres*, the four major urban centres of the county which will continue to function as centres of administrative, educational, cultural, industrial and commercial activity;
2 *Area centres*, twenty-six settlements acting as service centres to serve populations within both the settlement and the surrounding rural area.
3 *Selected local centres*, thirty-eight focal points in the rural areas where the policy is to ensure a priority in the provision of educational, social, health and postal services outside area or sub-regional centres.

Elsewhere, the names and numbers of selected settlements vary but the concept remains similar. For example the Durham (1978a) plan lists twelve major towns and eighty-eight other settlements for potential development; Humberside (1979), seventy-five selected settlements; Salop (1980), forty-two main villages; Somerset (1980), seven main rural centres and sixteen local rural centres; Staffordshire (1978), twelve key villages and twenty-one moderate growth villages; Suffolk (1979), forty-three major centres; South Wiltshire (1979), seven centres for major growth and four for minor growth; and Clwyd (1979), twenty-one main centres and many other main villages. In Cambridgeshire (1980) a fairly typical classification of

1 Ten major centres and market towns;
2 Sixteen key rural centres;
3 Twenty-one minor rural centres

is made interesting by two innovative phenomena. First, the sixteen key rural centres are divided into those selected for further housing growth (nine) and those where no further growth is encourages (seven). This represents a bifurcation of the roles of selected settlements (in this case between service provision

Figure 6.5 Settlement-plan policies of the Devon Structure Plan

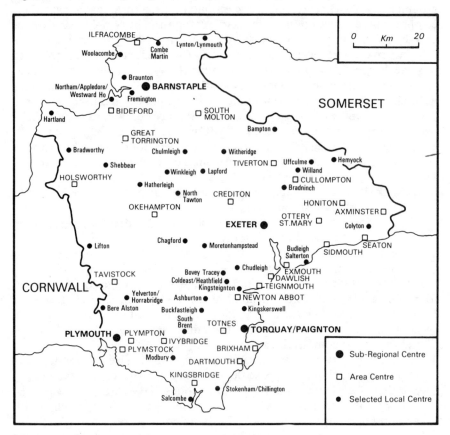

Source: Devon CC, 1981, 62

and housing) rather than the previously common preference for comprehensive key settlement functions. Second, the Secretary of State's approval of the plan deleted the selected settlements under the 'minor rural centres' category and substituted general criteria by which minor rural centres were to be selected. The letter of approval (Cambridgeshire CC, 1980, para. 3.2) states that

> One of the purposes of a structure plan is to provide a framework for local plans which should be left to deal with matters which are not of County significance. The Secretary of State is of the opinion that, by listing settlements as low in the hierarchy as minor rural centres . . . the Plan as submitted embodies a fineness of detail which is inappropriate for inclusion in a Structure Plan and which would prevent the District Councils from playing their proper role in the evaluation of each settlement in local plan preparation.

This decision reduces the role of small rural growth centres within the overall county strategy and increases the responsibility of district councils for the important developmental decisions concerning smaller rural settlements. Despite this deletion of named minor rural centres from the plan's policies, the county authority's preferences for minor rural centres remain in the text of the approved written statement (p. 40) giving the impression that county-level influence over rural settlement strategies might not be forfeited without a struggle.

Both of the innovations contained within the Cambridgeshire policy are repeated elsewhere. The district council responsibility for naming small centres also occurs in respect of Clwyd's main villages. Moreover, a bifurcation of growth settlement roles is also preferred in the Norfolk (1980) policy which seeks to direct population and employment into six small town growth centres and thirteen small town local centres, but in addition lists twenty-four settlements which are potentially suitable for residential estate development and twenty-six villages which act as service centres. Despite the recent indications that the service-centre policy has proved ineffective and might be abandoned in subsequent plan reviews, the plan as approved attempts to spread growth into more settlements by separating housing and service roles. Nevertheless, growth and investment is being concentrated into selected centres and in this sense the policy follows many aspects of the key settlement concept.

It is worthy of note that key settlement type policies have also been adopted in counties which suffer the problems of urban pressure. Leicestershire County Council (1976) recognized twenty-eight small towns and villages which were to receive the greatest proportion of future development in rural areas and which represented the best locations from which to serve the wide ranging demands of the rural population. Smaller numbers of growth centres were designated in Northamptonshire (1977), with six rural service centres and three limited growth villages, and Nottinghamshire (1980) where fourteen 'appropriate centres' for growth (mostly over 5000 population) were to act as the providers of services and facilities for surrounding smaller villages. The adopted policy for Warwickshire (1975) selected eleven first-tier and eight second-tier key settlements. This policy has been modified (Warwickshire CC, 1980) to recognize eleven settlements for housing growth, twelve for employment growth and sixteen for service growth, which demonstrates a more functional procedure for the differentiation of settlements even if the categories do overlap to some extent.

The criteria for the selection of settlements to accept resource concentration have not changed radically from those used in the preparation of development plans and their reviews. Avon County Council (1980), for example, requires a primary school, a bus service suitable for work journeys, main drainage, a post office and a foodshop for a settlement to be selected for secondary growth, and an additional doctor's surgery, shop and bus service suitable for shopping journeys for selection for primary growth. In both cases the character of the settlement must be maintained and public services must be adequate for the proposed development. For selection as a selected local centre in Devon, a settlement must fulfil rather more strict criteria, generally meeting six of the following attributes:

1 Basic facilities (primary school, post office, and resident or frequently visiting doctor);
2 Eleven or more shops;
3 Dispensing chemist;
4 Bank;
5 Local employment in the parish of 100 or more jobs;
6 Daily bus service;
7 Place of worship, inn and village hall

There is, however, dispensation for potential centres in remoter areas of the county to meet fewer than six criteria although a threshold of at least five shops is stipulated. Elsewhere, particularly in the pressured areas, greater emphasis is granted to constraints on development and existing commitments in the selection of growth centres. Very few counties have adopted the Warwickshire (1973) system of quantitative analysis of development potential to select key centres (which in any case proved less than successful (Cloke, 1979)) and so the actual decisions as to whether to invoke the various stated criteria and elect a particular settlement for growth remain *political*, and as such shrouded from the knowledge imparted by the written statements.

One significant difference in structure-plan policies of the key settlement type over their development-plan predecessors concerns the official planning attitude towards settlements which are not selected as growth centres. Previously, there has often been a presumption against any development in these non-key settlements, but the structure-plan policies herald a change in this presumption. The Cambridgeshire written statement (1980, 33–4) admits that:

> The strategy which has been chosen follows a concentrated pattern, *modified* [author's italics] to afford some choice in housing location and to provide a basis for establishing a network of at least minimum social facilities throughout the County, for the benefit of people who will continue to live in the rural areas.

This intention takes shape by permitting groups of houses and small-scale industrial or commerical developments in the larger of the non-key settlements where a good service base and appropriate sites exist. In other villages, many lacking even basic services, housing development will normally be restricted to infilling. Again, this seemingly more flexible policy towards unselected settlements is tempered by the fact that over three-quarters of the villages in Cambridgeshire fall within the 'infilling only' category.

This apparent trend towards allowing small-scale development in most rural settlements within a county is found elsewhere in policies of this category. Salop (1980) state the intention of ensuring that small scale developments in the form of infilling (one or two houses) or small groups of dwellings (three to five houses) should normally be allowed in most villages of the county. The detailed handling of this policy is left to district councils who are charged with giving priority to:

1   The provision of an adequate supply of houses in rural settlements for local needs – especially for people who work in the area or have strong local ties with it;
2   The provision of houses which are suitable for the young or the elderly;
3   The location of new housing so as to provide additional support to existing services and facilities – especially primary schools and rural transport services.

The real value of these policies cannot be fully assessed by these statements without regard to the manner in which they are implemented. Are developments of one to five houses sufficient for these purposes? Will criterion 3 lead to a concentration of development even among non-selected settlements so as to achieve scale economies? These questions are further discussed in chapter 10, but they form the nub of interpreting the policy intentions of most counties in this respect. Somerset's (1980) plan mentions 'infilling' and 'the erection of groups of houses' in some small villages and the Devon (1979) policy refers to 'infilling' and 'rounding off', but both policies suggest that any such development should be on a scale related to the existing size and character of the settlement, including the important factor of satisfactory servicing arrangements which in the past has been a major element in the prevention of development in smaller villages. Similar safeguards are imposed on the possibility of permitting small-scale proposals which are likely to provide local employment.

The survey to county planning authorities highlighted two contrasting plans where levels of development in non-key settlements is regarded as a vital factor in the overall policy of resource concentration. First, the Nottinghamshire County Council reply stresses that the structure plan is the wrong vehicle for pursuing detailed planning policies, which should be left to more local planning studies and initiatives. This sentiment is supported in the plan (1980) which makes allowance for housing and employment provision in *all* rural settlements subject to normal planning considerations. On the other hand the Northamptonshire (1977) policy suggests a strong presumption against growth outside the selected centres. Once again, however, techniques of implementation are quite able to ameliorate or even reverse these seemingly opposing attitudes, as is shown in the case of the Clwyd (1979) plan. Here a presumption against significant development in small settlements is being challenged by one of the district councils (Glyndŵr) which is operating the policy. In search of a more liberal policy for non-selected settlements this district council has produced its own settlement policy report and is challenging the submitted county policy at the statutory Examination in Public. This dissent at district level has meant that the county council has been unable and unwilling to enforce a rigid interpretation of the structure plan classifications. The Clwyd example serves to reinforce the observation that written policy statements should be viewed as guidelines rather than blueprints for what actually happens in the management of rural settlements. Thus the variations in detail among key settlement-type policies may indeed result in localized differences in outcome, or as has been suggested by some critics of the concept, policy detail may turn out to be insignificant as the underlying structural processes of resource concentration (which bind the above policies together) take their toll on smaller settlements.

Tiered policies

The survey of county planning authorities uncovered several instances where a policy of settlement tiering was preferred yet, for one reason or another, the authority considered its policy to be significantly different from the key settlement policy as traditionally viewed. Some overlap inevitably occurs between those key settlement-type policies which include liberal attitudes towards development in non-key settlements and other policies which are placed in this 'tiered' category. Nevertheless sharp differences do occur between the general tenors of the two categories and so it is important to differentiate between them rather than group them together in one key settlement type.

Three particular county policies appear to fall close to the border between key settlement and other classificatory strategies. The plan for Dorset (1980) (excluding south-east Dorset) recognizes four main local centres and four other settlements where growth is proposed. It is hoped that these centres will perform a service function for surrounding rural areas but there is no suggestion that the development of housing and employment opportunities in other settlements should be unduly restricted. Indeed it is the intention that the needs of all rural communities should be met by permitting limited residential development and by giving favourable consideration to proposals for small-scale developments which would lead to an increase in rural job opportunities. The centres for service growth and the potential housing and employment growth in other settlements both constitute a widening of opportunities away from established 'key' settlements and therefore the policy is appropriately placed in a non-key settlement-type category. In a rather similar manner, the plan for Northumberland (1980) nominates main and minor service centres yet is sufficiently flexible to permit development to take place across the whole spectrum of settlement types and sizes. The Gwent rural policy (1978) follows a comparable pattern. Figure 6.6 shows a three tier system of selection for village housing development outside of which a presumption against new dwellings in any village prevails. However, the plan does not seek to concentrate industrial, infrastructural or social and retail service provision in these selected centres, and so the key settlement concept strictly does not apply.

In two other areas, the intervention of the Secretary of State has served to modify policies away from the classic key settlement blueprint. The Mid Hampshire (1980) plan originally listed seventeen settlements for further development and seventy-two for limited infilling only. Similarly, the North-East Hampshire (1980a) policy initially recognized sixteen locations for small-scale housing development and twenty-six for infilling. In both cases the lists

Figure 6.6 Village development policy for Gwent

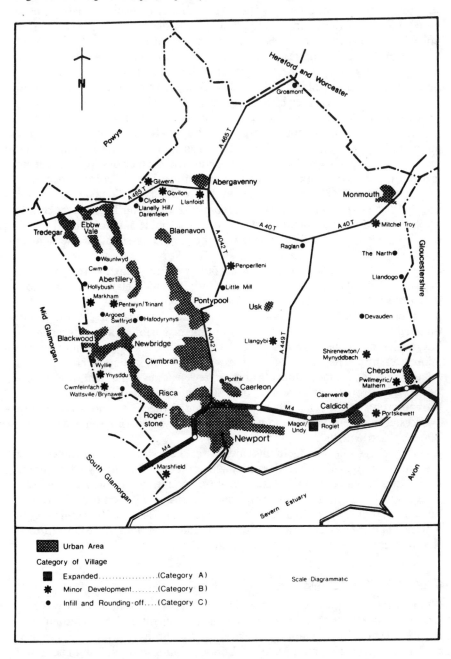

Source: Gwent CC, 1978, 87

of settlements concerned were removed by the Secretary of State from the structure plan, and although in Hampshire the settlements in question have been retained in the county's (1979) non-statutory coast and conservation policy, the transposition of responsibility to the district councils has meant that an overall policy of resource concentration cannot effectively be maintained at county level. A parallel situation has occurred with the Gwynedd plans for Caernarvonshire (1980b) and Anglesey (1980c) where the principle of categorization was accepted by the Secretary of State for Wales but the specific allocation of villages to the categories was not. The survey response from Gwynedd (personal communication) notes that: 'This is a somewhat anomalous situation and has rendered the operation of the settlement policies ineffective. Local plans, in effect, provide the framework for settlement growth in areas covered by them.' It may well be that the political decisions taken at district level as to which and how many settlements are to be selected for growth will be different from those previously taken at county level. If so this switch from district to county is capable of incorporating additional localized flexibility into a rather rigid system of settlement categorization.

Two further instances of this broad policy genre occur in areas of some urban pressure. The East Cleveland Structure Plan (Cleveland CC, 1980) does direct resources to particular settlements but only in terms of commercial development policies. The bulk of housing and industrial growth is not directed towards areas with high tier shopping provision so no comprehensive key settlement policy applies. Parallel claims are made on behalf of the Worcestershire (Hereford and Worcester CC, 1975) policy where the eight villages selected for more housing are not viewed as key settlements in the sense of being foci for resources and services. Instead, they are designed to serve as growth points in the relatively urbanized area to the south and south-east of Worcester in order to absorb some of the pressures from other, more vulnerable, rural settlements.

As a package, the policies in this category are cohesive more in terms of what they are not than of what they are. Nevertheless, the survey of planning authorities revealed a definite sub-group of counties who denied that their strategies were akin to the key settlement concept, and it is on the basis of this perception that a separate category is recorded here. The final assessment as to whether a policy is or is not a key settlement policy lies both in the definition of that concept (chapter 7) and the implementation of the policy (chapter 10).

Severe restraint policies

A rather more cohesive group of policies are represented in this analysis by a central policy thrust of severe restraint on development in all rural settlements. Figure 6.4 shows this grouping to be prevalent in those counties which are near major urban centres, mainly around London, but also on the south coasts of England and Wales and in one part of Lancashire. In some cases, a policy of blanket restraint on all village development (other than the ubiquitous 'infilling') has been adopted. The *raison d'être* behind this type of policy is suggested in the East Berkshire plan (1980, 28):

> A restrictive approach to future development will help protect the environment and natural resources of the area. In addition, the developing regional framework re-emphasizes the importance of areas of restraint as essential elements in the structure of the region. These policies, strengthening the Council's existing restrictive policies set out in the First Review of the County Development Plan (1960), are intended to give effect to these regional and local planning roles. . . . If regional and local obejectives are to be achieved, the restraint policies will have to be applied more effectively than in the past.

This tightening of the development net has meant that the three Berkshire plans (1979; 1980; 1980a) contain no selection of villages for growth, and intend only to permit development in certain urban areas. In this manner, rural settlements outside the metropolitan green belt suffer equality of restriction with those inside. Comparable policies of restricting rural growth to small degrees of 'local needs' development have been followed in South-East Dorset (1978), South Hampshire (1977), Mid Glamorgan (1978) and South Glamorgan (1977).

Elsewhere, policies within this category are slightly more complex because of green-belt arrangements. In Bedfordshire (1980) a general presumption against further residential development in rural areas has been modified by the Secretary of State to allow some further residential development where specialized local housing needs occur and some limited industrial development within villages. The county council in conjunction with the district councils affected, is now considering whether either or both of these policies should apply within the green belt, either as a generality or in relation to specific settlements. It appears likely that green-belt areas will be additionally protected from such developments, as is the case, for example, in Buckinghamshire (1980). Here the presumption against rural development in the green belt is slightly eased in residual rural areas, where the policy is (p. 81):

> to limit the provision of new housing to an amount, type and rate of development which is consistent with local community needs, the existing size, character and appearance of each village or hamlet and the availability of services and infrastructure.

Just how limited this provision will be is dependent upon the level of flexibility employed by district councils in the interpretation of these criteria.

There do appear to be trends towards a tightening of restrictions in these pressured rural areas, both within and outside the designated green belts. The North-East Lancashire plan (1980, 30), for example, categorically states that 'within the green belts planning permission will not be given, *except in very special circumstances* [author's italics] for the erection of new buildings'. Moreover, in the case of Kent where the structure-plan policy (1980) was modified by the Secretary of State to repeal the lists of settlements suitable for infilling (thus removing some of the county's power to restrict development), the first review of the structure plan includes a toughening of rural restraint policies to include all of the rural area. Thus green-belt-level restrictions are likely to be imposed over the whole of the rural county.

The policies within this category clearly place more emphasis on controlling the rate and location of new development than on the stabilization of rural services. However, in the final analysis service policies tend to be strongly linked with those for other development. Thus in areas such as Essex (1979) the strong service criteria which need to be satisfied before any rural growth will be permitted in a particular settlement tend to ensure that investment priority is concentrated into existing areas of rural population. These policies therefore proliferate the settlement rationalization trends found in less pressured areas, although in peri-urban areas planners are able to take 'comfort' that small settlements will be preserved through processes of gentrification.

Hierarchical restraint policies

Elsewhere in England and Wales, counties containing pressured rural areas have opted for a more hierarchical view of potential development within the general ambit of an overall restraint on growth. This can take the form of permitting limited general development in a series of small towns and villages (Central and North Lancashire, 1980a) or of selecting a limited number of settlements for development above the level of infilling, as was the case with the three selected villages in the East Sussex plan (1978). It is interesting to note, however, that the 1979 Review of the East Sussex policy subsumed the 'new development' and 'infilling' categories into one grouping, and indeed the bulk of policies adopting development hierarchies within an overall restraint strategy are those where green belt policies intervene.

A case of green-belt influence on rural settlement policy occurs in Hertfordshire (1979) where the ongoing structure plan review process has already led to modifications (1980). The county's stated policy is to 'retain a green belt extending over the whole of the rural county' (Policy 2) and so even though the metropolitan green belt is not designated to include all the county, similar levels of control are suggested for settlements both inside and outside the green belt. In the event this equality has not been strictly adhered to, with the adoption of a loose hierarchy for three levels of potential limited development:

1 The selection of twenty specified settlements for limited growth within the green belt;
2 The option to select settlements for growth to meet community needs beyond the green belt;
3 The option to identify large and small villages for the location of any development to meet community needs.

The interpretation of this hierarchy has proved troublesome to district councils and so the 1980 policy alterations have clarified that the third-level identification of large and small villages will relate only to *smaller* villages within the green belt if appropriate in local plans, and to *selected* villages beyond the green belt, again dependent upon local plan policies. This complexity of options stems from an acknowledgement of, and concern for, localized problems in Hertfordshire's rural communities, but it serves to demonstrate both the magnetism of significantly high restraint levels within green-belt areas, and the specific devolution of power over rural settlement planning to the district authorities, whose task in Hertfordshire is to interpret these policies, to assess community needs, and therefore to encourage and channel development where required.

In other policy categories, the handover of powers of settlement selection to district councils has often been at the prompting of the Secretary of State in his modifications to the structure plan. A particularly important example of these processes is shown by the Derbyshire policy (1980). As submitted, the plan's overall strategy for restraint of growth was tempered by a policy whereby. 'In some larger villages, small scale development within the existing built up area of the settlement may be allowed to meet the needs of local people, particularly provision of public sector housing' (Derbyshire CC, 1977a, 36). In addition it was considered necessary to state that: 'Consideration will be given, where appropriate, for limited infill housing development in certain smaller villages outside the main development pattern' (p. 36). This specific response to the existence of specific local needs was not translated into a list of settlements, although criteria and characteristics such as good accessibility, public utility and service capacities were suggested as being relevant to the settlement selection process. In the event, even these criteria were rejected by the Secretary of State and the resulting policy is a non-discriminating and ambiguous statement that development will be restricted to that which can be accommodated within the built-up framework. Just as other counties have sought to side-step such debilitating modifications, it seems likely that the rural settlement policy in Derbyshire will be closely reviewed during the monitoring stages.

A further interesting example of hierarchical restraint policies is afforded by Cheshire (1979) which has also been the subject of restrictive modifications from the Secretary of State which have served to:
1 Include a policy of general presumption against development in green belts;
2 Delete the lists of named villages lying within the green-belt area but which will not be subject to green-belt policies (inset villages);
3 Provide stricter control of development for employment purposes in inset villages.

The idea of inset villages (seen also in the Hertfordshire policy) was, where a local need existed, to give specific settlements limited development opportunities similar to those that were granted to non-green-belt settlements. The approved policy reduces the possibilities of active planning responses to employment problems in rural green-belt communities and submits the level and frequency of inset-village development to the political perceptions of the district councils. Inset villages also form part of the Surrey (1980) policy where the onus is again on district authorities to provide the impetus for any growth outside the normal presumption against development.

Oxfordshire County Council has attempted to impose rather stricter guidelines on district level decision-making than is the case in other policies in this category. The structure plan (1979) sets a ceiling figure on the overall amount of development per district and proposes that this limited amount of development in the rural areas should be used to meet local needs and to maintain existing services and infrastructure. A number of factors are laid down as relevant in the selection of a particular settlement for growth, and taking all these factors into account, the plan suggests that each rural settlement be placed by district councils in one of three categories:

1   Villages where no development will be permitted unless absolutely essential;
2   Towns and villages where development to meet local need only will be permitted;
3   Villages where some growth over and above local need might be permitted.

This attempt to impose strict conditions on district council planning decisions highlights the complex dualism which now exists between county and district authorities in rural settlement planning. In areas of blanket restraint this division of authority may be more easily brought into relative harmony, but where specific exceptions are to be made within an overall no-growth strategy, particularly where green-belt and non-green-belt areas are involved, the propensity for conflict between county and district objectives is exaggerated (especially with the trend of plan modifications from central government).

Special cases

Although the taxonomy used here constitutes only a loose framework for the analysis of rural structure-plan policies, particular facets of the strategies developed by various counties isolate them as worthy of special consideration. The five categories reviewed thus far have been firmly based on the resource concentration ethic, even though the level and degree of concentration vary between, and indeed among, policy types. This final category highlights instances of greatest movement *away* from the concentration ethic within structure plan policies for rural areas. This is not, however, to say that resource dispersal is the binding factor in these special policy cases, but rather that the degree of concentration is potentially reduced in some way or other.

An example of this wish to spread the benefits of rural investment is found in the submitted policy for Powys (1979). At first glance, the selection of 'area centres' in the county accords with traditional resource concentration methods. However, the idea behind these area centres is that those jobs which cannot be achieved in the rural areas themselves may be provided in a conveniently close town or village (termed accordingly the area centre). The encouragement of employment is thus *not* place-specific in the first instance, and the plan's aims and policies could be well satisfied if the bulk of development and investment occurred in settlements which have not been pre-selected. Similarly, policies for housing development allow development in unnamed settlements, even if the proposed development is linked to new jobs in area centres. Given this innate flexibility for the location of development in and around the designated area centres, the Powys policy breaks new ground towards the settlement cluster concept. In practice, however, many perceptual and decision-making barriers have to be broken down before investment agencies (such as the Development Board for Rural Wales – now Mid-Wales Development – whose policy is to concentrate effort in selected and sizeable rural locations) can be persuaded that the area centre is not the automatic choice for resource allocation in the area. Similarly, there remains a doubt as to whether settlements remote from area centres will be able to share any potential benefits. Nevertheless, the Powys policy is both innovative and appreciative of the problems to be found in smaller rural settlements and it remains to be seen whether policy implementation is able to translate these intentions into actions.

The dilemma between recognizing that selection and choice are integral parts of the planning process, and that the tiering of settlements recognizes the reality of functional differences between settlements, and wishing to avoid the artificial concentration of development and investment, is clearly shown in the case of the submitted Gloucestershire plan (1980). Here, twenty principal settlements are recognized as major growth centres, but additional residential development is permitted both in villages with a primary level of local community facilities and services and, to a lesser extent, in other villages where a specific local need is identified. This classification is designed to ensure a wide spread of development opportunity, with no spurious restriction of opportunity among the smaller settlements. For example a 'primary level' of services is interpreted as a school, post office and shop – a level that applies to many villages (this category is undefined, but probably over 100 villages are involved). In practice, even if one of these services is missing, a village is still able to qualify for development if such a service exists in an adjoining settlement. This practice marks the acceptance of village cluster ideas in the county. The 'other village' category does not incur a presumption against growth as would be the case in some key settlement type policies. Relatively high levels of county growth are allocated to village locations in the structure plan and so even the bottom tier of the classification is plentifully supplied.

This settlement system and the attitudes which accompany it make significant progress away from the previously rigid stereotype of rural settlement policy. There is, however, one further policy in Gloucestershire (also found to a certain extent in Gwynedd (1980; 1980a)) which offers a new form of policy response to rural problems:

> In areas of rural decline, particularly within the north and south Cotswolds, residential development will be encouraged in villages and groups of villages where additional housing can contribute to alleviating the causes of that

decline. The following factors will be used to identify the areas of rural decline where residential development will be encouraged:

A   An actual or threatened loss of important local community facilities and services, including schools, shops, post offices, public transport, health facilities and library services;

B   A static or declining population including a high proportion of elderly people;

C   An insufficient supply of appropriate housing to meet the needs of the local population; and

D   A rural area where the county council or district council proposes to promote employment opportunities.

(Gloucestershire CC, 1980, 38–9)

This policy is important because within the restricted options open to county planning authorities it represents a real effort to promote positive action in areas of need. The restricted options are relevant here because the policy relies on the ability of new housing inputs to revitalize an area where rural deprivation occurs. Although the plan also considers that all rural settlements have potential for some local employment growth, careful co-ordination of these policies will obviously be required, particularly in the prescribed areas of rural decline. The integration of various functional policies is made easier in this case by the support for village clusters:

> a single village may not have all the basic services and facilities considered necessary to serve the needs of both the existing and future populations, although a group of villages in proximity to each other may well do so. This [areas of rural decline] policy therefore requires that, in appropriate cases, village groups should be defined where housing, transport, community services and facilities and employment Policies can be integrated. It is considered that only through such an approach can the full benefit of the Policy be achieved. (Gloucestershire CC, 1980, 39)

The Gloucestershire plan as described here has yet to be approved by the Secretary of State, and the evidence of the North Yorkshire (1980) structure-plan process might suggest that modifications will be forthcoming. The preferred strategy in North Yorkshire was a redistribution of opportunity and development in favour of the less prosperous rural areas through specific policies for the scale and location of new housing development and the growth and distribution of employment. These policies included the identification of socio-economically cohesive village groups which alongside particular individual settlements would act as service centres for the less prosperous areas. The fact that the plan proposed a framework for a significant redirection of resources by the various agencies responsible for service provision in the rural areas generated some opposition to the policy, as did the uneven distribution of potential investment between districts. As a result, the outcome of the Examination in Public, and the government's now-predictable desire to enhance the district council powers of local planning, led the Secretary of State to eliminate the selective elements of the policy before granting his approval. Thus the teeth were removed from a potentially innovative policy and the outcome in rural areas is dependent upon local-plan implementation by district councils.

One final special case is also still in the 'intention' rather than 'action' stage. Structure-plan preparation in Cumbria forcefully proposed a policy of regeneration and remedial work in rural areas, including the promotion of further investment amongst groups of villages and the encouragement of local initiatives for self-help schemes. The submission of the Cumbria and Lake District Structure Plan (1980), however, came too soon for the completion of relevant survey work in rural areas. The rural policy included therein consists of a series of holding statements until the results are published of an investigation to 'determine whether future investment should be concentrated in key villages, dispersed more widely, or be distributed in some other way' (Cumbria CC and Lake District Special Planning Board, 1980, 55). Essentially, the feasibility and desirability of supplying a more dispersal-oriented policy is being scrutinized, and it is likely that policy innovations will result if this investigation supports the intentions outlined previously (Cumbria CC, 1976).

How much progress?

The degree to which these various written statements of policy intention constitute beneficial progress in rural settlement planning is difficult to assess without a concomitant view of how the policies are implemented at ground level. However two generalizations may be made. First, those rural areas under extreme urban pressure, often falling under the umbrella of green-belt legislation, do not show many indications of a redirection of policy away from the restriction and concentration of growth promoted in the development plans and towards more specific policy responses to problems encountered in rural communities. Although minor concessions have been made for small-scale infilling developments in small villages where a specific local need has been identified, these moves are more than offset by a general tightening of the overall restrictions on development in these areas. Second, in other areas the general adherence to classificatory settlement policies is tempered in many counties by some relaxation of previous presumptions against growth in small villages. In some cases this trend merely legitimizes the seemingly unstoppable trickle of permissions granted in small settlements for one reason or another. Elsewhere, there appears to be a genuine policy intention to allow small-scale developments to ease local housing conditions and to support existing services in the smaller villages. In the special cases mentioned above, this intention has been promoted up the batting order of policy intentions so that the emphasis of implementation is redirected towards encouragement of development in more needy settlements. Moreover, many counties appear to have rejected the traditional umbrella approaches to rural settlement planning in favour of a more flexible search for solutions (albeit limited) to problems experienced in specific places by individual communities. Trends such as these do represent an awareness of the socio-economic problems faced by small rural communities and mark the first faltering steps towards an intended shift of planning emphasis in favour of direct policy response. Many counties now recognize the potential offered by mobile services and small-scale rural employment, but recognition is an easier process than adoption or implementation. The overall resource constraints described in pp. 142–4 continue to restrict any initiatives involving public expenditure, and any reallocation of resources within the public-sector agencies at county level has been made more difficult by transferring to the district councils many of the important locational decisions with guide public resource allocation. The true worth of these apparent policy progressions, then, will only be known as the effectiveness of local planning both as an identifier of local need and as a co-ordinator of resource agencies becomes more clear.

Another method of assessing progress in British rural settlement planning is to compare developments with those occurring overseas. Although many nations continue to be characterized by an absence of effective planning controls (see Armstrong's (1976) account of French rural planning) there is some evidence that elsewhere the British planning system – for so long the doyen of developed countries – is being caught up and even overtaken in certain respects. Information exchange about rural planning in various parts of the developed world is sparse and unconsolidated, but several advances are becoming apparent (Moss, 1980). For example, rural planning in North America retains its reliance on zoning ordnances (see chapter 5), but in certain peri-urban areas, imitations of British-style village classifications have been produced. The plan for Ottawa–Carleton (Regional Municipality of Ottawa–Carleton, 1974), for example, selects certain villages to accommodate future population increases in the rural area, and aims to restrict growth in other rural settlements which are usually those which are less well serviced. This rather rudimentary system heralds the beginnings of comprehensive resource concentration akin to the development plans in Britain.

Grafton (1980) reports on the experience of rural planning in Switzerland, where a policy of *dezentralisierte Konzentration* has established a number of rural growth centres including twenty-one of population sizes between 1000 and 5000, where services and employment are encouraged. He notes (p. 4) that:

> in stark contrast to the situation in Britain, it is accepted that one of the crucial determinants of the quality of a service is the degree of access to it. Hence the improvement of accessibility by both public and private transport to the regional centre from its hinterland is seen as a vitally important complementary policy to that of concentrating resources in the chosen centres.

The Swiss emphasis on providing accessibility from the rural hinterland to selected centres highlights one of the major weaknesses of resource concentration in rural Britain, although the difference between stated policy and implemented policy is stressed in Grafton's conclusion (p. 22) that:

> Theoretically, the policies . . . appear highly decentralized and highly attuned to the local social and cultural fabric. In practice, however, the reliance on the free-market mechanism produces outcomes not always in keeping with planning aims.

One of the options offered by political theory (chapter 3) for more socially just systems of resource allocation and distribution is that of increasing public control over investment. The example of Hungary (Moseley and Smith, 1979) indicates a rural planning system which is used explicitly as a means of redistributing resources between people and areas. Just as in more mixed economies, however, socialist ideals of equality are frequently compromized by economic reality. In Hungary rural infrastructural services receive less subsidy than their urban counterparts and so with, for example, electricity and transport being more expensive in the country, new investment is largely channelled into selected rural centres which serve surrounding settlements. The centralized socialist system appears to be strong on regional planning but less exemplary on local aspects of development co-ordination and control.

Other areas of a more positive form of rural planning are evident in Scandinavian nations. Green (1977) notes that Norwegian planning codes make a firm distinction between rural development concerned with indigenous inhabitants living and working in rural areas and that connected with long-distance commuting, holiday homes and the leisure market. There is a strong parallel here with the rather ubiquitous concession made towards small developments for 'local needs' in non-selected settlements under the British structure-plan system. A further instance of Scandinavian directness and positive attitudes towards rural rejuvenation is shown in the subsidies offered by the governments of Finland, Norway and Sweden to improve the viability of small rural shops (Ekhaugen *et al.*, 1980).

In these and other examples, individual elements of rural planning may be seen as comparable or more advanced than the British structure-plan system. The main difference, however, is the comprehensive coverage of British planning in one form or another. Tilling's (1980, 19) description of rural planning in New Zealand emphasizes the problems to be found elsewhere:

> Planning is beset with a multitude of uncoordinated, overlapping government departments, organizations and local authorities. The mechanisms to resolve the inevitable conflicts within and between these departments and organizations do not work efficiently. The structure and responsibilities of these bodies are long overdue for reform.

The formulation of British structure plans has shown that an efficient system of land-use control is available in Britain. There is a suspicion, however, that an over-emphasis on tightening up the *organizational* deficiencies of the previous development-planning era has led to rural planners missing the boat so far as *positive social* planning in rural communities is concerned. If British rural planning is not to be overtaken by its overseas counterpart, planners need to use their roles of co-ordination and persuasion to induce positive action from resource allocation agencies with responsibilities for rural communities. Such a task may be aided by a further review of rural planning frameworks for resource concentration and dispersal (chapter 7) or by widening the scope of current policy implementation processes (chapters 9 and 10).

SEVEN

Establishing a policy framework

Key settlement policies

Chapters 5 and 6 have demonstrated that post-war rural settlement planning in Britain has been dominated by the use of concentration policies (particularly of the key settlement type) as frameworks for resource allocation. The key settlement concept has been the subject of detailed analysis elsewhere (Cloke, 1979; Martin and Vorhees Associates, 1981) but it is important in this context to highlight various salient features of this form of rural settlement planning in order to provide a foundation or viable and useful comparisons which alternative policy proposals.

The conception of the key settlement type of policy can be traced back to two far-sighted personalities of the inter-war and immediate post-war period. Harold Peake provided the academic germ for key settlements at the end of the First World War. He was foremost in campaigning for a structured planning policy for rural settlements at a time when village planning was given little priority in national affairs. In particular, he directed attention towards both the creation of rural settlements of sufficient size to overcome service thresholds (Peake, 1922), and the necessity for regional-scale rather than local-scale management of rural areas (Peake, 1916–18). Peake's contribution to the history of rural settlement planning is considerable. He prophesied the changes which were to occur in rural areas, and he outlined a form of planning action whereby rural imbalances could be accommodated gradually on a day-to-day basis rather than in retrospect.

Peake's visions of the future were granted practical expression by Henry Morris, who as Chief Education Officer for Cambridgeshire from 1922 to 1952 was in a position to implement a policy of resource concentration in the provision of educational services. He believed that 'the village has ceased to be an independent social unit' (Morris, 1942, 18) and that 'the only alternative to the complete subordination of the countryside to the town is the adoption of the rural region as a cultural and social unit' (p. 19). Accordingly he instigated the concept of the 'village college' (Morris, 1925) which was to be the centralized secondary school for a number of contributory villages by day, and a social and cultural centre for residents of the surrounding area outside school hours. This initiative to provide centrally located focal points for rural areas was a precursor to the broadened key settlement concept.

It is important to note that both Peake and Morris envisaged a strong *social* orientation for resource concentration policies, with a definite emphasis on using rural centres to service outlying villages. However this social component became diminished as the key settlement idea was adopted by county planning authorities in the impressionable period of the early 1950s. At this time, key settlement policies were regarded as a planning panacea for the physical and economic ills of the countryside (Cloke, 1980a; 1981a). Remoter areas were seen to benefit from a planned concentration of housing, services and employment, if only because of the consequent economies of scale and retention of service thresholds. Equally, a successful centralizing policy in pressured areas was seen as a mechanism to ensure the conservation of settlements whose environmental quality was such that further large-scale growth would be inappropriate. The wish to achieve these advantages, when allied with the perceived need for policies of economic and administrative expediency, led to the widespread use of key settlement policies in rural planning.

More recently, a body of professional opinion has condemned the key settlement approach as short-sighted and prejudicial to the long-term health and stability of rural settlements. The substance of these criticisms may briefly be reviewed under a series of functional headings.

The theoretical argument: key settlement policies have no theoretical basis

An enigmatic and indistinct relationship exists between so-called 'theoretical' arguments and other, more practical, *raisons d'être* for key settlement approaches to rural planning (Cloke, 1980). On the one hand, theory and practice have been inextricably linked in the formulation of key settlement policies by planners in some counties (for example Bracey's use of central-place theory in Somerset). On the other hand, most professional planners and planning committee members would agree that their views on planning policy options are not governed by seemingly esoteric theory, but rather on the more realistic matters of economics and the social consequences of resource allocation.

Given this complex dualism, it does appear that key settlement policies were originally introduced simply as a convenient blueprint at a time when planners were searching for a definitive and innovative policy with which to demonstrate to all concerned that rural problems were being tackled. Thus the development of an industrial estate and new housing estates in key settlements constituted visible signs of rural planning in action, and this high public profile was one of the major reasons for adopting strategies of resource concentration. As a result, there is a strong suspicion that the subsequent conceptualization of key settlements has been a cosmetic justification for a policy created merely out of economic expediency and administrative pragmatism. Theoretical justifications for key settlements should be viewed against the background of this intricate historical relationship.

The search for a conceptual approach to key settlements has led to the amalgamation of a wide range of socio-political, economic and spatial theory as justification for this approach to rural settlement planning. On the left of the political spectrum, the inevitability of eliminating social, economic and cultural differences between town and countryside by rationalizing rural settlement patterns has been strongly argued by Marx, Engels and Lenin. On the right, the free-market political theorists (see Turner and Collins, 1977) would appear to support a non-interventionist policy of decision-making in the market place which would manifest a similar trend of scale-orientated selectivity in the rural settlement pattern. Between these two extremes, followers of the more liberal approaches to geography and planning (see Smith, 1977) have argued that one potential method of supplying welfare opportunities to rural residents in small villages is to ensure accessibility links between these villages and sizeable rural service centres (Cloke, 1977a).

Given this broad range of political theory which has been manipulated in support of key settlements, several more specific questions remain to be answered before the approach may be deemed justified in theoretical terms. For example, the inherent contradiction between key settlements acting contiguously as both *provider for* and *destroyer of* small villages has been tackled by adopting the precepts of growth-pole and centre theory (see chapter 3) which illustrate two opposing forces governing the movement of economic prosperity. First, *backwash* forces, where central nodes attract factors of production from their surrounding areas, has been used as an analogue model for pressured rural areas where economic and population overspill needs to be controlled and channelled into suitable reception centres. Similarly, *spread* forces, which describe the transmission of economic prosperity from centre to periphery, have been used to model the remoter rural situation.

However, the implementation of backwash and spread effects has been problematic in rural planning, and research (notably by Moseley, 1974) has shown that growth-centre attributes have little effect on settlements of less than 13,000 population – a size not attained by most key settlements. Central-place theory has also been invoked to justify the reinforcement of 'natural' service centres in the countryside, but as was demonstrated in chapter 3, the concepts of thresholds and ranges tend to be evaluated using economic rather than spatial or social criteria.

Such evidence as there is suggests that support for key settlement policies has been hidden behind a rather hastily erected facade of theorization. In consequence, any attempt to establish a policy framework for the future planning of rural settlements might do better to concentrate on the more telling economic, social and political arguments which constitute rather more practical considerations in the continuing use of key settlement policies.

The economic argument: key settlement policies are not the most cost-effective mechanism for rural resource allocation

The traditional wisdom embodied by the key settlement concept is that economies of scale exist in the development in key settlements of large centralized resources (such as schools, housing estates, sewerage systems) but are lost in small-scale equivalent developments dispersed between a greater number of villages. For example, Ayton (1980, 99) argues that:

selective settlement policies are the only practical means in which fixed services and infrastructure can sensibly be maintained or provided in rural areas and by which the effects of 'run-down' caused by fundamental economic and social changes can be, at least partly, offset.

However, this conventional wisdom is now being effectively challenged by critics of the key settlement concept. For example, Gilder (1980) points out that many of the economic truisms underlying resource concentration policies can be contested. Although admitting that economies of scale in the provision of public services do occur in the case of individual fixed services such as schools, he suggests that only a few services concur with traditional notions of scale economies. Moreover, when the cost curves of several rural services are amalgamated, no relationship is evident between the size of settlement and the cost of service provision. This apparent absence of scale economies for services in rural settlements is in part explained by the non-existence of distinct population thresholds for particular services (again contravening traditional rural planning wisdom). It has been argued that resource concentration policies are far from the only practical means of providing fixed services and infrastructure in rural areas, and that key settlement economics have been grossly oversimplified.

This polarization of opinion is not easily unravelled. One investigative route is to undertake comparative economic evaluations of settlement policy frameworks (see pp. 183–9). Another more tangential but still important route is to survey the evidence presented by the use of key settlement policies in various counties. After all, it has been noted above that ever since the initiation of key settlement policies, planning practitioners have been pre-occupied by the economic and physical aspects of their work and we would therefore expect considerable achievements from the key settlement policy from the economic point of view.

Case studies in Devon and Warwickshire (Cloke, 1979) suggest that, by and large, the co-ordination of residential and employment growth in centres where services and infrastructure have been provided do represent a significant achievement in rural settlement planning. The economic priority given to key settlements has ensured that a majority of rural residents now enjoy urban standards of infrastructure provision. The concentrated effort of house-building and establishing industrial estates in selected centres has meant that some success has also been achieved in ensuring that rural people have an opportunity to live and work in the rural milieu rather than migrating to higher-order urban centres. The provision of health centres and other public services, along with the retention of private-sector retail and service outlets in key settlements have also created some degree of economic vitality in the rural settlement pattern. Thus it seems fair to accept Woodruffe's (1976, 26) conclusion that 'many village groups have benefited from the improved facilities and amenities that have so far been constructed in the key settlements'.

However, the apparently simple and expedient planning task of concentrating resources into key settlements has itself suffered a number of drawbacks. For example the economic priorities expressed by planners have not always coincided with those expressed by agencies governing the provision of public services such as water, education, health and highways, with the result that the planned development of key settlements has sometimes been delayed or even halted due to the lack of school, sewerage or bypass facilities. Another failing of key settlement implementation concerns the planners' ability to restrict house-building in non-key settlements, especially where infrastructural capacity exists and where an impetus for growth has been established under previous policies. This trend might be seen to represent a sympathetic response to social need in specific villages, but is more likely to be brought about by economic pressure from developers and potential middle class in-migrants. Moreover, key settlement protagonists would generally argue that:

> Although concentration and selection would need to be backed by programmes to maintain reasonable social services in settlements not selected . . . it would not seem sensible to accept development where it would add to the numbers of people in the smaller villages who would have to depend on such services, imposing extra cost to receive a lower level of service. (Ayton, 1976, 67)

Two reactions arise from these problems with the economic implementation of key settlement policies. First, the key settlement strategy is relatively straightforward in that the location of growth is largely predetermined. If problems of co-ordination between resource agencies occur in such a simple locational system, how much more difficult would co-ordination be within a more complex dispersal of growth over several rural locations? Second, any failure of policy implementation brought about by economic pressure rather than as a specific response to social need, rather devalues the idea of an overall resource location strategy for rural settlements. In fact these reactions are not as simple as they might appear. As the processes of co-ordination and implementation are improved, the economic limitations for rural policy frameworks are relaxed. Indeed, technological and political change affecting rural service provision could also alter the economic basis of rural settlement planning, and so past and present economic conditions should be viewed within the bounds of current administrative and technical levels which may change at any given time in the future. As usual in rural settlement planning, many questions remain unanswered. Key settlements have shown some evidence for the success of resource concentration economics. However, there is no proof that such achievements could not have been bettered by a more relaxed framework policy. The simple answer is that conditions vary in different rural areas, and scale economies may therefore be more applicable given certain sets of circumstances than elsewhere. This conclusion is important in the interpretation of economic policy evaluations outlined on pp. 183–9. It is also crucial that the social costs of rural planning policies be taken into account in any overall economic evaluation. The less obvious costs caused by opportunity deprivation in small villages, and the intangible benefits of living in a rural environment, with accompanying low rates of crime, and family break-up, all have to be recognized within the economic arguments concerning key settlement policies.

The social argument: key settlement policies exacerbate social problems encountered by many rural residents

McLaughlin (1976a, 56) provides a succinct summary of the perceived results of key settlement policies. He describes a situation

> where an increasing number of people, particularly the non-mobile, are faced with the choice of either moving to the key village or staying behind to suffer increasing social deprivation, as transport services, employment opportunities, and social, educational and commercial services withdraw to the relative security of the key village.

A similar conclusion is reached by Rawson (1981, 9) who considers that 'the policy has been powerless to mitigate the social problems which characterize most of the remoter parts of rural Britain'. Once again, evidence from detailed case studies of the key settlement policies of Warwickshire and Devon (Cloke, 1979) may be summarized here to highlight the social issues raised by key settlement planning. In both counties it was evident that the concentration of resources into selected centres has not been complemented by the establishment of linkages between key settlements and hinterland villages. For example, public transport in both case studies proved hopelessly inadequate for the basic needs of non-mobile groups living in small rural settlements. Thus the concentration of services and facilities in key settlements without concern for hinterland transport links does appear to have exacerbated the plight of the non-mobile population in small villages. Even so it is doubtful whether the need for periphery–centre transport links would be disposed of under a policy of resource dispersal, and it would therefore appear that whatever framework is selected for the planning of rural settlements, a solution to the problems caused by rural inaccessibility will remain a vital issue in the successful implementation of settlement policies.

Employment problems have also persisted under key settlement policies. In Devon, for example, new employment has mainly been guided into the larger market towns and to a lesser extent the key settlements. Although some success was achieved in the 1960s and 1970s in attracting employment to the rural areas, it is noticeable that the city-based regions of Exeter and Plymouth have creamed off the major in-migrant sources of employment, while the concerns guided into rural centres have been of a much smaller nature. Therefore the impact of key settlements in the provision of new rural employment has often been limited. At an even lower level, criticism has arisen from the planners' reluctance to allow small-scale workshop enterprises to locate in non-key settlements because of their overriding preference to channel all new employers into the key settlement industrial estates. Again the incidence of this trend varies from area to area, but it is clear that the *attraction* of employers is one vital element of the problem which cannot be attained by framework policies. Specific policies within the locational framework strategy are required for this task.

In the housing sector, key settlement policies have been criticized for concentrating low-cost owner-occupied and rented housing into selected centres while failing to provide similar housing opportunities for the local needs of low-income groups in non-key settlements. In this way, planners have in some cases created an exaggerated breed of rural housing problems in small settlements. Some young families have been forced to migrate to key settlements or urban areas, while processes of gentrification have led to social polarization in favour of higher-income groups in small villages. This type of policy-induced deprivation in non-key settlements has occurred but is not universal. In some cases, planners have been unable to prevent housing development in small villages, and elsewhere a sympathetic implementation of a key settlement policy has permitted small amounts of housing in non-key settlements to cater for local need. However, special policies are required in these situations to ensure that permitted housing is suitable for local people rather than taking the form of expensive, (and therefore profitable) luxury housing which developers prefer.

A further social issue arises from the fact that key settlement policies have coincided with a continued decline in the level of services and facilities in rural areas. Critics of key settlement strategies view them as a major contributory factor to the continuing demise of service levels, particularly in small villages, while protagonists suggest that service decline is a 'natural' response to underlying socio-economic structures and that resource concentration is able partly to offset the dire consequences of these natural processes. Again it is clear that although planners have channelled new services into key settlements and thus inherently prevented the improvement of local services in non-selected villages (Cloke, 1981; 1981a), the nub of the problem lies not with the planning framework policy but with the need for *specific initiatives* to improve service levels (or accessibility to services). All framework policies will be handicapped without such initiatives.

The positive social contributions of key settlement policies (such as the retardment of depopulation in some areas, and the conservation of environmentally fragile villages elsewhere) have thus been counteracted by an apparent exacerbation of a wide range of social problems in small rural settlements. Unfortunately our current state of understanding of these matters does not permit a definitive answer to two important questions in this context. First, to what extent are these various social problems actually *induced* by the use of key settlement strategies? Research evidence suggests that the link between policy and problem is *indirect* rather than direct (see chapters 2 and 5). Second, can any alternative framework policy create conditions which are more conducive to the successful establishment of specific policies with which to tackle the specific problems of accessibility, housing, employment and services? The success of social planning in rural areas largely depends on a better understanding of these two issues.

The political planning argument: key settlement policies are a politically unworkable planning technique

The social, economic and theoretical aspects of key settlement policies have received the bulk of attention from the critics of the technique, but it is also important to examine the policies' performance within the post-war political planning framework. If the key settlement concept suffers from intrinsic faults which inevitably lead to social problems for rural dwellers then a more acceptable alternative framework should be found on which to base the planning of rural settlements. However, if the social and economic ineffectiveness of key settlements has been at least partly due to deficient policy implementation and co-operation then, if these shortcomings are rectified, policies of resource concentration could still be important in rural planning.

A close look at the operation of key settlement policies in various counties over the years reveals several crucial weaknesses. The high opinion in which key settlements were held during the 1950s and 1960s led to expectations of almost instant results, regardless of the supplementary policies needed to achieve these results. Early key settlement planning suffered from inexperience and misunderstanding of the rural environment, but greater experience and expertise have brought improved co-ordination of planning tasks. In addition, the initial procedures for selecting key centres in many counties were at best sub-optimum and at worst subject to considerable political pressures, from both influential groups and individuals. Apart from these historical reasons for ineptitude, there are two other reasons for the continuing failure of the key settlement policy to respond to changing social and economic circumstances. First, planners have not been able to adhere to planning strategies in the day-to-day decisions which are the basic task of rural land-use control. Second, the scope of rural planning has not been sufficiently broad to deal with problems of transport, housing, employment and services.

In many ways, failure to keep to overall policy directions is understandable, given the British planning system. The alternation of free enterprise with socialist ideals within planning committees may well have interrupted the long-term application of key settlement policies in some areas, and the often troubled relationship between district and county levels of planning has also contributed to the defiance of a given planning policy. These administrative and political hazards can disrupt even an unidirectional policy, but where discretionary flexibility is possible, for example over housing development in non-key settlements, the different levels of planning often disagree, to the detriment of the policy as a whole.

In addition to these problems of co-ordination and co-operation, there is general recognition that the scope of rural planning is too narrow to deal effectively with countryside problems. The reliance on restrictive rather than positive rural planning has kept vital stages in developing key settlements and the spreading of opportunities to their hinterlands out of present planning systems. To fulfil its true potential, the key settlement policy should be supplemented by specific positive policies to combat specific problems. Transport and peripatetic service links between key settlement and hinterland need a positive impetus from planning authorities. The establishment of suitable small-scale housing projects and workshop employment also demands policies of attraction rather than mere permission should any application arise. There have recently been isolated cases of such positive planning, but tough financial and administrative barriers still prevent a co-ordinated approach to rural planning.

Given the constraints within which planners have been working, some overall merit may be recognized in their use of key settlement policies. Tangible indicators of growth have been nurtured in remoter key settlements and considerable steps towards conserving certain rural environments have been taken in the more pressured areas. However, planning priority to date has been directed mainly to problems of the past and the present, and when the whole *future* of rural settlement planning is under debate it would be unwise to continue key settlement planning without regard to its shortcomings, both intrinsic and implementative. It is particularly important to recognize that, despite some relative successes in some areas, key settlement policies may not be a viable planning mechanism in other rural areas where specific spatial and social problems occur. Therefore, before conclusions are reached as to what is and what is not an acceptable policy framework for rural areas it is necessary to consider the various alternative policies which have been proposed as successors to the key settlement concept.

Alternative framework policies

In view of the almost unquestioned support for key settlement policies during the 1950s and 1960s, it was perhaps not surprising that the tide of critical opinion should turn against the concept in the following decade. It is an almost institutional reaction for planning commentators to be visibly antagonistic towards current policy conventions for fear of their commentary being branded as sycophantic and unthinking. The trend of rural planning thought has been no exception, as witnessed by the stream of key settlement disapproval which has flowed across the pages of rural planning texts and journals. Indeed, the situation has now been reached whereby the traditional blind faith in the key settlement approach has been replaced by an equally benighted reliance on any policy with avoids key settlement philosophy or nomenclature. It would, however, be superficial to brand key settlement critics as mere reactionaries. The desire to improve on the situation brought about through resource concentration stems largely from both a deeper understanding of the complex social, economic and political systems of which the countryside is a part, and a heartfelt desire to provide greater benefits and opportunities for disadvantaged rural people. As a consequence a series of alternative concepts has been proposed which might replace key settlements as the dominant framework strategy for rural areas. These alternatives may be reviewed individually, although as figure 7.1 demonstrates, they may be placed on a form of continuum between the opposing attributes of resource concentration and resource dispersal.

Greater resource concentration

It should not be forgotten that a significant body of opinion lends itself to the

Figure 7.1 Alternative rural settlement strategies

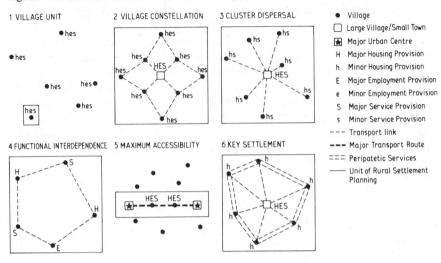

Source: Cloke, 1979, 219

view that the establishment of rural key settlements as small-scale growth centres does not take the ethic of resource concentration sufficiently far. Although alternative rural settlement planning policies in the British context have favoured a greater degree of resource dispersal, many European nations have adopted an opposite tendency which finds some sympathy from right-wing political factions in Britain. After all, belief in a free-market economy might well be logically extended into a policy of allowing market forces to run their course in rural areas. In this fashion, rural services would be supplied from profitable locations, and small rural settlements would receive even fewer resources than at present. It should be stressed that no mainstream political party in Britain has yet openly suggested that rural areas be abandoned in this manner, although the suggestion is commonly made by (usually highly affluent) individuals in the rural context. In some ways, rural settlement planning in Britain has already travelled some little way along this road of rural settlement abandonment. Elsewhere in Europe, stronger initiatives have been taken in this direction. Darley (1978, 303) reports that:

the French, dealing with a particularly vast problem of rural depopulation – both in numerical and geographical senses – have left many outlying settlements to the natural processes of disintegration and atrophy. Areas such as the South-West, south of the Dordogne, have traditionally farmed in small units – on a scale roughly comparable to Mid Wales. Now the hamlets are frequently entirely deserted, though sometimes a house has been restored for a second home, while the villages are shrinking or, at most, remain stable.

If rural settlement planning (in the broadest senses of these words) fails to provide public services for rural residents, and guide private sector resources into rural areas, this end result of rural desertion may act as a model for the future state of rural areas in Britain. In this manner, rural dwellers would become self-sufficient and therefore a seemingly efficient planning system would evolve. But, at the same time the opportunity to live in these rural environments would be restricted to those sectors of society whose personal resources enabled them to purchase their self-sufficiency or accessibility to urban services and facilities. As yet, Britain is not ready to grant overt political sanction to this extreme form of class division in the countryside.

A slightly 'softer' approach to the strengthening of resource concentration policies for rural areas is offered by the German model of *maximum accessibility*, which, as the name suggests, highlights the importance of public transport services in rural areas. In essence, this form of policy divides rural areas into viable and unviable settlements according to whether they are located on or near the seemingly permanent transport routes between urban centres. Settlements with favourable locations continue to receive public investment and are scheduled for future growth, while support for the remainder is withdrawn as part of a positive rationalization process. Although the linearity of this model is more suited to valley-dominated rural areas in upland situations, it does represent an alternative policy for parts of rural Britain, and is attractive to policy analysts striving for greater economic efficiency in rural planning. By these means, public support could be maintained in accessible components of the settlement pattern (where such support can be linked with easy accessibility to higher-order facilities and is therefore relatively inexpensive) and only the more remote (and thus more expensive) villages are surrendered to gentrification processes. There are, in fact, many parallels between the maximum accessibility approach and current British rural settlement planning; the main difference being that some settlements currently selected for growth (particularly in remoter areas) are not blessed with good public transport routes. Certainly, if future planning of rural areas is to be based on the social needs of rural residents, the overall planning strategy should not be controlled by the whims of public transport service operators. Rather, such services should be tailored to meet the needs of rural communities wherever they are located.

Greater resource dispersal

The majority of proposals for alternative policy frameworks have arisen out of criticism of key settlement policies on the grounds that they do not permit sufficient resources in non-key settlements. Therefore the balance of opinion has been firmly tipped in favour of framework policies which permit a greater dispersal of resources to small settlements. These proposals take many forms.

The village unit

The village unit concept stems from the belief that people who live and work in the countryside have a right to the continuation and proper functioning of their village. This desire for village viability stems from two main philosophies. First, many people retain a folk image of the countryside which incorporates the view of villages as an essential part of man's natural environment which must be preserved from the interference of twentieth-century urbanization. This back-to-nature philosophy is shown by Burton (1973, 185) who describes the village unit as 'the type of community that for well over 1000 years was unquestioningly accepted as man's "natural" home'. Second, the Schumacher philosophy of 'small is beautiful' suggesting that economics and planning should be studied 'as if people matter', has attracted considerable support from both traditional and adventitious rural residents. Although it is simple to discard the former philosophy as rampant idealism, and the latter as economically unsound, a great deal of public pressure is generated over village issues, and if this were ever organized into a coherent national lobby for the retention of the village as a planning concept, then rural settlement planning might have to rethink the role of the village in late twentieth-century society.

The concept of the individual village's role in the community, and the minimum of facilities and services required *in situ* for that role to be performed are issues which have only been outlined in a vague manner. For example, Peel and Sayer (1973) suggest that a village must have:

1 Adequate accommodation;
2 A church, a sub post office, a shop and a public house;
3 A village, hall;
4 Wherever possible a school;
5 An adequate water supply and methods of waste disposal;

and admit that 'clearly with the pressures that exist today, these components of the unit will not survive or be brought back into existence without a definite policy' (p. 2). This definite policy would, in fact, require several interacting components. Small villages would need a certain amount of housing development which should be carefully managed so as to meet the needs of local people. Public transport services would need to be maintained and enhanced by low-cost accessibility schemes. Infrastructural services, either on mains systems or at a smaller scale (such as septic tank sanitation) would need to be provided so that future growth was permissible. Perhaps most difficult of all, services and employment would have to be enticed back to small villages. Community action or public subsidy might provide a minimum service base when supplemented by mobile facilities and peripatetic professional services. Employment might stem from a new pattern of rural industry whereby both small-scale modern industries and revived craft industries would be attracted into villages to supplement the jobs accruing from a more labour-intensive form of agriculture (Venner, 1976).

It is easy to agree with MacGregor (1976, 524) that 'it is doubtful if the village has ever been a self-sufficient unit in social or economic terms', and therefore presume that attempts to restore the village as a viable unit of planning are impracticable and politically and economically naïve, but if villages are adopted as being socially necessary (as is argued by the Council for the Protection of Rural England (CPRE)) then the political and economic practicalities of re-establishing each and every village may well become the priority task for the positive social planning of rural areas in the future.

New villages/rural resettlement

Closely allied to the village unit concept are alternative policy proposals for the establishment of new villages, either on greenfield sites or as refurbishment of previously settled locations. Such proposals are obviously location-specific, and therefore represent partial rather than holistic framework strategies for rural settlement planning. Nevertheless, it is possible to envisage the majority of new developments in pressured areas being centralized into new purpose-built and well-serviced settlements, thereby conserving environmentally attractive villages whilst continuing to provide adequate levels of services and facilities in the area. Similarly communities in all types of rural area might benefit from the creation of largely self-sufficient villages through the resettlement process. Thus this group of policy alternatives is potentially capable of playing a significant role in the future of rural planning.

Experiments in rural resettlement have already begun to appear. Darley (1978) describes the situation in the village of Papworth St Agnes in Cambridgeshire which had become almost entirely deserted and derelict but which in recent years has been revived by piecemeal building and restoration. Hancock (1976; 1976a) presents evidence of participant observation in two such schemes. The Park Hall Army Camp (Shropshire) plan to build a craft-based garden village on the site of old barrack buildings was defeated by a single vote on the county planning committee. It was hoped that a combination of agriculture, horticulture, purpose-built retail facilities and craft industry would create a relatively self-sufficient village unit where experiments with alternative technology might be carried out to achieve a low energy form of rural living. The Dartington Cluster scheme (Devon) is also based on low-cost housing and alternative energy sources. In this case it is hoped to complement the existing village and surrounding hamlets with partially self-contained clusters of housing with associated workshops, nursery school, community centre and plots of land for small-scale agricultural production. Neither of these imaginative schemes has yet been approved by the local planning authority, and the reluctance of political decision-makers to give positive support to resettlement schemes is further demonstrated by Smigielski's (1978) failure to convince the local planning authority that his plan for a self-supporting co-operative village in Stanford Hall was worthy of planning permission.

Despite the relatively unsuccessful nature of these experiments, their inherent worth should not be underemphasized, and indeed a specific pressure group – the Rural Resettlement Group – now acts strongly on behalf of these concepts:

> the Rural Resettlement Group . . . has found a wide range of professionals, as well as those wishing to take practical steps towards living in the countryside, interested in the practical steps towards achieving these aims and

wishing for information and supportive evidence of activity in this area. Plainly it is unrealistic to dismiss the inclinations of very considerable numbers of people and the underlying motive behind their wishes to settle in the countryside. (Darley, 1978, 309)

The importance of this group and of the concept it represents has not received the attention it deserves as a vital component in the future of rural settlement planning. It is quite possible to foresee the establishment of many such schemes in rural areas where suitable conditions and suitable demand prevail.

Experiments in building new villages on greenfield sites have been more successful in receiving the recognition and backing of planners and politicians. The best known examples are New Ash Green (Kent) and Bar Hill (Cambridgeshire) which on the surface have successfully achieved the accommodation of commuter pressure without the despoilation of existing villages. Indeed, the actual development of houses, shops, a school, a health centre and (in Bar Hill) an industrial estate has received critical acclaim. However, Moss (1978) poses several fundamental questions concerning the Bar Hill project in particular:

1   Why was public and private investment on this scale put into a new village rather than into existing villages where houses and essential facilities were lacking?
2   Why should 200 acres of agricultural land be used up on a needless project?
3   Why build luxury properies and market them through exclusive estate agents in London thereby 'transferring urban ideals into the countryside'?
4   Why was provision not made for agricultural workers in the new village?
Moss concludes (p. 112) that:

the type of village resident would increase the cost of living in the area. Its industries would attract employees from outlying villages, would be generally harmful to existing rural industry and its labour requirements and create commuting between Bar Hill and outlying villages.

Clearly, not all new villages serve to enhance the opportunities available to local residents, and care should be taken to select a suitable context for any new village scheme. With this caveat, there would appear to be considerable scope in the concept of new or refurbished settlements as focal points for future patterns of rural settlement planning.

The village constellation

Although the re-establishment of viable villages in one way or another constitutes one major area of rural settlement reform through resource dispersal, there remains the task of constructing a framework policy within which resource dispersal can act to greater effect than was the case with key settlement policies. Three alternative frameworks have been proposed, although they are not mutually exclusive nor have they benefited from a period of planned implementation during which time the exact details of the proposals could have been worked out. Nevertheless, each is worthy of close attention as a potential future framework for rural settlement planning. The village constellation concept is founded on the linking together of small rural settlements so that services and facilities are shared on a communal basis. Hancock (1976a), for example, argues for the abandonment of key settlements and other settlement classification policies in favour of a planning framework based on groups of settlements which are interrelated both to city regions and to small towns and villages. Once these constellations are recognized the provision of social and infrastructural facilities should be made within these groups of settlements and should involve co-operative enterprise and voluntary effort as well as public support.

The appeal of the village constellation is largely dependent on the potential ability of planners to recognize functionally linked settlements. This ability has been noticeably lacking in the establishment of many key settlement policies where the arrangement of selected centres and hinterland villages was often not conducive to the development of centre–periphery linkages. As a consequence, functional boundaries for the spatial delimitation of rural settlement planning often and had little meaning when translated on the ground. A constellation approach would place much greater emphasis on the acknowledgement of existing interrelationships and wherever possible would seek to use these 'natural' patterns as a basis for the provision of housing, employment, services and community transport schemes. An integral part of this system would be for each constellation to form a unit for local political representation through strengthened parish or neighbourhood councils.

In theory, a series of settlements interlinked into a form of constellation does offer some practical advantages in comparison with the superimposition of key and non-key categorizations. However, the extent to which this alternative strategy could be successfully implemented is closely linked with the cost of providing statutory services to every village. Hancock (1976, 523) suggests that 'the broad concept of a varied constellation of villages in rural areas would be helped by the rapid development of appropriate technology for sewage disposal and, possibly, energy supply'. These developments certainly would add a degree of practicality to the constellation concept, as indeed they would to all resource dispersal options. Even without such technological advances, village constellations might appear attractive to planners in their search for a more socially oriented rural planning strategy, and certainly warrant further detailed and serious investigation and evaluation.

Cluster–dispersal

One realistic alternative to the dispersal of a minimum resource base to every individual village was proposed by Parry Lewis in his study of the Cambridge sub-region (Department of the Environment, 1974). He recognized the social advantages of a dispersed pattern of investment through which the inherent privileges granted to key settlements could be broken down. Accordingly, two potential strategies were developed for rural settlements around Cambridge (excluding the inner ring of villages which were considered to have expanded to physical and social capacity). First, a dispersal approach was attempted whereby new development was spread as widely as possible throughout the sub-region. However, even with the objective of dispersal in mind, only twenty settlements were zoned to receive moderate or major development with minor growth detailed for a further twenty-three locations. Sixty-four other settlements were to receive growth restriction under this strategy. In essence, the dispersal option represented a compromise between a theoretical obejective of scattered resources, and the current economic and political realism which ensured that growth could not, in fact, be supported in every village.

Parry Lewis's second approach, therefore, was based on the supposition that clusters of villages would represent a combined population sufficient for the attraction of central service facilities and public and private investment. In this way, villages could share dispersed facilities within a clustered planning unit which would focus on established and new rural settlements in which service and employment growth would be attracted so as to serve the whole cluster. In theory such an approach ensures that more villages would enjoy a collective share of growth benefits because together they provide a population threshold equivalent to that offered by one larger key settlement. In practice, however, with only seven proposed clusters, and nine other growth villages, the majority of settlements in the area (some fifty-five villages) are subject to a restriction on growth. Therefore, in this particular interpretation of cluster–dispersal policy, several small settlements are not accommodated within the clustering framework. On a more general level, the concept of village clusters offers apparent advantages stemming mainly from the freedom of choice offered by housing and service development in several locations within the cluster. However, cluster–dispersal *per se* does not necessarily match the incentives offered by single growth centres for the attraction of employment or housing investment, neither does it lend itself easily to efficient public and community transport services. Perhaps most important of all, unless all rural settlements are included within clusters, the policy does not represent a socially acceptable form of resource dispersal because it is the smaller more remote villages which are both the main locations of opportunity deprivation and the components of the rural settlement hierarchy which are often most difficult to cluster with more advantaged settlements.

Functional interdependence

A more all-embracing framework for a greater dispersal of rural resources is offered by the concept of functional interdependence. The core of this alternative is that the superimposition of a hierarchy of centres and hinterlands within the rural settlement system constitutes a complete misunderstanding of the interactions between rural settlements in that it disregards the fact that most villages however small make some service contribution to the surrounding area. Martin (1976, 80) stresses that:

> For these unique functions, a village will have a much wider catchment area than its own residents, and people in adjoining villages, instead of going to progressively higher order and, probably, more distant centres for specialist

services, may turn to neighbouring villages; to one for electrical goods, to another for furniture, to a third for shoe repairs and so on.

Building on this theoretical interpretation, McLaughlin (1976; 1976a) has revived the idea of an alternative policy framework based on a functionally interdependent unit of perhaps five or six contiguous settlements each providing services and facilities for the others. The cluster would then in turn be linked to higher order urban centres for more scale-specific services. This idea is similar to Parry Lewis's cluster–dispersal in that it proposes a collective population threshold to replace the single threshold offered by the traditional key settlement. However, the functional interdependence concept has been developed as an all-embracing policy (in contrast to the rather piecemeal proposals for the Cambridge sub-region), and figure 7.2 reflects that all rural settlements would be functionally allied to one particular cluster. Gilder and McLaughlin (1978) suggest that the minimum range of services for each cluster would include:
1   A primary school;
2   Medical services (doctor's surgery/health clinic);
3   A post office;
4   Shops;
5   Community facilities (probably linked with school provision);
6   A stock of private- and public-sector housing;
as well as sites where employment opportunities could be developed.

   Two sets of problems might be viewed as reducing the apparent attractiveness of rural policies based on functional interdependence. First, although the concept of multi-unit growth centres in rural areas offers considerable hope for the future viability of smaller settlements which individually could not expect to receive significant investment, the practical difficulties of recognizing functionally interdependent settlement systems are considerable. Second, as is readily admitted by its protagonists, the spread of development within five or six clustered settlements requires specific and positive action to ensure accessibility throughout the cluster as well as to link the cluster with higher-order settlements. Given the solution of these problems, functionally interdependent clusters of rural settlements represent a future policy for suitably settled rural areas which is both capable of implementation and advantageous for many of the more deprived sectors of the local community. As such it should be closely considered as an integral component of future rural settlement planning frameworks.

Economic evaluation of policy alternatives

With this range of proposed policy alternatives with which to replace the old key settlement-type system, rural planners are faced with the task of evaluating the various possibilities with regard to their own spatial context. Although in an ideal world, evaluation would be carried out so as to maximize social benefits to rural residents, the evaluation of rural settlement policies which has taken place during the development-plan and structure-plan eras has been

Figure 7.2 Suggested rural servicing clusters

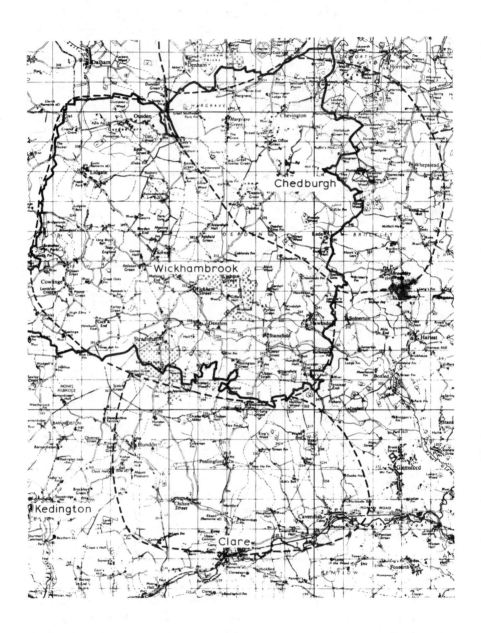

Source: Gilder and McLaughlin, 1978, 56

essentially economic in nature, and with the current financial stringencies imposed by government, it seems likely that economic analysis of public policy will continue to perform an important role in rural areas.

There has been relatively little research carried out into the economics of rural planning strategies, although Whitby and Willis (1978), amongst others, argue that 'there are many public decisions in rural areas which would be improved by economic analysis' (p. 56). Most attention in this context has been directed towards empirical analysis of rural public-service costs as it is the allocation of these particular resources which, when allied to similar decisions over housing and employment, tend to govern the underlying spatial pattern of rural settlement policy. Three distinct approaches to economic evaluation have been presented to rural settlement planners as potential models for assessing various policy options. These approaches concentrate on

1   Cost–benefit analysis;
2   Public-cost optimization; and
3   Economies of scale

as the basis for the measurement of investment appraisal. Each approach has been supported by empirical evidence, and a brief review of three studies serves to illustrate the conceptual complexities and pitfalls which are endemic in this element of decision-making in rural settlement planning.

Cost–benefit analysis: the South Atcham study

The first example represents an approach which attempts to predict the likely costs and benefits of various settlement and resettlement options in a particular rural area. The work of Warford (1969) in the South Atcham area of Shropshire was prompted by realization that the level of cost involved in providing piped water to remote unserved dwellings might be circumnavigated by rationalizing the settlement pattern into a more concentrated form. As a result, he set out to measure the impact of various relocation strategies on the provision costs of water supply, sewerage disposal, education facilities, housing, transport services and so on. Using a cost–benefit approach, it was concluded that:

> Within the policy limitations accepted in the context of the study, the results show that relocation would be preferable to the water supply scheme so far as quantified factors are concerned, for most of the possible sets of circumstances examined. (Warford, 1969, 170)

Thus, economic analysis in this case *appears* to endorse a rationalization of the rural settlement pattern rather than a dispersal of infrastructural resources to meet the needs of small remote hamlets.

Although the South Atcham study represents a landmark in the economic analysis of rural settlement strategies, there have been many criticisms of its all-embracing mode of analysis. These shortcomings are fully reviewed elsewhere (see in particular Willis, 1980) but some notable factors deserve brief mention here. For example, the emphasis on capital costs over budgetary costs inherent in the assumption that relocation investment would be immediate rather than spread over a long period of time has led to certain ambiguities in the final evaluation of options. Furthermore, the difficulties in making meaningful policy statements from a raw cost–benefit analysis are also highlighted in this study. The South Atcham planning options of *status quo* or relocation at various scales, when ranked in terms of net social benefit, presented a near-perfect inverse correlation with the ranking of options by decreasing budgetary cost. Therefore the ascendancy of any one option is totally dependent upon the selective criteria adopted by decision-makers. A least-cost approach would entail sub-optimum social benefits, and vice versa. In effect, Warford's technique has given order and pattern to the rural services problem, but does not help in the decision as to which policy option would best be employed as a problem-solver. Certainly the breadth of analysis does not allow specific evidence in favour of either side of the concentration–dispersal debate.

Public cost optimization: the North Walsham study

The second example of economic analysis in the evaluation of rural settlement planning alternatives was carried out in the North Walsham area by Norfolk County Council (1976). Rather than studying the costs and benefits of a fixed population under various relocation options, planners in Norfolk projected a level of population growth for the North Walsham area and then attempted to assess the additional public-service costs associated with the accommodation of this population within different settlement patterns. The study set out to achieve a positive link between analysis and policy in that 'the strategy which achieved the highest return on public spending, by producing the most effective provision of services in relation to their cost, was judged to be the "optimum" strategy' (Norfolk CC, 1976, 4). Four settlement pattern options were analysed (Shaw, 1976):

1   Concentration – concentrating growth in the largest settlements;
2   Dispersal[1] – allowing a standard rate of growth in all villages;
3   Dispersal[2] – making use of spare capacity in services, taking account of physical constraints;
4   Dispersal[3] – developing villages of 500–800 population.

For each of these four options, the capital and revenue costs of various public utility and community services were considered, and in addition several other social costs were assessed in non-monetary terms. The general conclusion reached by this study was that policies of concentration are less costly in both capital and revenue terms than policies of dispersal. However, strong social arguments were also found in favour of accepting the higher cost of dispersal. In fact, the difficulties of attaching comparative priorities to social or economic costs again served to cloud the policy impact of the study, as was highlighted by its final conclusion which states that:

> for those who would prefer the closer and more personal atmosphere of village life the dispersal strategy would be the most desirable, while for

those others who value greater independence and a wider variety of organizations and people, the concentration strategy would be best. (Norfolk CC, 1976, 87)

The North Walsham study has been heavily criticized, notably by Gilder (1979). The major grounds for complaint revolve around the fact that in assessing *future* costs of servicing the various settlement pattern options, the study omits those costs incurred in maintaining services for the *present* population of the study area. Such an omission tends to emphasize capital investment for additional services to the exclusion of future revenue costs of existing services. Gilder also points out that the North Walsham study assumes the continuation both of existing levels of service provision, and of the current balance of public and private sector contributions towards the cost of those services. Both of these assumptions may be arguable in a flexible view of future rural settlement planning. Thus, although this second example of economic analysis of rural settlement options appears to offer direct evidence in favour of concentration policies, sufficient methodological doubt has been cast upon the study to reduce the importance of its findings in a more general context.

Scale economies: the Bury St Edmunds study

The third and most recent example of economic appraisal of rural planning policies was carried out in the Bury St Edmunds area of West Suffolk by Gilder (1979) who undertakes two distinct stages of empirical analysis of public service costs:
1   The detailed investigation of public service costs in the area covering a single year;
2   The analysis of public service costs under different population strategies (including those of constant or declining population).

The first stage is an important prerequisite in that it affords both a relative scaling of the costs of various services and an opportunity to standardize the results of conflicting accounting techniques used by different public authorities. Services selected for analysis represented the education, sewage disposal, transport and community health sectors, and an integral part of the overall assessment was a cross-sectional analysis of the cost of these services in relation to settlement size. In effect a 'full costing' approach is used (in contrast to the relocation of present population in South Atcham and the additional costs of future growth in North Walsham).

The conclusions drawn from the Bury St Edmunds study are clearly in sharp contrast to those from South Atcham and North Walsham:

the accommodation of future growth will be less costly if that growth is dispersed widely throughout the area, than if it is concentrated in Bury St Edmunds and the larger villages. The marginal costs of making better use of existing schools and other fixed assets is likely to outweigh the benefits of concentrated development policies, even if economies of scale within services exist. The relative costs of maintaining services at existing levels for present population far exceed the costs of accommodating new growth. (Gilder, 1979, 264)

The fact that these results flatly contradict the conventional wisdoms of rural settlement planning makes the Bury St Edmunds study an important milestone in the analysis of rural planning strategies. Although the research is seen as the initial stage of a much fuller examination of the costs and benefits of rural settlement policies, if further usage of the full costing technique confirms these pro-dispersal conclusions then the economic basis of key settlement policies will have been severely weakened, and the need to consider alternative rural settlement strategies will be stronger than ever. Once again, however, certain methodological aspects serve to cloud the results of the Bury St Edmunds study and illustrate the technical difficulties which currently prevent the presentation of clear and unequivocal economic advice to rural settlement planning. Cloke and Woodward (1981) suggest that there are four main areas where the methods used in the study may be open to question:

1 The costs of providing public services are perhaps best estimated as *economic* costs rather than as public sector or budgetary costs (the use of which can lead to inconsistencies because of variations in the element of direct charging);
2 The relationship between economies of scale and increasing settlement size is not easily testable as any test of this correlation is bound to be dependent upon rather arbitrary accountancy procedures;
3 The identification of scale economies requires that great care be taken in standardizing for other factors in the analytical equation (e.g. by using proxy variables in regression techniques);
4 Although cost projections are a useful way of looking at the alternatives which face a local authority in providing public services, it is essential that the *best* alternatives are considered. There is not much point in evaluating the costs of second-best projects.

These implications should not be seen to suggest that the conclusions of the Bury St Edmunds study are necessarily erroneous. Indeed, the scholarly and inventive nature of the study has lead to significant improvements in the technical expertise available for economic evaluation in the rural context. However, it is suggested that a mere repetition of this methodology in other rural locations would be insufficient to justify the unquestioned acceptance of these conclusions. The technical ambiguities which have clouded many central issues in the Bury St Edmunds area, would necessarily do so in other areas without some improvement or substantiation of the methods used. Although this research task is under way (e.g. Curry and West, 1981) there is still some progress to be made before an acceptable method of economic evaluation of rural resource allocation can be presented to decision-makers.

Finally, attention should be drawn to the fact that any costing of the provision of public services has very few implications for rural development policies. In the last resort an evaluation should be based upon the full spectrum of costs and benefits. The costs of providing public services are no doubt an important element of cost in such an evaluation, but they are only one such group of items.

Evaluation and rural policy-making

The three studies reviewed in pp. 185–8 appear to suggest that scientific investigation is able to produce an objectively derived optimum pattern for the distribution of resources in rural areas. This view is effectively dashed by Jenkins (1978, 228) who places policy evaluation back into political reality:

> a positive advantage of evaluation would be to depoliticize a situation, to provide a cold rational appraisal of policy alternatives or policies *per se* outside the steam heat of emotion and ideology. Sadly, this is very much a false hope, a product of technocracy and scientism pushed forward by those who hanker after a managerial outlook and who fail to appreciate that there is really no such thing as an apolitical arena.

Thus, however effective rural researchers are in producing research evidence pointing to one particular framework policy as the optimum basis for future planning, planning authorities are required to take other, less 'academic' factors into account. This procedure is readily admitted in many county structure plans. Hertfordshire County Council (1976, 10), for example, outline four alternative strategies, but reject a methodological, evaluation of these alternatives. Rather, it was recognized that:

> the real decision about the basis for this Plan hinged upon reaching a compromise on various features of all four strategies. This compromise has to reflect a position of public and political acceptability, and a willingness by the many implementing agencies to operate within it.

Given the political nature of evaluation in the policy-making process, it would be naive to expect planning authorities to divulge the exact details of how a preferred strategy was arrived at. Indeed, the compromises between resources, implementation and acceptability mentioned in the Hertfordshire plan are often of an intangible nature which is difficult to measure or document. However, most county structure plans give some explanation of evaluation procedures, largely following central government guidelines. The Department of the Environment (1972) *Structure Plans Note 7* (para. 4) advises that 'to reach decisions through an explicit evaluation process the alternatives must be set out, the likely consequences must be predicted on a comparable basis and the extent to which they meet aims must be determined'. Most counties have followed this three-stage process.

The alternatives

The manner in which policy alternatives are described imposes an important influence on the evaluation process. A great deal of variation occurs in different county structure plans, demonstrating how perceptions of potential policy frameworks can vary from authority to authority. The Hertfordshire plan (1976), for example, establishes four *area-specific* alternatives:

1 The achievement of a balance between employment, housing and population growth by tight controls in both urban and rural areas;
2 The channelling of industrial development and housing growth into the already thriving towns along the line of the A1 road;
3 Minimal change, with no further land allocations for housing or employment;
4 High population and employment growth in north and south-west Hertfordshire.

Other themes formed the basis of policy alternatives elsewhere. For example, the East Berkshire plan (1980) chose to evaluate policies of no growth, limited growth, controlled growth and high growth without specific reference to the zoning of these growth levels within the structure-plan area. Cambridgeshire County Council (1980) selected three *functional* strategies for evaluation in comparison with existing policies:

1 To give high priority to the conservation of both manmade and natural resources;
2 To exploit fully the county's economic potential by encouraging further growth;
3 To give priority to social objectives by attempting to reduce social and spatial irregularities in living standards.

In fact very few plans outline alternative strategies using concepts of concentration and dispersal which have formed the nub of more academically based evaluation procedures. Even where this does occur, the variation of potential rural framework policies is often overshadowed by the search for county-wide development proposals. Thus the North-East Lancashire plan (1980) suggests a *conservation* theme, which favours a cautious attitude toward change and new development; a *compact town* theme, which permits new development in urban areas and market towns, but only in such a way as to avoid coalescence and sprawl; a *rural dispersal* theme allowing more development in rural settlements where it can be serviced at a reasonable cost; and a *peripheral expansion* theme which permits new housing and industrial expansion along the edges of urban areas. It should be noted that even within a theme of 'rural dispersal', new development in the countryside would in fact be concentrated in those locations where service provision is seen to be viable. In fact, rural issues *per se* appear to be given low priority at this stage of presentation of alternatives. Needless to say, the omission of rural details at the beginning of county policy evaluation has important ramifications for the way in which specific rural policies are subsequently generated to fit in with the selected county-wide policy.

Comparison of the likely consequences

The second recommended stage in the evaluation process involves comparing the likely consequences of each of the selected alternatives. It is at this stage that use could be made of academic studies which present evidence of the outcome of various policy mechanisms in rural areas. However, county planning authorities have understandably tunnelled their vision towards trends and phenomena within the area of their own jurisdiction, and so the likely consequences of policy alternatives often constitute informed speculation of a low-key nature. A brief review of the expected consequences of Cornwall County Council's (1976) analysis of policy choices demonstrates what can be achieved at this stage of the process. Table 7.1 shows the predicted consequences of three possible strategies for the county, and suggests that in attempting to simplify these outcomes for the benefit of public participation, the inherent complexity and inaccuracy of growth predictions can be reduced to a range of achievements of various planning objectives. The comparison of these consequences is therefore inevitably based on the chosen priorities between different *objectives* rather than different ranges of *outcomes*. Thus the third stage of the evaluation process is where choices are actually made between alternative strategies.

The achievement of planning objectives

Structure Plans Note 8 (1972) from the Department of the Environment suggests that planning authorities should use a matrix model to compare how alternative policies perform in relation to various planning objectives. Most structure plans show evidence of this advice, but a good deal of variation is shown in the actual manipulation of the matrices. In some cases, the underlying assumptions of the exercise are such that subsequent evaluation becomes a foregone conclusion. For example, the Somerset Structure Plan (1980) takes a prospective population increase of 45,000 as the starting point of its

Table 7.1 Predicted consequences of Cornwall's policy alternatives

---

Choice A: to promote maximum economic growth and efficiency
8,000–17,000 new manufacturing jobs, 1975–91
18,000–38,000 new job opportunities
1,400–4,200 annual in-migrants
NB Environmental considerations would have less priority.

Choice B to remedy deficiencies and achieve economic stability
4,500–12,000 new manufacturing jobs, 1971–91
11,000–33,000 new job opportunities
800–3,600 annual in-migrants
NB Development would be restricted to a limited number of settlements as a result of the need to concentrate the use of resources.

Choice C: to maintain the physical character of the county
'The more stringent environmental controls on industry might tend to inhibit growth in employment opportunities, leading to a lower rate of net migration by the economically active' (Cornwall CC, 1976, 18)
NB Environmental considerations would lead to a greater level of resource concentration, meaning a more economic provision of a wider range of services.

Source: After Cornwall CC, 1976

evaluation of alternative policies. However, the options to be assessed were limited by this figure as 'It was agreed that there was little scope for presenting radically different strategies because of the relatively small population change expected and the numbers of commitments already incurred' (p. 7).

Elsewhere, a range of planning objectives has been identified in order to test various alternative strategies in terms of their environmental, social, economic and management performance. Avon County Council (1980), for example, outlines twelve such objectives (table 7.2) which create a platform for a comparative analysis of four differing strategies. Although this method did not establish a clear advantage of one strategy over the others, it did suggest that two strategies were more appropriate to the overall planning objectives than the remainder, and so a preferred strategy was created out of the most favourable aspects of these two. The Avon process is duplicated in matrix form in the East Berkshire plan (1980) where four alternatives were measured against six planning objectives in terms of being unacceptable, marginally acceptable or broadly acceptable (figure 7.3). The preferred strategy was that of limited growth, which permitted the achievement of all objectives bar the 'discretion for meeting local needs category' (which was only satisfied by a high growth-level approach). A similar technique has been operated by the North-East Lancashire Structure Plan (1980) which quantifies evaluation ratings gained by four strategies and concludes that Strategy 2 (the 'compact town' theme) is the most successful and thus forms the basis of the preferred strategy (table 7.3).

Perhaps most typical of the current breed of alternative policy evaluation techniques is that employed by Northamptonshire County Council (1977). The evaluation was based on a quantitative analysis of how individual alternatives performed against each objective. Three generic groups of alternative (social, economic, and environmental) were used, and the results of the exercise are

Table 7.2   Avon's twelve measures for testing alternative strategies

1   Physical and social disruption of existing communities caused by development
2   Amount of land or building dereliction created or land left vacant and unused in the urban areas
3   Operational implications for the highway network in terms of traffic loading and journey time
4   Amount by which it would be possible to reduce undesirable existing development commitments
5   Costs of servicing development
6   Level of employment opportunities identified
7   Opportunities for reducing unemployment and underemployment
8   Level of local job opportunities provided
9   Influence upon levels of public services to existing and new development
10   Economic benefits to transport users
11   Ability to absorb changes in circumstances without the strategy being affected fundamentally (robustness)
12   Ability to amend policies to meet changing circumstances ('flexibility')

Source: Avon CC, 1980, 26

Figure 7.3 Summary of the evaluation of alternative strategies in the East Berkshire Structure Plan

ASPECTS OF THE KEY ISSUES	ALTERNATIVE STRATEGIES			
	NO GROWTH	LIMITED GROWTH	CONTROLLED GROWTH	HIGH GROWTH
COMPATIBILITY WITH REGIONAL PLANNING FRAMEWORK	Incompatible with regional policy, which envisages some limited development for meeting certain aspects of local needs.	Basic approach compatible with underlying aims and policies of regional planning framework, subject to available discretion being used for meeting local needs.	Generally consistent with SPSE intentions, although diverging from developing regional planning framework (1976 Review) because of higher level of growth and associated net immigration.	Incompatible with regional policy. Ignores 'Restraint Area status of the area. Would encourage/facilitate significant net immigration and undermine basic policies for concentration of development in growth areas.
DISCRETION FOR MEETING LOCAL NEEDS	Offers little scope to meet housing needs which would then have to be met outside East Berkshire, inflexible employment policies would allow little scope for accommodating needs.	Offers reasonable scope in overall terms for meeting housing needs, subject to implementation considerations. Some limited employment growth to meet local requirements could be allowed.	Provides more opportunities for meeting housing and employment needs through the release of additional land, although this discretion could be taken up by wider pressures for development.	Affords most discretion for meeting local needs within a growth framework.
POTENTIAL ENVIRONMENTAL IMPACT	No further development. Possible blighting of land already committed and pressures for alternative ad hoc releases. Restrictive employment and shopping policies would allow no scope for town centre developments which they facilitate environmental improvements.	Expansion of urban areas restricted to land already committed and some limited small-scale development. Some town centre development could be allowed if considered desirable.	Involves development of unconstrained land which might not be most environmentally suitable. More discretion for employment growth, with potential problems and opportunities for urban environments.	Involves significant further development of rural (Green Belt) land.
IMPLICATIONS FOR TRANSPORT PROBLEMS	Minimises impact on transport problems, although these likely to increase due to other factors influencing trips.	Problems created could be minimised through policy and infrastructure developments within the financial constraints.	Problems made marginally worse than with the Limited Growth approach.	Problems made worse than with the Limited Growth approach.
IMPLICATIONS FOR THE PROVISION OF COMMUNITY FACILITIES AND SERVICES	Impact on social and community services minimised, although resources might not be available to deal with existing shortfalls. Possible underutilisation of committed infrastructure. Significant over-provision of shopping facilities.	Existing standards of provision of social and community services could probably be maintained, with possibly some scope for improvements. Infrastructure requirements adequately covered by existing commitments or programmes. No discretion for additional shopping facilities.	Existing standards of provision of social and community facilities could probably be maintained, with possibly some scope for improvements. Additional areas for development may be comparatively costly to service, with potential localised problems.	Unlikely that even existing standards of provision of social and community services could be maintained. Potential localised difficulties in providing necessary infrastructure. Some discretion for additional shopping facilities.
IMPLEMENTATION AND UNCERTAINTY	Requires revocation of existing commitments, offers no flexibility and does not provide a workable planning framework.	Provides a workable planning framework, but requires specific measures to meet housing needs within discretion provided. Longer-term flexibility is provided by not being over-committed.	Provides added short term flexibility for resolving local issues within a growth framework but in the longer term would require release of Green Belt land to provide flexibility.	Difficult to protect Green Belt once some released. Over-committed if economic growth does not occur as anticipated.

Unacceptable approach in relation to criterion ■ Marginally acceptable approach in relation to criterion □ Broadly acceptable approach in relation to criterion ▦

Source: Berkshire CC, 1980, 20

summarized in table 7.4. As might be expected each generic alternative performed best when measured against its 'parent' set of objectives, although the social alternative performed least well overall. The usefulness of this technique is openly doubted by the authors:

> the differences in the level of achievement of objectives between Alternatives was only marginal, since in relation to the overall level of growth up to 650,000, differences in population and job distributions between the alternatives were relatively small. (para. 15.77)

In the end, Northamptonshire's preferred strategy was most strongly influenced by the 'economic' alternative, not apparently as a result of the technical evaluation, but because it was the *safest option*:

> Insomuch as the Economic Alternative had a pattern of development which was an extension of use of the existing infrastructure, and used established agencies to promote employment growth and concentrated population growth in areas where knowledge and control were relatively comprehensive, this Alternative handled uncertainty best. (para. 15.80)

Table 7.3   North-East Lancashire Structure Plan (a) summary of the strategic evaluations and (b) overall assessment of the strategy evaluations

(a)

Evaluation criteria	*Strategy*			
	1	*2*	*3*	*4*
Public acceptability	Good	Fairly good	Fairly poor	Poor
District acceptability	Poor	Moderate	Fairly poor	Good
Social impact	Good	Fairly good	Fairly poor	Poor
Economic impact	Poor	Fairly good	Moderate	Good
Flexibility and robustness	Fairly good	Moderate	Poor	Poor
Environmental factors	Moderate	Good	Poor	Moderate
Financial resource implications	Good	Good	Fairly poor	Poor
Risk in implementation	Poor	Moderate	Fairly poor	Moderate

(b)

Strategy	*Evaluation rating*				
	Good	*Fairly good*	*Moderate*	*Fairly poor*	*Poor*
One	3	1	1	–	3
Two	2	3	3	–	–
Three	–	–	1	5	2
Four	2	–	2	–	4

Source: Lancashire CC, 1980, 22

   In chapter 1 it was suggested that policy precedent was a strong determining factor in the preparation of new planning strategies for rural settlements. This brief review of evaluation methods adopted by structure-plan teams tends to confirm this view, with the innovative and socially oriented strategies generally being rejected in favour of the more easily predictable and manageable extensions of current policy directions. This trend strengthens the inevitability that rural settlement policy will increasingly evolve at local level rather than as an integral part of a county strategy which is determined by wider structural issues. Nevertheless, it should be recognized that these wider decision-making processes are likely to place severe restrictions on the available options for local-scale rural settlement planning.

Table 7.4 Technical evaluation of the Northamptonshire Structure Plan alternatives

Objective	Performance measure	Order of achievement		
Social objectives				
1 Channel resources to disadvantaged areas and social groups	Population outside New and Expanding Towns, 1991	Social	Environmental	Economic
2 Encourage the provision of a range of employment locations and opportunities throughout the county	Improvement of job worker ratio, 1971–91 (average per policy areas)	Social	Environmental	Economic
3 Maintain the viability of existing commercial and employment centres	(i) Growth in population in centres not benefiting from planned expansion, 1975–91 (ii) Growth in jobs outside New and Expanding Towns 1971–91 (iii) Net outward commuting journeys, 1991	Social	Environmental	Economic
4 Ensure that every household has good access to employment locations	Increase in commuting trips between policy areas, 1971–91	Social	Environmental	Economic
5 Ensure that every household has good access to shopping, educational, recreational and other community facilities	Population growth in New and Expanding Towns, A6 Towns and Key Centres	Social	Environmental	Economic
6 Ensure a choice of residential types and locations	Population growth in rural areas in relation to all growth outside New and Expanding Towns	Social	Environmental	Economic
Economic objectives				
7 Make the most efficient use of available resources	Population growth Northampton and Corby, 1975–91	Economic	Environmental	Social
8 Ensure the efficient operation of new industrial and commercial development	Job growth in New and Expanding Towns, 1971–91	Economic	Environmental	Social

9 Minimize the impact of development on agriculture	(i) Residential land take in New and Expanding Towns, A6 Towns and villages classified as Key Centres and Moderate Growth villages in the Alternatives (ii) Residential land take in 'Remainder of Villages', 1975–91 (iii) Land take for industrial use 1975–91 (iv) Land take for all other purposes 1975–91	Economic	Environmental	Social
10 Prevent the sterilization of workable mineral deposits	Mineral areas safeguarded in all Alternatives	All Alternatives perform equally well		

Environmental objectives

11 Protect and enhance the existing character of the villages and the rural environment	Residential land take in New and Expanding Towns, A5 Towns and villages classified as Key Centres and Moderate Growth villages in the Alternatives weighted by landscape quality 1975–91	Environmental	Economic	Social
12 Minimize the loss of high quality landscape	Population growth in Key Centres and Moderate Growth villages 1975–91 within areas for landscape protection and conservation	Environmental	Economic	Social
13 Improve the quality of the urban environment	No measure	No measure		

Source: Northamptonshire CC, 1977, 152

EIGHT

Rural settlement planning in practice

Participant planning agencies

At the beginning of this book, a heterodox view of the planning process was suggested (figure 1.2) which sought to combine factors of policy precedent, policy preparation, policy statement, policy implementation and policy result into a systematic framework which aids the identification of previously under-emphasized elements of rural settlement planning. Although at one level this view of planning applies neatly to the physical and land use planning process carried out in planning departments and committees of central and local government, at a more realistic level the model should be applied to all decision-making processes which affect resource allocation in rural areas. It has become clear from chapter 7 that progress in the formulation and enactment of appropriate *framework policies* for rural settlement systems is dependent on the close co-operation of all decision-taking agencies with jurisdiction over rural communities. Physical planning authorities have been established as the focal point for the co-ordination of these various agencies, yet planners themselves have little direct power of resource allocation apart from the development control process. Figure 8.1 identifies the multiplicity of government agencies with an interest in rural affairs, with central departments establishing policy guidelines which are often sieved and modified two or three times as central and regional agencies perform their allocative roles before responsibility reaches the elected local government authorities. In addition to these channels of power, there are the numerous private sector organizations which operate within rural settlements.

In order to gain some understanding of the practice of rural settlement planning, it is therefore important to give brief attention to the processes of decision-making which, in fact, dictate whether strategic framework policies are carried out at ground level. Separate consideration is given here to the formal *planning* agencies within central and local government whose roles are reasonably well established, and to other *resource allocation* agencies about which far less falls into the realm of common knowledge. Finally, the problems of co-ordination between various agencies is briefly discussed as a precursor to the more detailed analysis of policy implementation in rural areas in chapter 9.

Central government level

Central government responsibilities as a formal planning agency have been the

Figure 8.1 Central and local government responsibilities in rural areas

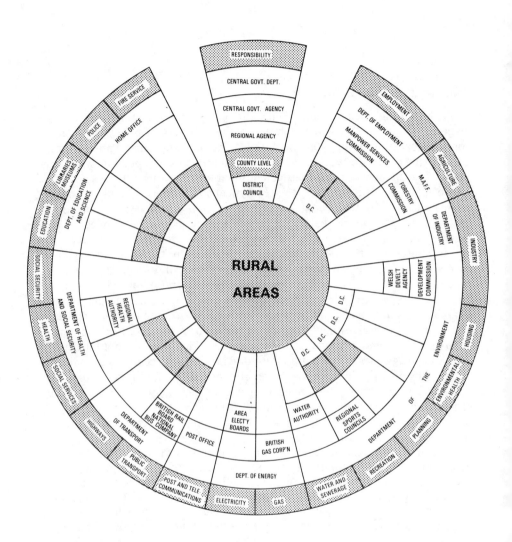

Source: Association of County Councils, 1979, 47

subject of considerable organizational change over the post-war period (table 8.1). Whether these changes represent a concerted attempt to introduce relevant institutional processes with which to tackle current planning issues is a moot point. A less charitable but perhaps more realistic interpretation might be to ascribe many of the reshuffles to the predilection shown by successive British governments for esoteric bureaucratic reorganization which tends to occur when previous administration processes have been made the scapegoat for any failure to tackle socio-economic problems. Nevertheless, the Ministry of Housing and Local Government and now the Department of the Environment have acted both as clearing houses for planning responsibilities and as foci for the delimitation of government planning duties.

In some instances, these duties have not changed. Ratcliffe (1974, 86) notes that the Department of the Environment's task of 'securing consistency and continuity in the framing of a national policy with respect to the use and development of land throughout England and Wales' has remained unaltered since the 1943 Ministry of Town and Country Planning Act. This suggests that the core responsibilities for planning have changed little despite the numerous discontinuities of nomenclature, buildings and staff involved. In Scotland and Wales, the Scottish and Welsh Offices have important responsibilities which replace or reduce the Department of the Environment's jurisdiction in these areas.

Six main responsibilities are shouldered by the Department of the Environment (or its surrogate agencies) which have direct bearing on the rural settlement planning process (Department of the Environment, 1975):
1   The Secretary of State has responsibility for approving the structure plans submitted by county council authorities. He can stipulate modifications to

Table 8.1   Changes in the organization of central government planning duties

1947	*Ministry of Town and Country Planning*: the initiating agency for development plans and post-war renewal
1951	*Ministry of Housing and Local Government*: responsible for town and country planning, housing and local government finance and services
1864	*Department of Economic Affairs*: with responsibility for the proposed regional economic planning system (withdrawn in 1969)
1965	*Ministry of Land and Natural Resources*: took over administration of National Parks, water resources and responsibility for the Land Commission and Leasehold Enfranchisement Bills. These roles were returned to the Ministry of Housing and Local Government in 1967
1969	*Department of Local Government and Regional Planning*: given powers over the Ministry of Housing and Local Government and in addition assumed responsibility for transport and previous duties of the Department of Economic Affairs
1970	*Department of the Environment*: the new Conservative government subsumed the short-lived 1969 structure into one overall organization with three subsections: planning and local government; housing and construction; and transport
1976	*Ministry of Transport*: achieved partial independence from the Department of the Environment

the plans either on the basis of the need for national co-ordination of policies or as a result of objections received from the public. It is important to note that central government acts in a quasi-judicial manner in this instance, and indeed there is considerable evidence that the Department of the Environment has increased its requirement for the modification of rural strategic plans in the late 1970s and early 1980s than was previously the case;

2   The Department of the Environment offers a broad guiding framework of land-use and development-policies for rural areas. This guidance usually consists of advice in the form of departmental circulars and bulletins, which have played a major role in the shaping of rural settlement policy trends, particularly in the development-plan period (see chapter 4). More recently, the department has sponsored research programmes in order to offer current information and advice to local authorities;

3   The department is responsible for formulating planning regulations which take the form of delegated legislation. For example the General Development and Use Classes Orders have simplified development control practices by isolating 'permitted development' for which automatic planning permission is granted and by ensuring that the changes of use of buildings do not require planning permission if the new use is of the same type as the previous use;

4   The department has powers to 'call-in' particular applications for planning permission which are considered to be of such outstanding importance that they should be decided at central government level in the first instance;

5   Normally, planning applications are dealt with by local authorities and the department again adopts a quasi-judicial role as the body to which appeals against refusal of planning permission are brought for decision. Planning appeals are dealt with by a special inspectorate either at local public inquiries or by correspondence, and local authority decisions may be reversed, modified, remodified or even reinforced in cases where it is thought that a permission with modifications should not have been granted in the first place;

6   Finally, the department through its regional offices and in consultation with other government departments is charged to produce regional strategies which will provide a contextual strategy for the county-based structure plans.

In many ways, the Department of the Environment has successfully preserved and enhanced its designated functions in times of economic recession, although Phillips (1976, 121) argues that the mere presence of the department has fostered a misplaced complacency 'that the environment is adequately allowed for in the process of government by establishing a powerful department of state whose prime responsibility it is to be concerned with the protection of the environment'. The fact that both agriculture and forestry fall largely outside the ambit of planning, and indeed of the Department of the Environment, does have an important limiting effect on any comprehensive form of planning for rural settlements.

Local government level

Prior to local government reorganization in 1974, local authority areas had stood virtually unchanged since the nineteenth century. England and Wales (outside London) were divided into county boroughs and administrative counties with the latter being subdivided into municipal boroughs, urban districts and rural districts. The county boroughs represented all-purpose local government agencies whereas the administrative counties devolved certain functions (including some planning duties) to the lower scale districts. Gilg (1978, 66) notes that

> a major problem was the splitting of local authorities into rurally dominated county councils and urban dominated county boroughs, which in most areas led to a serious conflict of interest over the use to which land should be put – a conflict which often became polarized into a straight rural–urban conflict.

It might be added that the rural–urban conflict usually worked to the detriment of rural areas.

The Redcliffe-Maud report of 1969 acknowledged these difficulties and others concerned with anachronistic boundaries which presented both a piece-meal delegation of power and a glut of small, low-funded local authorities who were prevented from performing planning duties with any competence. The report produced a majority verdict in favour of a new system of unitary authorities based on city regions which would be of a size which would allow both the undertaking of broad strategic planning and of more localized personal services. These diagnostics were accepted by the Labour government of the day, but the incoming Conservative government opted for a two-tier solution to the problem, with a first-level authority (the *county*) of substantial size for planning purposes, and a second smaller agency (the *district*) for local-scale planning and service provision (figure 8.2).

The new counties were subdivided into metropolitan counties (an entirely new structure, covering built-up conurbations) and non-metropolitan counties (which were based on the previous shire counties). In terms of their role in planning, there is no difference in the powers granted to the two types of county. Their three major tasks cover:

1 The preparation of structure plans;
2 The administration and decision-making roles connected with important items of development control;
3 The agreement of frameworks for local planning and small-scale development control carried out by the district councils.

In Scotland, the two administrative levels are slightly different in that a two-tier system of *regions* and *districts* was adopted. However, in areas of sparse population as well as in the three island regions a general planning authority was set up at regional level, and where districts were superimposed at a lower scale, they were not given planning powers.

In most areas of Britain, the new districts became the 'front line' of planning. They were granted responsibility for the two main planning tasks:

Figure 8.2 Stages in the progress of a planning application

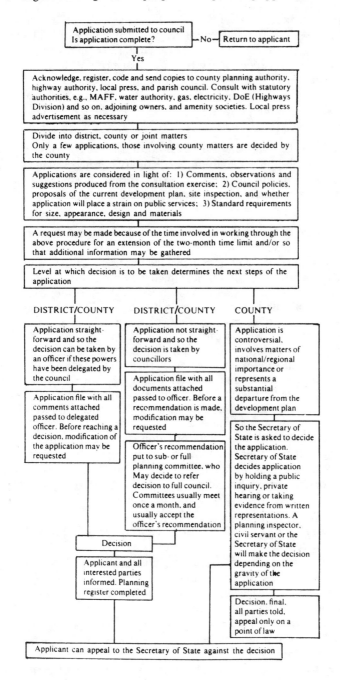

Source: Gilg, 1978, 70

1   The detailed local planning of the district in accordance with the broad policies outlined in the county structure plan;

2   The administration of development control (apart from major county-responsibility applications) and the enforcement of building regulations.

District councils should not be viewed as a homogeneous group, as the quality of development control and local planning will inevitably vary as indeed will the supervision of these tasks by different counties. It is also often the case that public opinion is more persuasive in the smaller local authorities than the larger ones. In this context the third tier of local administration – the *parish* or *community councils* – can play an increasingly important role. Providing that they inform the district council that they wish to be involved, parish councils may be notified of planning applications in their area. This permits some participation by local rural communities in the planning of their settlements, and co-operation between parish and district authorities is one area in which the 1974 reshuffle has improved local aspects of rural settlement planning. In many cases parish participation has been prompted by the work of Rural Community Councils and in particular their Countryside Officers. Although these organizations have been established at county level, their task has been to promote localized involvement with the planning process, and their success in this task perhaps points the way towards greater government sponsorship of community co-operation and administration in rural areas.

Development control processes

Development control is the principal method of policy implementation available to participant planning agencies. Without decision-making powers in the allocation of resources, the most significant impact that planning departments and committees can make is in their decision to refuse, accept or modify development applications which are made to them. An often-forgotten yet very important process concomitant to development control is that of development guidance, whereby informal discussion between planners and developers often results in the attraction of 'suitable' developments to cater for particular needs in certain settlements.

The 1962 Town and Country Planning Act defined development as 'the carrying out of building, engineering, mining or other operations in, on, over or under the land, or the making of any material change in the use of any buildings or other land'. This suggests that planners have powers over both building development and the uses made of buildings or land. In fact several exceptions exist to these seemingly comprehensive rules. For example, the General Development Order ensures that the way in which land is used for agriculture and forestry is exempt from powers of development control. In addition agricultural buildings (other than dwellings) not exceeding 465 square metres (5000 square ft) in ground area or 12 metres (39 ft) in height are similarly outside of planning control. The General Development Order also includes various developments by public authorities and nationalized industries. Phillips (1976, 134) notes one important exception in that 'minor – and sometimes not so minor – road improvements can be carried out without any form of supervision by the planning authority even though the cumulative environmental impact of minor road widenings and straightenings is considerable'.

Clearly, exempted developments of this nature can have important impacts for rural settlement planning. Similarly, the Use Classes Order represents a mechanism through which rural change can take place without recourse to planning consent. Classes of building use are prescribed, and change is permitted within but not between these classes. The classes most often encountered in rural settlements are outlined in table 8.2, from which it can be seen that a change of use from a solicitors office to an insurance office does not require planning permission, and that the change from a clerical outfitters shop to a sex shop is similarly outside the planners' remit. The replacement of a travel agents by an estate agents does, however, constitute a material change in use requiring planning permission. Again it can be seen that many small-scale changes do occur in rural settlements without the permission of planning agencies.

Where development does require planning permission, two types of application are available:

1 *An outline application* may be submitted to secure permission in principle for a certain type of development on a certain site. As the name suggests, no formal plans are required at this stage, and outline procedures are often followed before 'the applicant' buys the land involved. If outline permission is granted, details plans must be approved before development is allowed to proceed;

2 *A detailed application* should include a comprehensive description of the proposed development including site plans and diagrams and a justification as to why the development is needed in that location.

Once an application has been received by the planning authority it is duly processed according to well-defined procedures which have been neatly summarized by Gilg's (1978) flow diagram (figure 8.2). These procedures take

Table 8.2   Classes of development under the Use Classes Order

Class 1	Use as a shop (except hot food shops, tripe shops, pet shops, a shop for the sale of motor vehicles, etc.)
Class 2	Use as an office
Class 3	Use as a light industrial building (light industry is defined as that which makes little noise, smoke, smell, dust, vibration or other nuisance. It can be located in a residential area without harm)
Class 4	Use as a general industrial building
Class 10	Use as a warehouse
Class 11	Use as a hotel or boarding house
Class 13	Use as a church or for social activities connected with a church
Class 14	Use as an institutional home or hospital
Class 15	Non-residential use as a health centre, day nursery, clinic or surgery
Class 16	Use as a library, or public hall
Class 18	Use as a sports or dance hall

Source: Useful classes were selected by Devon Association of Parish Councils, 1976

account of both the strategic policies contained within the structure plan and the material considerations relating to the site or situation of the development. Gilg stresses that material considerations are sensitive to current government advice which may be time-specific, so that while the Department of the Environment's *Development Control Policy Notes* (various dates) urge planners to consider factors such as road safety, environmental impact, public services, alternative uses of land and so on before permitting development, specific advice (e.g. Department of the Environment, 1973) might urge a strong presumption in favour of housing in government approved growth areas which would be overriden only if exceptionally strong planning objections were raised. In fact the major overriding factor in many rural areas is the strong presumption against growth in green belts, National Parks or Areas of Outstanding Natural Beauty or Great Landscape Value. Similarly sporadic and ribbon development has been equally shunned (Manson, 1979). In addition to structure and local plan matters and material considerations, residential developments in rural areas are subject to a host of bye-laws and building regulations (detailed in Hobbs and Doling, 1981; and critically analysed by Pitt, 1979).

Having considered all the relevant evidence, the local planning authority can reach one of four decisions:

1   To grant the application unconditionally;
2   To grant the application with conditioning;
3   To grant the application temporarily;
4   To refuse the application.

The authority's power to impose conditions is rather a liberal one, as they are able to subject permissions to 'such conditions as they see fit'. The controversy over the Lake District authority's practice of granting permissions for new housing only on the condition that a Section 52 Agreement is signed to ensure that houses will be lived in by 'local' people, may be the tip of an iceberg in the use of the 'conditions' machinery for various motives in the planning of rural housing.

Until the 1968 Town and Country Planning Act there was no time-limit within which permitted development had to take place. The act, however decreed that permission would be revoked after 5 years (for detailed permission) or 3 years (for outline permission) unless respectively development is begun or detailed permission is granted. This regulation has frequently been circumnavigated. Manson (1979a, 22) notes that:

> what is needed to start a development, and so comply with the requirement to start work within the prescribed time, may be as simple as digging a trench for a foundation or a pipe. This simple operation is sufficient to preserve the planning permission and prevent it lapsing.

Despite the local authority's ability to issue a completion notice, many unused permissions for residential development have accumulated in rural settlements on this basis.

During the late 1960s and early 1970s, the development control process was subject to growing criticism (Blake, 1974) because of the increasing number of planning decisions to be made and the resultant delays in the reaching of those decisions. In 1973 the Department of the Environment issued *Circular 142* on 'Streamlining the Planning Machine' which urged planning authorities to consider applications expeditiously, and also expanded their inspectorate to deal with appeals. The department also appointed George Dobry QC to report on the state of the development-control process and to suggest any modifications which might reduce the pressure of planning applications and appeals. His final report (Dobry, 1975) vindicated the current development control system to a large extent, but suggested that a two-tier categorization of applications at district council level into Class A (minor and uncontroversial) and Class B (major or controversial or both) would speed up the overall operation. The Dobry report has been criticized for failing to place development control within the overall process of the planning system, and in the event his findings were largely rejected by central government. This was partially due to a change in circumstances from a Conservative government in the midst of a property boom to a Labour government whose attention was focused on legislation for community land. There was also, however, some horror expressed by district planning authorities who foresaw an increased workload brought about by having to differentiate between Class A and Class B applications. As a consequence the development control procedure has been left largely unchanged, although the recent Conservative government legislation to impose changes for the conveyance of planning applications, which ostensibly has been introduced to recoup some of the administrative costs involved, may be viewed as a scarcely veiled attempt to reduce the number of applications for planning development and thus create a more efficient system through market forces.

Political involvement in rural settlement planning

Over the past 20 years, a steady stream of literature has appeared in which political involvement in local government planning has been analysed (e.g. Bulpitt, 1967; Elkins, 1974; Gyford, 1976; Lee, 1963). It is therefore surprising that the full scope and importance of political action in rural settlement planning has been sadly underemphasized until quite recently when the work of Newby *et al.* (1978) and Blowers (1980) has served to shake off the lethargy of non-political analysis of rural planning. Levin (1976) sees the planning process as comprising three different kinds of sequence:
1   *The administrative process* consisting of acts, actions or activities which are statutorily or conventionally performed before implementation of a development may begin;
2   *The technical process* in which an action scheme is developed and a single preferred plan is arrived at;
3   *The political process* where the consumer and institutional interests of groups and individuals are partly or wholly aligned, accommodated or overriden.

The political process in rural settlement planning has been largely undervalued in our attempts to explain the actions and reactions of policies in the face of dynamism in rural communities. This is partly because the political process is manifested within the administrative and technical processes, where various interests are implicitly accounted for in decisions taken. Fay (1975) bemoans the fact that planning policy and politics have been viewed as separate entities in which politicians decide on the end result of planning activity and planners select the required techniques to achieve those ends. This traditional view ignores the fact that the means and the end are closely interrelated, and that judgements made in selecting certain methods of planning will almost certainly alter the end result of the planning process. These judgements are themselves political in nature in that they can lead directly to the advantage or detriment of certain rural population groups.

The practice of rural settlement planning at both county and district authority level is thus more complex than it first appears. In essence, professional planners are employed to service a functional committee (usually the 'planning' or 'environmental services' committee) of the authority which is made up of elected representatives of the council. The committee itself is answerable to the full council, although it is usual practice for committee decisions to be rubber-stamped by the full council meeting unless the issues involved are particularly contentious. Political involvement in rural settlement-plan decisions can thus issue from both professional planners and elected representatives.

The planners

Planning officials customarily place themselves in the role of neutral technicians, but by their very involvement in recommending various decisions, techniques and strategies, this neutrality is difficult to maintain. Blowers' experience as chairman of the Environmental Services Committee of Bedfordshire County Council led him to this considered judgement.

> It is easy to caricature town planners as content to ensure the continuity of policy, anxious to dissuade politicians from introducing party ideology into policy-making. In my experience, planning officers recognize the necessity for politics. They acknowledge the need for political support and initiative to get things done but tend to disclaim any political inclinations themselves. (Blowers, 1980, 3)

However, to disclaim political involvement is to ignore the fact that planning officials in practice wield considerable power in the outcome of planning debates and decisions. Figure 8.3, for example, demonstrates how a local authority often delegates power of decision-making to planning officers in cases of 'straightforward' development applications. Where applications are not deemed straightforward, the planning officer's recommendation is put to the sub or full planning committee where the recommended decision is usually accepted.

Figure 8.3 Suggested departmental structure for a Shire County

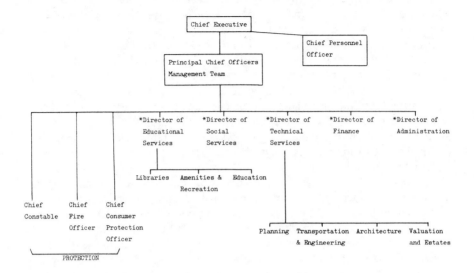

* Members of Management Team

Source: Hobbs and Doling, 1981, 27

It is in the allocative processes of strategic planning that planning officers
are able to wield considerable influence over the broad decisions made in
structure-plan framework policies. In the selection of a starting point for
strategic policy debate; in the narrowing down of infinite theoretical possibilities to a small range of alternative strategies; in the evaluation of these
strategies and the final recommendation of preferred policy, planning officers
are engaging in politically determined (if not strictly politically motivated)
tasks which inevitably reduce the scope of elected representatives in the determination of final policies. Planning officers, as members of the Royal Town
Planning Institute (with its own vigorously defined training and examination
procedures) will be subject to certain ingrained professional standards as well
as to their own ideological or theoretical opinions as to how resources should
be shared out between rural settlements or population groups. Moreover, there
are many ways in which particularly the senior members of planning
departments can gain the ear, and often the sympathy, of elected
representatives on planning committees, and thus ensure a direct input into
decision-making at local authority level. Hobbs and Doling (1981, 202) note
that:

> Much of the work of local authorities is carried out in committees and in
> working groups of officers and elected representatives. There are
> mechanisms by which issues can be discussed, opinions formed, ideas
> floated and resolutions made. In this the officer frequently is in an

advantageous position because he has access to the authority's data base, and any studies undertaken; and it is his full time occupation to consider the planning of the local authority. . . . In such circumstances an officer may deliberately distort, omit or misrepresent the real position in order to lead councillors to the decision which he thinks is the correct one.

This is not to suggest that the determination of planning policy is characterized by wholesale corruption. However it should be admitted that mechanisms do exist through which non-elected planning officers can play a significant, if not dominant, role in the decision-making processes of local authority planning. The extent to which this occurs varies between different authorities. It could be argued that the most common form of political involvement on the part of planning officers is the inherent acceptance of the political *status quo* in their authority. In most instances, planners will be well aware of the political nature of their committee and will tailor proposals to ensure that they have a reasonable prospect of adoption at committee stage. This process tends to prevent radical policy suggestions from reaching decision-makers and works in favour of compromise solutions which prop up current allocation policies however unjust or regressive these might be. Thus, through both positive and negative procedures, professional planners are continually engaged in tasks which require political reactions, recommendations and decisions.

The elected representatives

Political activity is like lightning, in that it may suddenly strike into any corner of the administrative system, but only rarely does so. (Self, 1972, 151)

Self's analysis of the interaction between professional administrators and political decision-makers appears particularly apt when applied to the planning process. For the most part, the symbiosis of planners and elected representatives is a relatively smooth process based on the avoidance of conflict and following conventions of *modus operandi*. In order to ascertain the most likely circumstances in which local councillors exert political power over the bureaucracy of planning we have to delve into the constitution and workings of local authority politics – a task which is again hampered by the degree of variation exhibited by individual authorities, some of which cover predominantly rural areas while others regard rural settlements as only a small element within their representative area. Some general considerations can be made however.

First, as local councillors are elected to make decisions on behalf of their electorate, it might be expected that the elected representatives would reflect the balance of interest in the community concerned. However it is usually the case (although some notable exceptions do occur in rural areas) that local elections are not decided on local issues, but rather that voting is more influenced by national issues and may thus follow party political lines. For instance, local elections in the mid-term of central government frequently favour opposition parties, and local issues are often overpowered by the electorate's wish to show dissatisfaction with national policies. Rural areas have traditionally spawned a host of independent councillors (and some still do) but the research of Blowers (1980), Dearlove (1973), Blondel and Hall (1967) and Buxton (1973) suggests that political parties now form the characteristic feature of the organization of politics in local authorities. The manifestation of party politics in local decision-making is seldom straightforward. Although Conservatives would be ideologically constrained to view local issues through the eyes of ratepayers and landowners while Labour councillors might stress the local authority's role in terms of service provision, these deep-rooted differences tend to assume a high profile in conflicts over housing, education and social services. The formal planning process, however, constitutes less of a potential conflict area between political parties.

A second generalization to be made about local councillors is that whatever their political party they tend to be drawn from the ranks of the better-educated and better-heeled elements of the community. This under-representation of the working class has been regarded by Hindess (1971) as the major reason for the absence of class conflicts in a local government system which tends to operate on a basis of consensus. Where a limited number of representatives are elected on a platform of local issues, they are often denied access to decision-making power by local authority committee structures. The work of Parsons (1966), Buckley (1967), Newton (1976) and others shows that a few well-organized individuals in positions of power (termed 'gatekeepers' by Pettigrew, 1972) can dominate a less organized majority. Thus the chairmanship of all committees and the membership of key decision-making committees is crucial in analysing the basis of political power in local authorities.

The lightning strikes of political power suggested by Self certainly do occur in rural settlement planning at local authority level. When county authorities consider draft structure-plan proposals, the full weight of council meetings is frequently exerted to oppose development proposals or features of budgeting arrangements. Positive pressure may also be exerted by powerful councillors on local planning issues affecting their electorates. However political power also takes the form of long-term pressure in favour of certain political aims and objectives. Newby *et al.* (1978) studied the power held by farmers and landowners over decisions reached by the district and county councils in East Anglia. They found that landowners and farmers were extremely well-represented at all levels in the region's local government structure. Moreover, this representation was strengthened by the potential power provided by key gatekeeper positions where again the farming interest was very marked. This power is often put to use. In Suffolk, for example, by a strong and steady pressure for policies of conservation and restriction of large-scale housing developments (both in the private and public sectors) these agriculturally based groups were seen to be imposing their own view of the needs of rural communities on the will of the councils and of the electorate. In the event, these restrictive residential policies led to an artificial scarcity of private housing, and an under-provision of council housing which was viewed by gatekeeper councillors as preserving the *status quo*. Rose *et al.* (1979, 16), however, point-out that this maintenance of restricted development policies was not merely maintaining an equilibrium but rather *redistributive* in its ramifications: 'At one extreme those in expensively priced private housing have seen their environment retained or even enhanced; while at the other low-paid workers have been forced to leave the area'. Rural areas are particularly prone to such political leverage because of their relatively stable patterns of political representation. Less predictable are the peri-urban counties and districts which are less exposed to long-term political domination by one group. It should be noted however that representatives for rural areas tend to lend support to planning strategies of conservation and restriction of development. Even where landowner power is declining, local authority places are being secured by middle-class environmentalists (Newby, 1979) who show remarkably similar policy leanings to the more traditionally dominant groups. Conflicts of interest arise less over representation of non-affluent and other groups in rural settlements than over the problems of rural versus urban representation in the mixed-area districts. In these cases, the dominance of urban problems and planning needs is the major stumbling block to the formulation of rural policies.

It is clear from this brief review that political involvement in rural settlement planning is shared between planning officials and local politicians. In many ways the distinction between these two groups is unnecessary as the most important consideration is the relationship between planner/politician and the prevailing social and economic interests of the society in which they are planning. Blowers (1980, 38) summarizes these elements:

> Bureaucrats can command the loyalty of subordinates, can control the flow of information, can assert professional values that they consider (and may be accepted by others) as incontestable, and can profess the technical expertise and political neutrality that enable them to appeal to such persuasive notions as rationality and public interest. Politicians can claim the support of a popular mandate, the ability to represent particular interest, and the backing of an organization which can deliver (on most occasions) a decisive role. Each has need of the other's skill and support. Together they form a powerful combination, substantially free from electoral pressures and able to co-opt or assume popular support for their policies.

Planning and rural people

One method of participation in the planning process for rural people is the exercise of their democratic right in local authority elections. However, with the traditionally low turnout in these ballots, the planning process in all areas has appeared to be stigmatized by its negative aspects of control and compulsion. These appear increasingly severe without positive feedback or communication from the planned public. The problems of non-participation are exacerbated in rural areas, where any development permitted or refused has a high marginal effect because of the small scale of settlements. The 1947 Town and Country Planning Act paid little attention to the need for consultation and communication with constituent communities, apart from allowing the consideration of objections before the development plan was submitted to the Ministry. As very few social groups have the time, expertise and resources to make their feelings known through the appeals or objection mechanisms, rates of public participation in the 1950s and 1960s were extremely low.

Some amelioration of the nature of planning was heralded in the report of the Planning Advisory Group which was established in 1964. The group called for better communication between planner and public in terms of both the aims and the ramifications of planning policies, and recognized that such communication amounted to a major public relations exercise. These sentiments were given practical expression in the 1968 Town and Country Planning Act (re-enacted in 1971) which introduced public participation as a statutory process in the preparation of structure plans. The act required that in drawing up their plan local authorities should ensure:

1 That adequate publicity is given in their area to the report of the survey . . . and to matters they propose to include in the plan;
2 That persons who may be expected to desire an opportunity of making representations to the authority with respect to those matters are made aware that they are entitled to an opportunity of doing so;
3 That such persons are given an adequate opportunity of making such representations;
4 That consideration be given to any representations made to them within the prescribed period;
5 That the plan be submitted to the Secretary of State together with a statement of the steps which have been taken to comply with the above requirements and of consultations which have been carried out with other persons.

Similar procedures were to be adopted for local plans except that in this case the adoption of plans is usually carried out by the local authorities themselves. A corollary of these regulations was the commissioning of a report from a committee headed by Arthur Skeffington which published its findings in 1969. The main recommendations of the Skeffington committee (as highlighted by Hobbs and Doling, 1981, 205–6) were couched in vague and almost evasive terms. For example its conclusion that 'people should be kept informed throughout the preparation of a structure or local plan for their area' and that 'local planning authorities should seek to publicize proposals in a way that informs people living in the area to which the plan relates' appear mundane if not substantiated by discussion of actual procedures which might achieve these objectives. Little attention was given to methods of participation except that 'people should be encouraged to participate in the preparation of plans by helping with surveys and other activities as well as by making comments'. Other recommendations have far-reaching implications for the issue of community government, an issue which is largely ducked by the report. For instance, the requirement that 'the public should be told what their representations have achieved or why they have not been accepted' highlights the difference between a public relations exercise of listening to views of the public, and a participation exercise in which comments are heeded and included in the planning process, either positively or negatively.

Two opposing reactions have arisen from Skeffington's proposals. To many, the report was seen to encourage a realistic participation in the planning process not only from active minorities but also from the passive majority of the planned public. This view was reinforced by the proposed appointment of community development officers who were to assist planners in accommodating the interests and aspirations of traditional non-participating groups. An alternative reaction (Ash, 1979) is that some visually effective but functionally weak move towards participation in planning represented a necessary legitimation of a policy-making process where there is a clear inbuilt incentive for planners to prepare their plans in secrecy and then to impose them on the public at the latest possible date. According to this view, therefore, Skeffington's proposals were introduced as a token delegation of planning powers in order to forestall any revolutionary moves towards citizen power over the planning process (Sewell and Coppock, 1977).

Evidence of these opposing reactions can be seen in the steps taken to include rural communities in the rural settlement planning process (Whitehead, 1976). It is certainly clear that a great deal of time, money and effort has been expended by county councils to ensure participation in the structure plan process and also by district and sometimes parish councils in local planning. A variety of techniques have been adopted. Exhibitions of maps, diagrams, free literature and other displays of problems or proposed policies have frequently been used to convey information to the rural public. These have often been established in mobile caravans which tour villages and towns to ensure exposure to as many rural groups as possible. These exhibitions are often accompanied by questionnaire surveys designed to ascertain the views of rural people on planning matters. Rural areas have also been treated to the sight of senior planners travelling the circuit of village halls in an effort to invoke local interest and both to explain and receive feedback on policy proposals.

On the whole these participation methods have been less than successful. Exhibitions tend to be rather superficial in nature and do not attract representative cross-sections of people. Public meetings have proved to be a useful technique but are often drawn into tangential issues which are only loosely connected to the plans under discussion. Questionnaire surveys have been subject to very low response rates, usually reflecting the views of the more articulate and more highly motivated social groups, and almost always restricted because the information collected is predetermined by the completion of the questions which can be manipulated to ensure a certain kind of answer from respondents. Such results can lead to bitter disappointment for planners who genuinely wish to bring about public involvement in the planning process. Simmie (1971; 1974), for example, takes a pessimistic view of a participation exercise in the Oxfordshire parish of Wheatley:

> nearly half the population never discovered, despite extensive publicity, that the plan was in preparation. Of those who actually participated in its

preparation, the leaders were normally drawn from the higher social classes while those who followed them were drawn disproportionately from the lower social classes. Of those who followed the preparation of the plan and who would therefore at least monitor their interest, again a disproportionate number were professional and intermediate workers with only a relatively small number of unskilled manual workers. (Simmie, 1974, 37)

The assertion here is clear and unsavoury. Less-affluent and deprived groups characteristically do not compete in the struggle for power over rural resources. This inability to compete has led to their interest being under-represented in planners' and politicians' definitions of public need, and because the views of these groups are not significantly included in the resolution of conflicting interests in rural areas, they receive less and less positive benefit from rural resource allocation.

An acknowledgement of the deficiencies of these direct methods of participation has led some local authorities to opt for a programme of participation based on local organizations and interest groups. Blowers' (1980, 169) account of participation in the Bedfordshire structure plan suggests that such organizations and groups largely reiterated previously known opinions on their specific interests:

The groups concerned with the countryside, agriculture, and conservation were in favour of low growth and generally restrictive policies. Housing interest showed concern for the homeless and the problems of the construction industry. Industrial and labour organizations favoured a permissive attitude towards industrial development. Political parties adopted ideological positions which found some echoes in the council chamber.

The danger here is that the well-known and well-advocated demands of predominantly middle-class interest groups such as the Council for the Protection of Rural England and the National Farmers' Union will swamp the less well advocated interests of other rural community groups. Even where parish councils represent active local pressure groups there is a likelihood that in some cases the formulation of parish council attitudes will be controlled by similar sections of the community to those represented by national interest organizations. Some parish councils have been able to make an effective case for action against deprivation, but this voice is seldom heeded in the midst of higher-level resource conflict resolutions in planning authorities.

Despite the good intentions of many rural planners, present forms of public participation are instrumental in legitimizing the traditional actions of decision-makers. Participation is geared towards achieving consensus and thereby curbs any opposition to the decisions reached and prevents political debate on more radical and positively reallocative planning proposals. Several issues demand resolution before this state of affairs will be significantly altered. How can planners accurately obtain information on what each individual wants? How can individual preferences be aggregated into a preferred policy which best represents the wishes of the community as a whole? If pressure-group views are sought, should there be active encouragement of groups to represent rural interests which are currently undervalued? At what stage in the planning process should participation be sought? The answers to these questions have yet to be clearly laid down either by central or local government and thus participation remains in a messy and uncoordinated state. Perhaps the most fundamental issue which remains unresolved is that of who should hold the balance of power in society, and therefore who is responsible for resource allocation in society. Hobbs and Doling (1981, 214) stress that 'if . . . participation is not to be intended, in fact, to give real control over planning matters to the population then it cannot be expected that the population will willingly participate at all'. If on the other hand some measure of control is delegated to the public, then fundamental repercussions would result for the interrelationships between local and central government in various policy areas. At present the former scenario holds sway and despite the active and well-intentioned efforts of many planners, participation conjures up images of window-dressing and legitimation rather than of active public involvement.

Resource allocation agencies

Most of the important locational decisions concerning the basic resources which affect rural life-styles are taken *outside* the formal planning process by agencies other than planning departments and committees. The role of these agencies has been underemphasized in the study of rural settlement planning even though it is increasingly recognized that what actually happens in rural areas is largely a function of decisions made in this sphere of operation. Moseley's (1979, 86–7) discussion of agency decisions affecting accessibility emphasizes several general factors which attribute importance to informal planning organizations:

1   No single agency is alone responsible for, or capable of, maintaining the welfare, wellbeing and general livelihood of rural communities;
2   For most relevant agencies, decisions affecting rural areas (and certainly individual rural settlements) are usually secondary considerations, if they are considerations at all: other objectives are usually paramount, or better defined;
3   In consequence of 1 and 2, decision-making tends to be fragmented and ill-focused on rural problems;
4   While there is no shortage of literature on the powers and policies of individual agencies, how they interact (or fail to interact) with one another has received little attention;
5   While in the medium or long-term a more integrated and purposeful process of rural planning and management might be developed, in the short run policy measures cannot be more comprehensive or ambitious than the present institutional context allows.

Thus the tasks performed by resource allocation agencies are crucial to any consideration of practical rural settlement planning. These tasks are briefly outlined below, but the interaction between different agencies, or between agencies and planning authorities is the subject of more detailed discussion in chapter 9 where co-operation between decision-makers is seen to be a major strand in the implementation of rural planning policies. A review of figure 8.1 gives some notion of the plethora of public sector agencies with responsibilities in rural areas. These are briefly described here in a hierarchical format.

District councils

As the parish councils have very few statutory powers of resource provision (apart from in matters of roadside furniture and public open space, which can indeed be locally important), the lowest-level public agency with resource allocation duties is the district council. Figure 8.1 shows that in addition to formal planning, district level responsibilities occur in the areas of employment, housing, environmental health, recreation and to some extent transport. Perhaps their most important function is in *housing*. As housing associations as yet only play a limited role in the provision of rural housing, the district councils are fully responsible for coping with most rented sector housing needs in their area, either through the allocation and management of existing council housing stocks or through the purpose-built construction of new dwellings for local need. Hoath (1978) describes four main types of allocation scheme for council housing: 'date-order' schemes (a first-come, first-served basis); 'points' schemes (where allocation is made to those amassing sufficient points which are gained, for example, for overcrowding family size and so on; 'merit' schemes (where each application is treated on its merits); and 'combined' schemes (e.g. a points scheme for families, a date-order scheme for single applicants, and a merit scheme for homeless applicants). However in rural areas, allocation processes are complicated by locational factors. The bulk of new council-house building is concentrated in the market towns or other selected centres such as the key settlements, and so even though house allocation may go to the most needy, if the recipients happen to live in a smaller village or hamlet they will often be required to move to one of the larger selected centres to receive their alloted dwelling. If district councils attempt to overcome this problem of building council houses in small villages they run the risk of placing tenants in settlements which are not properly serviced by other agencies. Furthermore, building to cater for small local needs in small rural settlements has its pitfalls.

> It is difficult for the local housing authorities to determine where to build small groups of dwellings in small villages. Housing waiting lists are notoriously inaccurate as indicators of housing need and as the demand in small villages is usually very small and can be highly volatile, new council houses in them may eventually be tenanted by households who could be better housed elsewhere rather than by those with genuine local needs. (Association of County Councils, 1979, 30)

The degree to which district housing committees conform to structure-plan resource-concentration policies, or indeed pay lip-service to theories of economies of scale in house-building (which would have the same effect), does differ according to the political make-up of the committee, the resources at its disposal and the extent of its perceived need to co-operate with other resource agencies. Indeed this location–allocation–co-operation equation is now complicated by the decision on how rigorously to pursue the selling of council houses.

Some district council duties require fewer location decisions than in the housing sector. For example the provision of various environmental health services such as refuse collection and septic tank cleansing is undertaken to every rural dwelling if required. Although it is costly to service scattered rural populations with these facilities, the main decision to be made at district level is whether the frequency and standard of service can be maintained at urban levels. In other duties, the district role is either permissive or advisory. An example of the former is in transport, where the 1968 Transport Act allows districts to subsidize local bus services, either directly or through concessionary fare schemes, and to establish experimental transport schemes. Degrees of action in these areas vary greatly from district to district, but in general progress is hampered by lack of finance and by the need to work within the county council's structure plan and transport policy and programme. Advisory duties are performed in provision of recreational facilities and in the tempting of new employment to locate in rural areas, both by site and factory establishment and by wider advertising and attraction methods. In both of these cases, locational decisions are made which will potentially affect the livelihood of rural settlements.

County councils

The Bains Report of 1972 recommended a formula for county council decision-making which consisted of a chief executive along with a management team of departmental directors who would ensure policy collaboration between different county-level functions and prevent isolationism amongst the various sections of the authority (figure 8.3). Although some counties have responded well to this challenge of corporate management, there is evidence that some departments still tend to exist in mutual isolation. Moseley (1979, 90) suggests two reasons for this:

> First, the councils have extensive obligations over a number of important fields and the relevant departments which have emerged are largely concerned with the achievement of aims and standards in one particular field. Second, in order best to achieve the aims of each department, the majority of its staff are specialists in that field at an appropriate level. . . . Because of this, departments tend to work towards the achievement of standards in different aspects of life with little overall appreciation of implications for broader issues.

Figure 8.3 shows the diversity of tasks which the Bains Report was attempting to integrate. The council's protection services require decisions as to the placement of police and fire personnel throughout the county. It can be most comforting for village residents to know that there is a police house in the village and a fire tender not too far away, although there has been an increasing tendency for locational rationalization of these services which has added to the isolation of some rural settlements.

The education service fulfils a statutory need ranging from pre-school provision through to post-16-year-old opportunities and adult evening classes, the sum total of which accounts for around 65 per cent of expenditure in non-metropolitan counties. Important locational decisions are made by the education authority which can have widespread effects in rural settlements. Faced with a scattered population and an ageing stock of school buildings many of which need refurbishing or replacing, rural education services are characterized by 'a downward spiral of numbers and resources' (Association of County Councils, 1979, 7). These circumstances have led to the closure of village schools and the likelihood of further closures in the future, all of which present the need to transport children to centralized school premises where economies of scale prevail. This rationalization is more or less complete in secondary schooling where the retrenchment of facilities in larger settlements results in the rigours of long-distance travel for rural children and the absence of choice as to which school to attend. Thus although school age education is mandatory, the allocative decisions taken by education authorities affect the life-styles of rural people, and can reduce the growth prospects of rural settlements particularly where the absence of a primary school leads to a refusal of planning permission for residential development.

Social services departments provide a host of services based on the concept of community care. Adoption, foster home placement, homes for children and the elderly, domiciliary and day care services for disabled and other client groups all come under this heading. In some cases, social service provision in rural areas tends to be at a low level. Shaw and Stockford (1979, 125) suggest that

> in terms of the community/domiciliary services for Home Helps and Meals-on-Wheels, concentration of population appears to be a significant factor in determining, in the case of Meals-on-Wheels, the provision of the service, and, in the case of Home Helps, how many clients are helped.

In addition to this population factor, the provision of social services in rural areas has traditionally been low level because it is considered that *demand* for these services is substantially lower in rural than in urban areas. However, Stockford (1978) refutes this conventional view and provides evidence that discrepancies between need and demand for social services owe less to the strong family and community structures of rural areas than to the physical accessibility of the services concerned. Thus, non-mobile groups in rural areas do not have the accessibility to reach centralized social services and therefore do not make as much use of them as might be the case if the services were more accessible. As with education, social service clients living in rural areas have little choice between services and are often faced with a situation whereby certain services are not available to them. On the positive side, some county councils (notably Hereford and Worcester, 1978) have deliberately allocated resources to local community care projects in rural areas. In many ways, social service departments have a significant part to play in changing overall policy in rural areas. The Association of County Councils (1979, 16) recognizes that:

> Their influence upon the kind of community settlement pattern which exists is overwhelming. Location of housing, employment opportunity, service provision and transport are all affected and since these factors influence the viability of a community, and its ability to help itself, a social work input to these plans must become a necessity.

The final area of county council resource allocation which is important in the context of rural settlement planning is that of transportation and engineering. County responsibility over rural transport first became important after the 1968 Transport Act, Section 34 of which established that county councils should make the final decision as to whether a rural bus service was essential or not. The councils are thus permitted (but not obliged) to subsidize the losses incurred by supported bus services. In fact many counties were slow to react to these permissive powers and as a result many rural bus services have disappeared through lack of sponsorship. Section 203 of the 1972 Local Government Act strengthened the involvement of county councils in transport policy. It dictated that counties 'should develop policies which will promote the provision of a co-ordinated and efficient system of public transport to meet the needs of the county'. This mandatory requirement was supported by an increase in the flexibility with which counties could allocate finance to transport purposes, and the end result was the production of annual transport policies and programmes (TPPs) which were to outline county strategy for transport development. Although these powers represent considerable potential for improvement of accessibility in rural areas, the promotion of rural transport at county level has not been significantly improved. Moseley (1979) gives three reasons for this trend:

1 Other claims on rural transport expenditure (especially road maintenance) are expensive and often unavoidable;
2 The personnel in the surveyors' and engineers' departments of most counties relates more to road and traffic management than to socially oriented accessibility systems;
3 There is often an ideological dislike of subsidy payments on the part of the predominantly Conservative-controlled councils of non-metropolitan counties.

However the decisions made at this level have crucial ramifications for all other sectors of rural living and are thus vital to the achievement of an equitable form of rural settlement planning.

County councils also play a vital co-ordinating role in employment provision in rural areas. They can participate in the development of fully serviced industrial sites with advanced factories. Indeed, more than one third of non-metropolitan county councils in England and Wales are currently acquiring land for this use, and in many other cases, similar efforts are being advanced through the co-operation of the Development Commission and local authorities. Investment is also required from counties for local access roads and other road improvements to ensure that available land can be used for industrial use. Once again, it is the co-ordination between counties and other agencies which will be the deciding factor in the success of these schemes.

Regional agencies

Brief mention should also be made of a series of other agencies which make decisions affecting rural communities and which tend to be responsible to government departments rather than the democratically elected local authorities. The two most prominent agencies at the regional level concern water and health although utility services (gas and electricity) also have regional components. Regional water authorities have control over water supply and sewage disposal provision. It is now the case that most rural properties are connected to mains water supplies, even though connection charges for isolated dwellings are extremely high. Resource allocation decisions by water authorities, therefore, are largely confined to sewerage considerations. The importance of this factor as a determinant of rural development should not be underemphasized. One major reason for refusing planning permission for residential developments in rural settlements is the absence of mains drainage capacity, and the ponderous progress which has been made in providing sewerage schemes to cope with rural growth has often led to strategic policies for rural growth centres foundering on the lack of co-operation from water authorities. This mismatch between planning policy and sewerage provision policy is always likely as long as water authorities base their allocation on their definition of needs caused by present low water quality rather than taking similar account of proposed future requirements.

Regional health authorities and their subsidiary agencies (e.g. area health authorities and family practitioner committees) are responsible for similar duties to those of water authorities: namely, the everyday management and longer-term planning of health services. A complicated structure of decision-making exists at different levels of this hierarchy. Ultimately it is the general practitioner (guided by the Family Practitioner Council) who decides where to set up practice and how to allocate surgery hours. The trend in rural areas of replacing single practices with group practices centrally located in larger settle-ments (thus reducing small village medical facilities) has thus largely arisen from decisions taken by medical staff, often based on the need to improve their own working conditions. At a larger scale, the decisions to build, extend or relocate hospital facilities are made by the regional health authority, usually following guidelines laid down by the Department of Health and Social Security. Most areas have opted for a centralization of such facilities (thus imposing accessibility discrimination against rural residents, particularly non-mobile groups) but the idea of re-establishing rural community hospitals has been contemplated by some authorities (Haynes *et al.*, 1978).

The regional scale has also spawned a new breed of resource management and allocation agency which is represented by the Highlands and Islands Development Board, and more recently the Development Board for Rural Wales (DBRW). Using central government resources in co-operation with local government resources, these boards have sought to establish widespread initiatives in their constituent areas. Attention has been primarily given to economic improvement, through the attraction of new industrial employment and the financing of other employment generating enterprises, but significant efforts have been made to underpin economic progress with concomitant social development. The DBRW, for example, plans to build homes in locations where industrial development is being expanded, and is also financing small-scale community welfare projects. The boards do appear to offer one method of ensuring a comprehensive type of approach to the planning of rural settlements, yet they inevitably introduce complexity into decision-making process by superimposing yet another planning agency into an already crowded area of allocative agencies.

National agencies

Decision-making which functions at national level, but which takes effect in rural settlements and communities can be divided into three main forms. First, the government itself continually acts as decision-maker for rural areas. This involvement can assume many forms. Most government departments take direct action which has ramifications in rural areas. The Ministry of Transport, for example, makes key decisions regarding the road network, and the Department of Employment encroaches into rural communities through the workings of job centres. Alternatively, central government holds the purse-strings of various agencies and of many local government functions. Consequently, guidelines and budgetary measures decided at national level filter through to smaller-scale decision-makers who often find their options narrowed accordingly.

The second major sphere of national decision-making takes place through government agencies. For example, the Manpower Services Commission has been instrumental in setting up various schemes which have provided short-term employment for various groups (particularly school leavers) in rural communities. In many ways the most important government body in this respect is the Development Commission which is concerned specifically with rural problems. Many of the initiatives for rural economic development have stemmed from the commission, particularly through the work of its subsidiary, the Council for Small Industries in Rural Areas (CoSIRA) and in turn through CoSIRA's county Small Industry Committees. The acquisition of land for industrial purposes, the building of advance factories, the provision of infrastructural backup, as well as numerous tasks of advice, information and advertisement are all functions undertaken with some success by this group of government organizations. They are, however, limited by the resources which are made available to them by their parent department.

The third main type of national influence is exerted through the various public corporations. The Post Office has obvious connections with rural areas, with the village post office representing a rallying point over the decline in rural services. The financial sponsorship of rural shopkeepers for providing post office facilities has maintained the viability of many village shops, and the decision to maintain this financial backing is in the hands of the Post Office Corporation. However, rural areas are likely to receive the brunt of any cuts in Post Office expenditure. Although the mobile collection and delivery of mail services still cover almost every rural property in England and Wales, the frequency of service is already less than that in urban areas (once as opposed to twice per day) and it is likely that rural post offices will be similarly vulnerable to the 'second-class' level of postal service. The Gas Corporation also attaches a secondary importance to rural areas. They have a statutory obligation to provide natural-gas supplies to any dwelling within 25 yards (23 m) of an existing main, but very few rural areas are actually served by mains. Finally, British Rail and the National Bus Company (NBC) both have obvious relevance to rural accessibility. The rail network has now contracted to the extent that many rural areas are devoid of rail services. However, British Rail is required to maintain unprofitable services, and many of these have a rural component. Similarly NBC services can be subsidized by local authorities, although the 1980 Transport Act may complicate this relationship by permitting private bus operators to compete with NBC services.

The private sector

With this multitude of public sector agencies whose decisions take effect in rural settlements, the fact that the private sector is an equally important decision-making power in rural areas is often neglected. Public- and private-sector activities are often interlinked. For example, public-sector efforts to entice employment into rural areas are usually dependent on individual entrepreneurs or private companies to respond to the incentives provided. An even more symbiotic relationship occurs between the post office and village shopkeepers. Whether in harness with public agencies, or working independently, the decisions made by agents and agencies in the private sector are of far-reaching importance to rural people. The decisions of firms of all sizes and key individuals (notably farmers) influence the availability of employment. Of particular importance here is the high-level decision of multinational organizations to establish branch factories in rural locations offering financial incentives. This type of employment has proved vulnerable since the decision to close a small rural manufacturing operation is far more easily made by the large-scale institution whose major interests are elsewhere than by the local entrepreneur whose livelihood depends on the continuation of the business. It might be argued that security of development is greatest where the workers themselves participate in decision-making processes.

Accessibility provision in rural areas is heavily reliant on independent bus operators who by using family labour and multiple role employment methods generally enjoy lower overheads and average costs than NBC subsidiaries. The importance of these operators to the maintenance of a rural bus network is recognized by many local authorities who have shown some willingness to subsidize certain independently run services. Other rural services also fall within the private sector. Rural retailing, for instance, is dominated by the various decisions made by both independents and multiples, with individual entrepreneurs being essential to the upkeep of shopping facilities in villages.

One final sector where private-sector decisions are important is rural housing. Local authority planners can devise strategic policies for residential development, but the decision to develop lies elsewhere. District housing committees allocate council houses, but private developers supply the applications which planners permit or refuse. In this instance, it is private sector agencies (again ranging from small local concerns to international companies) who decide on the number, type and purpose of residential proposals. However much informal consultation takes place between planners and developers on the subject of desirable types of housing in particular areas, the profit motive must be satisfied before the private-sector development takes place. Underlying the decisions made by developers is the rather more obscure influence of the financial institutions which provide both backing for private companies, and are also often instrumental in controlling the release of rural land (a good proportion of which is institutionally owned).

It is clear from this brief review that decisions made in the private sector are equally important in their outcome to rural areas as those produced by the public sector. The traditional view of rural settlement planning as a process carried out in local authority planning offices cannot be upheld in view of the complex interconnectivity of decisions which take effect in rural areas. Indeed, the agencies which, in reality, have the power to control the allocation of finance and other resources in rural settlements are those over which the formal planning process has least control. The interaction between all these agencies and the ability of planners to implement rural settlement policies is discussed in more detail in chapter 9.

NINE

Policy implementation

The policy–implementation gap

> The test of the value of any plan, policy or strategy is the extent to which it influences the making and taking of decisions. (Glasson, 1979, 32)

The degree to which rural settlement policy has been converted into action through implementation processes in planning has been questioned on several occasions in previous chapters. Despite a significant upturn in the importance which has been attached over the last decade by policy analysts to implementation procedures (e.g. Jenkins, 1978; Dunsire, 1978; Levitt, 1980), implementation in rural planning has been underemphasized to the extent that Pressman and Wildavsky's (1973) suggestion that 'the implementation of planning policies has been much studied but little understood' is positively flattering if applied to the rural context. It is only recently that researchers in rural settlement planning have fully acknowledged that written policy statements do not necessarily reflect the planning decisions made at ground level, and that a rather murky divide exists between policy formulation and policy implementation. This chapter discusses some of the issues involved in the study of implementation processes, with the intention of attempting to illuminate some of the inherent complexities in this subject area rather than providing answers to questions that remain under-researched and prone to untenable generalization.

Two recent research programmes in Devon serve to amplify the existence of a policy–implementation gap in rural settlement planning (the fact that both refer to Devon indicates the richness of research effort in that county rather than any inherent peculiarity in the planning taking place there). The work of Blacksell and Gilg (1977; 1981) provides a fascinating insight into the spatial distribution of planning permissions and refusals in selected areas of rural Devon. Their general hypothesis was that the county-wide key settlement policy adopted by the county council (for details, see Cloke, 1979) should result in a concentration of new housebuilding in the selected centres while development in other villages should be limited accordingly. Similarly, those areas within a designated National Park or Area of Outstanding Natural Beauty (AONB) might expect to receive additional restrictions on new development, particularly in smaller settlements and in the open countryside. Making meticulous use of planning application records which had been maintained by the county council since 1964, Blacksell and Gilg were able to test these hypotheses and produce firm evidence as to whether any gap existed between policy and implementation in this case.

Figure 9.1 demonstrates the pattern of outline planning *permissions* which were plotted for four selected study areas.

1 The *East Devon* area is partly designated an AONB and contains a dense network of pressured settlements which in total attracted 81.3 per cent of outline planning permissions in the area over the study period. A relatively low figure of 18.7 per cent of total permissions were granted for new building in the open countryside which suggests that measures of landscape protection were being implemented in this instance. The area's two key settlements, however, showed varying success as growth magnets. Woodbury in the west provided a focus for 18.7 per cent of all permissions but Newton Poppleford in the east failed to act as a significant growth centre for new development;

2 The *Dartmoor* area has a more sparse settlement pattern including three key settlements (Moretonhampstead, Dunsford and Christow). Here non-key settlements accounted for 33.9 per cent of permissions compared with only 22.0 per cent in the selected centres, of which only Moretonhampstead (the largest) dominated in the manner suggested by the county council policy. An astounding 44.1 per cent of permissions were granted in the open countryside of this National Park area. Blacksell and Gilg attribute this phenomenon to heavy pressure for housing both from the area's

Figure 9.1 Outline planning permissions in four areas of rural Devon, 1964-74

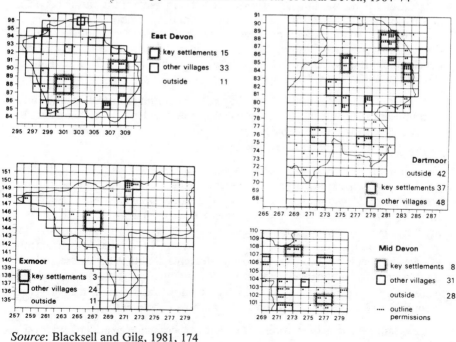

Source: Blacksell and Gilg, 1981, 174

agricultural population and from commuters to Exeter and Torbay, and they recognize a clear conflict between these expressed needs for development and the objectives of the Devon key settlement policy;

3   The *Exmoor* area experienced less demand for growth than the preceding areas, with the bulk of existing development being concentrated in the coastal resort of Lynton–Lynmouth. The one key settlement in the area, Parracombe, attracted only three permissions and does not represent the expected implementation of key settlement planning. In contrast to the Dartmoor case study, only 28.9 per cent of new development was permitted in the open countryside;

4   Finally, the *Mid Devon* area, where no landscape-protection policy was pursued, revealed that 41.0 per cent of permissions were granted in the open countryside, 50.8 per cent in non-key villages and only 8.1 per cent in the two key settlements of Lapford and Copplestone. Here there is little indication of any rural settlement policy in action (at least in terms of new housing).

These results have been reproduced in detail as evidence that in this one facet of rural planning, the stated objectives of the planning authority strategy have in almost every case *not* been fulfilled by the implementation of the planning-permission mechanism. Moreover, new residential development represents an area over which planners supposedly assume considerable powers of control and yet even when tested on this most favourable parameter, the formal planning process exhibits a significant gap between policy and outcome.

More light is thrown on the motives for planning decisions in Blacksell and Gilg's analysis of planning *refusals* (table 9.1). In general the ratios between permission and refusal for the East Devon and Dartmoor areas are high, reflecting the wish to protect these 'pressured' areas from indiscriminate development. In the Exmoor area the ratio is lower, as less pressure for development is experienced here. Blacksell and Gilg (1981, 142) note that the relative lack of development pressure in Exmoor

has produced a situation where villages are beginning to fail as viable communities through emigration and a lack of new residents to replace them. In such circumstances it is patently self-defeating to refuse applications on purely aesthetic and landscape grounds.

Only in the Mid Devon area do permissions exceed refusals and significantly this is the only case study of the four where no additional landscape-protection measures are in operation. Thus one general conclusion from this research is that a major motivator of planned implementation of decisions in these four areas is a desire to ensure that new development does not intrude into aesthetically valued landscapes. This motive appears stronger than that of concentrating development into the selected key settlements. Table 9.1 shows very little difference between the refusal ratios for key and non-key settlements, and this evidence is supported by figure 9.2 which demonstrates a significant level of refusal in key settlement locations. The authors conclude that

few examples have been found of villages experiencing a sudden and totally

Table 9.1   Ratio of refusals to permissions of outline planning applications in four areas of rural Devon

	Permission	:	Refusal
East Devon			
Total	1	:	3.9
Key settlements	1	:	2.7
Non-key settlements	1	:	2.5
Elsewhere	1	:	7.1
SE Dartmoor			
Total	1	:	2.8
Key settlements	1	:	1.6
Non-key settlements	1	:	1.7
Elsewhere	1	:	6.9
Western Exmoor			
Total	1	:	1.2
Key settlements	1	:	1.3
Non-key settlements	1	:	1.2
Elsewhere	1	:	1.4
Mid Devon			
Total	1	:	0.6
Key settlements	1	:	0.5
Non-key settlements	1	:	0.7
Elsewhere	1	:	0.5

Source: Blacksell and Gilg, 1981, 176

Figure 9.2 Planning refusals in four areas of rural Devon, 1964–74

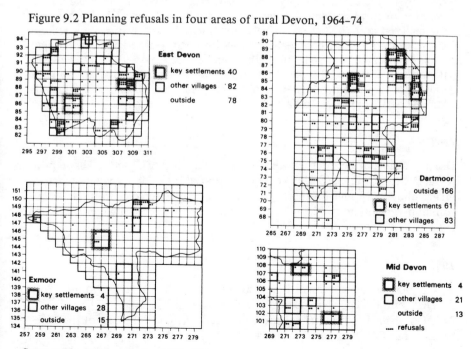

Source: Blacksell and Gilg, 1981, 177

> unprecedented spurt of growth after being designated a key settlement . . . what planning has done is to hold that demand (for housing) within bounds, so that distribution of population does not become too divorced from the distribution of services. (Blacksell and Gilg, 1981, 178)

This deviation between written policy and implemented action should not be considered surprising. Any detailed study of planning in a rural area is likely to uncover similar discrepancies and indeed it would be astonishing to discover a policy which *had* been directly translated into action without alteration at the implementation stage. What this Devon study does show is the extent of the policy–implementation gap in one element (granting or refusal of planning permission) which is under the direct control of planning authorities. In fact no planning element can be treated as an independent phenomenon, and in this one set of research results, evidence has arisen of discontinuity of policy (e.g. between landscape protection and low rates of pressure for new housing in Exmoor), lack of inter-agency co-operation (particularly where planning permission has been refused in key settlements due to a sewerage embargo), and discretion within policy so as to permit development in areas of decline.

The interconnectivity and conflict between various agencies and their resources, opinions and decisions within the implementation stage of rural settlement planning are highlighted by further research in Devon by Glyn-Jones (1979). In an extremely detailed case study of Hatherleigh (a settlement of around 1000 population, north of Okehampton) she plots a well-documented history of development planning at a local level which is characterized by its inclusion of many typical difficulties experienced in the implementation of rural settlement policy. Her account of planning in Hatherleigh between 1964 and 1973 is extensively summarized here to provide a second detailed example of the policy–implementation gap. Hatherleigh was selected as a key settlement in 1964 and might therefore be expected to receive sympathetic consideration for new developments. A chronological account of detailed local planning, however, demonstrates some of the many pitfalls which lie between policy and action.

1963

Discord occurred between Devon County Council (DCC) and Okehampton Rural District Council (ORDC) over the proposal for a county-wide key settlement policy. Although Hatherleigh was one of the selected centres, ORDC in common with other district councils would have preferred a wider spread of growth.

1967

1 No Outline Development Plan was produced for Hatherleigh until 1969. DCC and ORDC were deadlocked over several issues;
2 DCC wished to maintain the form of Hatherleigh to the east of the River Lew but ORDC wished to make use of land for development across the

river to the west (thus expanding and changing the settlement's spatial structure);

3 ORDC acquired land west of the river for council housing;
4 ORDC wished to approve a scheme for some fifty privately developed houses on a site adjacent to their own, to the west of the river. DCC refused planning permission;
5 The developers who owned the fifty-house site were connected with a newly opened abattoir (Devon Meat Co.) in Hatherleigh and stressed that these new houses were needed for key workers as the abattoir was expanded. They had already been refused permission to build houses on several sites and requested that ORDC might sell them a suitable council-owned site.

January 1968

1 ORDC agreed to sell their west-bank council-house site to Devon Meat Co. provided that it was used solely to house employees of the abattoir and the associated market and that no part of the site was subsequently sold off;
2 Hatherleigh Parish Council (HPC) protested that this transfer from local authority to private ownership would neglect the needs of the local aged and young married population;
3 Devon Meat Co. objected to the conditions for the sale of the site, because they could not afford to develop it themselves and would have to hand it over to a developer or offer plots to individual employees.

March 1968

1 Devon Meat Co. rejected ORDC's offer and pressed for the approval of their own fifty-house site (already refused by DCC);
2 Meanwhile, ORDC reactivated its own council housing proposals on the site rejected by the company;
3 DCC finally rejected the company's proposal on the grounds of an unsatis- factory road junction, a deleterious impact on the landscape, and the fact that development would be unrelated to the existing community.

May 1968

1 Devon Meat Co. submitted a renewed application for 160 houses, both on the same site and extending onto land nearer the town. The submission was backed by ORDC, HPC and the National Farmers Union;
2 DCC reiterated its previous objections and raised two more. First, the settlement's sewerage plant had insufficient capacity to cope with the new development. Second, sixty-eight permissions had already been granted in Hatherleigh since 1964 and only four houses had been built. Thus housing opportunities were already available for key workers.

July 1968

Devon Meat Co. passed into the hands of a receiver after less than a year in operation. The company claimed that they had to turn work away because they did not receive planning permission to house the men needed to operate the abattoir. Glyn-Jones (1979, 20) however suggests that 'it cannot be concluded that development control was the sole or even main reason for the collapse of the abattoir.'

June 1969

1 Throughout 1968 discussions were taking place over the proposed Hatherleigh Outline Development Plan. DCC wished to restrict development to sites east of the river, both because of the potential imbalance caused by growth on the west side and because any such growth would be isolated from the settlement core if a bypass was ever built along the preferred route close to the river. ORDC already had permission for thirty-five council houses on the west-bank site and wanted further development on adjacent sites including a 9-acre industrial estate. These proposals found support from HPC, Devon River Authority and the local Ministry of Agriculture representatives;
2 The plan was agreed in June 1969, but of 63 acres scheduled for development, only 27 were to the west of the river (much already committed), and ORDC failed to establish the 31 additional acres on the west bank which they favoured for development;
3 As part of the plan preparations it was recognized that expansion of sewage disposal arrangements would soon become a priority.

May 1969

While the outline plan was being thrashed out, planning permission was sought for land immediately adjacent to the west bank council house site (part of land ultimately zoned for residential development in the plan).

December 1969

1 Outline permission was granted for this development, partly due to an apparent assurance from ORDC (who had responsibility for the sewage works) of sufficient sewerage capacity for thirty or forty new houses;
2 The principle of an expanded sewage works was by now accepted as some plots were excluded from the permitted site due to their proximity to the works expansion site.

Autumn 1972

1 The developers submitted a detailed application for their outline permission, proposing 106 units on the site;

2   The size of the proposed development reopened the question of sewage disposal capacity. In September 1972, ORDC suggested that a first phase of twenty units could be accommodated by the present works. The river authority insisted that the works must be enlarged immediately and urged an embargo on any new development in Hatherleigh. Such an embargo could not prevent the granting of detailed planning permission, where outline permission was already held (as in the 106 unit site).

Glyn-Jones (1979, 23) explains the ORDC attitude in two ways:

> the Rural District had doubts whether the big development would really go ahead – and it may be assumed too, that as least some councillors must have reflected that within a year this costly exercise would no longer be their responsibility, but would pass to the newly constituted Water Authorities.

So ORDC did not initiate extensions to the sewage works, and the new South West Water Authority, on assuming responsibility, placed an immediate embargo on new development in Hatherleigh.

October 1973

By this time the developers had received detailed planning permission for their site (amended to 113 units) but the company's financial circumstances were such they they chose not to proceed with the development and the prospect of a grossly overloaded sewage works was avoided.

Such a string of circumstances is not unique or even unusual in local-scale rural planning. The Hatherleigh example is, however, important because of the detailed research attention devoted to it, and those who seek to understand rural settlement planning owe a debt to Anne Glyn-Jones for providing this example. Although the presentation above glosses over an intricate maze of negotiation, advice, parochialism, lack of co-operation and so on, it does serve to merge the aggregate and local levels of rural planning. At one level, a county-wide policy is favoured with the seemingly simple aim of promoting the growth of housing and employment in selected key settlements. At the lower level, one of these growth centres, which has the bonus of pressure for new development (not found in many of the more remote key settlements) experiences great difficulty in achieving the desired growth because of various conflicts between agencies and resources within the implementation process. The 'many a slip twixt cup and lip' adage may be a simplistic one, but the extent of the policy–implementation gap in the past has severely reduced the effectiveness of rural settlement planning, and only a greater understanding of this gap will change this situation and permit a more effective employment of desired policies in the future.

The concept of implementation

The term implementation has been used rather loosely in the context of rural settlement planning. A dictionary definition suggests a verb meaning to 'carry into effect' or to 'complete, perform, fulfil', and indeed the recent rise of interest in what we term implementation arises largely from a recognition that planning policies have been less than successful in their completion, performance and fulfilment. Traditionally, the phenomenon of implementation has fitted snugly into the rational decision-making model of planning. Simplified models like that suggested by Jenkins (figure 9.3) view implementation as one particular stage in a logical sequence of events in the policy decision-making process, falling between the arrival at a decision as to the optimum policy, and an evaluation of how that policy works when enacted. Within this paradigm, implementation has been described as:

1 'Those outputs (actions) of an agency which derive from a particular decision sequence, the outputs being supposed to achieve, or implement, the policy' (Healey, 1979, 5);

2 'The ability to forge subsequent links in the causal chain so as to obtain desired results' (Pressman and Wildavsky, 1973, 15);

3 'Those actions by public and private individuals (or groups) that are directed at the achievement of objectives set forth in prior policy decisions' (van Meter and van Horn, 1975, 447).

The assumption that action follows logically from decisions, and that clearly identifiable policies can thus be accurately translated into planning action, leads to an expectation that planning aims and objectives can be fulfilled through the implementation process. If the rational decision-making framework is followed, the policy–implementation gap becomes an illogicality in a logical system.

Critics of the rational model (e.g. Braybrooke and Lindblom, 1963; Boaden, 1971; Davies, 1978) suggest that the actual nature of implementation has often been subsumed by the need for it to act as a logical stage in a sequential process. As Lewis and Flynn (1978, 5) point out:

In reality there are disagreements about policy goals and objectives, vagueness and ambiguity about policies and uncertainty about their operationalization in practice; procedural complexity; inconsistency between powers available and existing problems; and conflicts arising from public participation, pressure group activity and political dissensus.

Recognition that these important factors tend to transpose implementation from a neat stage in a logical positivist process into a function of the political and organizational mechanisms by which decisions are reached has led to a search for new frameworks within which to search for an understanding of the concept (Rhodes, 1977). If, for example, implementation is viewed as part of a political decision-making process rather that a stage in an end–means process, then the policy–implementation gap is less important *per se*, as the focus for study is more on decisions which actually allocate resources rather than on the frameworks within which resources are allocated. In this way, policy is not artificially separated from implementation (Hambleton, 1981), and thus, an understanding of how decisions are made may be seen as one key with which to unlock the complexities of the implementation process.

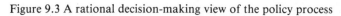
Figure 9.3 A rational decision-making view of the policy process

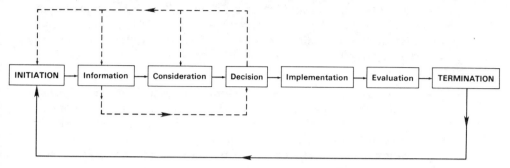

Source: Jenkins, 1978, 17

.Even this decision-making perspective has its limitations. Healey (1979) stresses that decisions are merely an outcome of interactions between different interests in society as expressed through particular agencies. In this case, the influence of economic and political institutions on the activities of decision-making agencies also becomes an important focus for study. She summarizes the current understanding of implementation (1979, 11) in this way:

> What we are looking for are better ways of understanding the interrelationship of policies, actions undertaken to achieve policies and the outcomes of these actions than those provided by procedural planning theory and the rational decision model.

In the limited space available here, two particular approaches to the understanding of implementation are advanced as being particularly relevant to the rural planning context. First, a model based on factors influencing the behaviour of decision-making actors in planning is described, and, second, a number of constituent foci of current implementation processes within different planning options are reviewed. It is hoped that both approaches, albeit from different angles, will throw light on what implementation is and how it is carried out.

A behavioural model

Following the social action approach adopted by some sociologists (Silverman, 1970) the research of Lewis and Flynn (1978) led them to present a behavioural model of policy-making in order to develop an understanding of the process of implementation as 'action' or 'getting things done'. The model's premise is that action will be explained by the study of the differential commitments and goal orientations of individuals concerned with planning. Accordingly the model focuses on the individual within an organization and analyses the dual concerns with which he or she is faced, namely the exterior world and the interior institutional context within which he or she works (figure 9.4). Although these two concerns are relatively fixed constraining factors, a great deal of flexibility and variation occurs because the actors will perceive courses of action and situations in different ways. As Lewis and Flynn (1978, 11) point out:

> The key feature is that an individual actor is not just a cog in a machine but is the mediator between the world outside the organization and the organizational structure which channels the available responses. The way in which the individual, and the multitude of individuals within an organization, mediate between these two sets of concerns are key processes in the understanding of what 'gets done'.

Thus, according to this model, the matching of problems and channels of action is the essence of implementation, and this alliance is in turn dependent on the three main blocks of the model.

Institutional context

All agencies and organizations which participate in rural settlement planning (see chapter 8 for a detailed breakdown) are seen to exist within an environment or context of other organizations with which a relatively structured set of relationships exists (Friend, 1980; Leach, 1980; Rhodes, 1980; Stewart, 1980). Accordingly an organization will develop a 'mode of action' which dictates its dealings with other organizations within that environment. Lewis and Flynn identify eight common modes of action within planning (table 9.2) which constitute an important backcloth to the problems of inter-agency co-operation discussed below. These modes of action are dynamic within particular policy fields (witness the rise of district council powers in town and country planning) and often hierarchical in nature so that one institution is in a position to dictate the terms of any interaction (Elkins, 1975). Where no such authority exists, the bargaining mode of action is used and the outcome is less predictable. Again the county/district relationship is important in this respect, with each agency governed by its own objectives and neither having sufficient power over the other to impose its will without bargaining.

The individual within the organization

The various modes of action which constitute the institutional context are

Figure 9.4 A behavioural model of policy-making.

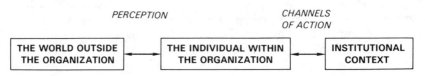

Source: Lewis and Flynn, 1978, 11

Table 9.2   Modes of action within the institutional context of planning

1 *Regulation*   Where the mode of action is legal and limits are set by law, such as pollution levels or local byelaws; sanctions are available through the courts
2 *Judicial control*   Where one organization can reassess decisions taken by another through legal or quasi-legal procedures, e.g. call-in procedures and appeals
3 *Procedural control*   An organization defines the way in which something should be done, but not what the substantive output should be, e.g. development control in the DoE
4 *Hiving-off*   An organization allocates responsibility for particular functional areas to some other body which 'administers' within policy guidelines laid down by the first organization, e.g. the Countryside Commission, or agency agreements made by county councils
5 *Consent*   One organization sets the policy guidelines for other organizations but leaves it to the latter bodies to define the specific problems and take the action, e.g. conservation in the DoE
6 *Bargaining*   Where two organizations have to reach some kind of accord over the actions to be taken, and each have a stake in achieving some outcome
7 *Execution*   Where one organization is concerned to define the problem, specify details about the way action should be taken and see particular kinds of outputs from other organizations, e.g. the first 2 years of the Community Land Act, or local authority house building
8 *Finance*   Where one organization can offer financial inducements to other organizations in order to achieve some actions rather than others

Source: Lewis and Flynn, 1978, 17

themselves modified by the individual's perception of 'the problem' and 'the appropriate channel of action'. For example, the gentrification of small rural settlements may be viewed as an appropriate trend in that it counteracts a position of depopulation, or as a harmful one in that it restricts the opportunities of less affluent population groups to live in that location. According to which view is adopted, opposite decisions on the need for planning action and the type of such action may occur. The factor of perception may be analysed according to:

1 *Personal attributes*, including political and ideological dogma, personal values and so on;
2 *Occupational role* in terms of job specifications and responsibilities, past professional experience and the so-called 'deeper structures' within the organization (Klein and Lewis, 1977); and
3 *Organizational context*, often relating to divisions of responsibility within and between departments.

The world outside the organization

This final section of the model stresses the variation in areas to be planned. Physical and demographic characteristics will obviously vary between the rural uplands and the rural–urban fringe; expectations will vary between middle-class rural residents, perhaps wishing for better environmental provision and more access, and working-class communities desiring different trade-offs between economy and landscape in rural areas.

Lewis and Flynn's model highlights several important aspects of implementation, not least the potential variation that occurs where seemingly similar sets of circumstances are dealt with by different individuals within different organizations. It focuses on the important question of why and how decisions are made in the enactment of preconstituted policies and offers the idea that policies are often reformulated during the implementation process. The behavioural approach does, however, have limitations. First, it tends to neglect private-sector decision-makers on whom many of the positive aspects of rural planning depend and where considerable power of implementation is bestowed on an individual entrepreneur both when initiating a development or service and when withdrawing it. Although the 'individual' and the 'organization' in the model can be transferred into the private-sector context, the modes of action are less easily applied to the profit motives of business, and the monetary motives of financial institutions. Second, and perhaps more important, there is some evidence that variations in implementation occur *before* individual perception plays its part. Pressures are often brought to bear on individuals to make a particular decision. These pressures are usually political in nature and may stem from both inside and outside of the institution involved (see chapter 8). Furthermore, the definition of 'planning problems' and 'planning possibilities' are often institutionalized before individual perception becomes important. Thus the resulting decisions are likely to conform to pre-existing types of planning from which it is difficult to escape.

Implementation and different types of planning

The thesis that implementation will show radical variation according to the type of planning which is adopted is advanced by Minay (1979a, 43–4). He stresses that

> there is, in fact, a conceptual difficulty about defining implementation without first determining one's theoretical stance: the idea of policy making implies an identifiable outcome which represents implementation, but as one moves away from this concept towards one of continuous planning, implementation and policy making become less easy to distinguish until ultimately they merge

and identifies four views of planning which each encompass different notions of implementation:

Planning as a response to private action involves a form of implementation which is brought about by the initiatives of private and public sector developers. The principal mode of action here is one of control either through land-use zoning or other regulatory mechanisms such as planning and design standards. This form of implementation is constrained by legislation and administrative standing orders as well as by a requirement that the planner should consult other interested or technically expert bodies during the decision-making process (for example other departments within a local authority or other levels of the local authority hierarchy). The major factor of variation in this case is that of the *discretion* of judgement exercised by the actor or actors concerned, and the question of whether discretion is technically or politically motivated is unanswerable at the aggregate level as little research effort has been directed towards the determination of how such decisions are made (see McDougall, 1979 and Glasson, 1979 for different views on this issue).

Planning as the positive promotion of environmental change is based on some dissatisfaction with development offered by the private sector and indicates a wish to bring about certain planning objectives through direct action. The importance of this form of planning is stressed by the Working Party on Rural Settlement Policies (1979, 14): 'Positive rural strategies have been much less successful than development-control policies, yet in many ways the implementation of positive policies is the most crucial element in rural settlement planning'. The lack of success in positive rural planning suggests that a very different type of implementation process is required in this case. Minay (1979a, 46) views this process as where:

> the planner assumes the task of carrying through his plans from formulation to execution, and in so doing he moves from regulation to entrepreneurship. The implementation task is one of mobilizing the necessary resources and ensuring that they are available in the right form and at the right time: the planner becomes a developer.

Although this form of implementation has been adopted, for example, in the inner-city and new-town programmes where resources have been made available to planners for the implementation of specific objectives, there is scant evidence of similar resource allocation in rural areas, and so the aims of 'positive planning' have tended to be pursued through the medium of co-operation with agencies where resources for rural improvement are available.

Planning as co-ordination Chapter 8 devotes detailed attention to the multitude of agencies which are able to effect change in the rural environment, and with the powers and resources of rural planning authorities usually being of an insufficient level for direct action of a positive nature, it is the degree to which planners can successfully co-ordinate the actions of these other agencies which has formed the yardstick against which implementation is measured. As each agency will have its own aims, policies and implementation methods, the major task for planning is to achieve consistency and compatability between the various policy strands. The example of development control in Hatherleigh (pp. 228–31) demonstrates very clearly that the actions of one agency are quite capable of preventing the fulfilment of the objectives of another, and when several quite different agencies are involved concurrently in a particular settlement then the difficulty of co-ordinative planning (as well as its essential nature) may be appreciated. The planners' task in this case goes beyond that of negative regulation to include the *identification* of areas where policy incompatability is a problem and *encouragement and persuasion* of certain agencies to reconstitute their policies and actions into a more conforming pattern. Another, more radical, solution to this dilemma is to reorganize the powers and resources vested in these various agencies into a more unified and 'controllable' structure. This represents one instance of many in which contrasts exist between change within the current planning system and changing the system itself (Lefebvre, 1978; Olsson, 1974).

Planning as resource management is an ambitious concept which suggests that planning might act as a management system, at least for resources of the physical environment and maybe even for the total resources of society. Minay (1979, 51) suggests that as yet this role for planning has been suppressed deliberately:

> One reason why governments opt for a relatively low level of co-ordination between agencies is no doubt the problem of resource management: the more co-ordination, the more arguments over the use of resources. Organizations which are reasonably autonomous can get ahead and implement whatever seems important to them with the resources they possess without arguments that the resources would be better spent on something else.

Were planning to assume the role of resource management, implementation would represent the process by which resources are allocated. Two factors make this approach unrealistic in the current context. First, a large proportion of the resources underlying rural life-styles and communities belong to private-sector organizations ranging from local to multinational scales. These resources, therefore, currently evade public-sector control. Second, even within the public sector the competition for resources is a *national* one in which rural areas are often given low priority. As such it is not a reallocation of resources within rural areas, but a reallocation within society which is required to meet the needs of deprived sectors of rural communities. This centralized resource reallocation is a governmental issue which if achieved would reform localized planning implementation, but at present the lack of resources stifles positive forms of implementation in rural areas.

These four different views of what might be involved in implementation may usefully be compared with the performance of post-war rural settlement planning. Generally, the main emphasis has been on the functions of control and co-ordination, of which the first has been more successfully achieved than the second. What is more, the impressive array of planners, government representatives and rural experts which formed the Working Party on Rural Settlement Planning appear to continue the priority given to co-ordination as the major factor in future implementation processes (1979, 15):

> Successful policy implementation clearly depends on an acceptance of a policy and a desire to make it work on the part of the public, local authority, statutory undertakers and central government, together with the right tools

for the job. The means include efficient communication between the various bodies and organizations involved in rural development to ensure a common approach to problems, and effective financial management to ensure that the availability of funds is flexible enough to cover factory buildings or services when suitable opportunities present themselves.

The recognition, however, that effective financial management and a unified desire to see a policy made to work are essential prerequisites for successful implementation practices suggests that planning as a positive promotion of change and ultimately as an agent for equitable resource allocation may not be a redundant concept in the future of rural settlements. This impression is reinforced by a brief review of the major problems associated with current implementation practices.

Common problems in implementation

Theoretical discussion of the nature and content of implementation in planning is useful in that it emphasizes the internal complexities to be found in the enactment of policies in different contexts and following different objectives. Problems experienced during implementation are very often conveniently labelled as 'technical difficulties' rather than political conflicts within prevailing socio-economic structures and the institutions and agencies which they spawn. In fact the theoretical study of the implementation phenomenon (both in America, and pioneered in Britain by researchers at Bristol and Oxford) has uncovered three particular focal areas where problems might be expected to occur. These foci are particularly relevant to the past performance and future efficiency of rural settlement planning in Britain (see pp. 242–56).

The first general area of concern relates to the cohabitation of policy and implementation. In simple terms there is very little credit in developing an all-embracing and all-conquering policy for rural settlements if it is impossible for that policy to be successfully implemented. Pressman and Wildavsky (1973, 143) point the way forward.

> The great problem as we understand it, is to make the difficulties of implementation a part of the initial formulation of policy. Implementation must not be conceived as a process that takes place after, and independent of, the design of policy. Means and ends can be brought into somewhat closer correspondence only by making each partially dependent on the other.

Clearly, post-war rural settlement planning has encountered this problem. Policies of resource concentration have been adopted largely for pragmatic reasons, yet the means of implementing such policies, so as to achieve growth in the selected centres and to ensure that the new centralized opportunities were made available to rural communities resident in other settlements, were not an integral part of the policy itself. The danger inherent in this criticism is that future policies for rural areas might be so constrained by the low level of available implementation machinery that they become totally negative and ineffective counter-measures to the problems and their underlying structures encountered in rural areas. This outcome would be even less acceptable than that current, the endorsing of equitable social and economic objectives for the countryside even though few means are available to carry these objectives into action. Another hazard of the policy–implementation relationship is an over-indulgent use of available channels of action. This problem is parodied in Cohen *et al.*'s (1972, 1) garbage-can model of organizational choice, according to which

> organizations can be viewed for some purposes as collections of choices looking for problems, issues and feelings looking for decision situations in which they might be aired, solutions looking for issues to which there might be an answer, and decision-makers looking for work.

What would seem to be required, therefore, is an interrelated consideration of ends and means, rather than the more traditionally linear ends–means, or indeed the more radical means–ends approaches.

The second area of conflict concerns the level of powers and resources which are made available to policy-makers. Continuing with the example of rural resource-concentration strategies used above, the development of housing growth, service rationalization and employment provision in selected rural settlements (which was the stated aim of some development-plan policies) requires powers and resources that are outside the scope of local planning authorities. In terms of housing growth, Wheeler (1977) shows that the implementation of development is largely dependent on there being sufficient demand for such development, and that demand is usually generated by private sector businesses and not by the local authority. If demand exists, then the influence of planners is strong; if not, there is relatively little that can be done to induce it. Local authorities have some considerable power over the services which they provide (the problem here is more one of co-ordinating different service agencies) but have no direct control over water, electricity, post and telecommunications, and most health services and again can do little about the closure or initiation of private-sector services where no entrepreneurial demand exists. Although private transport services are eligible for subsidy from public funds, this valid form of encouragement has not been extended to other services in the private sector. Thus although a degree of power is exerted through public-sector service provision, planners have had to resort (often unsuccessfully) to various forms of persuasion in the hope that a reasonable service base can be developed in the selected rural centres. The attraction of new employment has been pursued by similar means, with local authorities often providing a site, related infrastructure and possibly advance factories (usually with the co-operation of other development agencies) along with other forms of aid, and yet the final powers of decision-making lie with the potential entrepreneur concerned. In some locations these measures have failed to secure participants for industrial-estate schemes in selected rural centres. Planners involved in rural settlement planning are thus hamstrung by deficiencies of power and resources. An oversimplified answer to this dilemma would be to suggest that more power and more resources be allocated for the response to rural problems, and yet this would be no more than to duplicate the demands made by every other claimant on public resources. There is, however, some evidence to suggest that experimental involvements in socio-economic planning by local authorities are not wholeheartedly welcomed by central government, and that more flexibility could be instilled in this attitude. Despite the central backing for experiments such as the RUTEX schemes in the transport sector, there is a continual fear by local authorities about overstepping the mark in this respect. A public agency which acts beyond its powers may be punished by law, and an authority which spends beyond its means is now liable to a claw-back operation through the withdrawal of rate support grants. The relationship between central and local government is a subject worthy of closer future attention (SSRC, 1979). The scope for local authorities' support for rural revival schemes is outlined in chapter 12 but at present the greatest opportunity for direct action appears to be a co-operative effort between planning and other agencies to which resources have already been allocated.

A third common problem in the implementation process is that of achieving consistency in decisions made by various participant agencies. The most obvious example of this potential conflict is clearly outlined in Healey's (1979, 8) discussion of the relationship between the strategic framework of the structure plan, and the more detailed approach of local plans which have some discretion in the interpretation of structure-plan objectives:

> Development-control decisions are then made within the framework of both, although here there is a more apparent discretion as the plans are only one consideration a local planning authority should take into account when making a decision. In practice . . . there is considerable tension between the structure plan and the local plan, district planning authorities often stretching the discretion available to them as far as they can. Development-control decisions may subsequently undermine the policies of both plans. In other words, local-plan and development-control decisions can distort or override policies defined in a strategic framework, thus redefining policies.

These difficulties are also found in the interaction between planning authorities and other agencies such as water authorities and education departments. Agencies responsible for individual resources and services have their own policy objectives, their own assessments of 'need' and 'priority' and their own long-term investment programmes, all of which cannot easily be overridden by the seeming whim of one local authority department (namely planning). Conflicts such as these tend to occur where the channels of action presented in Lewis and Flynn's behavioural model are least well-defined and consequently the processes of bargaining or discretion are predominant. Inconsistent decision-making has been rife in the development-plan era of post-war rural settlement planning. The co-ordinated growth or conservation of a settlement can be broken down by the dissenting action of just one participant resource agency as is clearly shown by the sewage-disposal embargo in Hatherleigh and the high levels of housing growth in Devon's non-key settlements highlighted in pp. 224–8. Any improvement in this situation depends on an ability to harness the power and influence of these agencies into the pursuance of a series of agreed objectives, and this is now being attempted within the strengthened co-ordinating role for planning encouraged by the structure-plan system. Indeed the three problem foci outlined here are by now acknowledged and understood within formal planning, and some steps have been taken to remedy some of the more glaring deficiencies.

Implementation in current rural settlement planning

Structure plans

Section 7(4)(b) of the 1971 Town and Country Planning Act requires that:

> The Structure Plan should be framed realistically having regard to the likely availability of resources. . . . It should, as far as is possible, state the implications for the public and private sectors relating both to current and capital expenditure. It should also state the assumptions the County Council have made regarding the resources likely to be available.

This formal condition has ensured that all county structure plans devote detailed consideration to matters of implementation, with particular emphasis being placed on the resource levels required to enact proposed policies. It is therefore customary to find a chapter devoted to implementation in most structure plans, and these might be presumed to offer some insight into the implementation mechanisms to be adopted for rural areas. In fact, there is very little recognition that rural settlements require any purpose-built planning actions in that a general assumption prevails that rural implementation is merely a scaled-down version of urban implementation. All structure plans acknowledge the variety of agencies, both public and private, which are involved in the enactment of structure-plan policies (table 9.3) although there is an interesting perceptive contrast between counties which view these agencies as influences on policies and those which see them being influenced by policies. In fact both interpretations are relevant since the existing commitments of resource agencies have already been found to be a significant factor in structure-plan formulation (see chapter 6) while future resource programmes will inevitably take account of structure-plan strategies. Devon County Council (1979, 167) points out that:

Within the framework provided by the Plan the agencies referred to above are likely to prepare their individual resource programmes, including capital expenditure. The County Council itself has a 3-year capital programme which is rolled forward on an annual basis, and similarly District Councils have capital programmes. Apart from these, particularly important for the implementation of the Structure Plan are the Capital Programme of the South West Water Authority, the County Council's Transport Policies and Programme (TPP), and the Housing Investment Programmes (HIP), prepared by each of the ten District Councils.

Within this general framework, the specific role of the planning authority is recognized as being complex and often elusive. Although many counties optimistically claim (e.g. Derbyshire, 1977, 333) that 'the means of implementation are co-ordination, land-use control, investment and persuasion', this armoury is somewhat blunted by the candid admission that: 'The implementation of the policies and proposals in the Plan is dependent, to a great extent, on the ability of the various agencies involved in development in the County to secure funds for investment' (Gwent CC, 1978, 166). Therefore the roles of control and co-ordination are given greatest emphasis in the practicable enactment of policies. A brief review of important policy sectors corroborates this trend.

Housing

Part of the structure-plan team's task is to ensure that projected housebuilding rates fall within the capacity of both the private sector construction industry and the public-sector housing capability. Even if these overall requirements are

Table 9.3   Agencies involved in the implementation of structure plans

1   *The county council*: In its expenditure on the provision of most additional transport, waste disposal, and education (capital expenditure) facilities, and in future its contribution to industrial promotion; To a lesser extent the plan will also influence expenditure on social services, fire, police, libraries and other services, in their relation to the pattern of future development in the county
2   *The district councils*: In their public sector housing activities, particularly in the preparation of housing strategy and investment programmes, and for industrial promotion and the development of recreation facilities
3   *The water authorities*: In assessing their investment priorities [in Gloucestershire] for sewerage and sewage treatment provision, water supply, and land drainage (where related to development)
4   *The health authorities*: By setting a context for the formulation and implementation of regional and area policies and programmes
5   *The statutory undertakers*: In their planning of investment for telecommunications, electricity and gas supplies
6   *The private sector*: In its various developments, and in particular any investment decisions which relate to population and employment growth in the county

Source: Gloucestershire CC, 1979, 191

met, however, the provision of adequate and suitable housing in rural areas is an extremely difficult task. If no pressure exists from private developers to build on sites in rural settlements where growth is planned, the positive forms of encouragement are required from planners to attract development. Most planning departments have established some rapport with local and even national building organizations, and these contacts along with a smooth path of land availability and planning permission can be used to encourage new development where it is needed. Where demand already exists, the main task is to ensure that the more profitable larger (and thus more expensive) dwellings do not dominate housing opportunities where the need is for smaller, cheaper dwellings. There has been a noticeable lack of success in this respect over the last two decades in British rural settlements. In the public-housing sector, the housing investment programme submissions often militate against rural locations. In the case of Gloucestershire (1979, 201):

> The Housing Authority has to demonstrate a need, and to be able to indicate that the proposed development will in fact be carried out in the period proposed. However, these criteria do pose a number of problems, namely that it is more difficult to demonstrate need in small dispersed communities than in larger ones. Land assembly in numerous small packages is more difficult than acquiring sites in established urban areas, and it is more difficult to demonstrate need in small dispersed communities than in larger areas.

Gloucestershire's proposed answer to this dilemma is to assess need on the basis of groups of villages, and to encourage district councils to promote their own cheap-housing schemes (such as starter homes and self-build schemes) as well as to give financial assistance to housing associations which set out to provide mixed tenure type and size of dwelling units. Some examples of these types of scheme are described in the 'kit' which accompanied Westward Television's *Village Action* series (National Extension College, 1980). Many counties offer similar advice to their districts, yet implementation powers ultimately rest with the lower tier of authority in this case.

Employment

There is a shared responsibility between county, district and central government authorities for the encouragement of employment and in rural areas this initiative generally takes the form of developing industrial estates in the larger growth settlements. Industrial estates involve the acquisition and servicing of land, the possible construction of advance factories, and expenditure on advertising, and once again there appear to be inherent disincentives connected with rural locations. Devon County Council (1979, 176) explains that:

> The degree of financial commitment by the County Council will be related to the commercial attractions of each individual site. In order to attract private sector investment to less favoured locations the council must be prepared to contribute a greater sum towards their development costs.

In that rural areas tend to be perceived as 'less favoured', a great deal of the factory building on rural estates has been carried out either by the private sector or by government agencies including the Department of Industry, the Development Commission, CoSIRA and the rural development boards in Scotland and Wales. Close co-operation is required for these joint enterprises, and collaboration is often institutionalized as in Gloucestershire where CoSIRA, with support from the county and district councils, have prepared a strategy for the county which identifies pockets of need. The Gloucestershire County Council (1979, 200) reflect, however, that

> this is not the case with all agencies, and there clearly would be gains to be made by establishing a framework which ensures a co-ordinated and con-centrated effort to secure a greater impetus in the development of employ-ment opportunities. It is therefore the intention of the County Council that a joint working group from the County Council, District Councils, the Manpower Services Commission and CoSIRA be formed for the exchange of information and the co-ordination of action with respect to industrial development.

It is to be hoped that one result from this form of co-ordination will be the provision of smaller workshop-scale employment opportunities to suit the needs of some rural settlements, although at present the major emphasis con-tinues to be the industrial estate.

Education

Implementation procedures are more simple in this case as education is a county responsibility and a statutory obligation. Consequently, the policy co-operation required is a direct link between planners and the education authority who are obliged to provide education services for school-age rural dwellers wherever they live. Lack of primary school capacity, therefore, cannot place a direct embargo on new development, although it often has an indirect effect on refusals to allow development on the grounds of inadequate local services. In general, structure-plan predictions are confident that educa-tional facilities can be provided for any growth in population over the plan period, but there is less optimism for any improvement elsewhere. In the case of Norfolk (1980, 153)

> the Plan recognizes that, despite the urgent need for replacement outside the growth areas, there will be limited scope for replacement and improvement, and that reorganization which is dependent on new buildings in these areas is not likely to be completed during the Plan period.

Such policies do not, however, rule out reorganization without replacement, a process which has led to the progressive closure of small rural primary schools. Few counties echo Gloucestershire's (1979, 203) support for the small school:

> Small schools have higher unit costs than average . . . so that their retention beyond the point of educational justification could be regarded as an

additional cost. Against the overall education budget, figures are small per school – the annual running costs of a very small school being in the order of around £15,000 within a primary-school budget of some £18 million. Hence, it is not felt that revenue considerations are particularly important compared to, say, the quality of education provided at small schools.

Another result of aiming education priority at growth areas is the continuation of long bus journeys to school for rural children, and prolonged use of temporary buildings when they get there.

Water services

In most cases the current state of sewerage facilities has been an influential factor in the planning for future settlement expansion within the structure-plan period. In Essex (1979, 85) for example, 'the existing Water Authority Development Programmes . . . have generally been accepted into the Structure Plan as they will implement the strategy by overcoming the more important existing problems and removing some constraints on development'. Once again there is a general optimism that sewerage facilities will be provided to accommodate planned growth, but it is clear that schemes to service rural settlements where no major growth is envisaged will be given little priority on the grounds of high cost and low strategic need.

Health services

Implementation of structure-plan policies takes note of available health services but does not permit the lack of local facilities to prohibit housing development and population growth. In rural areas, a doctor's surgery forms an important part of the local service base and therefore the lack of such a facility may indirectly mitigate against planning permission for new development in that settlement. In general, however, there is a sentiment of *hope* for new investment in health services rather than any implementation capability in this matter. The Devon plan (1979, 173) admits that 'The South West Regional and Devon Area Health Authorities have expressed concern that future levels of population will place increasing difficulties upon them in meeting their obligations for the provision of medical care'. The lot of rural areas would appear to be to make do with long journeys to medical facilities during a period of rationalization of health-care centres. There is an obvious need here to fill the gap with specific transportation services which will permit non-mobile groups the necessary access to health care. Schemes along these lines are provided in many rural areas but are not stressed as implementation mechanisms within structure plans.

Social services

A similarly dismal picture is portrayed in the influence of available social services on the implementation of structure-plan policies. Once again it is Devon County Council (1979, 172) that have the honesty to suggest that:

> At present the level of expenditure on the various social services in Devon, in common with all Local Authorities, falls substantially short of the national minimum guidelines laid down by the Department of Health and Social Security. Improvements need to be made in both the quantity and quality of the services provided. Demand will undoubtedly continue to outstrip supply, and this basic difficulty will be exacerbated by the increased number of very old people anticipated by the end of the Plan period.

Any improvement in the quality of social services is largely dependent on available levels of investment and, for the usual reasons of scale, expense, perceived need, and lack of political power, rural communities are likely to be given low priority in any programme of growth.

This array of difficulties and conflicts in the implementation of various facets of structure-plan policy highlights a number of practical outworkings of the foci established in the discussion of implementation theory in pp. 239–42. For planning in rural areas, the principal methods of implementation are co-operation and control. If co-operation with resource agencies fails to secure the provision of a particular resource in a rural community, then there is always the back-up of control of development on the grounds of the absence of that resource. Positive persuasion and encouragement are piecemeal and localized in rural settlement planning, although these channels of action are obviously becoming more important as co-operation between resource agencies and planners becomes more institutionalized in the form of various joint working parties and committees. The concept of direct action through investment is almost non-existent and is likely to remain so in a depressed economic climate in which rural areas are generally afforded a low priority. Actors in the current planning system may be seen as generally continuing to conform with the traditional genre of rural settlement planning as a negative and restrictive practice rather than as a process which is able to respond to specific problem areas.

Two major deficiencies in the implementation of rural settlement planning are just beginning to be recognized. First, the search for more efficient co-operation with other resource agencies has in the past tended to ignore the fact that rural communities themselves are a valuable resource. Voluntary organizations and self-help groups in rural settlements are able to play a major role in community service provision and therefore form a significant factor in the implementation process. Many structure plans make mention of the self-help phenomenon but do not advance their support as far as allocating financial resources either to self-help projects or indeed to the establishment of a reasonable liaison with village groups as a supplement to the efforts of the rural community councils and countryside officers. The second glaring deficiency is the neglect of the interdepartmental approach similar to that of the Hereford and Worcester Rural Community Development Project (1978, 1980, 1981). Here, an interdepartmental and inter-agency exercise, with funding initially from the county council and subsequently from the Development Commission, was able to appoint community staff to work in a particular depressed rural area in order to promote community awareness and self-help schemes. A similar initiative is being planned in Derbyshire under the auspices of an experimental Social Priority Areas programme. By establishing an inter-agency body, often via the reallocation of staff from participant agencies, th co-ordination mode of action can more easily be translated into a direct action or investment mode through which more positive results may be achieved. The themes of self-help and inter-agency projects are taken up in more detail in chapter 12.

One final fragment from the theory of implementation which is relevant in the structure-plan context concerns the consistency of decision-making between different levels of the planning hierarchy. Department of the Environment (1974) *Circular 58(1)* recommends that county planning authorities should prepare a non-statutory planning brief which details the aims, objectives and policies of the structure plan which are appropriate to subsequent local plans. Oxfordshire County Council (1979, 87) amongst many others have decided to follow their recommendation, in view of the fact that: 'Much of the Structure Plan will be implemented by the District Councils, both through their role in preparing local plans and through their exercise of the majority of development-control functions'. Chapter 6, however, revealed that however close the co-operation between county and districts, the potential for conflict between them remains because of differences in political and technical appreciation of each other's plans. Technical appreciation in particular is dependent on the levels of discretion which are permitted in the wording of policies. A poignant reminder of the gap between policy and implementation is provided by Somerset County Council's (1979, 178)) explanation that the wording of policies expresses the degree of flexibility appropriate and the measure of control that can be exerted:

> Only when there is a specific intention to make resources available, are the words 'WILL PROVIDE' used. In most situations the words 'WILL MAKE AVAILABLE' indicate that indirect action will be taken through co-ordinating the investment of other parties. Otherwise the policy would be worded 'WILL ALLOCATE'. Where a policy is not directly within the power of the planning authorities to be achieved, the words 'WILL ENCOURAGE' are used.

Unfortunately it is often the case that there is too much *encouragement* and insufficient *provision* in the implementation of rural settlement policies.

Local plans

The *raison d'être* of the 1972 structure-plan/local-plan partnership was to introduce a localization of the detailed planning process whilst retaining the necessary strategic guidelines at a higher level. Many structure plan policies are thus implemented through local plans, and although 'local' in this sense ranges from a form of miniature structure plan right down to a small-area development programme (see chapter 10) it is to be expected that implementation at the smaller local-plan scale will exhibit some differences from that discussed above. The local plan is designed to display a greater awareness of particular local problems and needs. It offers an area-based approach to resource agencies rather than the agency-based approach to areas as is found in structure plans. Perhaps most importantly, it offers scope for more direct channels of action, particularly in terms of housing where planning and housing responsibilities are both vested with the district councils. As with the structure plans, local plans are obliged to produce policies which are capable of implementation within existing resource constraints, and it is usual for a formal statement of compliance with this obligation to accompany the details of the plan. For example, the plan for Norton–Radstock (Wansdyke DC, 1980, 89) clearly suggests that: 'In terms of the ability of both private and public sectors to fund the implementation of the proposals during the period to 1991 the District Plan is considered realistic and achievable'. The difference between an 'ability' and a 'willingness' to fund local-plan proposals is crucial to the successful implementation of localized policies. Very often the availability of even district council resources is a matter of competition between the requirements of several local plans and therefore the priority which is advocated for a particular project is crucial to its resource attraction and ultimate implementation. The task of the planning authority is thus to suggest proposals to agencies and persuade the agencies to accept them.

One method of smoothing this collaboration with other local authority departments or institutions is to provide a programme of plan proposals which require positive action. An example of implementation programming is found in the Interim District Plan for Bruton (Yeovil DC, 1980) a settlement in Somerset of some 2200 population. In this case, the planning authority have designated three levels of priority to aid the attraction of resources and ultimate enactment of their proposals:

A   Delay in implementation should be avoided. These are the proposals which are most important in terms of solving problems or using sources of finance which are immediately available;

B   Important proposals – immediate implementation desirable but not essential;

C   Desirable proposals – could be delayed but should be implemented in the Plan's 5-year period.

Table 9.4 outlines the proposals, the suggested priorities, and the agencies

Table 9.4 Implementation proposals in the Bruton District Plan

Priority	Policy number	Policy	Responsibility for implementation					Comments
			District council	County council	Department of the Environment	Parish council	Private agencies	
A	3	Renovation of dwellings	X	X	X		X	Grants already available from public funds, but these are limited and a contribution is also required from the property owner.
A	4	Industry, saw mills site	X				X	Yeovil District Council can encourage firms to locate on this site, but it is privately owned and would require private investment (perhaps with CoSIRA assistance where appropriate).
A	12	Extension of conservation area	X					
A	13,14	Enhancement of conservation area	X	X	X		X	See Policy No. 3. Introduction of a Town Scheme would require the support of property owners and the commitment of a specified amount of public funds each year for a fixed number of years.
A	15	Riverside walk	X				X	Agreement of landowners desirable. An early start would permit use of Special

	No.	Scheme				Notes
						Temporary Employment Programme (job creation) labour and District Council (Amenities Committee) funds for materials (available immediately, in the present financial year).
B	17	Time-limits on parking	X		X	The County Council's regular triennial review of traffic management in Bruton takes place in 1979/80. Parking restrictions cannot be introduced unless a new car park is provided.
B	18	Car park, Higher Backway	X	X	X	Agreement of landowner desirable. Could be undertaken by Parish Council instead of District Council. If undertaken by Yeovil District Council, will require commitment of funds by Works Committee.
C	19	Children's play area, near Uphills	X	X	X	Agreement of landowner desirable. Normally a Parish Council responsibility, but grants may be available from Yeovil District Council (Amenities Committee). New footpath required for access.
C	20	Uphills–Burrow field footpath	X		X	Agreement of landowners desirable.
C	21	Dual-use of schools' sports facilities	X	X	X	

Source: Yeovil DC, 1980

responsible for their implementation. The comments on each proposal give a firm indication that although local-plan implementation deals with more direct forms of action than its structure-plan counterpart, the advocacy role of planners is consistent in both forms of implementation.

The propensity for direct action in local plans in rural areas stems from both the detail of plan proposals and from the harnessing of district council resources from within the local authority by district council planners. Apart from the negative management powers available through the development-control process, the principal area of action in local plans concerns housing. The scope for local authority intervention in local housing markets is stressed in the *North York Moors Local Plan* (North York Moors National Park Authority, 1980) which mentions aid to housing associations, local authority mortgages, building for sale, intermediate forms of tenure, and 'local-need' planning conditions as possible channels of action through which district councils can respond to housing needs which have been isolated by local plans. In the North York Moors context (p. 46), it is suggested that: 'Such discriminatory intervention would only be justified if it can be shown that prices are rising in such a way that local people are being squeezed out of the housing market'.

Housing-policy implementation in local plans can therefore be seen to hinge on the interpretation of 'local needs'. Elson (1981) argues that 'local needs' has become a complex concept which encapsulates a *political* decision on the acceptability of the level, type and phasing of housing development in rural settlements. This issue is discussed in more detail in chapter 10 (see also Winter, 1980), but two aspects are particularly important in connection with local-plan implementation. First, the perception of local housing needs may vary significantly between county and district authorities, with the result that the spirit inherent in a 'housing for local needs' policy at structure-plan level may be ignored or even deliberately reversed by a more liberal interpretation of the policy within local plans and detailed development control. Second, despite both a willingness on the part of district councils to intervene directly in local housing markets, and an ability to do so through current implementation channels, there appear to be grave doubts as to whether district councils are able to call on sufficient financial resources to support direct intervention on any appreciable scale. The examination in public of the North Yorkshire Structure Plan (Department of the Environment, 1980, para. 2.7) discussed possible methods of intervention with this conclusion:

> we doubt whether many of these methods could be implemented in practice. Most of them seem to rely upon the provision of some kind of local authority financial aid; and we consider it unrealistic in the current, and likely future, financial climate to expect that there would be any significant increase in the availability of funds for this purpose.

For these reasons, many structure-plan policies restricting rural development to local needs have been deleted by the Secretary of State who at this time views with some ideological horror a situation whereby a restriction on the availability of private-sector housing opportunities might lead to a considerable increase in local authority spending on direct intervention into the housing market. Consequently, a lack of resources and an absence of government-policy support constitute significant hindrances on district council action to provide housing for local needs in rural areas. Normal council housebuilding activities are being curtailed, the sale of council houses is diminishing current stocks, and local-needs policies are increasingly being narrowed, as in the North Hertfordshire District Plan (1980) where the current building programme is largely directed towards the construction of small units of accommodation, mainly for elderly people.

If direct housing action is proving financially difficult to implement, despite the relative ease of communication and co-operation between planning departments and housing departments, it is not surprising that many local plans resort to development control as the main channel of implementation, particularly in view of the inherent difficulties in obtaining policy and financial support from other agencies. A selection of implementation statements from the Norton–Radstock Plan (Wansdyke DC, 1980), illustrated in table 9.5, corroborates this trend. The commitment to development control as the principal implementation tool is clear, and although some public-sector housing development is scheduled, the direct action to be taken by the district council mainly relates to projects (such as car parks and sports complexes) for which finance had already been sanctioned. New areas of direct action are qualified with the words 'may', 'will require' or 'will depend', and give little hope of major initiatives. These extracts from one particular plan are fairly typical of approaches to implementation in local plans in general. The suggestion arises, therefore, that local plans can be firmly implemented in their role as detailed guides to development control (often effectively altering structure-plan policies in this respect), but that a rather more loose and optimistic approach towards implementation occurs when local plans assume the role of policy-respondents to particular socio-economic problems in the area concerned. Successful implementation of positive local planning will therefore largely depend on the skill with which planners are able to encourage the allocation of internal and external resources to the area concerned.

Conclusions

The heterodox model of the planning system outlined in chapter 1 isolated implementation as an obscure stage between the written policy and what actually happens in rural areas. It was further suggested that implementation is the most clouded area of the planning process, and the preceding discussion of the theory and practice of implementation tends to support this initial hypothesis. Although evidence is available to show that stated rural planning objectives are not being achieved, and that written policies are not accurately enacted in the various decisions which influence the life-style of rural

Table 9.5   Implementation in the Norton–Radstock District Plan

---

'Wansdyke District Council will be substantially involved in the implementation of most of the District Plan policies and proposals through its powers to control development'.

'the District Council will be directly responsible for the development of some of the land allocated for housing, the scale of construction depending on the Block Capital Allocations. Local authority development is likely to concentrate on accommodation for elderly people'.

'After 1981 reduced Block Capital Allocations covering the whole of the District Council's functions will result in greater competition for resources'.

'Growth in employment opportunity will be primarily dependent on the private sector'.

'There may be a need for Wansdyke to make a contribution to particularly beneficial highway schemes, although the provision of roads is primarily an Avon County Council function'.

'The District Council will be responsible for new public car parks in Midsomer Norton and Radstock centres'.

'Regarding the maintenance and improvement of the basic fabric of bus services, the District Council's role is principally an advisory one. A travel token system is operated for the elderly and any further subsidy of bus services or fares will require an increased financial outlay'.

'In appropriate cases the District Council could give financial help towards the cost of community halls'.

'Implementation of many of the recreational and leisure proposals will be carried out by the District Council'.

'The scale of financial involvement by Wansdyke in protecting, maintaining and enhancing areas of distinctive environmental character . . . will depend on resources available during the Plan period and the District Council's assessment of expenditure priorities'.

Source: Wansdyke DC, 1980, 89–92

communities, there has been insufficient study of where, how and why these decisions are reached, and of the degree to which they are influenced by the planning process. This dirth of understanding of implementation in the rural context prevents any definitive analysis of either the major deficiencies in policy enactment or of the measures required to bridge the policy–implementation gap. For example, many studies (including the surveys of county planning authorities described in chapter 6) have hinted that the use of 'special cases' and 'extended discretion' on the part of decision-makers has permitted private-sector development of a type and location that appears to contravene an overall rural settlement policy. Unfortunately, there has been little direct evidence of this understandably 'sensitive' area of decision-making, and so no degree of accuracy has been possible in assessing whether this phenomenon may be attributed to technical difficulties in the monitoring of rural development or to political influences on the degree of discretion permitted in individual cases.

Two general conclusions may however be gleaned from the conceptual and practical evidence which is available. First, the notion that a lack of co-ordination and co-operation between resource allocating agencies has been a major hindrance to effective implementation of rural policies, is confirmed by this analysis. The dissipation of decision-making powers creates extreme difficulty in assembling a comprehensive approach to the welfare of rural communities. The Working Party on Rural Settlement Policies (1979, 20) concurs with this finding:

> We suggest much of the failure in policy realization may be attributed to a lack of co-ordination between the many bodies involved in plan implementation, and to an imbalance between long-term plans and short-term financial programmes. Even within a single organization there is still often a lack of policy harmonization and co-ordination in forward planning. Each internal department tends to see its plan as the plan, although the constraints perceived as dictating this kind of approach are often more imaginary than real.

Some of the formal and informal interchanges between agencies during the preparation of structure plans indicate that this problem is recognized by planning authorities, but it would be erroneous to predict wholesale improvements in co-operation until a more corporate approach to decision-making is brought about (see chapter 12).

The second generalization inevitably concerns the extent of resources available within rural settlement planning. A recurring theme in this chapter is that a much more positive response could be made to rural problems (and even to their underlying structures) were higher levels of finance to be allocated to this role for planning. In particular, local plans present interesting new channels of action, particularly for direct intervention in the housing sector but also for a co-ordinated approach to a small area. Even if no additional finance was available, the existing system of sectoral accounting could be merged into a more corporate approach to rural settlement planning, which is again favoured by the Working Party on Rural Settlement Policies (1979, 23).

> Costs would then be examined in terms of benefits and trade-offs between the various services to provide an overall financial assessment for a given policy package and, as necessary, a comprehensive analysis of its likely effects on individual groups or areas.

Reallocation of agency staff to administer this corporate effort and to sponsor a closer liaison between decision-makers and decision-receivers would be another method of diverting a resource towards a comprehensive planning effort. If resources can be reorganized in this manner, rural settlement planning is not short of ideas and initiatives which would put these resources to good use. Many of these innovations are contained in, and may potentially be enacted by, the new series of local plans which now adorn some rural areas.

TEN

Local planning in rural areas

Village plans

> It seems that better rural settlement planning can be achieved either by reducing pressure on villages or by more vigorous initiative and control at local level. (Thorburn, 1971, 48)

> Authorities have wasted considerable effort on abortive local planning. (Green, 1971, 55)

These two polarized views indicate the rather chequered development of early forms of local planning in rural areas. A trickle of village plans were prepared alongside the original county development plans and many more accompanied the development-plan reviews, particularly in areas which were experiencing pressures for housing and population growth. Village plans were introduced with high hopes, but within 10 or 15 years of operation the limitations of the techniques used in the preparation and implementation of the plans had led to a general cynicism as to their effectiveness and to a general re-evaluation of the role played by local forms of planning in rural areas. Not all counties chose to use village plans in tandem with their development-plan policies, preferring to judge applications for development on their individual merit. Sufficient plans were produced, however, for them to be an important phenomenon in rural settlement planning, not only because they represent a precursive training ground from which important experience has been gained for the new forms of rural local plans following the 1968 Town and Country Planning Act, but also because they were circumstantially responsible for the shape of village development in some locations and contributed some village planning guide-lines which have found their way into currently accepted policy principles through the practice of trend planning.

Little government advice was available to aid the conceptualization of village plans, although technical procedures were outlined by the Ministry of Housing and Local Government in 1967. There were, however, several expectations inherent in the use of individual plans for rural settlements. At a general level, it was hoped that a comprehensive approach to the development in a village would avoid piecemeal decision-making and allow local residents to participate in the planning of their community. In addition, Thorburn (1971, 47) outlines several practical reasons for preparing a plan:

1 To provide the planner concerned with an opportunity to draw up policies

258   *An Introduction to Rural Settlement Planning*

which will lead to the preservation and improvement of the existing environment, and a high standard of new development in the village;

2   To indicate to property owners the planning authority's views on matters affecting the value of their property or their peace of mind;

3   To guide prospective developers, local authorities and others concerned in development or the provision of services and amenities;

4   To avoid the planning authority having to re-examine every issue bearing on the planning of the village each time a planning application is received.

This heady mixture of environmentalism, control and administrative convenience can, with hindsight, be seen to ignore the crucial socio-economic elements which underlie physical development. Thorburn (1971, 47) offers a partial explanation for this deliberate omission:

> Some planners have also suggested that we should encourage the growth of a satisfactory social life in the village, although planning authorities have been wary of trying to do this. It entails the adoption of some social objectives, and this leads to the danger that the preferences and attitudes of a dominant sector of the community (often the professional classes) will be imposed upon those with different views on the desirable way in which to live.

If this reasoning is a valid reflection of prevailing rural attitudes, it follows that the public participation objective of village plans (see 1–4 above) may be seen to refer to views on *physical* planning expressed by *one part* of the community, and that the plans themselves sought to avoid sensitive political judgements on the type of opportunities to be presented by new development.

The different types of village plan have been discussed comprehensively elsewhere (Woodruffe, 1976) and are thus only briefly summarized here. In fact, although several definitive categories of plan have traditionally been recognized and accepted, these categories are rarely mutually exclusive, with the later plans in particular adopting hybrid versions of these basic techniques. Four approaches are relevant to this discussion.

Layout design or outline structure

This approach, often linked with the work of Sharp (1953), seeks to take account of the form and layout of the village concerned by ensuring that sites selected for development conform to an acceptable overall settlement shape. Elements of this approach can be seen in the Sawtry Village Plan (Huntingdon DC, 1976) which is illustrated in figure 10.1. Here, the suggested sites for new housing development tend to take the form of infill at the edge of the settlement, thus retaining its elliptical shape. Woodruffe (1976, 50) assesses the results of this approach as being that 'the original structure has not been obliterated so much as enclosed, whereas it might have been augmented and enhanced'. Perhaps more important, the approach has proved difficult to implement, particularly in the persuasion of developers to follow the planned

Figure 10.1 The layout design approach: Sawtry Village Plan

Public Open Space................ POS   Allotments............ O/A

Secondary School Playing Field SS/PF   Industry...............

Site for Health Centre........... HC   Residential..........

Junction Improvement............ J

Land with Planning Permission as at December, 1975......

Source: Huntingdon DC, 1976

layout design. To achieve a preconceived structure, the land required for development or infill has to be made available at the right time in the plan programme, and this is rarely the case when land is in private ownership. There have also been some qualms amongst planners (on theoretical grounds) and developers (on financial grounds) about whether a very traditional village form is appropriate to the needs of twentieth-century rural communities. Thus although this approach was adopted by various planning authorities, it proved rather inflexible to the actual processes of development in rural settlements.

Capacity or village envelope

A more widely used approach to village plans sought to define a strict boundary for a village beyond which development would not be permitted. Buckinghamshire County Council's (1973) plan for Tingewick (figure 10.2) incorporates a village limit of this type in its overall consideration of development and design. Capacity approaches vary enormously, and their effectiveness is dependent on the nature of this variation. For example, the boundary may be abrupt or gradual; it may enclose sites where development potential is recognized, or it may only include small infilling plots; and it may be continuous or open-ended to cater for unseen future demands. Although most of these variations will serve to prevent the merger of separate settlements, and to maintain a certain compactness of village structure, no specific assessment of this category of approaches is prudent because of their widely differing natures. Individual problems have been encountered, however, particularly due to the (often false) impression given by the plan to developers that all sites within the envelope are fair game for new residential use. This approach also offers little scope for achieving new development at the right time and of an appropriate character. Another problem arises when the envelope is drawn without regard to service capacities (for example relating to sewerage or education) prevailing in the settlement. In most of its forms the approach has proved inflexible, as might be expected when social and economic needs are sacrificed on the altar of visual conservation of the village. This inflexibility proved the major factor in the demise of the village-envelope plan, but the nature of its successor demonstrates that a greater influence over *visual* and not socio-economic flexibility was being sought in the change of approach.

Visual appraisal

The visual-appraisal approach differed from previous methods in that the idea of a rigid and fixed blueprint for future development was replaced by a series of evaluations of a village's visual character which were then used to guide development-control decisions. In this way a physical appraisal of building and townscape, and a landscape appraisal of view, vegetation and vista forms the basis for village planning decisions. An example of this approach is found in figure 10.3 which illustrates the Cheddington village appraisal

Figure 10.2 The village envelope approach: Tingewick Village Plan

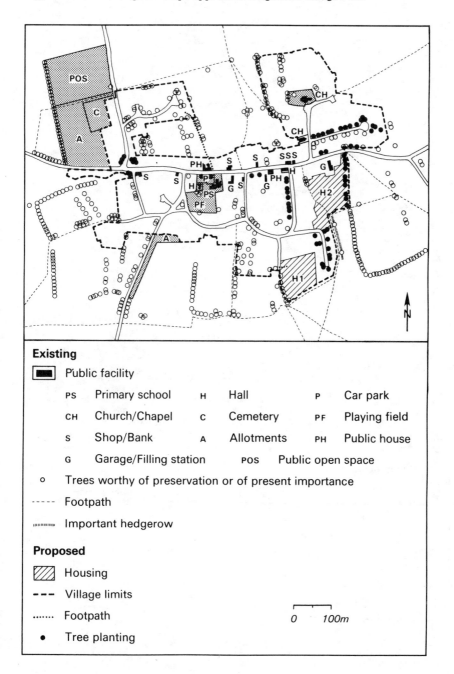

Existing

▨ Public facility

PS	Primary school	H	Hall	P	Car park
CH	Church/Chapel	C	Cemetery	PF	Playing field
S	Shop/Bank	A	Allotments	PH	Public house
G	Garage/Filling station		POS	Public open space	

o   Trees worthy of preservation or of present importance

\- - - -   Footpath

ıııııııııııı   Important hedgerow

Proposed

▨ Housing

\- - -   Village limits

....   Footpath

•   Tree planting

0   100m

Source: Buckinghamshire CC, 1973

Figure 10.3 The village appraisal approach: Cheddington Village Plan

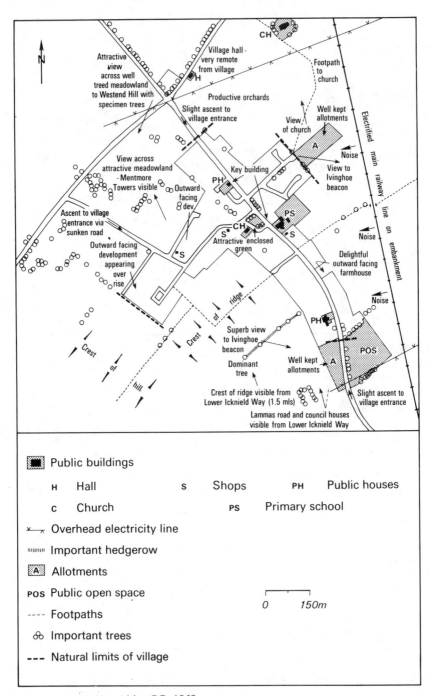

Source: Buckinghamshire CC, 1969

(Buckinghamshire CC, 1969). A flavour of the detailed treatment included in this plan may be gained from the following excerpt (p. 5):

> There are two threads which lead us to an understanding of the High Street. The first clue is to realize that the west side of the street is negative and the east side is positive. On the west side the buildings are mainly recessive and indeterminate, they are in the shade, orchards and gardens come up to the road and confuse the clarity of the buildings; the Green is on this side. Note also that the curve is convex so that half the length is hidden; it is never seen as a whole. Opposite on the east side the buildings are in the sun, bold, vigorous and continuous. The curve is concave so that the whole length of this side is revealed at one glance. This basic pattern is in sympathy with the overall landscape pattern, the great slope of the hills falling into the village, percolating through the west side of the street to be contained by the vigorous concave arc.

In case any reader of the plan is sufficiently foolish to suggest that the second clue to the understanding of the High Street might be the interaction of village residents, both one with another and with important village services such as the school, shops, church and public houses, it is in fact 'the organizing power of those buildings which abut right up to the road. They create the impression of unity and continuity by their dominance' (p. 6). Although this approach appears anachronistic and meaningless to those whose main concern with village planning is the equitable management of resources and opportunities within rural communities, it should be judged in its historical context of reacting against previous methods of inflexibility. Even when measured against its own objectives, however, it is clear that visual attributes differ according to the individual perception of the agent of appraisal, and that, at best, such an appraisal merely isolates visual quality or lack of it and requires statutory back-up for any ensuing policies.

The fourth approach to be isolated by some commentators centres on the specific nomination of *policy areas* and *conservation areas* which represent the subdivision of villages into broad policy zones or the recognition of above-average rural character in the specific designation of an area for stricter planning practice under the Civic Amenities Act of 1967. The effects of conservation-area status are discussed in chapter 11, and these techniques in reality are almost always used in conjunction with one or more of the above approaches. The hybrid nature of village plans should not be under-represented. The three examples illustrated in figures 10.1–10.3 all suggest a multidimentional approach even if one element is emphasized in each case.

Several general limitations of early village planning methods can be recognized. Although village plans were often prompted by a pressure for residential growth, Green (1971, 55) also notes a tendency 'to prepare local plans showing in great detail proposals where there was no great likelihood that development would be carried out, or where there were not the means to implement or enforce the plan'. Thus, early village planning in some instances suffered a similar malaise to that encountered in development planning, namely that the bulk of planners' effort and achievement was exhausted on the production of the plan itself and not on its implementation.

In more pressured rural situations the evidence of Essex County Council (1978) is salutary. Fifteen approved and forty draft village plans were used to guide development control with the following result (p. 118):

> The Village Plans showed areas where residential development could be permitted and were intended as a guide to development control on the basis that pre-war house-building rates would continue so that areas allocated would last many years. There was no programming, and, indeed, the Ministry of Housing and Local Government would not support on appeal any kind of programming. The Draft Village Plan went through a consultation process and since developers had the houses built within 2 or 3 years, the Village Plans only served to accelerate development. Consequently, the sewage works could not cope, drainage embargoes were applied in about three-quarters of the County and the Ministry of Housing and Local Government supported the drainage embargoes on appeal.

The need for a stricter control on development than that afforded by village plans in Essex led to their withdrawal and replacement with a categorization policy which was accompanied by formal maps of committed village development limits. A similar pattern was followed by Kent County Council who proposed the definition of village envelopes as the normal limit for any new development as part of the 1963 review of the development plan. This method of village planning was abandoned in the 1967 revision of the development plan in which village policy was based on treating development applications on individual merits. The evidence from the Essex and Kent examples suggests that, even judged by their restricted physical planning-oriented objectives, village plans were unsuccessful in establishing control over the rate and type of housing to be built in villages.

The other major limitation in village plans concerned the objectives which they pursued and the methods adopted to achieve these aims. Village plans were rural *settlement* planning in its 'purest' form since the only consideration was for the physical structure of nucleated settlements in the countryside. Two deficiencies ensued from this adopted stance. First, a considerable level of physical development outside established rural settlement slipped through the net during this period when attention was firmly focused on villages. Second, and more important, the emphasis on physical development overrode any parallel focus on social and demographic problems in the villages concerned. Only the later village plans began to present information on village services and facilities, migration rates and age structure of the population, and other crucial socio-economic factors. Moreover, in the few cases where such information was collected there was no real attempt to link problems with policies in the village plan. Consequently, although village-plan preparation has often been spotlighted as an example of the craftsmanship of rural planners and their consultants, in practical terms they fulfilled few of the objectives required of rural local planning in the 1970s and 1980s and were (apparently) revolutionized with the arrival of the structure-plan/local-plan system in the 1968 Town and Country Planning Act.

The local-plan concept

The term 'local plan' was introduced by the Planning Advisory Group (1965) and was formally instated in the British planning system by the 1968 Act. Loew (1979) suggests a multiplicity of practical and ideological reasons for the acceptance of the need for some form of local planning. At one level the localization process is viewed as one element of a much wider socio-political trend of devolution from centralized power to decision-making by local communities. When this process is allied to the ideology of man–environment interaction which has been a constant focus of planning philosophy, the concept of local control over physical environment becomes difficult to avoid. From a more practical point of view the notion of a structure plan containing only general policy guidelines will be complemented by more detailed guidance at the smaller-scale level of planning, and the resultant local plans were inevitable once the new format for structure plans was decided. The exact combination of these reasons for the acceptance of local plans is difficult to discern, but it is clear from their nature that no great stress is laid on socio-economic problems experienced at a local level and therefore requiring a local response. Physical management of land and development continues to be the major theme of the new mechanism for local planning.

The absence of socio-economic objectives is notable in the four local-plan functions described in the government development-plans manual (Ministry of Housing and Local Government, 1970).

1 Applying the strategy of the structure plan: giving particular attention to the proposed changes in development and use of land;
2 Providing a detailed basis for development control: local plans will be the official development-control documents, giving precise information concerning the uses allocated to particular sites, planning density standards and so on;
3 Providing a basis for co-ordinating development: to build co-ordinating links between public and private resource agencies and add positive elements to development control;
4 Bringing local and detailed planning issues before the public: showing in particular how various interests will be affected by the outworking of the plan.

The current Department of the Environment requirements are that local plans should be presented according to a rigid land-use format rather than extending their ambit to other, socio-economic matters (as suggested by function 3). Local plans are, however, 'the only vehicle by which policies and suggestions affecting all types of agencies and leading to investment of many different kinds can be brought together' (Caddy, 1981, 16), and many authorities recognize the need to promote positive action in socio-economic planning as well as negative control in land-use planning within the local-plan framework.

Thus, although incurring official disapproval, local plans can legitimately be viewed as possible *de facto* vehicles for a range of planning approaches and techniques.

A more detailed analysis of the legislative obligations attached to local plans is presented by Loew (1979), but it is important to note that three distinct types of local plan are available for use in different planning situations.

District plans are characterized by the need for comprehensive and often long-term planning of substantial areas covered by a particular structure plan. It was envisaged that a large area of a county (often the entire area of a district planning authority) would be dealt with by one such plan, but in practice considerable variation of plan scale has occurred. The specific aim of district plans is to provide a link between the generalized objectives of the structure plan and the detailed proposals which can form the basis of development control.

Action area plans refer to more restricted geographic areas and are designed to cover particular forms of development over a 10-year time-span. A wide range of development, redevelopment and improvement action is catered for and the plans are intended as catalysts for comprehensive planning within formulated objectives, standards and layouts. They cover the public-sector proposals for infrastructure, services and access within which private sector developers can operate in a co-ordinated but flexible manner.

Subject plans are designed to cater for one particular planning problem or issue. The scale of the plan is flexible to include a wide area or a small locality, and indeed it has been suggested that subject plans need not be area-based at all. Subject plans differ from district and action-area plans in that they operate either when a comprehensive plan is deemed unnecessary, or where local policies and proposals are required in advance of a comprehensive plan. There are also limitations on the type of issue which can legitimately be dealt with in a subject plan. Department of the Environment (1977) *Circular 55* sees this plan as appropriate where the subject has such limited interaction with other planning matters that these will not suffer if the subject is planned in isolation. According to these guidelines, matters of rural housing and rural services are deemed structure-plan topics whereas housing design guidelines and mineral-extraction site controls might legitimately be viewed as subject plans by local planning authorities.

The local-plans system has been adopted as a national mechanism for small-area planning in Britain, with the inherent presumption that the three plan types are equally appropriate to inner-city and remote-rural locations. In fact, action-area and subject plans have as yet been used very sparingly in the rural planning context. Although stretching the credibility of rural–urban definition and differentiation, one example of a rural action area plan might be seen in the Friars area of King's Lynn (West Norfolk DC, 1980) where a late-nineteenth-century housing area is scheduled for improvements in housing, recreation areas and levels of through traffic. This use of action-area planning conforms to the general impression that this particular mechanism is primarily designed for built-up areas of an urban nature. Subject plans are more common within rural environments. The Avon Valley plan (Stratford-on-Avon DC, 1978), for example, seeks to regulate issues of recreation, leisure and tourism in an area dominated by important waterways, and a similar, though informal, approach has been adopted in the Wear Valley (Wear Valley DC, 1981). It is the district plan, however, which has dominated the attention of local plans in rural areas in the late 1970s and early 1980s, and most district councils have at least begun the technical process of district-plan preparation. Figure 10.4 demonstrates the complex and involved nature of this process and offers a very clear step-by-step description of the tasks performed in the development and approval of a local plan. It is important to note the two main areas of consultation which are encapsulated in this process. First, the local plan is required to adopt the strategic policies of the county structure plan, and therefore the iterative process of discussion between county and district authorities is often a difficult one. As Beardmore (1976, 74) points out, 'Where the political control of the county authority differs from that in any large district within it, the potential for inter-authority friction is at its greatest', and the preparation of a local plan is often an ideal vehicle for the insertion of this friction into the consultation system. The second area of consultation is that of formal public participation in which two techniques are usually adopted. One method of participation involves the direct consultation with individuals and organizations at the draft proposals stage. The size and scope of this operation may be illustrated by the list of consultees contacted by South Norfolk District Council (1980) during their preparation of the West Costessey, Wensum and Yare Valleys Local Plan (table 10.1). The other source

Table 10.1   Consultation in plan preparation: consulted institutions and individuals

County Planning Officer	National Farmers Union
County Surveyor	Royal Norfolk Agricultural Association
County Education Officer	Eastern Council for Sport and Recreation
County Estates Officer	Norwich Sports Council
Chief Constable	The Caravan Club
Chief Fire Officer	The Norfolk Archaeological Unit
Chief Planning Officer, Breckland District Council	The Costessey Society
	The Norfolk Society
Planning Officer, Norwich City Council	The Ramblers Association
Chief Executive and Clerk, Broadland District Council	Norfolk and Norwich Naturalists Society
	National Federation of Building Trade
Bawburgh Parish Council	Employees: Eastern Region
Costessey Parish Council	Builders Direct Supply
Colney Parish Council	The Gun Room Rifle and Pistol Club
Easton Parish Council	Messrs Hill and Perks
Ringland Parish Council	The County Landowners' Association
Hellesdon Parish Council	The Norfolk Naturalists Trust
Drayton Parish Council	The Council for Small Industries in Rural
Anglian Water Authority	Areas
Nature Conservancy Council	University of East Anglia
Forestry Commission	Eastern Omnibus Co. Ltd
Countryside Commission	*Detailed comments also received*
Ministry of Agriculture, Fisheries and Food	South Norfolk Constituency Labour Party
	A major agricultural landowner in the area

Source: South Norfolk DC, 1980, 50–1

Figure 10.4 Procedure for the preparation of local plans

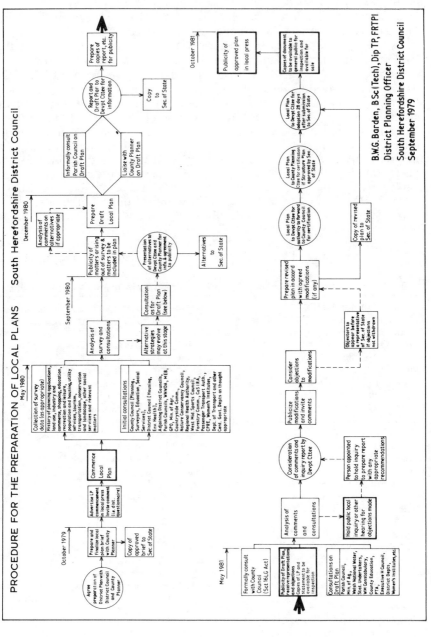

PROCEDURE FOR THE PREPARATION OF LOCAL PLANS   South Herefordshire District Council

B.W.G. Barden, B.Sc (Tech), Dip TP, FRTPI
District Planning Officer
South Herefordshire District Council
September 1979

Source: South Herefordshire DC, 1980, 10

of local opinion is secured through such media as questionnaire surveys, public meetings and exhibitions (e.g. Warwick DC, 1978).

The successful implementation of publicly acceptable local-plan policies will depend in no small measure on the course taken both by county council consultations, particularly in view of the commitment of resources to the plan, and by public participation procedures, which are capable of demonstrating the real problems in an area but are frequently biased in favour of the environmentalist and anti-development views of the articulate and adventitious middle class. Certainly the task of marrying strategic country-wide policies with localized needs and problems creates a tremendous variety of plan format and emphasis between different plan-making authorities.

The content of rural local plans

The early 1980s represent a transitional period in local planning. New guidelines for district plans are well established and most district authorities have at least made a start on preparing local plans dealing with rural areas and settlements. There are insufficient completed plans, however, to establish whether local planning in rural environments takes the form of a number of recognizable approaches to rural problems, or indeed whether the parochialism inherent in the local plan process tends to negate general policy-based planning in favour of individualistic area-based planning. To add to this complexity, the time-lapse involved in structure-plan completions has meant that some local-level plans have been produced before the approval of their parent strategic document. The situation has thus arisen that interim policies and plans have become an essential ingredient of local planning in rural areas, resulting in both statutory and non-statutory plans being operational at the small-scale level. In addition, certain authorities have chosen to insert yet another plan type into the structure-plan/local-plan arrangement, in the form, for example, of a district settlement policy or of very detailed and localized development briefs. The various types of local rural plan and their content are briefly described here, using a limited number of examples. By these means some impression may be gained of the type of issue and policy dealt with in local plans, but no nationwide analysis of policy categories is attempted. Indeed it will be quite some time before sufficient statutory local plans are published for this task to be fulfilled with any expectation of success.

Interim local policies and plans

Several local planning documents for rural areas have appeared in the vacuum between the outdating of development-plan reviews and their associated village plans and the approval of submitted county structure plans which form the framework for statutory local plans. These interim policies and plans vary according to scale, format and relationship with forthcoming structure-plan policies. Some of the earliest interim plans were, in fact, a continuation of previous village planning techniques. Cambridgeshire County Council produced a number of such village plans in the early 1970s (e.g. the plan for Linton, 1971) which differed from their earlier counterparts in that topics such as population growth and structure, employment and industry, shopping needs and additional facilities were included alongside the more traditional concerns of housing development, conservation and landscaping. These plans have been superseded by the approved Cambridgeshire County Structure Plan (1980), but represented the basis for localized rural settlement planning during its preparation. Similarly innovative village plans have been adopted by district councils during this interim period. For example, West Dorset District Council produced a series of village plans (e.g. Charmouth, 1976) which were linked to the Dorset County Council interim rural planning policy of 1969, and West Somerset District Council (e.g. 1979) similarly published interim settlement policies to provide local detail within the county-wide interim strategy. Although not intended as statutory local plans, there is little doubt that these interim village plans had a significant precursive effect on subsequent local planning in these areas.

If the village plans described above represent a point halfway between the plans illustrated in pp. 258–65, and the new statutory local plans, a further advance is marked by a series of similarly named 'village plans' prepared by district councils as an official first stage in the local-plan process. The Sawtry Village Plan (Huntingdon DC, 1976, 1) was prepared for this purpose: 'The Plan and Proposals contained in this report can form the basis for formal Local Plan Proposals suitably revised and updated when the County Structure Plan is approved', and other examples of this type include the Ronaldkirk (Teesdale DC, 1981) and Redmire (Richmondshire DC, 1981) Village Plans. Although principally concerned with the urgent need for development-control guidelines, these village plans assume many of the characteristics of the forthcoming local plans, with similar consultation procedures and a well-developed interest in socio-economic as well as physical characteristics of the settlement. The proposals for Sawtry, for example, include the encouragement of industrial development and the persuasion of resource agencies to allocate priority to community service provision.

In general terms, interim local plans in rural areas have conformed to one of two broad models. First, many plans have been brought about by the need for a holding operation in areas of development pressure where structure-plan policies have not taken sufficient shape for prognostic local planning on the basis of suggested policies. Many of these plans are solely concerned with providing a continuous basis for local development control, and by their very nature are unlikely to be innovative in their approach to socio-economic as well as physical planning problems. Nevertheless, these plans represent important existing commitments in the ensuing local planning process and may hamper the instigation of more radical ideas and objectives due to the operational effects of trend planning. The second broad type of interim plan is more forward-looking and uses the guideline of draft structure-plan proposals to prepare positive and sometimes innovative comprehensive schemes for small areas over a 10-year period. An example of this latter type is the Appleby

Advisory Plan (Eden DC, 1980) which is set in the context of the Cumbria Draft Structure Plan (p. 1):

> Particularly relevant to the town are those Structure Plan policies concerned with the stabilization and regeneration of rural communities, the maintenance of existing population levels and the capitalization on potential to widen employment opportunities and utilize tourism as an important contributor to the local economy

and aims to provide a *positive* policy response (p. 1):

> The purpose of the Plan is to study these and other issues of importance to the town and to examine possible changes over the plan period, up to 1991, as a background to providing positive policies and guidance for such change.

This second group of interim policies, then, is much more closely allied to the aims, content and structure of the statutory district plans discussed below, and represents an important opportunity for change (and also innovation) in local planning techniques.

Guideline policies and plans

In some instances, district authorities have thought it necessary to give formal expression to their interpretation of county structure-plan policies in a published 'district settlement policy', which is not recognized as a formal local plan but rather forms a bridge between the structure plan and local plans for parts of the district. The District Settlement Policies and Plan produced by Caradon District Council (1980) is an example of this intermediate-plan scale, and is mainly employed in organizing the spatial aspects of housing development according to the submitted Cornwall Structure Plan's objective of relating new housing to job provision and real local housing needs. The Caradon plan translates structure-plan housing policies into six district council policies (table 10.2) which will form the framework for subsequent district plans. Moreover each area of the district is submitted to a rigorous examination according to these six policies, and strict categorization policies result. In the Liskeard area, for example, ten villages are committed to a policy wherein 'no housing development beyond real commitments . . . will be permitted except where it satisfies the real local economic or social needs of persons who find it necessary to live in the villages' (p. 17); and three more are named as locations where (p. 18):

> the amount of land allocated for housing development . . . be reduced, as and where possible, and that housing developments in these villages be related to the real local economic or social needs of persons who find it necessary to live in the villages.

The detailed consideration of the policies to be adopted for individual settlements reduces the role of subsequent local plans to one of transposing these

Table 10.2   Caradon District Council housing policies for local plans

1   'In view of the present day absence of an economic need for many people to live in rural settlements, and the comparative public costs of providing services in rural areas compared with urban areas, there should in general be a considerable reduction in the rate and amount of new housing development in rural settlements'.

2   Development in rural settlements should be related primarily towards local social and economic needs, and the development judged on its overall benefit to the community'.

3   'New housing development in both rural and urban areas should be of much greater quality (which does not necessarily mean greater cost) and at densities required to balance needs to conserve agricultural land to blend with the character of the settlement'.

4   'Where a local need for housing cannot be met in a local settlement because of non-availability for purchase of sites or dwellings, the council should closely examine the advantages of acquisition itself of suitable sites or dwellings to satisfy that local need'.

5   'Urban development and redevelopment should be encouraged'.

6   'Housing development, and redevelopment for housing, for year-round occupation will be encouraged in principle in the town-centre areas'.

Source: Caradon DC, 1980, 13–14

firm guidelines into development control decisions for individual plots of land, and assessing the real local needs in each case. Positive planning at the local-plan level is thus reduced in scope by the policy restrictions presented in these rigid district guidelines. A similar district level settlement policy has been formulated by South Pembrokeshire District Council (1976) which categorizes villages according to their capacity for residential expansion and assesses the priority for follow-up local-plan formulation.

Other guidelines for rural settlement planning within local plans are presented within a less formal framework. An interesting case of unpublished guidelines occurs in the deliberations undertaken by Eden District Council concerning the principles which should guide local planning within its jurisdiction. Since the mid-1970s Eden has been used by Cumbria county planning department as a pilot study area for the adoption of village clusters as planning units. In 1978, the preliminary results of this study were presented at a meeting of the district planning committee (Agenda Item No. 6, March 1978, p. 2):

> The village cluster system seems to provide a very useful tool for a planning authority whether it be County or District. It gets round the problems with the old settlement classification methods and it provides a framework for making development control and investment decisions. It may also be that in future local plans should be drawn up for clusters, rather than individual villages so allowing the spreading of resources, perhaps some housing in one village, industry in another, etc.

Although the suggestion for a cluster framework was viewed at the time to be tentative and requiring further study, the principle of a settlement-cluster policy was agreed subject to detailed investigation of individual clusters. This type of guideline inevitably structures both the format and content of ensuing local plans and in this case, the adoption of the village-cluster concept has resulted in an innovative approach to local planning even before the arrival of an approved county structure plan. The Eden example also demonstrates the progress which can be made when county and district approaches to rural settlement planning are allowed to proceed in relative harmony.

In fact, Eden District Council has also pioneered another form of 'guideline plan' which is able to exert influence on statutory local plans in rural areas. In March 1980, the council approached the parish councils of Kirkoswald and Lazonby with a view to a joint experiment in local planning, and the result of this co-operation virtually amounts to a 'self-help' local plan (Kirkoswald and Lazonby Parish Councils, 1981). A joint working party was set up with representatives from the district and the two parishes, and studies were undertaken of all aspects of community life in the area, culminating in the identification of problems and the generation of proposals for the area's development over the next 5 years. Policies which received local support included:

1 The provision of new local employment through the construction of small workshops by the Development Commission and the allocation of land and redundant buildings to industrial use;
2 The development of small groups of houses of varying size and cost;
3 The enhancement of the local physical environment, for example by tree-planting projects and the undergrounding of wirescapes;
4 The promotion of formal car-sharing schemes and the reopening of Lazonby station to passenger traffic;
5 Permitting small-scale tourist developments;
6 The retention of local primary schools;
7 The rectification of specific servicing problems, such as that with sewage disposal.

If the participation of parish councils is successfully able to present the views and aspirations of *all* sections of the rural community then the joint preparation of local-plan guidelines with district officials is an encouraging step towards the recognition of localized rural problems and (hopefully) the implementation of specific policy responses. The Kirkoswald and Lazonby working party suggest that the exercise 'has fostered a spirit of co-operation which it is hoped will continue into the future through the implementation of the proposals contained in the Report and through joint working on matters of common interest' (p. 2). It is certainly the case that guidelines from above in the decision-making hierarchy (notably from the county authority) should be carefully balanced with guidelines from below (the residents of the area concerned) in the formulation of local plans at the district level.

District plans

The mainstay of local planning in rural areas is the district plan. Although the other types of plan discussed above often impose important guidelines and restrictions on the scope of the statutory local plan for an area, it is the district plan that is put through the paces of co-operation and participation and which represents the basis for the implementation of localized rural settlement planning. Considerable variation exists in the approaches adopted by district authorities in the preparation of district plans. Some take the view that planning policies alone are insufficient to bring about any significant change within the short term, and designate their priority for resources accordingly. East Lindsey District Council, for example, place great emphasis on their ongoing 'Organization and Development Programme' which attempts to develop a more beneficial impact from national and corporate policies in their area. Accordingly, the district-plan mechanism is viewed as a less effective agent for change, and resulting plans (e.g. the Wragby Plan, 1977) are content to recognize land that has previously been allocated for housing and industrial development, and to permit implementation to take its course as and when private developers make use of their planning permissions, or when industrial entrepreneurs develop in the area. Direct spending in the Wragby plan is foreseen only for tree-planting schemes, and direct action of any kind is perceived as being outside the scope of the local-plan process.

In contrast to this approach, other district authorities have thrown the full weight of their effort behind the local-plan process, in some cases producing a series of studies and reports resembling a miniature structure plan. Horsham District Council, for example, have produced a series of detailed study reports on population and housing, employment and industry, recreation and open space, agriculture and the countryside, shopping and community facilities, design and conservation, transport and development land. These survey details have contributed to an examination of possible strategies (1979) which broadly favour the concentration of new development in the major urban area of Horsham Town and limitation of rural settlement growth to that dictated by local needs. Matters of public participation (1980) and implementation and monitoring (1980a) are also given specific report status, and the culminating Interim District Plan (1980b) gives the impression of being founded on the maximum possible effort and priority level available to the authority, who thus may be seen to rely on the district plan as the major planning tool at their disposal. It might be expected that the Horsham area, with a high degree of pressure for housing development, will require a planning mode of action which is dominated by *development control* and will therefore be well suited to the implementation capabilities of the district plan (see chapter 9), whereas in areas such as East Lincolnshire, the major requirement is for the *attraction* of suitable growth which local plans *per se* are less well-equipped to enact. In order to investigate this hypothesis, examples of district plans from three different types of rural area are briefly described here. The examples have been selected not as representatives of a generalized norm of local planning in a particular type of area (for it is too early to prove the existence of such norms in the parochial process of local planning) but rather as indicators of the issues and policy responses which may occur in areas of different needs. Categories of green-belt areas, pressured commuter areas and growth-need areas are neither comprehensive nor mutually exclusive, but are used here to give some idea of the variable content of different district plans.

Green-belt areas

A good example of district-plan preparation in a green-belt area is afforded by the East Hertfordshire District Plan (1980). The area has a history of green-belt restrictions, and although limited growth has previously occurred in some villages, these too have recently been included in the blanket green-belt policy. A continuing fear of encroachment from the expansion of London (figure 10.5) has resulted in both the county structure plan and the district plan adopting a broad objective of reducing the rate of growth in the area, but within this strategic remit, several more specific planning aims are suggested as suitable for the local planning process (table 10.3). Objectives 3, 5, 6, 7 and 8 demonstrate a wish to provide positive planning responses alongside the more negative mechanisms of development control, although it is admitted that 'the

Figure 10.5 East Hertfordshire's perception of an expanding London

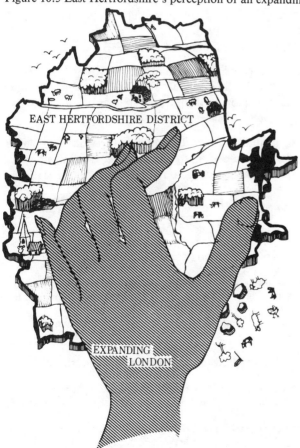

Source: East Hertfordshire DC, 1980, preface

District Plan cannot bring about a dramatic change in the pattern of modern life, nor would it be the intention to do so' (p. 8). The East Hertfordshire plan is thus an attempt to deal with the social and economic problems of a rural area within the structural restrictions of both the green-belt policy and the lack of comprehensive implementation powers. This complex interaction gives rise to a number of specific policies.

Rural land allocation is managed under an umbrella of presumption against rural development. The plan as originally drawn up treated all rural areas in the district as if they were green-belt areas, but the post-local public enquiry modifications to the plan (1981) ensured that rural areas outside the green belt were given separate policy attention which in effect resulted in a slight easing of blanket restrictions in these areas. Nevertheless both inside and outside the green belt, strict conditions concerning agricultural or community need effectively limit development in rural areas. Given this broad strategy the plan (p. 14) acknowledges 'the need to ensure to whatever extent may be possible that villages are not isolated in physical terms as preserved museum pieces of bygone architecture with no community spirit', and as a consequence of this view, any available development in rural areas would be (p 15):

> directed towards those settlements which are in need of limited growth to cater for local requirements; be they specific to meet a growing demand from new household formation, or for the purpose of arresting a decline, or level of social imbalance in the village community.

The plan therefore allows for small-scale development in three named villages and infilling in eight others, to a scale of up to ten and three dwellings respectively (although these definitions were removed in the 'modifications'

Table 10.3   Main planning objectives for the East Hertfordshire District Plan

1   To regulate the development and use of land in the public interest.
2   To conserve and protect a productive and attractive rural landscape and good environmental quality in towns/villages and to secure improvement to the environment wherever the opportunity occurs.
3   To attempt to maintain economic stability within the area in order to provide a sound background for continuing investments by commercial undertakings in the district (subject to the limitations of the council's powers and authority).
4   To secure the provision and maintenance of an adequate system of movement within the district.
5   To cater for the housing needs of the existing population.
6   To secure the highest possible standards of development and construction in the district.
7   In co-operation with other authorities, to encourage, maintain and participate in the provision of adequate welfare and social facilities for the elderly, deprived, disabled and handicapped.
8   To identify the needs for leisure, including sporting, recreational, cultural, artistic and tourist facilities in the district, and to endeavour to secure such facilities.

Source: East Hertfordshire DC, 1980, 7

document because of undue rigidity in development-control processes). Elsewhere, development will only be permitted according to strict local needs criteria, and in all cases planning permissions are only to be granted for 12–15 months so that a local need for new dwellings is not thwarted by land speculation. Within such an all-embracing strategic policy of growth restriction, the plan has made some effort to channel any available growth towards the specific needs of the local population, and the council aims to acquire land for local needs development in rural areas where the private sector is unable or unwilling to do so (Policy Rl). These efforts should be measured against other district plans in green-belt areas where the expectation that existing commitments and turnover of current housing stock will cater for local housing need, means that little or no new development will be permitted (Warwick DC's Lapworth Plan, 1980). Within the limitations imposed by the structure plan, East Hertfordshire's plan includes some resource redirection towards specific needs, although the ultimate test of this policy will be in its efficacy when implemented.

The land-use aspects of the plan are complemented by proposed action in other sectors. In *housing*, direct action by the district authority will provide new council dwellings for newly formed households and 'small' and 'starter' homes for first-time buyers (Policy H3) where a particular local need is identified in rural areas. In addition, special provision is made in Policy H4 for households in stress (e.g. the homeless) and special-needs groups (e.g. the elderly and the handicapped). Continuing the emphasis on fulfilling specific needs, the plan pursues a general policy of making full use of the existing housing stock (through grant aid for improvement, providing local authority loans for the purchase of older and/or cheaper property, and so on) and of enforcing a requirement that new residential developments include a proportion of small dwellings, presumably through the use of planning conditions such as the Section 52 agreement.

The area is seen as having a buoyant economy, reflected in high levels of *employment*, and the plan seeks to limit interference with this situation as far as practicable within the imposed strategic restrictions. Industrial, office and warehouse developments are limited to those which need to be located specifically in the area (particularly through linkage with existing concerns) or those essential to the national interest. In effect, these conditions mark a rather strict attitude towards the enforcement of low growth levels, although suitable small-scale or craft-type industries are not ruled out in rural settlements. There is certainly no perceived need to pursue a policy of active encouragement of suitable enterprises in this area where the market mechanism already creates a ready-made demand.

The plan's treatment of *movement and accessibility* is mainly concerned with highways (a district council responsibility). Public transport's role as a lifeline to many villages is, however, recognized, and the district authority pledges the maintenance of at least current real levels of financial subsidy for bus services which are responsive to local needs (Policy M11). The possibilities of private-sector and self-help schemes are also recognized and encouraged (p. 49):

> The District Council will investigate ways to support and license innovatory
> self-help schemes and private operators which would be intended to meet
> those transport needs not catered for by conventional public transport

but this support is conditioned by the disclaimer that the district authority's
scope in this field is very limited compared with that of the county council.
Similar succour is offered in relation to the retention of *shopping facilities* in
rural settlements, either by favourable planning consideration of proposals for
new or converted shops in villages (Policy S9), or by the consideration of
applications for special grant assistance to potential entrepreneurs when
village communities are either unable to attract a local shop or when existing
premises are under threat of closure (S10). This last policy, if implemented,
represents a new trend towards the subsidy of the local general store/post
office in rural communities. The plan also encourages the retention and
further development of *community facilities* in villages, but the enactment of
this policy amounts to a close liaison with the area health authority and the
county education authority to secure district objectives such as the retention of
village-based surgeries and schools through methods of co-operation and
persuasion.

This package of policies demonstrates that even within a county-level
strategy of very tight growth restriction, the district plan is able to channel
residual resources towards the specific needs of local communities in rural
areas. It might be argued that this residual is too small to have any noticeable
positive effect and that the various positive aspects of the plan are merely the
idealized mouthings of well-meaning but impotent planners. Such a view will
be untenable if sufficient resources are allocated to community need schemes
by county, district, statutory and private-sector agencies. Once again the
willingness of the spirit is demonstrated in written policy statements but the
willingness (or weakness) of the flesh will only become apparent as these
policies are implemented.

Commuter areas

It might be expected that commuter areas which are not shackled by green-belt
restrictions might require styles of planning within local plans which are very
different from the fine tuning of development which dominates the East
Hertfordshire plan. An analysis of district plans for commuter areas
uncovered a veritable *pot pourri* of policy emphasis according to the parent
structure-plan attitude towards growth, the political complexion of the district
authority, and the area's relative proximity to urban employment centres. Few
generalizations are warranted by this wide variation of district plans, but one
or two examples here suffice to demonstrate the nature and content of plans in
different parts of this spectrum.

One approach to district planning in a broad area of commuter pressure
is shown by the West Bassetlaw District Plan (Bassetlaw DC, 1978) which
covers an area of Nottinghamshire centring on Worksop. The area has
been the subject of a settlement classification policy under the *Plan for*

Rural Nottinghamshire (Nottinghamshire CC, 1966) and the issue of the future use of a classificatory system was seen as central to the content of the district plan:

> In terms of containing development within specific 'growth' villages the Plan has undoubtedly been successful. What needed to be decided was whether the policy ought to be continued and, if so, what level of development should be allocated to each settlement. (Bassetlaw DC, 1967, 6)

In conjunction with the structure plan it was decided that 95 per cent of future growth should be accommodated in Worksop and the other major settlements in the area, with the remaining 5 per cent designated to meet the local requirements of the predominantly rural areas covered by the plan. On the basis that 'experience suggests that policies in rural areas are best explained by a system of village groups' (p. 22) the plan establishes a classic hierarchical classification of villages into:

1 *Primary growth:* one village where extensive outstanding commitments prevail and where services and facilities will be maintained;
2 *Secondary growth:* two villages with some previous commitments and where small-scale growth will not harm village character;
3 *Limited growth:* ten villages where the intention is to maintain their present population or to show only slight growth; and
4 *Special amenity:* three villages where strict control will be exercised over growth.

Housing policy in the plan concentrates on a residential land search in the major settlements and it is considered unnecessary to define exact sites to meet the housing requirements in the rural areas. Broad guidelines for permitted rural housing (p. 19) suggest that permission will only be granted:

> where it is essential to agriculture and the maintenance of community services, to meet the local needs of the Council's Housing Waiting List, or, in the case of small infilling plots, where no harm will be caused to village character.

No specific proposals are included, however, which directly link rural housing policy with the requirement to meet other forms of local need than that expressed in the local authority waiting list. Similarly, broad policies are included to encourage some development of employment opportunities in the primary and secondary growth villages but no specific aid is offered to workshop-scale enterprises in smaller rural settlements. No active concern for rural community services is voiced in the plan, with the major village policy discussion being directed towards the physical conservation of settlement appearance. An inevitable conclusion is that the socio-economic concerns of the smaller rural settlements are subjugated by the priority given to the programming of growth in the major centres, and this might reflect more on the chosen *scale* of the plan (which is too broad for adequate attention to individual village problems) than on the political objectives of the plan-makers. One noteworthy exception to this trend is the Bassetlaw community bus, introduced on an experimental basis in 1978, which provides services for different functions (e.g. to shops, recreation centres, medical centres) on different days of the week. The service is operated by the joint action of county, district and parish councils, the health authority and voluntary organizations, and co-ordinated by the Bassetlaw Council for Voluntary Services. The district plan commends this scheme but makes no move to repeat it elsewhere in the area.

District plans dealing with smaller spatial units offer a much more detailed consideration of and response to commuter pressures. The West Costessey, Wensum and Yare Valleys Local Plan (South Norfolk DC, 1980) covers an area west of Norwich where a combination of 'fringe area' residential estate development and suitable small-scale development for local needs is advocated by the structure plan. The objectives of the local plan are to resist the pressures for undue commuter development outside the designated 'fringe area', kept deliberately vague so that individual applications are not predetermined by local-plan policy. Thus in the three major settlements in the plan area (p. 34):

> planning permission will be given, at the discretion of the district council, for individual dwellings or small groups of houses which will enhance the form and character of the village. As well as providing choice in terms of residential location it is felt that this policy will meet those demands for village housing often referred to as 'local need' though this normally accounts for a very small proportion of the total housing demand.

Outside these settlements, permission is restricted to dwellings connected with agriculture, forestry or the expansion of existing institutions, and in all cases high standards of design for new development will be required by the planning authority. The overriding theme of the plan may therefore be viewed as a concern for the conservation of settlementscape and the preservation of good agricultural land, rather than a perceived need to make special arrangements to meet local housing need. The provision of services and facilities is not overtly presented as problematic in any part of the plan, although it does seek to encourage workshop-scale industries in the villages provided that they are not detrimental to visual amenity or agricultural land loss.

A different response to commuter pressure is seen in the Steyning, Bramber and Upper Beeding plan (Horsham DC, 1978) which covers the three named villages in the West Sussex coastal belt. Several important issues are recognized as central to the plan-preparation process in this case (table 10.4), but the ensuing proposals are severely restricted by a number of specific constraints. Service deficiencies such as expensive drainage, no health facilities, limited shopping facilities, and a primary school operating at capacity are seen to 'constitute a significant constraint which, in the present economic climate, is unlikely to be overcome by further development' (p. 44); the need for a new bypass has effectively prevented new development; the parent structure plan permits only restricted development; and much of the area is designated an AONB and is thus subject to a firm presumption against new development.

Table 10.4   Main issues in the Steyning, Bramber and Upper Beeding Local Plan

1 An imbalanced aged structure
2 A need to control pressure for further planning permissions to be granted for speculative private housebuilding
3 A need to relate housing provision to meet local requirements
4 A lack of employment opportunities and suitably conforming sites for employment provision
5 The problem of heavy through traffic
6 Public transport frequency and costs
7 The lack of recreational facilities
8 The need for high design standards and environmental conservation

Source: Horsham DC, 1978, 33–4

These various constraints all point towards a policy of low growth levels in the area – a trend which is also demanded by the perceived paucity of financial resources (p. 45):

> the availability of public finance to provide additional facilities likely to be required as a result of future development is extremely limited and therefore such growth will only be able to take place where existing capacity in services is available or where the necessary infrastructure can be provided by the proposed development.

The end result of these deliberations is the preference for a policy of limited growth based on existing planning permissions. Indeed an option of *no-growth* is only rejected because it would 'involve payment of substantial compensation in respect of revocation of existing planning permissions and is, therefore, impractical in the present economic climate' (p. 46).

Within this strategy of limited growth, some attempts have been made at influencing the nature of permitted development, thereby fulfilling some of the objectives inherent in table 10.4. For example, the plan advocates a direct involvement in the housing market, if necessary through the acquisition of suitable land both for public-sector housing requirements and to be made available to the private sector. In addition: (p. 47):

> Planning permission would only be granted subject to Agreements under Section 52 of the Town and Country Planning Act 1971 ensuring that a contribution had been made towards meeting local housing needs and achieving other stated objectives.

The plan also aims to encourage rural crafts and small light industry to locate in the area. However, we are once again presented with the problem of assessing the likely efficacy of these policies when implemented. In that a paucity of available resources is stressed throughout the plan it is reasonable to suggest that few resources will, in fact, be available for housing projects or the encouragement of employment. This suggestion is given further credence by the plan's treatment of rural transport problems (p. 48):

The introduction of more frequent, cheaper services or concessionary fares for elderly people and school children would all have to be subsidized at considerable cost to the ratepayer and to introduce such a policy would be contrary to government advice.

Therefore direct action on transport is rejected in favour of a rather more easily implemented policy of general support for the introduction of legislation to aid private bus operators. In all these sectoral policies, this type of approach to district planning can be seen to be politically orientated towards monetarism and environmentalism, and although some steps are taken towards a fulfilment of local housing and employment needs, these appear to be subject to financial stringency and lacking in the more radical proposals for supporting self-help and direct intervention.

The suggestion that rural areas experiencing pressure from growing commuting populations might exhibit some degree of uniformity of approach to local planning may be disregarded on the evidence of available district plans. The potential unifying factor of pressure for development (rather than the need to encourage development as found in remoter areas) is initially manipulated by structure-plan policies (in which district authorities participate, but not always successfully) to restrict or channel growth, and then by the political motivations of the district authority themselves who are able to superimpose a *laissez-faire* or a direct-action approach (or, as is more usual, some compromise between the two) on their localized interpretation of the strategic policy. Rather than offering comprehensive responses to local problems as was the case in the East Hertfordshire plan (see pp. 275–8), at least in terms of subject matter, district plans in commuter areas appear to concentrate on particular issues of local importance. They therefore pursue the principal goal by moulding development control, by encouragement or persuasion, or by direct-intervention modes of action. This may, for instance, be a theme of concentration of available growth (West Bassetlaw), of consideration of individual developmental merits (West Costessey), or of minimum expenditure (Steyning). In this way, innovations of planning action tend to appear singly in district plans (mostly linked with the principal issues) rather than in any comprehensive manner. For example, the plan for Penrith (Eden DC, 1979) presents schemes for limiting new local authority housing to one- or two-bedroom dwellings, and for active co-operation with housing associations; Stratford-on-Avon District Council's (1978a) plan for Bishops Itchington stresses the usefulness of Section 52 planning agreements to obtain desired house types, and their plan for Southam (1979) outlines the implications of Community Land Act procedures (since repealed by the Local Government Planning and Land Act 1980) for settlement planning; and the Kempsey plan (Malvern Hills DC, 1980) shows how village community centres can be provided from the general allocation of playing field funding. The imagination and innovation collectively contained in these district plans is encouragingly widespread, but there would seem to be a deficiency in the local planning process that prevents sufficient resources being devoted to allow several innovations to be implemented together in a comprehensive programme of positive policy responses to particular problems experienced by particular rural communities.

Growth-need areas

A third category of rural area where one particular structural facet might be expected to pose common problems in district-plan preparation is the remoter areas where pressure for development does not necessarily exist on-tap and so growth, if deemed desirable, needs to be encouraged in one way or another. The lower level of developmental pressure allows considerable flexibility in the plan-making process, which, when released from the overriding theme of growth restriction, can roam the wider horizons of growth promotion based on various spatial models. This elasticity of potential policy for remoter rural areas provides a fertile habitat for discord between different levels of policy-makers whose judgement is based on contrasting political acumen, resulting in turn from widely varying perceptions of policy requirements. Thus it is common for district authorities in these areas to raise strong objections to the strategic principles imposed on them from the county level, and if district council objections are not heeded within the structure-plan process, the conflict of ideas and interests is continued during the preparation of district plans. Very often the remoter districts are least well endowed with plan-making resources, and so completed district plans for this type of area are as yet not in full flow. There is, however, a considerable body of evidence to suggest that county/district disputes are likely to have a traumatic effect on subsequent district plans and their outcomes.

A case in point is that presented by Torridge district in north Devon, where the approved structure-plan policy for rural settlements is to concentrate growth into selected local centres, while development in all other villages will only be permitted if infrastructure is available and the development is in keeping with the existing character and scale of the settlement. Indeed this approved policy offers a more relaxed policy for 'other villages' in which development was to be restricted to 'infilling and rounding off' in the submitted plan – a change promoted largely by strong local opposition to the policy for small rural settlements. This new flexible attitude to other villages means that some room for manoeuvre has (against the county authority's original wish) been instilled in the local planning process, and every indication suggests that in areas such as Torridge this opportunity will be grasped as firmly as possible. The district council's Rural Areas Study (1980) argues strongly for a change in the balance of residential and employment development in rural Devon, to allow appropriate small-scale growth in a much wider range of settlements than is proposed in the original, and to some extent even the amended, structure-plan policies. The reasons for this stance are summarized in two main prognostications:

1   The character of the rural settlements can be retained by ensuring that the scale of the development is suitable for a particular settlement and that the design and materials used are compatible. The appropriate scale of

development for each settlement should be determined by local studies, not stipulated at strategic level;

2   The spreading of development in a wider range of settlements will make more efficient use of previous public investment in infrastructure and services and in some cases will take up spare capacities (e.g. schools, sewage treatment works) (Section 8, para. 1.1).

The immediate concern for Torridge District Council is that only four selected rural centres were designated in their rural area, leaving most rural settlements with the prospect of restrictions on growth. It is, however, a thinly disguised distaste for the imposition of policies from above which underlies many of the specific criticisms of the county plan (para. 1.2):

> The District Council considers that it is the most suitable body to undertake the detailed appraisal/local plan work to determine the level of growth that is appropriate in the District. . . . The Structure Plan policies, in their present form, pre-empt such locally based studies.

As part of its drive to stem rural decline in its area, the district council has undertaken several detailed local studies and has isolated several types of settlement which although classified as 'other villages' in the structure plan are deemed capable of accommodating further growth. The conclusion (para. 1.2) is reached that:

> It is not appropriate to classify a large range of different settlements into one category as 'Other Villages' and that the suitable scale of development that is appropriate for each settlement is a matter to be determined at the local, and not the strategic level. A less concentrated pattern of development will not necessarily result in a larger amount of development overall.

The policy preferred by Torridge is for resources which are devoted to the provision of services and infrastructure to be allocated *by district council area* in agreement with detailed local studies. This strategy would then permit development in a wide range of settlements where service capacity exists, or can easily be restored. Such a strategy would allow greater scope for direct action by the district council (along the lines of their contribution in 1979 of £6000 for improvements to Bradworthy sewage-treatment works, which enabled 5 acres of land to be released for housing and industrial development), and would greatly enhance its existing programme and provide serviced industrial sites, housing land and housing and leisure facilities in settlements of particular need.

The Torridge experience is endorsed, albeit in rather less critical terms, by the *Tavistock and District Local Plan: Issues Report* (West Devon DC, 1981) in which the encouragement of a greater degree of self-sufficiency in terms of housing and employment in individual settlements is perceived as a central theme in plan preparation. In Devon, district council criticisms of county policy may have been assuaged by the modifications contained within the approved structure plan, which allow more leeway for district-level initiatives in small settlements. District-level disapproval of strategic policy, however, is by no means confined to one particular county. For example, South Herefordshire District Council (1980, 3) strongly recommends a different county-wide approach to that of concentrating development in the market towns of the area:

> The District Council would like to see a revision of the rural development policies in the Structure Plan in favour of a more positive approach towards what can best be described as community need. It is suggested that rural settlements should be classified, the range of facilities available or capable of provision identified and a case made, if appropriate, for additional residential development where necessary to support those facilities.

The plan suggests the recognition of 'capital villages' where job opportunities and concomitant housing growth should be encouraged to meet local needs, and of other smaller settlements where some new housing would help to maintain the viability of existing community facilities. Given a more flexible strategic framework, South Herefordshire's plan for the 'rural west' offers a checklist of action available to local planners, the salient socio-economic contents of which are repeated in table 10.5. Once again it should be realized that while these actions together would almost certainly benefit disadvantaged groups in rural communities, the limitations enforced by paucity of resources and the difficulties of corporate decision-making result in a general inability to enact all these innovative policies comprehensively where necessary. Therefore district councils are required to assess the priorities of various rural planning problems and concentrate on particularly important themes (as described on pp. 278–83 in commuter areas). In remoter areas, however, the selection of district-plan themes is often hampered and restricted by the differences between strategic and local-plan objectives and requirements. In short the checklist in table 10.5 will not become a complete reality until finance, administration and structure-plan policies are positively altered in favour of small rural settlements and their problems.

This rather gloomy conclusion is supported by those district plans which have been completed for remoter areas. Leominster District Council's plan for Kingston (1979) does at least show a realization of the need for a comprehensive planning programme at local level: 'Implementation of complementary housing and industrial policies and proposals together with an improved infrastructure, particularly the local highway system, will be necessary to achieve even the modest growth envisaged' (p. 10) but in general, matters of physical planning and negative control dominate published plans for this type of area, and the issue of positive action in smaller settlements is often either compromised or shelved in order to meet the required compliance with strategic policies, or is still in the melting pot and has thus delayed plan presentation. It remains to be seen whether forthcoming district plans for remoter rural areas can achieve the kind of agreed positive policies which have so far eluded many of the plans which are already published.

Table 10.5   Checklist for local-plan action in remoter rural areas

A   Rural housing
1   Establish local and community housing need
2   Examine how needs can be met within strategic framework
3   Examine means to meet local need other than by council housing (e.g. building houses for sale, partnership schemes with local builders or potential occupants, and use of existing powers to restrict initial sales to local occupants)
4   Improve existing housing stock
5   Promote policies to achieve dwellings of the right type and price for local people (perhaps though expandable or starter home schemes)

B   Employment
1   Establish type and level of employment need
2   Match need with development Commission programme to provide new employment
3   Promote additional jobs by attracting small, privately owned industries

C   Education
Pursue with local education authority policies to maintain existing schools

D   Transportation
Within limited resources consider optimum means of assisting rural communities, for example public transport, car-sharing and mini-bus service schemes

E   Social services
Discuss needs with relevant county council departments and parish councils and encourage positive ameliorative policies

NB The plan also discusses tourism, conservation, settlement patterns, and recreation and leisure.

After: South Herefordshire DC, 1980, 3–5

The effects of local plans

Owen (1980, 1), in discussing the historical development of planning culminating in structure plans/local plans, concludes that:

> There is a strong case for the slower, but more thorough, development of planning based on *evidence*. Although there are many environmental problems which require urgent attention, and planning must respond quickly to these problems, it should be a response that is based on careful sifting and distilling of evidence as well as on the pursuit of new ideas. Too many of the quick-fire responses that have occurred during the last 30 years have exacerbated rather than alleviated problems.

If this advice is heeded, the content and performance of local plans may be assessed according to two distinct criteria. The first basis for evaluation is that adopted by Barnard (1981) which is to test local plans against the objectives required of them by the Planning Advisory Group and developed in subsequent legislation and advice from the Department of the Environment. Such an approach stresses the quality of details for development control, translation of strategic policies, co-ordination of the development process and public participation, and is characterized by the identification of 'good planning practice'. In terms of the requirements of planning practitioners this approach is a most useful tool, providing important inputs into the iterative process of future plan modification and preparation. By adopting this criterion for assessing local plans, however, the merit of the policies contained therein and their contribution to the tackling of particular problems and issues in a local area is often ignored, and so the second basis for evaluation would therefore aim to investigate the scope of local plans as policy responses to local issues rather than items of planning practice.

Several problems are incurred when adopting this second approach. The criterion voiced by Owen concerning 'quick-fire responses' may, for example, be viewed as good reason for a conservatively safe and passive series of aims to be incorporated in local plans. Moreover, the Department of the Environment has continually urged a restricted view of local plans, and districts following this advice to the letter will also pursue good planning practice and neglect socio-economic issues and available channels of action to deal with them. In addition, to level criticism at local plans for a lack of positive action for which local planners have no direct implementative mode and for which they are often totally reliant on the goodwill and resource base of other decision-making agencies is merely to expose the weaknesses of the local planning system rather than of the individual plans and policies themselves. Nevertheless, at a time when the problems of rural communities have been given continuous exposure for at least a decade and experimental responses to these problems have been operative in specific locations for almost as long, to ignore the positive social-response potential of local plans would be to discard the slow and thorough development of rural settlement planning of which Owen speaks. Therefore, despite there being sound reasons for doing so, local plans which disregard factors outside a strict land-use framework are failing to exploit the full potential of local planning.

As yet, insufficient plans have been enacted in rural areas for many positive conclusions as to their effectiveness. It is however the case that land-use-only plans, even with favourable implementation conditions, will achieve less benefit to disadvantaged groups in rural communities than will similar plans with added components dealing with specific local needs for housing, employment or services, even though these additional factors are almost entirely dependent on implementation procedures and decisions operating outside the district planning authority. This brief review of local plans in rural areas has uncovered some of the basic difficulties in the successful achievement of a comprehensive form of local planning. Many of the issues raised above concur with the lessons drawn by Caddy (1981) in his account of the local plan programme in the Vale of White Horse District in Oxfordshire. In *political* terms he stresses the importance of ensuring a strong political commitment for proposals within local plans. Lack of support from the political arena will hamper or prevent the collection of a package of interrelated policies which will be implemented by a variety of agencies. In addition the difficulties of interaction between local and strategic authorities are given further emphasis (p. 12):

it was complicated by the political differences between County and District

on the interpretation of the Structure Plan which are not so much ideological but rather arise out of the different perceptions of, on the one hand
the County, which sees matters in a strategic light, and on the other, the
District which is concerned with local issues.

Caddy also notes that many districts have diverted local-plan resources into
opposing structure-plan policies and their modifications, thus retarding the
presentation of the local plans themselves. This problem will continue with the
regular review of structure plans, and it can be argued that the longer a plan
takes to prepare, the greater the probability that political changes will alter its
direction and policy priorities.

Technical lessons from the Vale of White Horse District highlight the
dilemmas faced by restraint planning in an area of developmental pressure.
Caddy describes this process as 'tugging in two directions' and suggests that
there is no easy compromise between the two, particularly in cases where
county and district wishes differ. In this context the grass always seems greener
on the other side of the pressured/remote 'fence'. Caddy enviously notes that
'in the poorer regions, local plans can concentrate more single-mindedly on
regeneration without being beset by fear of over-stimulation' (p. 14), but
unfortunately there is strong evidence to suggest that single-mindedness is
more often a figment of detached envy rather than a realistic platform for
growth stimulation in the remoter areas. Both county–district policy conflicts,
and lack of co-ordination in inter-agency resource allocation, have led to
delays and an absence of technical and political consensus in these areas. It can
only be concluded that local plans are an extremely difficult technical exercise
in all types of rural area (but for different reasons), and that a plan where such
difficulties are not encountered has probably not risen to the challenges of
local rural issues other than those strictly connected with development control.

A third set of lessons are *financial* phenomena linked directly to political and
technical difficulties. The fact is that the financial inducements to local
authorities in attracting growth are enormous (Caddy, 1981, 15):

> Additional development means extra investment, rateable value, and
> possible 'planning gain', and in times of economic stringency and cuts in
> publicly-financed schemes, private sources of finance assume greater
> significance.

Thus the permission for new development is financially attractive at district
level (especially where local authority landholdings are involved and
consequently capital receipts and revenue ensue), and also within districts
where competition for growth between settlements takes place not only on
grounds of need but also because of the financial loss and gain potentially
incurred by private-sector services under different plan regimes (witness the
strong involvement of chambers of commerce and trade in consultation exercises). Caddy once again summarizes these influences most succinctly (p. 15):
'planning solutions which could well lead to financial benefits can be expected
to receive Member encouragement'.

The final set of lessons drawn from the experience of local planning in the

Vale of White Horse District are *procedural*, and hinge on whether local plans should be restricted by a traditional land-use framework or whether they should actively pursue a promotional and advocative role which extends their ambit to wider socio-economic matters. Caddy argues for the use of local plans as a means of stimulating ideas and action which are not specifically connected with the allocation of land, and places this progression alongside the wider shift of emphasis in planning away from land-use and development-control domination and towards a reiterative process accentuating *planning* and not *plans*.

These conclusions from a planner who has been actively engaged in local planning are worthy of very serious consideration, and the fact that these various problems with the local plan process are now being recognized and publicized suggests that the lessons involved are gradually being learned, and that the inconsistencies and difficulties are slowly being overcome. There is a danger, however, of falling into the eternal trap of assessing policies without regard to their implementation. Chapter 9 examines local-plan implementation in some detail, and it is clear that even if local plans continue to progress towards a wider and more comprehensive response to localized planning issues and problems, there remain considerable difficulties in enacting these policies given current resource levels and bureaucratic administration of finance in rural areas. Many of the local plans described above have pinpointed a central theme of providing housing opportunities to meet particular local needs, yet the few observations that have been made of the implementation of local needs policies suggest that 'they are inevitably outside the strict scope of land-use planning powers and . . . there may also be policy reasons, for example the effect on house prices, and doubts about the possibility of implementing the proposed measures' (Elson, 1981, 65). In the more adventurous plans where direct action is proposed to provide particular housing opportunities, subsidize informal rural transport schemes or even rural shops, or service and encourage new employment, a very big question mark hangs over the sufficiency of resources for these projects. Undoubtedly one or two of these tasks can be performed in a local area but it appears most unlikely that a comprehensive package of direct-action policies will find an adequate resource base for implementation in the currently stringent economic climate. The overall conclusion to be made at this fairly early stage in the life of local plans in rural areas is that while current evidence suggests some promise for a constructive and positive local planning response to rural issues at some point in the future, the present paucity of effective and financially supported implementation channels for positive action mean that until changes in these underlying procedures and structures occur, development control will remain the kingpin of implementable local planning in rural settlements.

ELEVEN

Special cases:
the role of designated areas

Rural settlements in designated areas

> The human life of a rural community is as vital as the natural history of the area. The principle of making these towns and villages into show places lacks reality. One Rip van Winkle village cocooned as a museum of the past in each area might be able to pay its way if the old toll-gates were to be manned again and visitors had to pay as they entered, but in a countryside which is full of old villages conservation brings little benefit to the inhabitants and often results in extra costs to their public services. (Haines, 1973, 2)

The complex and conflicting dualism evoked by this passage from George Haines' *Whose Countryside?* is becoming an increasingly important issue in rural settlement planning. As more and more of rural Britain becomes designated as a special area, the trade-offs between physical conservation of settlements and their socio-economic health assume an ever more pressing priority for planners and rural resource managers. Within these designated areas it is generally assumed that the physical structure of settlements is viewed as more important than socially orientated issues, thus creating a situation which can lead to a congregation of the affluent in protected villages and all the problems resulting from trends of gentrification and geriatrification. This chapter briefly seeks to review the procedures and effects of rural planning in designated areas in order to test this hypothesis. Indeed there is evidence to suggest that the assumption of stricter regulation of village development in these areas may be overvalued. Blacksell and Gilg (1981, 123) suggest that:

> One of the more curious features of development control in rural areas is the small number of special controls in National Parks, Areas of Outstanding Natural Beauty and other protected landscapes. Despite the fact that nearly 50 per cent of the land area of England and Wales has now been designated under one or other of these protection orders and the strictures about the need for high standards of development control in the official guidance to local authorities, there are few extra powers available.

The Landscape Special Development Orders introduced in 1950 to reduce in certain areas the exemptions usually granted to agricultural and forestry-related development have, in fact, been used successfully on only three occasions and so any special restrictions in designated areas stem from the ordinary policy-making and development-control decisions which are operated throughout rural Britain.

The scale and variety of designated areas is considerable. In terms of landscape protection National Parks and AONBs are designated by the Countryside Commission (or its predecessor, the National Parks Commission); Heritage Coasts are also suggested by the Commission but regulated by county councils along with Areas of Great Landscape Value and Coastal Preservation Areas. More specific agents of development restriction are represented by green belts at a macro level and conservation areas at a more localized scale. In combination, these various measures exert influence over the bulk of rural areas in any particular county. Figure 11.1 shows the various landscape categories appertaining to Devon in 1979, although it should be noted that this distribution has been modified by the Approved Structure Plan, and by the effects of the Local Government Planning and Land Act of 1980 (which abolished the term 'Outstanding' when applied to Conservation Areas). In practice the rural settlement planning procedures within each particular designation are of widely varying importance.

National parks

The ten national parks in England and Wales cover some 13,620 square kilometres (5260 square miles) and represent 9 per cent of the total land area. Within their twin purposes of preserving and enhancing natural beauty within park areas and promoting enjoyment of these areas by the public, national-park authorities are also enjoined to have due regard for local social and economic needs. The resolution of the obvious conflicts between conservation, recreation and local needs has been central to the task of planners in national parks since their inception, and very often it is the local needs objective which has been the first to be sacrificed in the complex policy equations which delegate priority to landscape, townscape and recreation in these areas. The Exmoor National Park Plan of 1977 explicitly acknowledges this order of precedence for policy objectives (p. 51): 'It must be recognized, however, that to make the interests of local people the first objective of the NPA would be to defeat the purpose of the National Park'. It is therefore logical to expect that in addition to the 'normal' problems experienced in similar rural areas, rural settlements and communities in national-park areas will be subject to specific pressures arising from high levels of residential popularity and very restricted planning policy and practice. Such a generalization, however, is applicable in different measures to individual national parks. For example, Blacksell and Gilg (1981) highlight a strong contrast between the scale of development pressure in Exmoor and that in Dartmoor. Although rural growth restrictions prevail in both areas, the declining nature of rural communities in Exmoor has led to a general encouragement of new housing in order to bolster ailing settlements, whereas in eastern Dartmoor there exists a strong demand for permission to develop and therefore a policy of restraint rather than encouragement has been adopted. The Northumberland National Park

Figure 11.1 Specially designated areas in Devon

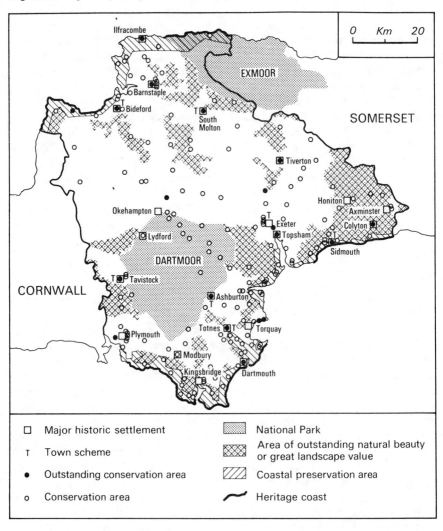

Source: After Devon CC, 1979, 127, 130

environment is different again, as no substantial settlements are included in the designated area and the pressures for housing development are slight: only twelve new dwellings being constructed in the whole of the park area between 1974 and 1979. In this case there has been no real need for detailed settlement planning policies to be defined solely for the park area.

Despite this wide degree of variation in settlement pattern and growth trends, some prevailing problems which affect many national-park communities have been isolated. For example, the Yorkshire Dales National

Park Committee (1979) lists several problems which reflect the geographical remoteness and lack of economic and social opportunity in the area. Table 11.1 lists some of these problems and clearly demonstrates the coexistence of 'rural' and 'national-park-specific' issues. Even in the remoter national parks such as the Yorkshire Dales, characteristic demands are made for holiday homes, second homes, retirement homes and commuter homes which arise because of the nature of the area and its national-park designation, and these demands may be seen to exacerbate existing problems stemming from remoteness and socio-economic decline (e.g. by 'pricing local people out of the housing market' as claimed by the Yorkshire Dales Committee). The question of park-specific pressures on local housing markets has been the subject of closely argued debate based on conflicting evidence from different national parks (Rogers, 1981; Shucksmith, 1980). The Lake District Special Planning Board (1979, 3) insists that:

> The popularity of the Lake District as a holiday and retirement area has put exceptional pressures upon the housing market . . . there is bound to be concern when people with local employment or local affinities find themselves unable to compete with other purchasers for local housing.

Penfold's (1974) study of housing problems in the Peak District National Park reaches a similar conclusion (p. 17):

> The Peak District is characterized by not only a policy of restricted supply

Table 11.1   Problems experienced by rural communities in the Yorkshire Dales National Park

Population
1 Total population is declining
2 Out-migration of younger persons
3 High rates of retirement age population

Employment
1 Lack of job diversity
2 Over-dependence on agriculture
3 Limited economic advantages of the area

Housing
1 Level of private rented accommodation is significantly high
2 Level of local authority housing is below average
3 Absent households and vacant dwellings suggest many second and holiday homes
4 Demands for retirement homes and for houses from commuters increases competition for local housing and may price local people out of the market

Services
1 Viability of village shops is declining
2 Remoteness from medical services
3 Primary school closures
4 Inadequate sewerage facilities
5 Inadequate facilities for formal cultural and recreational activities
6 Decline in public transport services

Source: Yorkshire Dales National Park Committee, 1979

of housing consequent upon its status as a National Park, but also a high level of demand generated by the commuting population of the surrounding conurbations.

The Peak Park Joint Planning Board (1976), however, takes a rather more circumspect view of this issue (p. 118):

> Some evidence was found to support the claims that local people were being priced out of the Peak District due to extreme competition for houses by persons from outside, but it was not overwhelmingly convincing. This is not to deny that needy cases and perhaps needy villages do occur. But in general terms there seems to be no reason for extreme pessimism about housing prospects in the Park.

The various opinions expressed in this debate merely reflect the fact that park-specific housing problems are sporadic both in intensity and spatial distribution. Even if local disadvantage in the housing market is not a current difficulty in some national parks it is generally acknowledged that

> there is a strong possibility that it will become a problem in the future, as more and more people are likely to want to live in the fine environment of the national park and acquire the means to do so. (North York Moors National Park Committee, 1980, 45)

The problems faced by local rural communities in national parks, therefore, appear to require two sets of policy responses from rural settlement planning within park areas. First, action is needed to promote the regeneration of declining communities suffering from the uniform ills found in remoter rural settlements. Second, specific measures are prompted by current or potential problems caused by successful external interference with local housing markets. The manner in which these requirements are matched against the strategic demands for visual and structural conservation of rural settlements in national parks will eventually decide whether the more desirable and accessible national-park areas maintain their local communities or become swamped by processes of gentrification, in which case the best rural environments and settlements will only be preserved for the affluent sectors of society.

A recent report by the Edinburgh-based Tourism and Recreation Research Unit (1981) focuses on the role of rural communities within national parks and gives a detailed analysis of three case studies in Exmoor, the Lake District and the North York Moors. Although the report is an important milestone in our understanding of the economy of national park communities, it tends to assume that an improved economy will inevitably also take care of social problems. This assumption tends to restrict the scope of the report in isolating the policy responses needed by park communities (Cloke, 1983). Another significant addition to national park literature has come from MacEwen and MacEwen (1981) who concentrate mainly on conservation aspects of the parks' objectives. Attention in this chapter is firmly planted on the planning policies which attempt to juggle with these various aims and objectives. These policies are formulated at three main levels.

National-park plans

The Local Government Act of 1972 required each national-park authority to produce a 5-year management plan which was to concentrate on the conservation/recreation themes of planning in park areas (Dennier, 1978; 1980; Hookway and Garvie, 1978). There have, however, been a wide range of interpretations of this mandate by park authorities, many of which have found it difficult to ignore their role as local planning authority and have thus dealt with issues in national-park plans which overlap with those found in structure-plan and local-plan policies. An example of how rural settlement policies are included in national-park plans is shown by the Brecon Beacons Plan (Brecon Beacons National Park Committee, 1977) which stresses that the two statutory national park goals of:

A   The presentation and enhancement of natural beauty; and
B   The promotion of its enjoyment by the public,

are subject to two vital qualifications:

1   That in situations where the two goals conflict and are irreconcilable, priority is given to goal A (conservation);
2   In pursuing goals A and B, the authority must have regard for the social and economic interests of the local population, *and in particular the interests of agriculture and forestry* (author's italics) (p. 13).

The definition of local interests in terms of agriculture and forestry is emphasized here because qualification 2 above can be interpreted as a back-door method of achieving goal A (conservation) in national parks. The Exmoor plan (1977, 51) admits that 'unless the people who live in it are prosperous the National Park would be neither a happy, nor a beautiful place', and this emphasis on the direct links between the socio-economic well-being of major land-users and landscape appearance is further stressed in the Brecon Beacons plan (1977, 15) which aims to 'safeguard the economic and social activities of the local population including farming and forestry particularly where these make an important contribution to the landscape'. Thus even the statutory requirement that national-park plans should consider national-park people can be interpreted selectively in some cases. This criticism, however, applies more to the relatively low priority given to socio-economic issues than to any lack of recognition that all sections of local communities in national parks do have needs of the planning system. Accordingly the Brecon Beacons Plan seeks to support the property and social balance of local communities by:

1   Encouraging *industrial activities* which do not by their nature or scale detract from the character or amenity of the park;
2   Ensuring that *new housing schemes* are for local needs only;
3   Encouraging the development of *services* to meet vital local needs.

This seemingly flexible attitude is, however, tempered by the development control details which are included in the plan. The tone is set by paragraph B28:

Government has concurred with the view of the Sandford Committee, also expressed in the National Park outline development control policy that 'acceptance of the philosophy of national parks must presume a stringent control of development'. While the National Park Authority will be most concerned to secure continued vitality of local settlements, substantial additional growth will only be acceptable in towns.

In fact, the Brecon Beacons Authority has made heavy use of conservation-area designations to control development in rural settlements, and growth elsewhere is restricted both by the policy conditions which have to be fulfilled before permission is granted, and by strict design guidelines which tend to steer developers towards the more profitable market for larger, more expensive dwellings. The Brecon Beacons example is by no means unique among national parks and merely serves to emphasize the ease of discord between conservation and local needs objectives. It also highlights the interweaving of special designations, with conservation areas also playing their part in arresting growth within a national park area. This doubling up of restrictive status also occurs frequently in other parks, notably the Exmoor 'Coastal Preservation Area' where planning permission for any development is only granted in exceptional circumstances.

Structure plans

Whereas national-park plans serve a quasi-advisory purpose and have limited direct means of implementation, structure plans convering national-park areas perform a statutory role and the policies therein, having been approved by the Secretary of State, form the basis for planning action at a strategic level. Structure-plan policies, and their interpretation in local plans, represent clearer and more realistic guidelines for rural communities and their settlements than the irreconcilable ideological differences in the national-park plans. Moreover, while park authorities have held complete responsibility for the preparation of national-park plans, their level of participation in structure-plan-making has been variable (Blenkinsop, 1978). Structure-plan policies for rural areas in national parks will, therefore, include the composite views of county planners and politicians alongside those of the park authorities. A further policy constraint has been introduced by central government. *Circular 4* from the Department of the Environment (1976) dictates that stricter development control procedures need to be applied in the national parks and that the development of new structure plans and local plans provides a further opportunity for strengthening such procedures.

Where national-park areas are included in the remit of county-based structure plans (and therefore form only one element of strategic decision-making) there has been a tendency for county-wide rural settlement policies to be made generally applicable to rural areas both inside and outside park boundaries, with stricter development control conditions being imposed within this broad framework for areas regarded as needing special protection. In this way, the Devon Structure Plan (1979) nominates selected area centres for its rural areas regardless of the boundaries of Dartmoor and Exmoor, and no specific national-park settlement policy was envisaged in the submitted plan. The

Secretary of State's modifications to the plan, however, despite relaxing the policies regarding development in rural settlements in general in Devon, advocate a marked toughening of policy inside Landscape Policy Areas (Devon CC, 1979, modifications appendix).

> In designated National Parks and Areas of Outstanding Natural Beauty, the preservation and enhancement of the landscape will normally be given priority over other considerations in the determination of development proposals. Within these areas outside Area Centres (none in Dartmoor) and selected Local Centres (six of the largest villages in the national park), these will be a presumption against development except where this is necessary to the economic or social well-being of the area or where it will enhance its character.

This centrally guided policy of minimum development in national-park areas is backed up by the imposition of strict criteria prior to the granting of any planning permission. Somerset's (1979) structure plan includes a typical list of criteria (table 11.2), and the policy for Exmoor National Park is to apply these criteria most stringently and to require very high standards of new development where permitted. Although seemingly rigid in theory these policies when implemented are prone to the fluctuations of pressure for development whereby the interpretation of development conditions may be relaxed if new dwellings are required to meet any local need which is not being fulfilled by the processes of the private-sector market. This situation has certainly arisen in that part of Exmoor that falls within the county of Devon (Blacksell and Gilg, 1981).

In some instances the national-park authority has a more important role in structure-plan preparation. For example the Cumbria and Lake District Joint Structure Plan (1980) results from the collaboration of the county council and the national-park special planning board, and the Peak District has its own structure plan (1980). In these cases, more specific attention has been devoted to strategic issues within national-park boundaries, and specific policy responses have resulted. Within the settlements of the Lake District park, for example, housing will normally only be permitted where:

Table 11.2   Development control criteria for Somerset

1 The nature and benefit of the proposal
2 The particular locational and functional requirements of the proposal and possible alternatives
3 The detailed siting in relation to the character of the surrounding area
4 The design of buildings and structures and use of materials in relation to the setting
5 The landscaping provision including consideration of both immediate impact and distant view of the development
6 The ability of rural access roads to accommodate traffic likely to be generated in terms of number, size and type of vehicles
7 Arrangements for access, servicing, parking and, as appropriate, provision for plant, equipment and storage of goods or materials

Source: Somerset CC, 1979, 27

1   The proposed development lies within the existing limits of each settlement;
2   The development is specifically intended to provide for the needs of the resident population or in association with the creation of new jobs in the locality;
3   The proposed houses are of a type and density which is appropriate to the needs of the local population and to the character of the village and its setting.

By pursuing a strict application of this policy, housebuilding can be limited to rates which are appropriate to local needs, but planning authorities cannot ensure that the houses which are built will be allocated to local people. Therefore the plan 'will seek means by which all further housing development can be retained for occupation by local people as full-time residents' (p. 55) – a task which has been attempted through the medium of Section 52 agreements. These are discussed in pp. 300–4 in the context of local plans. It should be noted, however, that although the special planning board continues to favour the use of Section 52 agreements in this context, the Secretary of State has deleted this policy in his modifications to the Lakes and Cumbria Joint Structure Plan.

On the surface, then, strategic settlement policies for rural areas in national parks follow a consistent format. New development outside designated growth settlements is to be severely restricted, and such housing that is permitted is to cater for local needs only. These superficially similar policies, however, are subject to varying degrees of commitment in the implementation process. A Northumberland National Park planner offered this comment in a personal communication:

> It may be true to say that development control policies in general are more strictly applied in the Park; certainly the practice has been to refuse permission for isolated residential development unless this serves the needs of agriculture and forestry. . . . The same general policies apply outside the Park for the rural areas of the County but I have no evidence that they are less strictly applied.

This view corroborates previous findings from rural settlement studies (e.g. Cloke, 1979), which suggest that development trends within national parks are often little different at an aggregate level from those in undesignated rural areas. Pressured areas within parks have often received similar planning treatment to commuter areas outside, and remoter park areas show little difference in policy implementation from that found in their counterparts beyond the park boundary. In some cases, therefore, specific national-park restrictions have resulted in no discernible differences in rural settlement planning on either side of the national-park demarcation. This is certainly true in the case of the purposeful allocation of development to local needs in some parks. At the other extreme, however, park authorities in areas such as the Lake District are bringing forward distinctive proposals to enforce the implementation of local needs development within a general framework of growth restriction.

These varying attitudes towards policy enactment are given further detailed expression in local-plan policies.

Local plans

It is the local planning scale which offers most scope for detailed policy, both negative and positive, for rural areas in national parks. Dartmoor National Park Committee (1977, 1) suggest that they, as the local planning authority, have a clear opportunity to promote the social and economic well-being of local rural communities.

> Through local planning policies and through decisions on applications for development, the Authority will need to take into account the needs of the people in relation to such things as housing, employment, essential public services and social facilities.

This then is the sharp end of conflicts between planning and management objectives in the parks. Decisions are made at local level which require the assessment of priorities relating to individual developments, and it is here that the implementation of policies designed to respond to local needs is either secured or ignored in the conceptual ferment of environmentalism and socio-economic welfare. Local plans pertaining to national parks occur at varying scales. The North York Moors National Park Committee (1979; 1980) have produced a district plan for the entire park area, whereas the Yorkshire Dales (1979) and Dartmoor (1977) authorities have preferred to rely on local plan policy frameworks covering national-park areas, to be supplemented by local plans for individual settlements (e.g. the selected local centres such as Ashburton, 1979, in Dartmoor) or groups of settlements.

Even with the strong socio-economic mandate of local plans, strategic conservation issues continue their overall domination of policy matters. The North York Moors National Park Committee District Plan (1979) outlines four specific policy objectives:

A   To conserve and enhance the natural beauty of the landscape of the national park;
B   To conserve and enhance the character of settlements in the national park;
C   To further and protect local economic and social interests;
D   To secure maximum efficiency in public and private investment;

and proceeds to discuss the relative importance of these objectives (p. 10):

> At times it will not be possible to meet all the objectives equally . . . throughout, special prominence will be attached to objective A (conservation and enhancement of landscape) . . . as this is one of the statutory duties of the National-Park Authority.

Against this background of physically oriented planning, national-park authorities have been eager to seize the opportunities for positive planning action within local plans, promoting mechanisms of both advocacy and control in the quest to secure the fulfilment of local needs. This willingness to stretch the official guidelines for local plans away from a land-use framework and towards more active involvement in policy-response stems partly from the acknowledgement that national-park areas do generate peculiar problems in rural communities, and partly from the increasing awareness by park authorities of public pressure for a realignment of policy benefit from visitor needs to full time resident needs. The efficacy of the proposed policy responses will, however, again depend on the implementation of detailed schemes.

The strategic patterns for permitted growth are handed down from structure plans and are generally mimicked reasonably accurately in ensuing local plans. Accordingly Dartmoor's (1977) settlement-policy advice accepts that new housing development will occur in the selected local centres, and the North York Moors (1980) plan allocates housing growth to its equivalent service centres. Policy differences occur below the growth settlement level. The Secretary of State's amendment of the Devon policy resulting in strict minimum growth attitudes to non-selected national-park villages has been noted above, and this contrasts with the North York Moors case where 'unless there are overriding environmental difficulties new small-scale housing development will not be opposed in principle at smaller villages' (North York Moors National Park Committee, 1980, 24). Both areas, however, are adamant that new growth in small villages should be inextricably linked to local needs, although the achievement of this stipulation is to be implemented by means of advocacy with private developers and housing authorities, as outlined in table 11.3.

An interesting facet of the North York Moors housing policies is the call for further research into various measures including 'local-need' planning conditions. Since November 1977 the Lake District Planning Board has revised its previous policy towards housing in view of the exceptional pressures caused by holiday and retirement demand, and has adopted the planning condition approach in an attempt to ensure that all future housing is channelled

Table 11.3   Housing advocacy policies in the North York Moors

Policy 1	'A programme designed to monitor house prices in the area will be considered, in order to attempt to quantify whether the area has undue housing problems'.
Policy 2	'District councils as local housing authorities are invited to consider whether local difficulties justify special housing policies being followed which could discriminate in favour of the local community, in particular in the construction of more council houses, the granting of more local authority mortgages and the introduction of programmes of building for sale and financial help with intermediate forms of tenure'.
Policy 3	'The Housing Corporation is asked to make more finance available for housing association activity in rural areas'.
Policy 4	'The Association of County Councils and Countryside Commission are asked to look into the special housing needs of rural areas and to conduct research into building for sale, "intermediate" forms of tenure and "local need" planning conditions'.

Source: North York Moors National Park Committee, 1980, 46

specifically towards people with a local need. The Draft Settlement Policy Statement for the Eden District (1979, 4) details the new policy:

> Whenever planning consent is sought for a new dwelling, or for the conversion of a building not previously in residential use, the application will be considered firstly in relation to widely used land-use guidelines. If the proposal meets these criteria, consent will be given subject to the signing of an agreement under Section 52 of the 1971 Town and Country Planning Act, that the dwelling will be occupied full-time by someone who is employed, to be employed or was employed locally.

This enforced allocation of new dwellings in the Lake District for full-time occupation by 'local' people has been widely publicized (although also used in a more 'back-door' fashion elsewhere) and is already the subject of controversy. One of the most difficult elements of the policy concerns the definition of 'local'. The Lake District Board have adopted a sliding-scale definition whereby in small settlements under heavy pressure the local area is equated with the parish concerned, whereas the term is more often related to the area of the district council, within the national park.

Clark (1981; 1982) has been one of the first to attempt an evaluation of the use of Section 52 Agreements in the Lake District context. He discovered that between September 1977 and August 1980 a total of 104 agreements were concluded covering 173 dwellings, although of these only 13 had been built, 45 were under construction and 19 had already obtained approval of building regulations. This low rate of building is explained largely by the fact that the legal standing of this use of Section 52 agreements is doubted in some quarters, and many local lawyers, estate agents and developers have been waiting to see if the policy would be deemed illegal in a test case. National-park planners clearly believe that the local full-time occupant condition is a logical progression from the use of Section 52 agreements to reserve new dwellings for agricultural or forestry workers. Since July 1979, applicants who have refused to complete an agreement have been given planning permission subject to a condition ensuring sale to a local, which at some stage is likely to lead to a personal redress appeal to central government. While the legal outcome is awaited, the problem of enforcing the policy has also yet to be tested. Clark (1981, 10) foresees that 'the sanctions in the event of an unremedied breach of agreement would presumably be an injunction, damages or even eviction. It is not clear whether the policy would withstand the legal and political strains of such enforcement'.

Several other fundamental criticisms of the Section 52 policy have been loudly voiced, notably by Shucksmith. Noting the legal difficulties mentioned above, he states (1981, 100):

> The policy has also been criticized on the grounds that it is inequitable. It discriminates in favour of those who already own houses, in that their houses will increase in value as a result of the policy. Conversely, the policy discriminates against all those local people who aspire to own their own houses, and in two ways: firstly, houses will become more expensive as a

result of the policy, and first-time buyers will therefore find house purchase even more difficult; secondly, the purchasers of new houses covered by the Section 52 agreement have found difficulty in obtaining viable mortgages because of the restricted resale market.

Thus the policy not only appears to favour the wealthy at the expense of the poorer national-park residents, but there is a strong feeling that the principal beneficiaries of the policy are tourists and recreationists who visit the park from outside and gain most from a preserved landscape.

The analysis of the use of Section 52 agreements has led to two opposing conclusions. Shucksmith accuses the planners thus: 'The Lake District Special Planning Board, then, continues to operate a policy which tends to inflate local house prices, to the detriment of local people' (1981, 107). In the event, the Secretary of State has backed this conclusion in his deletion of the policy from the Cumbria and Lake District Structure Plan. The idea is far from dead, however, since planners are known to remain in favour of the policy and a different national government may take a different view of its use. A summary of this sentiment comes from Clark (1981, 11) who concludes that: 'there is no evident alternative way of helping local people, under current planning legislation, once the decision has been taken on aesthetic grounds to reduce the rate of private house building at a time when fewer publicly financed houses are built'. This parallel with the public-housing sector is an important one. One alternative method of securing accommodation for needy local families is through public-sector action (Phillips and Williams, 1982) which is currently reduced to a very small programme of council housebuilding in the Lake District due to public expenditure restrictions. Ironically, the sale of council houses at discount prices under the Housing Act of 1980 has presented opportunities for owner-occupation to non-affluent community groups, while Section 19 of the Act allows local authorities either to buy the property back or to ensure that it is purchased by local residents if it is put up for sale by the first owners. This scheme, however, operates at the substantial social and economic cost of further reducing the rented sector (Gillon, 1981), and there appear to be strong arguments for the reallocation of funds towards equity sharing and partnership schemes and in support of housing associations which collectively will do much more to secure housing for these local families who have the greatest need.

Although local planning policy in national parks has been dominated by housing issues, other initiatives have also been forthcoming. The policy statement for Eden in the Lake District (1979) offers evidence of an ability and willingness to encourage and provide small-scale workshop buildings and to attract entrepreneurs to them. Indeed, the planning board has already constructed small workshops in several rural locations in the national park (including two in Coniston in the Eden area) and depending on future levels of available finance hopes to initiate further projects of this nature as part of a drive to secure local employment for rural communities. In general, national-park authorities display a high level of awareness concerning the pressures and problems of their rural communities and of the various informal schemes for employment, services and transport that were detailed in chapter 10. More variation, however, is displayed in the propensity to permit these various developments in small villages or to concentrate the bulk of resources into key service settlements.

The initial hypothesis of this chapter suggested that rural settlement planning in designated areas overemphasizes the physical structure of villages whilst often ignoring important social issues. In the case of national parks this suggestion remains unproven for a number of reasons. First, there is clear evidence of substantial housing growth in some parks, certainly up to the late 1970s. In Dartmoor, for example, some 1795 new dwellings were constructed between 1963 and 1973 according to the Park Authority (1977). Although much of this growth was concentrated in key settlements there has been a continuation of the spread of new dwellings outside these centres. Given this rate of growth the type of development becomes important in determining whether local needs, particularly those of the non-affluent, are being catered for. In Dartmoor, the physical manifestation of growth can be seen in the mushrooming of housing estates on the outer fringes of key settlements, and where embargoes on new development in these locations have arisen, building pressure both for estates and single dwellings has switched to smaller villages. The Dartmoor Committee (1977, 9) note that 'this "stop–go" housing-development pattern, apart from the visual and physical impact, has created economic and social burdens too heavy for the communities and the responsible public service authorities to carry'. In addition, population growth has outstripped local employment opportunities leading to more commuting. Significantly the committee consider (p. 9) that 'there remains an unsatisfied need for additional housing on the part of people living and working in the Park'. Therefore prior to the new planning policies introduced in the late 1970s it appears that the supposedly strict physical planning guidelines for national parks proved incapable of restricting speculative commuter, retirement and holiday-oriented housing development in pressured areas. Thus up to this point, neither physical planning objectives nor socio-economic considerations of local communities were being satisfied.

There is now strong evidence to suggest that recent national-park plans, structure plans and local plans have laid the groundwork for a much more severe interpretation of development control in national-park areas. Although detailed research evidence is required to substantiate the claims made by county and local planning authorities, the tightening up of growth restriction policies would appear to leave fewer loopholes for unwarranted housing development in national-park settlements. Conversely, there is a much higher level of appreciation by planning authorities of the community facilities and life-style opportunities which are needed by the more deprived sectors of the local population within national parks. The advocacy policies presented in appropriate local plans are among the most comprehensive and convincing of any such policies put forward for rural settlements and communities, and specific control policies such as the Lake District Section 52 agreement experiment are at least founded on the best intentions even if the success of their enactment remains doubtful. Given suitable resources and political commitment, it appears that national-park authorities have paid as great or greater policy attention to the social aspects of rural planning than any equivalent planning authority with jurisdiction over rural areas. We are therefore left with a similar dilemma to that which was posed at the start of this chapter, namely the incongruous combination of conservation and welfare objectives. Plans developed since the late 1970s have tightened up on development restriction at the same time as giving higher priority for the provision of specific opportunities for local communities. Whereas both policy strands are designed to overcome previously encountered problems there still seems a high probability of conflict between them, in which case the strategic restrictions on growth are likely to dominate. Detailed research evidence is awaited to confirm whether local opportunities can be tightened for non-affluent groups or whether it is those affluent groups of local or quasi-local people who will thrive in this environment of policy incongruity.

Other designated landscape areas

Outside the national parks, special landscape designations have been growing rapidly both in numbers and in terms of land area covered. Figure 11.1 gives some impression of the extent of Areas of Outstanding Natural Beauty (AONBs), Areas of Great Landscape Value (AGLVs) and Coastal Preservation Areas (CPAs) in one particular county, and it is increasingly acknowledged that such areas represent an equal if not greater threat to the social welfare of rural communities than the national parks which have previously overshadowed them. Indeed, over 40 per cent of England and Wales now falls under the jurisdiction of non-national-park landscape restrictions, and in addition forty National Scenic Areas have now been selected in Scotland which may play a future equivalent role (Countryside Commission for Scotland, 1978). The danger inherent in the scale of landscape conservation represented by AONBs, AGLVs and the like is that specific development-control restrictions on new housing and employment will disadvantage local non-affluent population groups who are subjected to heightened competition from external demand for housing due to the specially attractive nature of the areas. The Standing Conference of Rural Community Councils (1979, 1) suggests that:

> In a number of AONBs, either because of the lack of housing for younger people, or the lack of housing at a feasible price, together with a lack of job opportunities or access to those jobs that exist, rural communities have been experiencing population decline and serious changes in the age structure of their population, although not all of these changes have been necessarily due to AONB designation.

It is therefore important to ascertain how strict the protective policies actually are in these areas, and to review the evidence of the extent to which these policies have been instrumental in promoting or exaggerating socio-economic problems in communities within designated boundaries.

The policies

In general, AONBs and AGLVs are smaller than the national parks and are administered by local planning authorities whose powers are similar to those of park authorities. Relevant policy decisions are thus made at both county and district level. County policies as expressed within structure plans tend to offer a rather constant level of restrictive attitudes towards development in designated landscape areas, although some variation does occur as a result of overlap strategies with, for example, national-park or green-belt areas. Devon County Council (1979, 131) proposed two policies to cover all so-called landscape-policy areas (including national parks) which aim

1   To conserve and enhance the landscape by securing the removal of eyesores and undertaking amenity tree planting, by not allowing incongruous development and by other suitable measures of enhancement (12 P 9);
2   To give particular weight to the scale of development, its siting, layout and relationship with existing development, its design appearance and the materials to be used in construction (12 P 10).

In this way, the severity of development control is viewed as similar for national parks, AONBs and AGLVs although in practice some differences may occur in implementation processes. Within green-belt areas, however, other special designations are used as additional restraint measures within an already protected landscape. Surrey County Council (1980, 101) require

1   A high standard of development in AGLVs; and
2   A particularly high standard of development in AONBs

just in case any development should slip through the net of green-belt restrictions. This rationale is echoed in the East Berkshire Structure Plan whose policy towards areas of special landscape character is clearly stated (Berkshire CC, 1980, 67):

> New development in the area will be strictly limited because it is in the Metropolitan Green Belt. However, in order to safeguard the landscape, it will also be important to exercise special care in considering the limited categories of development which might otherwise be acceptable in the Green Belt.

In the case of Devon's Coastal Preservation Areas, planning policy is even more prohibitive to new developments, with permission only being granted in exceptional circumstances for the specific and necessary purposes of agriculture, forestry and recreation services. This package of specially designated rural landscapes, then, represents an ability to restrict both the quantity and type of new development within and without constituent rural settlements which represent a large proportion of all such settlements in Britain.

These policies, when translated into decisions at local level, are dependent upon the implementation process for their outcome. Local-plan policies tend, however, to endorse the mechanisms and objectives offered by AONBs and AGLVs, and in some cases are actively promoting the further designation of these special zones. This attitude is shown by Caradon District Council (1980, 9) in Cornwall where, in AGLVs, 'the conservation of natural beauty and amenity will be given particular emphasis in considering proposals for development' and, in AONBs, 'the preservation and enhancement of the landscape will be given priority over other considerations relating to development and the management of change'. Moreover, figure 11.2 demonstrates that if the district council's recommendations come to fruition, well over 50 per cent of the area will be subject to these policies of further restriction on development. It would therefore appear that landscape-protection zoning policies are being strengthened and multiplied within the dual processes of structure-plan and local-plan preparation.

Socio-economic problems in designated areas

In July 1978 the Countryside Commission published a wide-ranging discussion paper on the future of AONBs which sparked off considerable debate concerning the plight of both landscapes and communities within designated zones. Although specifically concerned with AONBs, these recent discussions have a far wider relevance in view of the frequent overlap of development-control policies in all specially protected landscape areas. A summary of responses to their 1978 paper has now been published by the Countryside Commission (1980), but in terms of socio-economic problems experienced by AONB communities, the contribution of the Standing Conference of Rural Community Councils (1979) is particularly important in presenting evidence of the nature and extent of AONB–related problems. The Standing Conference (1979, 2) succinctly reveals the major methodological difficulties in measuring the ramifications of AONB designations (as with national-park designations) on rural communities as being

> trying to disentangle what has happened in AONBs from what might have happened anyway, and separating AONB policies from those settlement policies which are likely to have as much effect on economic and social development. It is not easy to see what would have happened without AONB designation, since many villages within AONBs include conservation areas and much of the countryside would be included within AGLVs.

A starting point for evaluative research of the social ramifications of AONB designation has been the analyses of development-control decisions (Blacksell, 1979). Cornwall County Council (1976) for example, have noted an increase in the refusal rates for planning applications in Cornish AONBs from 20 per cent between 1959 and 1964 to 32 per cent from 1969 to 1974. This evidence should, however, be tempered by the fact that the total number of applications grew by 600 per cent over the same 15-year period, and so although rates of refusal were higher, a considerable absolute increase in the number of permitted developments occurred. Given the inadequacy of highlighting trends in one individual

Figure 11.2 Existing and proposed landscape designation in Caradon District

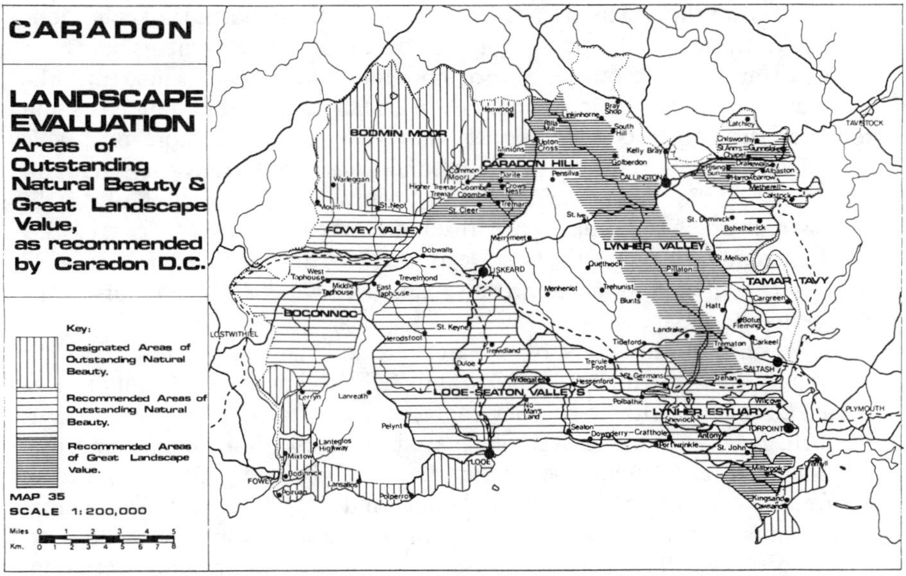

Source: Caradon DC, 1980, 116

area, comparative analyses of designated and undesignated areas have been attempted. Blacksell and Gilg's (1977) study of the East Devon AONB actually found a slightly higher rate of approval for all categories of application within the AONB than outside, although these rates were almost the same when residential applications were considered as a separate group. Similar results are presented by the Standing Conference of Rural Community Councils (1979), whose comparison of three equivalent areas in Lancashire with varying measures of development restriction found little difference in the manner by which planning permissions for new housing were granted or refused. Preece (1981) lends support to these findings in his analysis of development control in the Cotswold AONB. He concludes that AONB status does not necessarily restrict development any further than would be expected in a similar but undesignated rural area, this truism being particularly relevant in areas of low levels of developmental activity. Anderson's (1981) study of the Sussex Downs AONB offers a similar conclusion, but stresses that similarities between development control inside and outside the designated zone are due to a general strictness and effectiveness of strategic restrictive policies throughout the rural areas rather than to any laxity of approach within the AONB. These research results in combination would appear to suggest that socio-economic problems in AONBs are primarily related to the scenically attractive and often upland nature of the areas themselves rather than being initially caused by AONB status.

A rejoinder to this suggestion of AONBs exerting minimal intrinsic pressures on the communities living within them comes from the inclusion of *planning conditions* attached to permissions to develop in these areas. Even if new houses are allowed in special landscape areas, the imposition of conditions relating to the materials, cladding and colour of new developments may have an important bearing on the type of housebuilding which occurs, since the exaction of high aesthetic standards will usually add to building costs and result in the construction of larger, more expensive and more profitable dwellings. The importance of planning conditions in AONBs is stressed in two of the case studies mentioned above. In Cornwall, the proportion of AONB permissions which were approved with conditions rose from 44 per cent in 1959 to 97 per cent in 1976, and the East Devon AONB study uncovered a similar 97 per cent rate of conditional approvals, compared with 88 per cent outside the designated boundary.

The results of this body of research are an interesting antidote to the commonly held myth that AONBs and AGLVs have been maintained as barren landscapes with no new development. The evidence, however, remains inconclusive as to the exact role played by these designations on rural community life. It should be stressed that AONBs and AGLVs include an enormous variation of area and landscape, and not all have significant rural communities within their boundaries. Even where such communities do exist, the problems existing therein are also the subject of considerable variation. Therefore, to claim that AONB or AGLV status exerts one 'model' effect on rural communities is nonsense. Nevertheless many commentators continue to believe that areas of special landscape designation are conducive to the exaggeration of various community problems. The Standing Conference of Rural Community Councils (1978, 2) suggests that 'while AONBs may not be the cause of the problem *per se*, we believe they certainly contribute to the scale of it, and can locally exacerbate difficulties caused by other external pressures'. This conclusion is founded on three perceived trends within AONBs. First, a study of population change for AONBs in three counties led to the guarded conclusion that the designation has attracted retired, well-off people and tended to drive out younger, less affluent members of the local community. Again it is not possible to substantiate that AONB status has caused or even accelerated this problem, but the attractive nature of the areas along with the indirect restriction on the building of cheap houses cannot be ignored as potential and partial explanatory factors.

The second piece of the jigsaw concerns house prices within AONBs. Analysis of houses sold in five districts of the Northern Region containing substantial areas of a national park or AONB shows a considerable price premium in designated areas as compared with the regional average (table 11.4). A similar exercise for Devon and Cornwall national-park/AONB areas also shows above-average house prices in all but one case (table 11.5). These trends may be brought about by the reduced supply of land or the higher aesthetic standards attributable to development control policies in designated areas. It is, however, the case that the majority of dwellings sold in AONBs are existing stock and not the result of new development. It has been suggested, therefore, that AONB or similar designations have added a premium to the price

Table 11.4   House prices in Northern Region designated areas

District with large area in NP/AONB	Average house price 1974–5 £	As index of regional average	Average Floor-space m² (sq. ft.)
Alnwick	12,060	161	130 (1,407)
Tynedale	11,597	155	120 (1,318)
South Lakeland	10,555	141	118 (1,291)
Eden	9,767	130	133 (1,446)
Berwick	7,727	103	114 (1,242)
Northern Region (average)	7,491	100	103 (1,128)

Source: DoE/Inland Revenue 20 per cent Sample and Standing Conference of Rural Community Councils, 1979

demanded for houses because of the implication of a 'protected' environment which will not become spoilt by further development. An alternative explanation is that AONBs are attractive areas (with or without the status or planning restrictions brought about by designation) which *per se* are magnets for external demand for houses from commuters, retired people and so on and which inevitably are inflicted with the sellers' market syndrome of high prices. Whatever the particular combination of explanatory variables which is valid in any one area, it is clear that specially designated landscape areas are connected with discriminatory housing market pressures which limit the opportunities of some local residents, and that further restrictive policies in these areas will exaggerate this situation unless specific positive measures are adopted to satisfy local housing needs.

The third trend which has been used to implicate special landscape status with socio-economic problems in rural communities is the apparent correlation between some AONBs and AGLVs with low economic activity rates and income levels. If this link were proven there would be an inherent assumption that restrictive planning practice militates against local employment initiatives. Smith's (1977) examination of employment factors in the North Wessex

Table 11.5   House prices in Devon and Cornwall designated areas

District	Average price £	As index of regional average
East Devon	15,282	135
South Hams	13,869	123
West Devon	12,588	111
Carrick	12,194	108
North Devon	11,594	103
Devon and Cornwall (average)	11,298	100
North Cornwall	10,374	92

Source: DoE/Inland Revenue 20 per cent Sample and Standing Conference of Rural Community Councils, 1979

Downs and Cotswold AONBs uncovered significant economic underdevelopment in terms of income levels, economic activity rates and population changes. Furthermore this situation was found to be perpetuated by the political effectiveness of the environmentalist lobby whose anti-development arguments were largely founded on the importance of AONB status. Additional evidence of the connection between low economic activity and special landscape zones is cited by the Standing Conference of Rural Community Councils (1979, 5) with respect to the Lizard AONB in Cornwall:

> Unemployment levels are high in all of Cornwall but in the Lizard they vary between 16 per cent and 21 per cent in winter (1977/8 figures). Attempts by CoSIRA to get small businesses settled in workshop space have failed, and CoSIRA has a list of over a dozen applicants for such facilities in that area for which space cannot be found.

These examples are, however, balanced to a certain extent by the cases of the Northumberland Coast AONB and the proposed North Pennines AONB where a strong commitment to industrial development, particularly through the provision of Development Commission-financed advanced factories, has been demonstrated both in policy and implementation. This mixture of evidence is again inconclusive, but does demonstrate both the danger of allowing conservation emphases to deny reasonable and acceptable small-scale employment initiatives in rural communities and the possibilities for coexistence for conservation and local needs ideologies.

Clearly it is both tempting and simple to overemphasize the strength of links between AONB or AGLV development-control practices and the incidence of various inequalities and lack of opportunities in rural communities. Research evidence in this area suggests that direct links of this nature are often not proven, although there often remains a strong inference of the coexistence of designation and problem. The relationship is thus a complex one, in which it should be recognized that AONB boundaries are artificial and that areas within them suffer similar structural deficiencies to those outside. It does, however, appear that special landscape designations are liable in certain circumstances to aggravate pre-existing problems of population movement, housing markets and employment opportunities. As a minimum, it can be claimed that AONB, AGLV and other such zonations represent yet another hurdle which has to be overcome by the non-affluent, low-opportunity local population groups who are the focus of deprivation in most rural areas, and who have sufficient existing difficulties in gaining access to life-style requirements without the burden of this additional hurdle. It is to the needs of these groups that positive and specific policies within the umbrella of landscape protection in these areas should be directed.

Green belts

The background to green-belt legislation and development in England and Wales has been comprehensively covered elsewhere (e.g. Hall *et al.*, 1973;

Elson, 1979; Thomas, 1970), and the six Scottish green belts, although less well-publicized, are well described by Skinner (1976). Green belts in the context of this chapter are viewed as yet another policy stratum which is capable of polarizing socio-economic problems in rural settlements. Other landscape designations discussed above have been dominated by a centripetal pressure for housing development. In one sense, green belts demonstrate a marked propensity to deflect such development as well as maintaining strong internal demands for housing and industrial land usage. Dennis and Clout (1980, 124) stress the leapfrogging effect caused by 'the construction of large estates of detached and semi-detached houses at medium densities (8–12 houses per acre) beyond the Green Belt'. Similar, though less marked, deflections of development have also occurred beyond the boundaries of some national parks and this process should be seen as an integral component of the 'problems' arising from the designation of special landscape areas. A more direct confrontation of policies, however, occurs within the areas covered by green-belt status (Banks, 1980). Here, the now familiar restrictions on new growth have been strictly implemented in the face of consistent developmental pressures caused by inherent proximity to major urban centres. Accordingly, heavy pressure has been placed on the existing housing market, where prices have become inflated and non-affluent groups have become less competitive. One result of this chain of events has been the increasing incidence of hobby farming:

> Green-Belt legislation prevented 'desirable country properties' being constructed in close proximity to London but existing farm houses might be purchased to provide the ideal setting for realizing the dream of a secluded place in the country. Buildings have been modernized inside and preserved, or enhanced outside. The land has been farmed as a hobby or leased in part to surrounding operators. (Dennis and Clout, 1980, 186)

Even the less salubrious dwellings in green-belt areas have become desirable because of the environment in which they are placed and the attached community milieux in which they are perceived. Gregory (1973) offers evidence of the distributional consequences of green-belt policies on rural housing markets whereby middle-class commuters and other high-income groups have dominated both new and existing dwellings when they are put up for sale. As a result, problems of social bias and uneven age structure have become paramount (Pahl, 1965; 1966). For the non-affluent groups which remain, living standards have also been attacked from other directions. Buckinghamshire County Council (1976, 271) acknowledges that 'Limited growth . . . has rarely made it easier to provide the necessary services and has consequently placed more people at a disadvantage'.

The onset of the structure-plan era presented an ideal opportunity for an acknowledgement and response to these socio-economic inequalities within green-belt areas. Several factors, however, served to fudge these issues within the more structural uncertainties which tainted green-belt considerations in the local-plan/structure-plan tandem. Elson's (1981) succinct analysis of structure-plan policies for green belts isolates four important limitations which have led to such uncertainties:

1   No previously approved green belt is necessarily continued within a structure plan, which must therefore justify green-belt policies anew;
2   Structure plans can give only general guidance as to the boundaries for proposed green belts;
3   Structure planning authorities, although charged with providing a framework for local plans, must defer to the district council's detailed decisions on the precise form and extent of restraint;
4   Structure-plan policies will only be approved if implementable through the powers granted by the various planning acts. Thus policies to secure the provision of local needs through other means will not be retained in the final versions of the plans.

Given this climate of uncertainty, county structure plans have sought to achieve two main aims by using green-belt designations. First, county authorities have sought to secure significant extensions to existing green-belt areas. Elson calculates that some 2000 square miles (5180 square km) of additional green belt has been proposed in various extensions to the 6000 square miles (15,540 square km) in existence prior to the onset of structure planning (figure 11.3). The basis of government advice on the nomination of green belts (Ministry of Housing and Local Government, 1955) suggests that permitted justifications for new designations should be restricted to: the checking of urban growth; the prevention of mergers between adjacent urban centres; and the preservation of the special character of particular urban centres. The trend towards increased designation of green-belt areas stems from an attempt by local authorities to widen the scope of green-belt justification to include, for example, the conservation of environmental resources. So, the first aim of structure-plan green-belt policies has been to propose that larger rural areas should be covered by the designation. A corollary of this expansionism is a stated desire for stricter control of development within green belts (see chapter 6 for analysis of specific policies on this point), although there are obvious potential conflicts between this posture of increasingly diligent restrictions on growth and the recent growth-orientated policies on land allocation for new development expressed in the Department of the Environment's *Circular 9* (1980).

If this first objective is seen to stem from dissatisfaction with previous standards of development control in green belts, then the second major aim of structure-plan policies in this context is also a direct result of previous experience within green-belt settlements. Alongside the widened and stricter use of green-belt controls, county authorities have sought to provide opportunities for local needs, particularly in terms of housing. Specific examples of these policies are given in chapter 6, but the motives behind this emphasis on local needs are given by Healey (1980) as:

1   The protection of existing rural communities from additional intrusion from external urban influences;
2   The provision of housing for skilled workers in the local economy;

Figure 11.3 Proposed extensions to green belts

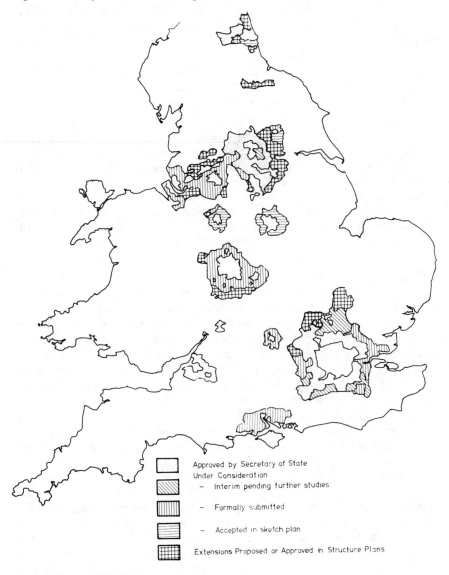

Source: Elson, 1981, 53

3   The reduction of housing growth rates;
4   The maintenance of a local councillor's ability to release land for planning applications viewed as special cases;
5   The maintenance of a balanced age and socio-economic structure; and
6   The provision of housing and job opportunities for local low-income groups.

In combination these factors provide a powerful incentive for local athorities to place a 'local-needs' tag on any permitted new development. Gault (1981) detects a 'local chauvinism' in this approach, and regards the anti-urban dweller policies which prevent the in-migration of newcomers while increasing the opportunities of the existing population as heavily politicized rather than necessarily being founded on a theoretical desire for positive discrimination towards needy population groups. His summary of the local-needs policy element highlights several potential difficulties (1981, 115):

> The common theme which runs through most of the arguments in favour of positive local discrimination is the perceived need to keep out regionally derived demand without stifling the local economy and displacing local people who wish to remain in the area. A main cause of the problem is that most restraint areas attract development by virtue of the restraint in operation. The local authority is then faced with the problem of how to institute restraint without declaring an absolute prohibition on all development. Local needs policies are therefore seen as a method of allowing some relaxation of the restraint without 'opening the flood-gates'.

Apart from the now familiar question of how to define local needs, a major problem occurs in the implementation of such policies. In terms of new development (where permitted) the sensitive use of planning permissions and related conditions can to some extent be instrumental in shaping the type of dwelling to be built, but there is evidence to suggest that the link between house-type and occupier-type may be less strong within the highly charged pressures of green-belt environments than elsewhere in rural areas. Moreover, even the use of Section 52 Agreements on new dwellings (although not yet anticipated in green-belt areas) may be less effective than in a national-park location where the gulf between the local population and second home or holiday demand is much wider than the grey area between locals and commuters in peri-urban locations. Moreover, none of these implementation channels purports to deal with the existing housing market where external demand remains highly competitive.

A further problem associated with restricting development to that required for local needs is the attainment of a worthwhile overall balance between blanket green-belt controls and localized development permissions. For example, if the balance is tipped towards allowing local developments than local-needs policies will act as an additional category exempt from green-belt control, and the overall policy mix may be viewed as more permissive than that within the development-plan era. Alternatively local-needs policies can be used to restrict green-belt controls even further in that they attempt to limit both the role and the occupancy of any permitted development. Fladmark's (1980, 71) analysis of the new strategic planning system in Scotland uncovers both trends:

> Two distinct approaches are discernible in the new plans: one adheres strictly to the minimalist principle of SDD Circular 40/1960, the other is based on the more pragmatic approach of allowing new physical development in selected areas.

As yet no clear trend is apparent which might indicate the likely future balance of conflicting green-belt policies in the rest of Britain. Few of those districts incorporating green-belt areas have produced district plans, and the policy intentions towards the extent of local-needs development will become more clear as these are prepared and as county authorities develop green-belt subject plans for the areas of proposed green belt within their jurisdiction.

The various uncertainties which generally cloud the likely impact of green-belt policies on constituent rural settlements and communities have not yet been subjected to detailed research scrutiny. Green-belt communities of the 1960s and their associated problems of in-migration of commuters, social interaction and so on have been immortalized in the work done by Pahl (1965; 1965a; 1966) in Hertfordshire. Development control during this period has been analysed by Gregory (1970), who found evidence that local authorities controlling the West Midlands green belt had been strict in their adherence to strategies of development discouragement, and furthermore that this rigid approach found support from central government when cases were taken to appeal. These results were corroborated by research undertaken by JURUE (Joint Unit for Research on the Urban Environment, Aston) (1974; 1977) which also painted a lucid picture of problems facing housebuilders in the face of rapidly rising property and land prices. On the other hand, Healey *et al.* (1980) suggest that local-needs policies are likely to allow more development in green belts than initially envisaged. Any assessment of the policy changes brought about within structure-planning exercises will require very thorough evaluation. The anticipation of significant socially oriented advances, however, would be rather more hopeful than realistic. An authority's ability and propensity to control carries far more weight under current planning regimes than its ability to instigate positive programmes to change existing trends. Therefore, it would not be unduly cynical to expect greater success in the use of local-needs policies as a control mechanism than in their use to ensure adequate housing and employment opportunities for local disadvantaged groups. Given this gloomy prognosis, the current discriminatory distributional outcomes of development restrictions in green-belt areas are likely to continue and even be expanded in proportion with the growth of designations. With the ever-present pressures of urban-based demand for housing stock in green-belt settlements, communities in these areas will be amongst the most difficult in which to survive as a low-income, non-mobile or otherwise disadvantaged local resident.

Conservation areas

Underneath the umbrella of the various landscape conservation policies discussed above there exists a more localized yet equally potent mechanism which serves to restrict development in rural settlements which might have provided opportunities for disadvantaged rural community groups. The Civil Amenities Act of 1967 made provision for the designation of special policy areas as conservation areas within which previously listed buildings of architectural or historical merit could be placed in a protected setting. Local authorities were required to nominate conservation areas where preservation and enhancement were desirable, and five general aims were promoted (table 11.6).

1981 estimates suggest that more than 6000 conservation areas have been designated or are in the process of designation in England and Wales, while a high proportion of the 400-plus Scottish conservation areas are located in small villages and country towns. This high take-up rate has been interpreted in different ways. Cantell (1979, 806) views it as 'an eager response to a new measure' whereas Eversley (1974, 14) considers the state of conservation areas as part of the wider conservation movement which is characterized by two disturbing attributes: 'First of all, the whole debate has become emotional. . . . Secondly, the desire to conserve every scrap of existing fabric has now become absolute'. Whatever the underlying motive, structure plans and local plans have continued the foregoing propensity towards an 'if in doubt, designate' attitude. In areas where no other landscape conservation policy is available, the conservation-area mechanism represents a convenient and logically plausible method of restricting the scale and type of new housing development in particular settlements. In green-belt, national-park or AONB locations, conservation areas are used to strengthen existing anti-growth attitudes in specific locations. The North York Moors Local Plan (1980), for example, makes use of conservation areas in its general drive to conserve and enhance the character of settlements in the national park. Accordingly, twenty-two villages have already been designated and a further twenty-three are proposed for later designation. The Kent Structure Plan (1976) is even more rampant in its recognition of conservation needs in rural settlements. As well as its full quota of conservation areas, the plan nominated sixty-two 'villages of special overall character' where (p. 325):

> the conservation and enhancement of general character and appearance would be the primary planning objective. In general, new development

Table 11.6 Conservation-area objectives

1 The safeguarding of listed buildings and other buildings contributing to the character of the area, both by statutory powers and by the use of grants and loans for improvements to or repair and maintenance of important buildings
2 A closer control over new development by insisting on detailed designs or sketches before any decision is given; particular attention will be given to materials and colours, building lines and height
3 A more critical assessment of existing development, including advertisements and 'permitted development'
4 A greater attention to detail – street furniture, signs, poles, wires and lighting can all detract from the appearance of an area; statutory undertakers, local authorities and developers will be encouraged to give priority to minimizing clutter and unsightliness
5 Local effort and initiative from individuals or local societies must be encouraged

Source: Woodruffe, 1976, 58

would be restricted to minor infilling and, in any event, would be required to be of a high standard of design, in sympathy with the existing village character.

Although the plan recognizes that some villages may need housing development to avert population decline or to support a recognized service function it is stressed that these factors 'should not be allowed to override restrictive planning policies in Areas of Special Significance to Countryside Conservation' [yet another landscape zone title – author] or 'Villages of Special Overall Character' (pp. 325, 327). Clearly in some rural areas it will not be long before conservation areas and other copycat schemes will cover the great majority of rural settlements.

Government advice on conservation areas (*Circular 53* (1967) from the Ministry of Housing and Local Government) recommends a two-stage approach to the enactment of this zoning policy. First, the area should be designated, a process consisting of marking the boundary and identifying special buildings and other features usually in map form. Second, plans should be produced both for detailed development control and for positive enhancement schemes in the area. In general, local authorities have been quick to designate, slow to provide control details and positively slothful in producing positive enhancement schemes (Wools, 1978). Although there are some notable exceptions (e.g. the Totnes Conservation Area which has become a model of positive conservation planning), conservation areas have more usually been viewed as agents of growth limitation in rural settlements.

An example of the localized detail of conservation-area status may be seen in St Florence Conservation Area (South Pembrokeshire DC, 1977). Typically, the area concerned previously contained six buildings which were listed as being of architectural or historic importance, and the conservation-area proposal was based on a special settlement character generated by four factors (see figure 11.4):

1 The relationship of the large number of roads and footpaths meeting at different angles in the older village area and, therefore, the enclosed nature of the built form;
2 The age of the settlement pattern;
3 That a number of buildings have a common and traditional architectural design and use of materials;
4 The importance placed by the community on trees, shrubs and flowers which complements and softens the building materials and metalled roads.

This last point is important, as support from the local community for conservation-area designation is both an important factor in the successful implementation of the mechanism and symptomatic of the environmentalist opinions of typical conservation-area residents. Very often local residents or their elected representatives are the initiators of moves to achieve conservation-area status, a fact which suggests both that they are unwilling to sanction any significant development in the area and that they are willing to undergo the financial implications which can accompany homeownership in this type of area. 'The positive attitude of the local community' (para. 4.20) is

Figure 11.4 St Florence Conservation Area

Conservation Area Boundary

Listed Buildings

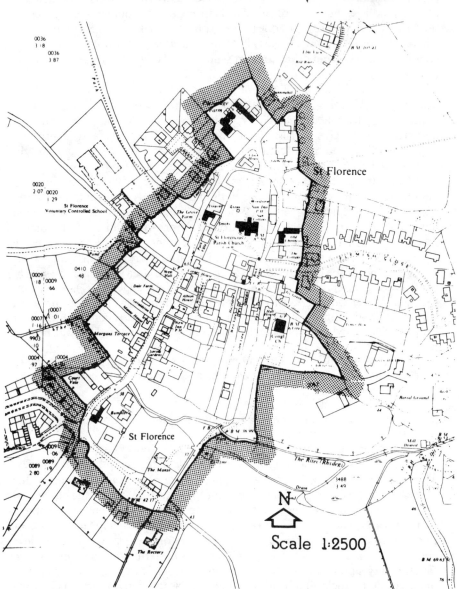

Scale 1:2500

Source: South Pembrokeshire DC, 1977

seen as one justification for the designation of St Florence. In general terms, the implementation of conservation-area objectives is undertaken primarily through the development control process which includes a legal obligation to give notice of proposed development which in the opinion of the planning authority would affect the character or appearance of the area. In effect the area's status could provide a convenient peg on which to hang planning refusals for unwanted developments. The preparation and discussion of preservation and enhancement schemes with interested organizations and individuals also forms part of the implementation process, but is often given only secondary priority.

Figure 11.4 shows that the St Florence Conservation Area covers only a part of the settlement, but elsewhere complete villages are included. Indeed much of the analysis of conservation-area performance has concentrated on narrow *physical* aspects of designation, such as where best to draw area boundaries (Thorburn, 1971), how best to select and impose desired design standards on new buildings (Blacksell and Gilg, 1981), and how to enhance existing ones (Wools, 1978). There are, however, other issues which have been neglected in these considerations. The most important of these concerns the impact of conservation-area status on the *communities* so designated. It might be expected that, as with other areas where artificial restrictions are placed on the housing market, existing housing in conservation areas would be the subject of extreme competition from affluent external groups and that gentrification will quickly occur to the detriment of disadvantaged local people. A complex dualism exists here. Conservation areas are only so designated because of their special architectural and environmental character and will thus *per se* be attractive to affluent residents, whether designated settlements or not. Thus it can be argued that conservation-area status makes little difference to socio-economic trends in the settlements concerned. This opinion, albeit in a slightly different context, is aired by Cantell (1979, 808):

> Even though designation brings protection, status and grants, a few places have resisted the idea. The village of Foy, in Hereford and Worcester, recently opposed the local authority's suggestion that a Conservation Area be designated because it feared an increase in tourist traffic and more bureaucratic control. Both fears are hard to substantiate. *Most tourists will never know which village is designated and which not because no signs are put up and no lists published* [author's italics].

It may be, however, that any threat that does exist will advance through insidious attack from within rather than through the attentions of transient visitors. Precisely because designation brings protection and status, houses within the boundaries become desirable, perhaps more so than if no conservation area existed. Cantell (1979, 808) concedes that: 'Even designation alone achieves something. Confidence is engendered in the future of the area, which encourages people to invest in and care for the fabric'. The fear here is that ability to buy and care for such fabric is only held by certain population groups, thus leading sooner or later to a discriminatory outcome for the conservation-area policy. Although generalization is difficult because of the wide variety of settlements and communities affected by the designation, the worst cases of conservation-area designation (such as Chilham in Kent, with its classic layout of buildings around the village square and a church that is often seen on the front of chocolate boxes – a place that displays the trappings of affluence and privilege, from the brass name-plates on the dwelling doors to the cars parked in front of them) represent a visual symbol of class structures and differential wealth levels in rural areas. Local people who wish to remain local, and yet who cannot compete with the gentry in an open housing market, are either forced into a clearly segregated part of the settlement, perhaps where the local authority estate is situated (well screened from the conservation area), or are given no option but to move to another settlement where suitably priced housing opportunities are being offered. If this process is allowed to continue, conservation areas will slowly but surely become microcosmic one-class communities where planning for conservation has only benefited the already privileged minority. There is also evidence to suggest that conservation-area status is manipulated by developers to obtain maximum profits from large, expensive but environmentally pleasing housing which can only be afforded by the 'right kind of people'. Figure 11.5 demonstrates the appeal of this type and price of house in a conservation area. This rather bleak outlook has as yet only reached fruition in a few conservation areas which are well known for their 'chocolate box' appearance. Nevertheless, so long as insufficient regard is given to the need for small-scale, cheap and mixed-tenure residential development in all rural areas, especially those with special designations such as conservation areas, the incipient creep towards a high-affluence polarization of rural living opportunities will continue.

Conclusion

Countryside planning in Britain may be likened to an onion. In order to get to the heart of it you have to peel off layer after layer of policy, and the nearer you get to the heart of it, the more it makes you cry. National parks, AONBs, AGLVs, green belts, conservation areas, and various copycat policies all represent layers of policy which in some circumstances are capable of producing gross inequalities of socio-economic opportunity in their attempts to conserve the rural heritage. Even when these policies are successively peeled away there still remains the influence of a widespread commitment to resource rationalization in county settlement policies and a general assumption against development outside established settlements apart from that which is warranted by agricultural or forestry requirements. The evidence presented in this chapter is insufficient to establish conclusive direct links between the various landscape and settlement designations and the outcome of resource redistribution towards more affluent and non-local groups in the community. A great deal more research into the causal structures and mechanisms of such redistribution is required before these links can be any stronger than inferential in nature. There are, however, clear indications that the types of areas and

Figure 11.5 Advertisement for new houses in a conservation area

Limpsfield Village

The Wates development at Limpsfield, Surrey is a unique opportunity to buy a new home in a conservation area. It is an outstanding example of the very best in modern housing specially built to reflect and complement an area of immense historical interest and natural beauty.

Wates are building three types of home at Limpsfield.

The Hazelwood: with 4 bedrooms, bathroom, shower en-suite, living/dining room, fully fitted kitchen, hall, utility room, study and double garage. From £71,950.

The Chevening: with 4 bedrooms, 2 bathrooms (one en-suite with master bedroom), large living room, fitted kitchen with breakfast area, study, utility room and garage. From £79,250.

The Chartwell: (as illustrated) with 5 bedrooms, 2 bathrooms (one en-suite with master bedroom), fully fitted kitchen, hall, utility room, dining room, living room, study and double garage. £123,000.

All houses have full gas central heating and cavity wall insulation for warmth and economy.

The fully fitted kitchens come complete with Neff split level oven, hob units, extractor hood and fridge.

Most of the homes surround a complete village green at the heart of the site. All have landscaped front gardens.

The village of Limpsfield, on the Surrey/Kent border dates back to the sixteenth century. Locally, Oxted (which is within walking distance) offers excellent shopping facilities and a regular train service to Victoria of only 37 minutes. The M25 is nearby if you want to go to Gatwick and within three years it will also take you to Heathrow.

If you'd like to know more about Wates at Limpsfield, visit our showhomes at Stanhopes, off High St, Limpsfield, **wates build with care** Surrey. Oxted 6506. We're open 7 days a week.

Source: *The Sunday Times*, 19 October 1980

settlements covered by the various designations are particularly prone to external pressures from affluent groups which frequently speed the demise of other groups particularly through the mechanism of the open housing market. Moreover there are at least firm suggestions that the actual designation of an area, with the resultant additional strictures of development control (although these are by no means universal), can exacerbate the problems of discrimination which may have been latent or occurring to a lesser extent before the designation. Again, this sequence of events occurs chiefly because housing within a designated area (particularly conservation areas) becomes increasingly prone to the advances of the new gentry wishing to secure a suitable rural dwelling in a suitable rural environment which will be protected by suitable rural planning policies.

The stance adopted in this analysis has been deliberately critical of the potential and actual outcomes of policies geared towards conservation. This approach is certainly warranted by the way in which specially designated areas have in the past continually been assessed according to physical and environmental criteria; an imbalance that should be rectified by a full discussion of social problems in these areas. It would, however, be equally as foolish to advocate an approach to rural planning geared solely to socio-economic demands as to continue with the current conservation-dominated approach. If rural environments and settlement (however defined) are to continue to act as alternatives to the predominant city/suburb existence, they should retain sufficient of their previous physical and land-use character to maintain the perceived gap between city and country which underpins the whole idea of such an alternative. What is clear is that the balance between conservation and social response has been markedly uneven in post-war planning and that conservation is being achieved increasingly for the privileged minority. In order to rectify this imbalance it is necessary for rural settlement planning in its widest sense to provide opportunities for all ages, classes and levels of affluence to enjoy the conserved rural environment both by living in it and by freely enjoying access to recreation within it.

Two fundamental changes in rural planning attitudes are necessary before an equitable balance is likely to be achieved. First, the notion of conservation should be examined for its distributional outcomes and its élitist nature. Eversley (1974, 15) suggests several targets for such an examination:

> A tiny minority of self-appointed arbiters of taste dictates what the living standard of the rest of us shall be. . . . One rapid glance at the composition of the official bodies which can prevent any plans for change by their edicts, the unofficial pressure groups which back them, the leading individual writers who monopolize the subject in the press, will show us who they are: the ever-present ancient establishment, the landed aristocracy, the products of Oxford and Cambridge, the landowners, the officer class, and, behind them, their hangers on: the trendy academics with less pretensions to gentility who prove their club-worthiness by espousing these élitist views.

The right of these groups to their point of view cannot be disputed, but does their point of view reflect the majority wishes of all sections of the community who require the provision of opportunities in and around rural settlements? The sooner conservation concepts, policies and practices are rid of their élitism, the sooner will a more balanced form of rural planning result.

Even if the environmentalist stranglehold on rural settlement planning is released, a second change of attitude is required before balance can be achieved. The evidence reviewed throughout this book has consistently suggested that market mechanisms act to the detriment of disadvantaged groups in rural areas. Judged by the private-sector standard of profitability, small-scale housing, employment, service and transport opportunities represent unwanted and unwarranted uses of precious resources, and therefore have been and will be increasingly phased out. Only by positive discrimination in favour of deprived groups, either directly by the public sector or indirectly through private agencies, will the necessary opportunities be provided in rural communities to allow all ages, classes and levels of affluence to be accommodated if they so wish. Once the prevailing attitude against positive discrimination is changed, specific measures to provide such opportunities can be introduced. Some of these measures are now discussed in chapter 12.

TWELVE

What future?

Current problems and issues: a reprise

Priorities for action

The problems which have beset post-war rural Britain have gone neither unnoticed nor unchallenged. Nevertheless this period has been characterized by growing recognition rather than increased action against rural social and economic ills. As a result, there is a spreading weakness among rural communities, often in a rather invisible manner because it singles out individuals and groups within a community far more often than afflicting a community in its entirety. Moreover the rural malaise is varied in intensity and thus rural people can be viewed as having few 'standard' needs to which 'common' policy responses can be addressed. Invisibility and variable intensity are ideal characteristics for undue optimism so far as policy responses are concerned. This lack of urgency for policy action might well be exacerbated by the resurgence in rural population shown by the 1981 Census in Britain. An undiscriminating interpretation of this trend might well result in the view that rural problems are solving themselves through the mechanism of 'natural' repopulation. Nevertheless, the research evidence analysed in earlier chapters confirms that a very real and pressing set of problems exists for certain sectors of the rural population in Britain, and Moss' (1980) wide-ranging study demonstrates parallel symptoms in Europe. In the United States similar trends have been described by Beale (1977), and have been attributed by Berry (1976) to the more general phenomenon of 'counterurbanization' rather than to rural revitalization *per se*. Indeed, Morrison and Wheeler (1976) question the motivation and the ramifications of selective rural growth as the 'answer' to rural problems.

In order to direct planning priority to the most urgent outcomes of rural change, it has to be recognized that rural areas show ever more marked divisions between the 'haves' and 'have-nots' (Lewis, 1981). These two headings are not representative of two mutually exclusive groups (if they were, then remedial action would be more easily distributed). For every element of rural life there are groups of have-nots, some who have always been in this position and some who find that access to a particular rural opportunity has been withdrawn by force of personal or structural circumstances. Moreover a combination of have-nots can lead to the more holistic state of deprivation (McLaughlin, 1981) which is exacerbated by market-prompted and politically connived processes of resource rationalization. Inevitably, low levels of disposable income induce a lack of opportunities. The Labour Party National Executive Committee (1979) stresses the importance of the perpetually low level of basic wages paid to rural workers in all sectors; and Newby *et al.* (1978) note that the desire to suppress rural wages has led farmers, in particular, to resist new economic development that might introduce wage competition within the workforce. The wide political divisions over the need for redistributive policies so far as income is concerned have indirectly hampered the progress of governments of either ideology towards the introduction of wider policies covering opportunities which are less responsive to basic income levels. Walker (1978, 107) has produced a telling summary of the problems of the rural disadvantaged:

> These problems stem from the dual failure to distribute resources according to need and the failure to prevent or ameliorate the differential impact of policy decisions in different income groups. One important reason for this failure is that in the location and allocation of services, planners have apparently ignored the question of inequality in the distribution of income and other resources, concentrating instead on what they believe to be the value-free questions of *efficiency* and *optimal* location. By ignoring the former problem they are allowing the social costs of their decisions to fall unevenly on the population and are therefore reinforcing and in some cases exaggerating the existing structure of inequality in income, wealth and life chances.

In addition, McCallum and Adams' (1981) statistics on rural employment and unemployment serve to underline the ailing economic structures which underpin these distributive deficiencies.

The problems suffered by disadvantaged groups in rural areas are undoubtedly accentuated by a political under-representation both locally and nationally. This mechanism tends to obscure the needs of those groups who should be given priority in rural areas, whilst maintaining the status and position of those already advantaged groups who wish to perpetuate their own priorities. Researchers have tended to produce conflicting evidence on the nature of local rural representation, with Green's (1980, 75) submission that the farming community 'no longer holds any effective control over the organs of local government' contrasting sharply with the work of Newby *et al.* (1978) in East Anglia which strongly suggests that landowners, both individually and collectively, still hold key positions in the local government decision-making process. What is clear is that landowners and articulate newcomers in combination are sufficiently powerful in rural politics to maintain the *status quo* for their own economic and environmentalist ends. Neate's (1981, 12) review of Trent parish in Dorset suggests that political under-representation

> requires planners, as long as they are concerned with meeting needs, to put more effort into identifying the problems and aspirations of those much less able to express themselves than the well-educated and better off 'newcomers' moving into most rural settlements.

Somehow then the conundrum of politics and participation in planning must be unravelled, so that the needs of disadvantaged groups are allocated a much higher priority in decision-making processes. Beresford and Beresford (1980) have suggested that genuine participation cannot be reconciled with political decision-making, and clearly no progress will be made in this direction before the barriers of dogma and privilege are broken down in in these areas.

What is needed?

Even if some priority could be achieved for action to alleviate the needs of disadvantaged rural groups, there is no consensus as to what these needs actually are. Once again, the expression of need is best discovered in the local context where a specific combination of opportunities and requirements will prevail, but some attempts have been made at a broad statement of need. A configuration of nine organizations (table 12.1), which represent a wide spectrum of rural viewpoints, have collectively called for new initiatives in rural areas (National Council for Voluntary Organizations, 1980; 1981). This 'rural voice' outlines one form of consensus view for the future of rural areas:

> We look to the maintenance or creation of rural communities which have a measure of social mix (in terms of age and income and occupation) in order to nurture that communal self-help without which very heavy burdens must fall on the statutory social services; in which people with roots, and in particular with jobs, in a locality can find housing there whatever their income; in which all groups in the community have effective accessibility (whatever their level of mobility) to all basic services; in which there is a reasonable range of job opportunies, particularly for the young; and in which there is effective partnership between the rural communities themselves and the official and voluntary agencies to enhance the quality of life.

As a vision this will find support from many individuals and groups connected with rural areas, but as a practical statement of what is needed (particularly by disadvantaged groups) in today's and even tomorrow's countryside it omits several important details. Dower (1980), the first Chairman of Rural Voice, expands on some of these trends which have been glossed over. He points to the shrinkage of public resources which is occurring without any assurance that they can be replaced by the private or voluntary sectors. He also spotlights the

Table 12.1   Organizations behind the 'rural voice'

National Council for Voluntary Organizations
National Federation of Women's Institutes
National Farmers' Union
National Union of Agricultural and Allied Workers
National Association for Local Councils
Country Landowners Association
Council for the Protection of Rural England
Standing Conference of Rural Community Councils

reduction in the volume of loans made to small businesses by CoSIRA and the sharp reduction in funds for local authority housing and housing association projects, and suggests on the basis of this evidence that the aspirations of rural areas will not be fulfilled through their own momentum. He concludes that 'a particular onus thus rests on government of ensure that the vitality of rural areas does not simply bleed away' (p. 178). We are thus forced to return to the idea of *priority action* to alleviate the problems of disadvantaged groups as a first step to a better future for rural communities. In this respect, Moseley (1980, 37) isolates *employment* and *services* as the factors which lie at the heart of the major issue for this priority action, namely: 'How far should the higher costs implicit in bringing standard levels of service provision and reasonable levels of employment opportunity into regions of wide population dispersal, be a charge on the state as a whole?' This issue not only raises further questions about what are reasonable levels and standards, but may also be expanded to include the housing sector, where higher rural costs also apply. Another valid question concerns the actual definition of localized expressions of these needs. Gault's (1981, 121) discussion of local housing highlights the essential differences between 'needs' and 'demands':

> To a large extent, housing needs are a result of high inelastic demand; there-fore, strictly speaking, needs constitute a facet of demand. Loosely explained, demand becomes need when either the demander no longer has the ability to compete due to the high prices demanded or because the market finds it more profitable to meet demands for other types of accommodation.

Even the recognition of local 'demanders' is not an easy task, especially in peri-urban areas where regional demand and local need often appear similar in nature.

So, the question of what actually are the needs of local rural people is not easily answered. Broad visions of the future are important, but tend to gloss over current priorities. Basic life-style opportunities such as employment, housing, services and accessibility are obvious necessities for a future rural existence, but the definition of priority local needs is difficult. Public expenditure levels are falling, yet in some areas of opportunity public-sector provision appears to be the only alternative. This sequence of dualisms often appears to defy consensus, and yet if some agreement is not reached (particularly at the level of identifying specific local needs in individual communities) then inevitable recourse will be taken to policies of expediency which are geared more to the convenience of the decision-maker rather than the needs of priority groups within rural communities.

A socio-cultural framework for the future

One further issue which is crucial to the future of rural settlement planning concerns the overall objectives which underlie these various attempts to maintain the presence of rural communities in Britain. In basic terms, is rural planning aimed towards preserving present life-styles or developing new ones within countryside locations? In what is now regarded as a slightly old-fashioned view Keeble (1969) summarizes planning as the organization of building and land use in pursuance of an express scheme of urban and rural evolution. However over-rigid such an 'express scheme' might turn out to be, this definition does at least serve to point planning in a certain direction rather than leaving it like flotsam drifting aimlessly on the tide, which is an image appropriate to the current state of the rural planning art. Moreover, the reten-tion of *status-quo* objectives appears increasingly difficult in the face of social, economic and cultural change. Green (1980, 82) offers a rather gloomy prediction:

> The concentration of jobs into the cities and towns is likely to continue in spite of the assistance given to small industries in villages. The city sub-regions will continue to grow relative to the remainder, and country towns will continue to grow at the expense of smaller places in both lowland and upland sub-regions . . . unless village regeneration is remarkably success-ful, a move to a city or country town may present the only local option to people who must look beyond the village for their livelihood.

Preserving present life-styles in rural settlements may well constitute a hard-fought but eventually unsuccessful rearguard action against the forces of change in rural areas. Rather than subscribing to this negative and probably fruitless (at least in the long term) exercise, it may be more profitable to plan for alternative future life-styles in rural areas which may offer a more just and equitable distribution of opportunities and resources.

Robertson (1978) polarizes future options into two genders. The HE option (hyper-expansionist) assumes that the post-industrial revolution will herald a super-industrial way of life: industry will be dominated by the high technology and service sectors, and social services will become increasingly institu-tionalized and professionalized. Robertson views this option as a mechanism which will accentuate élitism and domination in a class-oriented society, with a sharp division between the responsible technocratic power-base and the irresponsible unemployed masses with little to do but enjoy their leisure. The alternative SHE (sane, humane and ecological) vision urges a change of direc-tion towards increasing self-sufficiency, a more dispersed pattern of habita-tion, decentralization of power, alternative technology and a general 'back to the land' philosophy. This polarization almost parodies itself, and ignores middle-ground futures such as an extension of the *status quo*. The HE/SHE options do, however, provide fertile ground for debate concerning alternative rural futures.

Any realistic concern for future socio-cultural frameworks should recognize and account for potential forces for change. Moseley (1980) identifies three main headings.

Technology

Technological change is important in two areas. First, an increase in state-supported unemployment and lower retirement age thresholds could result in a substantial sector of the population being released from the constraints of having to live in or near the major employment centres. A significant repopulation of scenic rural areas could result, with concomitant pressures stemming from an intensification of demands for second homes and pre-retirement homes. Ellis (1975) suggests that rural areas in the United States have become increasingly characterized by in-migration, a process which he sees as being prompted by the onset of a post-industrial age. The second technological change involves a breakdown of economies of scale in infrastructure which, if achieved, could promote a more dispersed framework for rural living. Small-scale energy or sewage-treatment systems for individual dwellings, and the use of telecommunications for the interactive dissemination of information and opportunity needs and requirements (Clark and Unwin, 1981) might all encourage rural dispersal.

Behaviour/attitudes

Technological change must be accompanied by sympathetic attitudes and behaviour towards more dispersed forms of rural living if socio-cultural frameworks are to be reconstructed. One element of such behaviour may already be recognized in the increasingly steady flow of people who have 'opted out' of high-pressure city living and moved to remoter rural areas such as mid-Wales in search of a more relaxed life-style achieved by total, partial or minimal self-sufficiency. The manifestations of this process range from the Black Valley 'hippy' community near Llandeilo where a group of fifty or so people live in canvass tepees and pursue a simple trading and partially self-sufficient life-style, to the more 'conservative' migrants who wish to operate their own business in a rural setting (evidenced by the strong take-up rate of offers to small-scale entrepreneurs by the Highlands and Islands and Rural Wales Development Boards). These widely varying elements may be collectively viewed as searching for 'voluntary simplicity' which Elgin and Mitchell (1978, 207) describe as embracing

> frugality of consumption, a strong sense of environmental urgency, a desire to return to living and working environments which are of a more human scale, and an intention to realize our higher human potential – both psychological and spiritual – in community with others.

Voluntary simplicity is not directly equated with 'back to the land' or even rural movements, with many experiments taking place in urban contexts (Elgin and Mitchell, 1977). It is however likely to attract some future migrants to rural locations in Britain.

Degrees of self-sufficiency are also exhibited by *current* rural communities. The 'do-it-yourself' philosophy is already important in some areas (see pp. 340–4) and could be positively fostered by socio-economic planning policies. Indeed, several international organizations have already shown support for settlement reorganization on this basis (Economic Commission for Europe, 1978).

Politics/government

The attitudes of central and local government to a possible rural future based on appropriate technology and voluntary simplicity may be crucial to the achievement of new socio-cultural frameworks. Warren (1980, 182) is pessimistic about any change in government's failure to regard the countryside as a living and dynamic entity.

> This attitude is now enshrined in government policies which resist any new building in the countryside and exclude small industry from the villages. As a result, those villages too small to grow into towns are becoming gentrified. Rich commuters and retired people looking for attractive country cottages have pushed up property prices so that young local people can no longer afford to live in their own villages.

What is needed therefore is a reformation of political attitudes whereby the almost maniacal concern for resource rationalization is substituted by a more tolerant and positive stance towards the initial costs needed both to foster voluntary simplicity in all its forms in rural areas and to maintain opportunities for disadvantaged groups while the new social-cultural framework is being established. Chapters 6 and 10 show glimmerings of this kind of attitude but in general reflect a firm continuation of previous minimum-cost strategies. Without changes in government attitude, however, the opportunity to maintain a rural life-style either in voluntary simplicity or gentrification will largely be limited to those who can afford to establish themselves in an initially high-cost location.

These three forces of change give some indication of what is possible in the way of organizing future life-styles in rural areas. It seems likely that even given favourable economic, political and attitudinal conditions, voluntary simplicity and self-help can only form one part of a mixed economy future for rural settlements. Equally, basic resources such as land, housing and economic activity remain dependent on finance, and so currently disadvantaged groups will remain disadvantaged unless specific action is taken on their behalf to provide access to basic life-style opportunities. Therefore, rural planners are faced with several overlapping tasks, notably to secure a new future basis for rural areas; to secure a niche in that future for all individuals and groups, including those currently disadvantaged by structures and circumstances; and to take priority action in favour of deprived groups during the interim period between the present *status quo* and the new socio-cultural functions for rural areas. The exact nature of future rural areas is at present undecided, but unchanged attitudes and policy will certainly result in the eventual conservation of a gentrified relict rather than a living environment fostering equitably distributed resources.

Current policy responses and issues: a reprise

The performance of the policy-making and planning system in responding to the needs and disadvantages of the rural population may be assessed critically in a number of ways. For example, Shaw (1979) gives three reasons why the extent of rural deprivation has not been fully reflected in government policy:

1 Poverty is traditionally perceived as an urban phenomenon;
2 Rural problems are less visible than urban problems;
3 Rural deprivation is often too localized to be reflected in average statistics.

This view from the Chief Planning Officer of Norfolk (who is thus an important actor within the planning system) is predictably geared towards objective and normative explanations for the failure of policy-makers in this respect. At the other end of the critical spectrum, a neo-classical Marxist analysis would view planning as an internal survival mechanism which has evolved with the development of industrialized capitalism:

> The function of these internal survival mechanisms may be thought of as the transformation of the energy of opposing social forces into the defence of the *status quo*. By extracting those aspects of innovation which are likely to aid its organization and power, and by discarding those which are likely to remain troublesome, the dominant system is able to fulfil two crucial needs – the need to reinforce its defences and the need to neutralize the opposition. (Knox and Cullen, 1981, 183)

In the rural environment the planning process has quite clearly aided the maintenance of an inertia in social and economic relationships by sustaining different settings for different social classes, and has thereby fulfilled the role of the internal survival mechanism. It would appear that whatever the mode and paradigm of analysis most rural commentators are heavily critical of the failure to give formal policy representation to the opportunity requirements of disadvantaged groups.

Any attempt to prescribe alternative policy responses or structures is fraught with the very paradigmatic divisions which are so clearly demonstrated above. Within some analytical frameworks nothing less than social revolution would be viewed as an acceptable alternative to the present policy-making and planning systems. At a more establishment level, new policy proposals will only be considered if they present cost comparability with current policies, and if they offer more political kudos than gained at present. In reviewing existing policy alternatives for rural areas it is hardly surprising to find that they represent piecemeal measures *within* the present planning system rather than following a more revolutionary tendency. Indeed, if one role for the future of rural settlement planning is to take priority action in favour of deprived groups in the *interim period* while new socio-cultural patterns are established for the future of rural areas (see pp. 326–30), then urgent reallocation measures within current planning frameworks would seem to be required.

It has been argued elsewhere (Cloke, 1982) that one major reason for the retention of traditional rural settlement planning has been the failure to present *realistic* alternatives, including how such measures can be implemented under current financial and administrative regimes. This line of reasoning opens up the wider quandary to whether to work within the system and thereby attempt to change it from the inside, or whether to spurn internal participation on the grounds that acceptance of the system's framework will strengthen its existence and militate against change. At one level it may be argued that short-term gains *are* important provided that they do not conflict with long-term objectives. Therefore short-term measures to ease rural disadvantage may be beneficial even if they are treating the symptoms and not the causes of the problem.

To achieve some realism in the prescription of within-system policy alternatives, certain lessons may be gained from the experience of rural geography and planning in the post-war period.

1　We are in a period of strict financial control. Moseley's (1977) image of the bubble of public spending being burst was never more appropriate than in the current phase of low public spending power. Short-term action should, therefore, seek to offer realistic resource bases for suggested measures rather than indiscriminately prescribing a solution without regard to resources;

2　The ineffectiveness of rural settlement planning in the past has been as much due to problems with *implementation* of policies as with the inherent qualities of the policies themselves;

3　Rural planning experience has now been building up for 30 years or so. Rural commentators should make wise use of this hard-earned experience (even if on occasions experience appears synonymous with inertia). Both negative and positive experience is valuable;

4　Future rural settlement planning will require different types of policy for different types of area, rather than one centrally favoured all-embracing strategy;

5　Whatever overall policy trend is finally adopted, it can only act as a *framework* within which specific problems of inequality and disadvantage (e.g. connected with employment, housing or services) can be tackled by special initiatives within the planning system, within state policy or by community involvement. No framework policy can fully alleviate fundamental problems without these additional local-scale policies with which to tackle specific social difficulties.

Traditional suggestions for the within-system improvement of current rural settlement planning have followed two main themes.

Administrative reorganization

Many authors have regarded the administrative structure of rural planning as the chief stumbling block to the achievement of effective policy-making and policy-implementation. Davidson and Wibberley (1977) stress the temptation to argue that rural problems can be resolved by fairly simple bureaucratic reorganization. In terms of central government responsibility, an anomalous situation of rural policy-making exists at present. Agriculture and forestry have separate ministerial control and are largely exempted from formal planning controls. The Department of the Environment was established to co-ordinate environmental matters but has no control over such important matters as energy or farming development. Decision-making is thus widely fragmented, and Davidson and Wibberley suggest that a new 'super' Ministry of Agriculture (to include social welfare and environmental conservation among its duties) would greatly improve the co-ordination of rural policies. One problem with such an all-embracing rural ministry is that it could well be dominated by the needs and aspirations of one particular rural sector, such as agricultural concerns in the case of a super Ministry of Agriculture. There has, however, been a strong lobby for some form of centralized amalgamation of rural agencies (Gilg, 1978a). Cherry (1976) regards a strengthened Department of the Environment as the best form of policy co-ordination agency, and indeed the general concept of the Ministry of Rural Affairs or some similar institution has found wide favour (Wallace, 1981).

The counter-arguments to these proposals are also important. The Labour Party National Executive Committee discusses the concept of a new rural ministry and concludes (1979, 16):

> We believe that in the long run such a ministry would weaken not strengthen, the voice of the rural areas in central government. There would be unceasing conflicts with nearly all the other ministries – DHSS, DES, MAFF, DoE and the rest, about responsibilities, funding and so on. It would make the rural areas into a 'special case' – something we have always argued against, rather than allowing rural areas problems to be considered in a more general context and in relation to the urban areas.

It is generally agreed that there is scope for much greater co-operation between various government units, but no consensus has yet occurred over ministerial reorganization or indeed over how far rural policies should be separated from those for urban areas. Moseley (1980, 36–7) suggests that

> government departments could be required to have regard to the economic and social interests of rural communities in the formulation of new policies. Whether in practice this would give us a 'rural policy', analogous to the 'urban policy' towards which government seems gradually to be moving is unsure. But it would be one way of trying to safeguard the interests of a disadvantaged minority group, namely the rural poor.

The question of a specific 'rural policy' is returned to in pp. 344–8, but it is clear that some reorganization of policy-making and resource allocation procedure at central government level is long overdue. Equally, administrative reorganization alone will not solve the problems of rural areas, and it would perhaps be more beneficial first to decide on what forms of policy are required to meet the needs of rural communities, and then to model bureaucratic organization around those policy guidelines rather than *vice versa*.

Spatial framework

The debate concerning organizational reorganization spills over into another area which has traditionally been viewed as ripe for reform within rural planning, namely the spatial units within which policies are enacted. Almost as soon as local government had been reorganized in 1974, it became evident that the new county/district system had not satisfied the critics of the spatial distribution of governmental powers in Britain. Inevitably the two constituent parties each bemoaned the lack of real authority, with the Association of County Councils (1979, 46) arguing that

> County councils are in a unique position to play a pivotal role in a co-ordinated rural policy. In terms of scale, number and importance of services provided and accountability to the community, county councils are able to apply sensitively national policies and reflect local interests. They are also the only bodies which can start to look at the problems in total at a local level and take a lead in applying comprehensive solutions.

and the Association of District Councils (1978, 2) proposing that

> District Councils, however, with their responsibilities for local plan-making and development control, housing, industry, environmental health, tourism and recreation, and an important role in rural transport too, should be given the primary responsibility for co-ordinating the policies and program-mes of the various agencies . . . both in relation to the district as a whole and the individual towns and villages within it.

All in all it is the districts' star which is rising, with the district councils now being of sufficient size for most local government purposes. Indeed, Cherry (1976) argues that county councils are becoming increasingly redundant and should be abandoned in favour of *regional authorities* (three of four counties in extent) which would have the financial and geographical scale to undertake an effective form of strategic rural planning. A less radical proposal is to permit consortia of existing county councils to draw up strategic plans (Blacksell and Gilg, 1981). The regional or sub-regional approach mirrors one theoretical advantage held by the districts in that it attempts to integrate the problems of urban and rural areas, thereby recognizing the essential inter-relationships between the two. Although theoretically sound, in practice such a system can be dominated by 'urban' interests and can prove detrimental to rural areas through processes of resource starvation. These fears have to be matched against the obvious regional advantages of broadening the opportu-nities to be gained from urban-based economic activity (see Commins and Drudy, 1980).

The split between regional or county-based planning strategies is closely connected with the ever-present polarization between concentration and dis-persal of resources in rural areas (see chapter 7). Support for regionalism is partially based on the sentiment that resource rationalization is an inevitable process and that rural communities should be more closely linked with urban centres where opportunity provision will continue. Green (1980, 83) argues that 'all social and economic indicators point to the county towns as the only sensible location for new economic activity', and this theoretical stance is directly related to his support for a sub-regional planning structure. The middle ground of this debate is represented by Moseley's (1980) call for certain non-economic services to be provided as of right in rural areas, a call which is tempered by a recognition that a gradual process of spatial restructuring will have to take place with services increasingly being provided in or from key settlements. At the other end of the spectrum, the resource dispersal school with an inbuilt prediliction for the provision of opportunities *at source* for the needs of rural residents, tends to be related to support for small-scale local government which can be cued into localized requirements. An alternative spatial scale of operations is represented by the new villages movement, where the new socio-cultural framework discussed in pp. 327–30 can be initiated from scratch rather than by moulding a pre-existing pattern (Darley, 1978).

Again, the spatial framework for rural settlement planning should be determined by the policy requirements of rural people (particularly the disadvantaged) rather than by a pre-decided framework acting as a major constraint to policy alternatives (as is currently the case). Spatial structures have for too long dominated rural planning and the situation is overripe for social and economic structures to take the front seat in strategic thinking. In this way, spatial frameworks, though important, are secondary to a socially equitable distribution of opportunities and allocation of resources amongst rural people sometimes *within* a single spatial unit. Hence the traditional suggestions for within-system improvement of rural policies and planning, with their emphasis on space and not people are less important than some of the more recent ideas on redistribution of existing resources and the generation of new resources.

Harnessing existing resources

Given a task of alleviating the problems of the rural disadvantaged in the short term, and preparing a new socio-cultural framework for rural areas in the longer term, rural planners and decision-makers have two broad avenues of approach, of which the first is to make use of existing resources. How can new opportunities be provided on an equitable basis for rural residents given current resource bases? It might be expected that all worthwhile policies not involving additional resources will have already been utilized, but there do appear to be ways in which resources can be redirected to further the short- and long-term objectives outlined above. Potential reallocations of public and private resources is a subject which could fill a tome in its own right. Various possibilities may, however, be discussed briefly here under three headings.

New initiatives from existing agencies

Chapter 8 describes in some detail the duties and powers of various resource-allocation agencies whose decisions lead to specific outcomes in rural communities. With a reorientation of priorities, the decisions taken by these agencies could result in additional benefits to disadvantaged rural groups. Rural planning is commonly perceived as taking place within county and district planning offices, and yet planners thus defined have only negative powers of opportunity provision. They are able to decelerate development where it is not required but not to guarantee it where it is needed. In this context Moseley (1980, 30) notes that 'while rural planners are often criticized by the layman for their excesses, a criticism of their inadequacies would be a fairer appraisal'.

Planning officials do, however, play a important co-ordinating and advocative role within wider decision-making processes. They are in a position to ascertain the broad spectrum of needs within a rural community, either by formal surveying and informal contact (a process which could be aided by joint research projects with personnel from academic institutions (Cloke, 1979a)). Although the information gained by planners will never be totally detached or objective, it is able to serve as a counterbalance to the ideological dogma of elected representatives on planning committees. In some cases it is tacitly accepted that information and policy suggestions which do not accord with the prevailing political views of the planning committee are not deserving of the precious time and effort of planning officers. Indeed this pragmatic approach of 'only dish them up what they like to eat' is common in British formal planning relations between departments and committees. Nevertheless one important future task for local authority planners is to escape from this syndrome and champion the cause of the rural deprived. This can be done both by information gathering and by more sympathetic forms of advocacy and development control. Informal discussions with developers are becoming an increasingly successful tool of promotion for particular forms of housing, although this channel of operation is more suited to peri-urban or other residentially desirable areas where a greater pressure for development exists. Moreover, flexibility within development control might be used to permit socially beneficial schemes of varying scales (from single, inexpensive houses to more ambitious plans such as Smigielski's (1978) self-supporting co-operative village) which might not conform to *all* planning regulations or environmentalist visions. In the last resort, social needs should outweigh environmental benefits in such cases. Finally, planning officers can indulge in stronger advocacy with other agencies for resource-allocation priorities to be directed towards socially disadvantaged groups.

These changes in the attitudes and actions of formal planners will be thwarted by the internal-survival mechanisms of local authority politicians unless the ideological reservations of more conservative authorities can be overcome. A similar breakdown of convention is required if local authority resource agencies are to be persuaded to reallocate in favour of disadvantaged individuals and groups. Housing, education and social service departments already work to their own assessment of need (see chapter 8) and yet more can be done by these agencies in rural areas. For example, although local authority house-building rates are falling because of expenditure restrictions – a situation exacerbated in some areas by council house sales – many authorities have stockpiles of land under their ownership which could be utilized, at cost to reserves but not to revenue, for housing schemes of one form or another for local people (as has been the case in Tavistock, Devon). Similar flexibility and collaboration with the self-help instincts of rural people can be successful, and indeed have been shown in the retention of small village schools and in the use of transport subsidies so as to gain the maximum accessibility benefits (even if this means supporting unconventional rather than traditional transport and accessibility schemes). Local authorities are already heavily involved in job-creation projects, yet an active willingness to pursue the attraction of small-scale entrepreneurs for village locations as well as the more prestigious industrial estate enterprises would subtly, but crucially in some cases, reallocate opportunities to needy rural people. Finally, local authorities can do much by reorganizing personnel so that willing individuals can be made available for the task of localized community co-ordination so that the valuable work carried out by rural community councils can be continued and dramatically extended at the local level (see pp. 340–4).

Many agencies outside the sphere of local government are also responsible for decision-making outcomes in rural areas. In the case of the Development Commission, CoSIRA (Breakell, 1980; Clarkson, 1980) and the rural development boards, it could be argued that existing resources allocated to rural areas are being efficiently utilized, although the swing towards small-scale workshop employment is to be encouraged (see Hodge and Whitby's (1981) account of employment creation in the Eastern Borders). Elsewhere, the regional authorities covering water, health and so on tend to allocate low priorities to rural areas and improvement in rural opportunities in these areas may well come only through the attraction of new resources rather than through a rural reallocation process. What could be done, however, is to gain an acceptance of the need for flexible schemes in rural areas, which, in the two services mentioned, might lead to a recognition of the adequacy of one-unit sewage-disposal schemes (such as septic tanks) even for new developments, and to a greater willingness to provide peripatetic rather than centralized health-care services. In the private sector, the profit motive is not easily geared towards resource reallocation in rural areas, and public-sector subsidy may be required before private-sector opportunities are significantly improved in all but fast-growing areas.

Inter-agency experiments

Another usage of existing resources to further the short- and long-term objectives of rural settlement planning is through positive planning experiments backed by various resource agencies. One or two examples are briefly described here to demonstrate the scope of these projects. A revealing example of a small-scale scheme is offered by the East Fellside and Alston Moor Project, which covers an area of 230,000 acres (93,090 ha) in rural Cumbria. The area has shown a marked depopulation over the last 20 years, with some parishes losing over half their population in that period. These changes have led to increasing numbers of second homes and to the closure of schools, local stores, post offices and other vital services. The project has now employed a full-time officer whose task is to open up a whole range of opportunities to people who might otherwise leave the area, and to others who might be attracted in. Given funding from the Development Commission, the English Tourist Board and the Countryside Commission, and other forms of sponsorship from Eden District Council, MAFF, Cumbria County Council, Cumbria Tourist Board and the Forestry Commission, the project represents a 3 year pilot scheme which sets out to:

1   Confront the social and economic problems of the area;
2   Encourage community initiatives and new job opportunities;
3   Provide the means for people to earn a satisfactory living;
4   Encourage new farm enterprises which will provide continued employment for farm families; and
5   Maintain a high quality of life and a well-kept environment.

The employment of one locally based and enthusiastic project officer has already succeeded in establishing a useful information and advisory service in the area and has acted as an innovative catalyst for new forms of rural enterprise. Although the project has yet to be fully evaluated it seems clear that the provision of a locally acceptable co-ordinator in rural areas can go a long way towards bridging the gap between the planners and the planned.

The idea of placing a form of 'community worker' into rural areas where disadvantage occurs is now well founded in rural planning experimentation. In 1969 the Home Office launched a national experiment aimed at finding new ways of meeting the needs of people living in areas of high social deprivation. Of twelve participant areas only Cleator Moor (Cumbria) and perhaps Upper Afan (Glamorgan) can be described as 'semi-rural' settings, but the Cleator Moor experiment became part of a wider Cumbria Community Development Project which paved the way for social work approaches in rural areas. Two particular features of these experiments are worthy of mention here. First, a mobile 'information and action' van was established (Butcher *et al.*, 1975), which offered various peripatetic information and representation services in the Cleator Moor hinterland. The types of services involved, as portrayed by the team itself, are shown in figure 12.1. Second, a feasibility study was carried out into potential community action schemes in Cumbria (Voluntary Action Cumbria, 1974). The study concluded that many of the problems being experienced by rural residents could be removed or ameliorated both by encouraging greater participation by local residents in the making of planning decisions and the assessment of their own needs, and by enabling local residents to come together to provide their own services and amenities where these were not available from other sources. In addition, four main obstacles to the realization of these processes were recognized:

1   The lack of self-confidence within small communities, where vulnerability to criticism is high;
2   Apathy on the part of many residents, who feel that attempts at improvement are futile;
3   The lack of ideas as to what can be done and of information as to how to go about doing it; and
4   The lack of physical resources.

The study argued with some justification that these obstacles are precisely

Figure 12.1 Services offered by the Cleator Moor rural community project

FUNCTIONS

OF THE

CENTRE

dealing with enquiries

writing letters for people

telling people who they should see

speaking up for people

helping organise groups

dealing with personal problems

running benefits and rights campaigns

moving furniture

Source: Butcher *et al.*, 1975, 70

those with which a community work approach is best able to help, and for these reasons several community-work experiments have been initiated in different rural areas throughout the country.

One such community work scheme which has received widespread attention is the Hereford and Worcester Rural Community Project (1978; 1980; 1981) which was conceived as an interdepartmental, inter-agency exercise with wide representation from county, district and other authorities. Through a process of temporary and part-time personnel reallocation, a small study team was assembled, which consisted of a planner and a statistician from the County Planning Department, a community-work consultant from the County Social Services Department, and the director and countryside officer from the Rural

Community Council. Although the county council were unable to supply direct funding for the project, a Development Commission grant was secured in 1977 for the appointment of a rural community worker to work in the Wyeside area for a 2-year period. A publicity leaflet for the project makes several claims on its behalf:

> The Project was based on the idea that there was potential for greater involvement in the social and political life of the community, which could be released to the benefit of the areas. The experience of the Wyeside Project bears this out; by raising awareness, offering support and advice, increasing confidence and making available relevant information, it has been possible for local people to tackle a wide range of issues affecting this rural area. . . .
>
> The Project has led, amongst other things, to the establishment of a village newsletter, the rerouteing of bus services and introduction of a car scheme to carry children to a playgroup, the retention of a sub post office and a new local authority housing development in the area. (Hereford and Worcester Rural Development Project, 1981a)

Although these claims have been regarded as slightly over-exuberant in some quarters (e.g. Green, 1980), it does appear that the project can be well justified in traditional cost-effectiveness terms and, in addition, that some evidence is offered of the potential value of inter-agency experiments in general, and the community work approach in particular as a policy-making catalyst in rural communities.

Self-help and community approaches

The Wolfenden Committee's (1978) report on the future of voluntary organizations identified four mechanisms for meeting social need:
1   Informal (from family and neighbours);
2   Commercial;
3   Statutory;
4   Voluntary.
The last 15 years have seen a significant increase in the use of the fourth mechanism, with rises in both the numbers and types of voluntary agency and the degree to which central and local government have been prepared to support voluntary action (Dungate, 1980; Wilmers, 1981). In this way, the notion of mutual-aid projects has assumed a parallel importance in rural areas to the within-system improvements offered by the inter-agency experiments discussed above.

The fast-growing propensity to promote rural self-help and thereby shift certain responsibilities from government to community has led to a belated debate concerning the social and political equity of these approaches to rural planning. Wolfenden highlighted the major pros and cons. He regarded the substantial presence of existing self-help as a positive advantage, with the expenditure of registered charities representing the equivalent of 3 per cent of local and national government spending and with some sixteen million man or woman hours per week being devoted to formal voluntary work. Rural areas, although only receiving a *pro rata* share of this effort, cannot ignore its importance as a resource. Moreover, self-help schemes are able to be innovative and more closely conforming to the participation ethic than activities outside the voluntary sector. With community involvement or control, such schemes can not only be closely aware of local needs but also are able to indulge in lateral thinking in the search for the fulfilment of those needs. A third advantage of voluntary action is that it may be an efficient agent of welfare improvement in rural areas. Wilmers (1981, 59) gives enthusiastic expression to this possibility:

> The Voluntary sector may be able to draw on resources – money and volunteer effort – not available to the public sector. In some cases, voluntary action may be the only way of providing or improving a service, where the state feels action inappropriate or of low priority. It can provide a choice of service and commands political and media support. . . . It also abounds with great vitality and energy.

These various advantages should be weighed against some inherent difficulties with self-help operations. Wolfenden highlighted the potentially uneven distribution of voluntary effort whereby a social or spatial polarization of participation may lead to a similar concentration of benefits within particular community groups or settlements. The use of mutual-aid schemes within the overall rural planning process will lead to a haphazard allocation of resources rather than a planned system of response to priority needs. Furthermore, the relationship between the voluntary sector and government is often viewed as politically motivated. Fudge (1981) crystallizes this relationship in the form of three answers to the question of the context in which self-help activities should be developed:

1 Where government should do something but is not;
2 Where government cannot do anything;
3 Where government could do something, but it is preferable that it does not.

Option 1 suggests a clear-cut opposition to self-help in certain situations, particularly where government is seen to be shifting its obligations onto community groups. Many such groups, however, face the dilemma of possessing the will and the resources to provide an opportunity, yet regarding its provision as a task for the state and not for them. How long should they wait for government action and thereby prolong the unnecessary hardship caused by a lack of the particular opportunity concerned? In cases such as these, the decisions to be made are far from clear-cut even if ideological objections are strong. Option 2 seemingly represents an important niche for voluntary action, but will self-help in these areas be a question of 'sticking plaster rather than reform' (Wilmers, 1981, 59), giving temporary first aid where socio-economic structures require change so that government *are* in a position to respond? The safest bet for self-help, therefore, appears to be option 3 where, in cases such as the need for impartial information and advice, voluntary bodies like the Citizens' Advice Bureaux are better placed to undertake the task than more overtly political bodies such as local authorities. Shropshire Community Council for example, have recruited and trained a network of local residents to act as 'information representatives' for their villages. Even here, however, there are problems of how this kind of voluntary effort should relate to public-sector officials whose co-operation, if accepted, might lead to co-option or even partial control. This rather confused situation is nicely summarized by Fudge (1981, 61):

> mutual aid and community oriented alternatives, involving collective work and responsibility, should be advocated and fought for not because they are cheaper (because they may well not be!) or because they require less paid staff (because they should not) or because they relieve pressure on the statutory services (because pressure is needed for maintenance and improvement, and many will always rely on them) but because they are more sensitive services and they are often areas where innovation can occur. The doubt remains however that many groups only respond to symptoms rather than to underlying problems and that because of this the raising of consciousness among members leading to political analysis and action is unlikely to be forthcoming.

Despite the various theoretical and political caveats mentioned above, self-help has flourished in rural areas. Woollett (1981a) argues that the continuing decline in rural services has necessitated the development of an increasing array of alternative forms of provision – a situation which urban areas have only recently begun to face. the various experimental schemes in rural areas are too numerous for detailed attention here, but the breadth of the voluntary approach in rural areas is worthy of mention. Shankland (1981) and Pearce and Hopwood (1981) analyse the potential for community-based *job-creation schemes*, and rural areas have been the subject of some co-operative and entre-preneurial initiatives, often fostered by the rural development boards, CoSIRA or local authorities. Although the oft-quoted successes of the village co-operative workshop at Llanaelhaearn may have been overemphasized both in terms of the jobs created and of the stability of the enterprise (Cloke and Laycock, 1981), it is clear that some scope (albeit structurally limited) remains for small-scale self-help projects for employment generation in rural communities.

The service sector has experienced greater attention from voluntary activists, and Woollett (1981) has described a wide range of activities aimed at promoting self-help services. In addition to the information services mentioned above (Clark and Unwin, 1980) advances have been made in:

1   *Community shops*, often operated from a village hall and stocking exactly the products that local people require. Successful experiments in Devon have widened the role of the shop to provide an outlet for local produce, and have linked it with other facilities such as a concurrent playgroup. In some cases existing premises have been taken over by the community on the withdrawal of a private-sector operator. A North Wales settlement now supports its own public house through this mechanism;

2 *Community transport*, which takes many forms including: voluntary car schemes operated under the aegis of the WRVS, WI, Red Cross or other voluntary agencies; community minibus schemes whereby a locally organized group (perhaps with financial assistance from outside) will purchase, administer, drive and maintain a vehicle for use in the provision of accessibility links for the local community; and collection and delivery services for local residents who lack the access to centralized services;

3 *Community education*, where in extreme cases parents and local residents have bought redundant school buildings and established their own local school following the withdrawal of local authority support. More often part-time assistance by parents, both in teaching and in fund-raising, have been instrumental in keeping open state-funded primary schools in 'uneconomic' locations;

4 *Community health care* can similarly be promoted in rural areas through voluntary assistance and fund-raising on behalf of existing cottage hospitals, and by specific care schemes which often offer a mobile nursing service staffed by volunteers. Many such schemes are now recognized and grant-aided by local authority departments;

5 *Rural community care* is provided by a wide range of good-neighbour schemes and preventive care groups which can organize specific projects such as 'skill-swaps' or 'garden sharing' within rural communities.

Many of these self-help service schemes have now become semi-institutionalized with financial support from local and central government who realize that their own efforts are inferior in many respects.

Self-help experiments can also be important in providing *rural housing* opportunities (Kingham, 1981) either in participation with local authorities or other agencies such as housding associations, or entirely through the self-build process. A wide range of mechanisms are described by Clark (1981) and Winter (1980), but in general terms urban-based projects have been more prolific than those in rural areas, where a belated importance is now being attached to self-help groups. Once again, an informal partnership is now being established in some areas between local authorities and self-build or housing co-operative groups which represents an acknowledgement by local government that grant-aided voluntary initiative is an effective method of opportunity provision.

In all these cases, evidence is beginning to appear that self-help and community approaches can serve to benefit disadvantaged groups in rural communities. Moreover it is also becoming clear that self-help transcends the mere provision of opportunities, rather forming a type of 'social glue' (Russell, 1975) which is viewed by many as a necessary quality for the future of rural communities (Downing, 1979). These compound advantages have led some commentators to present self-help as the knub of future rural settlement planning. Shaw (1979, 204) suggests that:

The immediate need is therefore for each public authority to help identify problems, to ensure the coordination of activity, to act as a catalyst to spur other bodies into action, to encourage and assist self-help activities in all their forms.

However, the generalized limitations of approaches which attempt to harness existing resources apply equally to voluntary services, and as Shaw himself recognizes (p. 204): 'The solution to rural problems will remain partly a matter of resource allocation, particularly at national level'.

Attracting new resources

A review of the theoretical basis of current rural settlement planning (chapter 3) highlighted the stark reality that a strongly conservative political ideology with accompanying attributes of environmentalism, pragmatism and non-interventionism has dominated the structural constraints on decision-making for rural areas in post-war Britain. Given this course of events, it is not surprising to discover that most policy alternatives for rural settlement planning have been framed within the short-term, within-system, incremental-change category. In the event even these changes have largely been rejected by decision-makers as too radical, and so positive policy innovations have only been enacted in a piecemeal and experimental manner. The various policy options discussed in pp. 335–44 appear to offer considerable benefits to rural communities, but are hamstrung by the obligation that they operate within existing resource levels.

It appears increasingly clear that the problems of deprivation and disadvantage in rural areas can only be effectively tackled either by attracting substantial additional resources to the treatment of problematic outcomes of socio-economic and political structures, or by changing the nature of those structures so that more equitable opportunity-decisions become the norm; or indeed by both these measures together. It is a simple task to advocate glibly that rural areas need more resources, but far more difficult to justify the withdrawal of resources from elsewhere that would inevitably result. The attraction of additional rural resources thus involves a realignment of both theory and practice.

Rural–urban resource allocation

The appeal for increased state funding of rural areas is epitomized by the Association of District Councils' (1978) reply to the Countryside Review Committee report on *Rural Communities*. Three main financial conclusions are reached as to the financial imbalance between rural and urban areas:
1 There is clear evidence that rural areas in recent years have been increasingly starved of resources, and this has contributed to the decline of village communities;
2 The present rate support grant distribution system is too heavily weighted towards the conurbation areas;
3 Given the Government's highly selective approach to aid for the inner cities and other urban areas, there should be a similar form of specific grant available to those deprived rural areas in England and Wales where there is evidence of special social need.

These conclusions are strictly related to rural local government finance, and when wider servicing issues are taken into consideration the view of the Countryside Review Committee (1977, 10) may be raised as an alternative interpretation:

> It could be said that where the social and economic interests of rural settlements differ from those of urban communities, it would be wrong to lay more emphasis on one than another. There is, in any case, no hard evidence to suggest that the countryside has been starved of resources in the past. . . . In short, the case seems evenly balanced.

On one hand we are presented with a case of extreme resource discrimination against rural areas, and on the other, an evenly balanced picture. This dualism tends to act as an initial clouding catalyst in the debate as to whether rural areas should receive more resources. In fact much more is known about local government resource allocation than the wider distribution of public expenditure. Moseley (1980, 36) offers an explanation for this situation:

> We simply do not know how much rural Britain receives by way of public expenditure each year. Expenditure data are presented for a variety of different areas which embrace both rural and urban portions – health authority regions and areas, water authority regions, shire counties and districts, etc. Much less do we know whether this sum constitutes a 'fair share'.

From this position of ignorance we are prone to deliver broad generalizations about the visibility of urban problems (which are thus viewed as politically sound areas for extra expenditure), and about the existing implicit subsidies involved in maintaining statutory services in rural areas. For example, the Labour Party National Executive Committee's (1979) interim statement on rural areas points out that the provision of social services in rural areas costs approximately 25 per cent more in rural areas than in urban areas. Similarly, three employees in the personal social services are needed to cover the dispersed needs of rural communities whereas only two people are required for equivalent work in cities. This document does not, however, proceed to the crucial point of interpretation – namely, should rural areas thus receive additional resource equivalents to cope with their special needs, or does this form of distribution constitute an unwarranted subsidy of rural areas by urban areas? Many would argue that specific state resources for inner-city projects constitute one method of redressing an imbalance of resources which are already tilted in the rural direction because of higher servicing costs. If accepted, this point of view would nullify rural claims that equivalent resources should be directed towards rural-deprivation blackspots (in either geographical or social space).

The relationship between government policy and service expenditure in rural areas is an extremely complex one. The underlying issue involves decisions as to the extent to which consumers should pay for services, the extent to which nationally standardized charges should apply, and the extent to which certain services are essential for the upkeep of rural communities. If market systems are permitted to dictate the price and location of essential services then rural disadvantage will be further exacerbated. Even where standardized charges apply, the quality and location of services remain paramount for the provision of realistic opportunities to disadvantaged rural residents. Only, then, when there is a commitment to provide essential services (or access to them) for rural residents of all ages and social classes, will part of the deprivation problem be tackled effectively. Moreover, similar necessities have also to be catered for in other opportunity sectors such as housing and employment, but as Moseley (1980, 36) suggests: 'it seems inescapable that a 1 per cent variation in the level of public spending in rural Britain will have more effect on employment there, than would a doubling or even tripling of the budget of the Development Commission'. The rural system is thus complex and interacting, and no one opportunity should be viewed in isolation from the parallel needs of rural people.

In some ways, an acceptance of the need to provide so-called essential opportunities to all rural residents side-steps the theoretical issues of whether rural problems *per se* warrant positive resource discrimination. What is required is positive intervention to benefit *all* disadvantaged groups be they urban, rural, peri-urban or belonging to any other spatial category which is fashionable. Thus no 'special' rural case is needed, because the rural disadvantaged should be given equal benefit from the national movement towards the redress of opportunity deficiency. Some authors have suggested that rural areas are capable of raising more income internally. Green (1980, 84) recommends that

> new financial arrangements should provide for the revaluation of all country properties to bring rural rateable values up to urban levels, and authorities should be empowered to surcharge remote properties for their services, but with exemptions for farm and forestry workers, teachers and others providing direct personal service to the local community.

This rather sweeping attack on certain sections of the rural community seems likely to add to the already imbalanced financial burdens placed on rural dwellers, and in addition may instigate a series of unhealthy side-effects, affecting the continuation of the private rented housing sector and the attractiveness of rural areas to industrial entrepreneurs. It seems preferable that additional resources should be derived from national taxation mechanisms which are more closely related to personal income. A national commitment to positive equalization of opportunities obviously requires fundamental and radical changes in current political opinion, and implies some redistribution of wealth on a nationwide scale. It is equally apparent that decision-makers will strive to restrict any such redistribution to the minimum levels required by political acceptability and self-preservation. We are presented with the stark option of either continuing social disadvantage or precipitating some level of resource redistribution at a national and international scale.

Direct action

Even if some redistributive impetus is achieved, the question remains of how the direct intervention of national resources is best used in the treatment of the causes as well as the symptoms of disadvantage in rural areas. Most emphasis has been placed on the alternative methods of directly providing necessary opportunities to consumers, often through the auspices of local government intervention. A recent Royal Town Planning Institute report (1979, 33) suggested that:

> Planning in the last decade has been dotted spasmodically by a wide range of imaginative initiatives taken by various authorities more often than not within existing powers available to them. We are emboldened by these historical precedents to suggest that with increased political and professional will the scope for informal and local initiatives is enormous.

Morley (1981) outlines three reasons for an increased level of direct intervention by local authorities:
1 To ensure an adequate supply of suitable buildings;
2 To ensure control over design, quality of construction and tenant selection so that buildings produced are suitable to their requirements;
3 To reap the financial benefits of development.

Other commentators (e.g. Byrne, 1981) prefer the lower-risk and less-expenditure approach of partnership with the private sector to secure the same aims. Yet another viewpoint is expressed by Coopman (1981, 309):

> Do planners always know best? Are we doomed to live in a world of no choices, where planners not only decide what should be built but also go on to build it? In a market-oriented economy the producer ignores the consumer at his risk. If the consumer does not like a product he does not have to buy it, they are unlikely to encourage competition. We shall be completely at the mercy of the public sector.

This range of opinion offers many red herrings to the understanding of direct intervention as a means of securing the prevention and cure of rural disadvantage. The very mention of 'financial benefits' and 'competition' remove us from the realm of the need to provide opportunities *where they do not already exist*, and which have often already been abandoned by the private sector. Moreover, the focus on 'buildings' is also indicative of a rather old-fashioned approach to direct intervention which neglects the management and staffing of opportunities which are not necessarily tied to buildings. In many ways a more realistic debate should be initiated over the relative merits and disadvantages of direct intervention as opposed to the subsidy of other bodies (community, private-sector and public-sector organizations) in the provision of necessary rural opportunities.

What needs to be done? A vast literature is available on the subject of household and opportunity deprivation in rural areas, but no real agreement has emerged on what are the so-called 'necessary' opportunities which should be supplied. These should perhaps include:

1 *Employment*, where central and local government can establish their own nationalized or localized enterprises in rural areas to generate employment, or greatly increase efforts to attract and subsidise co-operative or private sector employment generators;

2 *Housing*, where local authorities can build dwellings for rent or purchase by local disadvantaged groups, or subsidize the efforts of co-operative groups, housing associations and self-build groups where a specific need can be established;

3 *Accessibility*, where provision should be viewed as a social service and where organization, training and finance is required to establish a package of informal transport services *in every rural settlement* so that non-mobile groups can gain access to centralized services and opportunities;

4 *Peripatetic public services*, where a collection of information, medical, community and other public and private services can be made available to every settlement on a regular basis in the form of a mobile services market (Moseley, 1979);

5 *Village shop/post office*, which although sometimes falsely perceived as a prestige symbol for a village, nevertheless performs a necessary function. It is important that rural small-shop price differentials with urban counterparts are equalized, perhaps by some form of small-shop subsidy as is offered in Norway (Kirby *et al.*, 1981) or more radically by a nationalization of small shops so that profit in one location can be used to offset loss in another, and costly distribution systems can be viewed partially as a social service.

This list is by no means comprehensive, but it is likely that if this nucleus of opportunities were to be provided for disadvantaged rural residents then other opportunities might follow in their wake. It is vital that some basis of rural opportunity is secured in the short term, so that a longer-term future, perhaps involving elements of voluntary simplicity (see pp. 327–30) will have a platform on which to develop. In some ways it is an easy way out merely to suggest that 'more research is needed'. There is however, a glaring need to investigate the structures and mechanisms required to permit this form of direct or indirect intervention on behalf of the rural disadvantaged.

Corporate management

Although many of the policies described above are several steps removed from current conventional thinking in rural settlement planning, there have been recent moves in the general direction of a corporate approach to the management of rural areas. Dissatisfaction with the glaringly obvious deficiencies in co-operation and co-ordination between decision-making agencies has focused the minds of many planners and government advisors towards various methods whereby decision-making can be made more comprehensive. After all, the structure plan was introduced as a vehicle for co-ordinating the programmes of all sectors involved with development, and so it has been argued that if the question of inter-agency and inter-authority relationships can be sorted out, the outcomes of structure-plan implementation will eventually come good.

Corporate decision-making *per se* is only a partial answer to some of the problems of rural settlement planning, but some form of corporate resource allocation would doubtless make a far more significant impact. The Working Party on Rural Settlement Policies (1979, 23) advocates both corporate decision-making and corporate resource allocation as the next stage in rural settlement planning progress. This would involve

> the relinquishing of the present system of sectoral accounting in favour of a corporate approach to rural settlement planning. Costs would then be examined in terms of benefits and trade-offs between the various services to provide an overall financial assessment for a given policy package and, as necessary, a comprehensive analysis of its likely effects on individual groups or areas. The final stage would relate the overall policy package back to the individual sectors for any necessary policy adjustments to be made. Such an approach will not be achieved easily, since it will require a major change of emphasis in financing on the part of a number of public bodies. Nevertheless we consider it essential if the present problems and future needs of rural areas are to be dealt with satisfactorily.

This viewpoint is reproduced at length here because it marks the small beginnings of radical thinking from a quasi-official body considering the future of rural settlement planning. If the recognition of a need for corporate action can be linked to a political willingness to direct rural planning and management towards the priority areas represented by deprivation and disadvantage, then the traditionally held view of rural settlement planning as a physically oriented process will eventually be broken down. The old notions that planning priority should be given to conservation and settlement appearance may at last give way to a more balanced view in which the welfare of rural communities receives its due import. Corporate rather than disparate resource management in rural settlements is a powerful tool for the fulfilment of needs, and thus an equable means of isolating and evaluating the priority needs of any rural community is a vital prerequisite for this new approach.

Conclusion

This chapter gives ample illustration to the fact that it is far easier to pinpoint the faults of current rural settlement planning than it is to offer potential improvements which are to be seen as realistic and viable to the majority of rural planners, politicians and scholars. Many of the alternatives outlined above bear very little relation to the way in which decisions are made in current rural resource management processes, and yet there appears to be overwhelming evidence that policy changes at various scales are necessary because of the progressive trends of imbalanced resource distribution and social inequity in rural communities. At this point, we appear to be faced with four broad political options:

1   Continue with a *laissez-faire* approach of exclusive rural conservationism. Resource rationalization will then continue under free-market promptings and small rural settlements will thus be conserved eventually only for those who can afford to live there. Rural areas will thus be subject to rampant gentrification and geriatrification;

2   Recognize the need for some additional opportunity provision in rural settlements to tackle rural disadvantage, but only within strict budgetary limitations. Emphasis here will be on the prompting of self-help and community-action schemes, perhaps through the formation of a comprehensive system of local administrators and community workers, acting as initiators for local efforts. These measures would seem to be a logical progression from the splendid work already being carried out by the Rural Community Councils (McLaughlin, 1979). However, such actions are often insufficient to provide more than temporary first aid to the symptoms of rural problems;

3   Realize that low-cost solutions are only a small part of the answer and bring about a resource reallocation in favour of measures directed towards the opportunity deficiencies suffered by certain disadvantaged groups in all locations. In rural areas indirect action through subsidy or partnership and direct action by government bodies can do much to provide essential services to such groups where the need exists, provided that sufficient resources are found for the task. This option requires that traditional views of rural settlement planning should be swept away and a new social welfare-oriented process be substituted in which the goals and objectives of planning are corporately directed at the wellbeing of rural communities;

4   Take the structural view that even if a combination of government action, subsidy and self-help were able to provide a satisfactory opportunity base in rural areas for all rural residents, some of the underlying causes of deprivation will remain. This is because certain sections of the rural community will have insufficient disposable income to make use of the opportunities, regardless of whether they be on site, peripatetic, or at the other end of some form of accessibility link. Such a situation requires radical policies of personal subsidy and wealth redistribution so that satisfactory incomes are available both to those in full employment and to those who choose the voluntary simplicity life-style which may be one cornerstone of the future of rural areas. Townsend (1979) has justifiably posed the question of whether welfare can be distributed equally to all in a capitalist society that is necessarily economically constrained by private and market interests, and sympathy with this view accords with a realisation that options 2 and 3 are insufficient.

These options in turn require political decisions which should be taken in the light of the opinions and needs of all sections of rural communities (and indeed of society as a whole). These decisions should also be made with a clear recognition that the needs of each community are different, and that the notion of a 'standard' solution to rural problems is meaningless in view of these differences. Moreover, the decisions have to be made soon, because before very long the eradication of poverty and disadvantage will have been achieved through processes of forced migration, and rural areas will have achieved the status fo havens for the affluent minority rather than harbouring opportunities for all who wish to live, work or otherwise participate in them.

Bibliography

Allison, L. (1975) *Environmental Planning: A Political and Philosophical Analysis*, London, Allen & Unwin.

Ambrose, P. (1974) *The Quiet Revolution*, London, Chatto & Windus.

Anderson, M.A. (1981) 'Planning policies and development control in the Sussex Downs AONB', *Town Planning Review*, 52, 5–25.

Armstrong, J. (1976) 'Rural planning: a French approach', *Town and Country Planning*, 44, 161–4.

Ash, M. (1979) 'Public participation: time to bury Skeffington', *The Planner*, 65, 136–9.

Ashworth, W. (1954) *The Genesis of Modern British Town Planning*, London, Routledge & Kegan Paul.

Association of County Councils (1979) *Rural Deprivation*, London, ACC.

Association of District Councils (1978) *Rural Recovery: Strategy for Survival*, London, ADC.

Atkinson, J.R. (1970) 'Planning problems in County Durham', in Dewdney, J.C. (ed.) (1970) *Durham County and City with Teesside*, Durham, British Association for the Advancement of Science.

Austin, D. (1979) 'The pattern of settlement – dispersal or nucleation?', Internal seminar paper, Department of Geography, St David's University College, Lampeter.

Avon CC (1980) *County Structure Plan: Submitted Written Statement*.

Ayton, J.B. (1976) 'Rural settlement policy: problems and conflicts', in Drudy, P.J. (ed.) (1976) *Regional and Rural Development*, Chalfont St Giles, Alpha Academic.

Ayton, J. (1980) 'Settlement policies can bring stabilization', *The Planner*, 66, 98–9.

Bailey, J. (1975) *Social Theory for Planning*, London, Routledge & Kegan Paul.

Bains Report (1972) *The New Local Authorities: Management and Structure*, London, HMSO.

Bajan, K. (1976) 'Egalisation des conditions de vie entre la ville et la campagne en Pologne', *Economie Rurale*, 111, 77–9.

Banks, P. (1980) 'Planning in the green belt', *Local Council Review*, Spring, 247–50.

Barnard, T. (1981) 'A review of local plans', in Fudge, C. (ed.) (1981) *Approaches to Local Planning*, Working Paper 17, University of Bristol School for Advanced Urban Studies.

Barr, J. (1969) 'Durham's murdered villages', *New Society*, 340, 523–5.

Barras, R. (1979) 'The first ten years of English structure planning: current progress and future directions', *Planning Outlook*, 22, 19–23.

Barras, R. and Broadbent, T.A. (1979) 'The analysis in English structure plans', *Urban Studies*, 16, 1–18.

Bassetlaw, DC (1978) *West Bassetlaw: Draft District Plan*.

Batty, M. (1979) 'On planning processes', in Goodall, B. and Kirby, A. (eds) (1979) *Resources and Planning*, Oxford, Pergamon.

Baynes, R. (1979) 'Housing policy in the Lake District National Park', Colwyn Bay,

Paper presented to the North Wales Planning Group conference on Rural Housing and Settlements.

Beale, C.L. (1977) 'The recent shift of United States population to non-metropolitan areas 1970-75', *International Regional Science Review*, 2, 113-22.

Beardmore, D. (1976) 'An uneasy partnership in development control', *The Planner*, 62, 73-4.

Beavon, K.S.O. (1977) *Central Place Theory: A Reinterpretation*, London, Longman.

Bedfordshire CC (1976) *County Structure Plan: Report of Survey*.

Bedfordshire CC (1980) *County Structure Plan: Approved Written Statement*.

Beresford, P. and Beresford, S. (1980) 'Public participation and local politics', *Town and Country Planning*, 49, 412-14.

Berkshire CC (1960) *County Development Plan – First Review*.

Berkshire CC (1979) *West Berkshire County Structure Plan: Approved Written Statement*.

Berkshire CC (1980) *East Berkshire County Structure Plan: Approved Written Statement*.

Berkshire CC (1980a) *Central Berkshire County Structure Plan: Approved Written Statement*.

Berry, B.J.L. (ed.) (1976) 'Urbanization and Counterurbanization', *Urban Affairs Annual Review*, 11.

Berry, B.J.L., Barnum, H.G. and Tennant, R.J. (1962) 'Retail location and consumer behaviour', *Papers and Proceedings, Regional Science Association*, 9, 65-106.

Berry, B.J.L. and Garrison, W.L. (1958) 'The functional bases of the central place hierarchy', *Economic Geography*, 34, 145-54.

Berwickshire CC (1972) *A Rural Policy for Berwickshire: Draft Report*.

Best, R.H. (1978) 'Myth and reality in the growth of urban land', in Rogers, A.W. (ed.) (1978) *Urban Growth, Farmland Losses and Planning*, Rural Geography Study Group, Institute of British Geographers.

Best, R.H. (1981) *Land Use and Living Space*, Methuen, London.

Best, R.H. and Rogers, A.W. (1973) *The Urban Countryside*, London, Faber & Faber.

Blacksell, M. (1979) 'Landscape protection and development control: an appraisal of planning in rural areas of England and Wales', *Geoforum*, 10, 267-74.

Blacksell, M. and Gilg, A. (1977) Planning control in an Area of Outstanding Natural Beauty', *Social and Economic Administration*, 11, 206-15.

Blacksell, M. and Gilg, A. (1981) *The Countryside: Planning and Change*, London Allen & and Unwin.

Blake, J. (1974) 'The development control crisis', *Town and Country Planning*, 42, 211-16.

Blenkinsop, A. (1978) 'The Peak District National Park – a challenge?', *Town and Country Planning*, 46. 392-4.

Blondel, J. and Hall, R. (1967) 'Conflict, decision-making and perception of local councillors', *Political Studies*, 15, 322-50.

Blowers, A. (1972) 'The declining villages of County Durham', in Open University (1972) *Social Geography*, Bletchley, Open University Press.

Blowers, A. (1980) *The Limits of Power: The Politics of Local Planning Policy*, Oxford, Pergamon.

Boaden, N. (1971) *Urban Policy-Making: Influences on County Boroughs in England and Wales*, Cambridge University Press.

Bonham-Carter, V. (1976) 'The changing rural community', in MacEwen, M. (ed.) (1976) *Future Landscapes*, London, Chatto & Windus.

Bowler, I.R. (ed.) (1981) *Social Problems in Rural Communities*, Rural Geography Study Group, Institue of British Geographers Annual Symposium, University of Leicester.

Bowley, M. (1945) *Housing and the State 1919–44*, London, Allen and Unwin.

Boyle, R. (1980) 'Examinations in public: Scottish practice reviewed', *The Planner*, 66, 73–6.

Bracey, H.E. (1952) *Social Provision in Rural Wiltshire*, London, Methuen.

Bracey, H.E. (1953) 'Towns as rural service centres: an index of centrality with special reference to Somerset', *Transactions IBG*, 19, 95–103.

Bracey, H.E. (1956) 'A rural component of centrality applied to six southern counties in the United Kingdom', *Economic Geography*, 32, 38–50.

Bracey, H.E. (1958) 'Some aspects of rural depopulation in the United Kingdom', *Rural Sociology*, 23, 385–91.

Bracey, H.E. (1962) 'English central. villages', in Norborg, K. (ed.) (1962) *IGU Symposium – Urban Geography*, Lund, IGU.

Bracey, H.E. (1970) *People and the Countryside*, London, Routledge & Kegan Paul.

Bracken, I. and Hume, D. (1980) *An Analysis of Welsh Structure Plans*, Papers in Planning Research 5, Department of Town Planning, University of Wales Institute of Science and Technology.

Braybrooke, D. and Lindblom, C.E. (1963) *A Strategy of Decision: Policy Evaluation as a Social Process*, New York, Free Press.

Breakell, M. (ed.) (1980) *Small Industries in Rural Areas: The Economic and Social Context*, Oxford University Department of External Studies and Oxford Polytechnic.

Brecon Beacons National Park Committee (1977) *Brecon Beacons National Park Plan*.

Broadbent, T.A. (1977) *Planning and Profit in the Urban Economy*, London, Methuen.

Broadbent, T.A. (1979) *Options for Planning: A Discussion Document*, London, Centre for Environmental Studies.

Brush, J.E. (1953) 'The hierarchy of central places in south-western Wisconsin', *Geographical Review*, 43, 380–402.

Brush, J.E. and Bracey, H.E. (1955) 'Rural service centres in South-western Wisconsin and Southern England', *Geographical Review*, 45, 559–69.

Bruton, M.J. (ed.) (1974) *The Spirit and Purpose of Planning*, London, Hutchinson.

Bryant, C.R. (1974) 'An approach to the problem of urbanization and structural changes in agriculture: a case study from the Paris region, 1955–68', *Geografiska Annaler*, 56B, 1–27.

Buckinghamshire CC (1969) *Cheddington Village Plan*.

Buckinghamshire CC (1973) *Tingewick: Village Plan and Conservation Area V46*.

Buckinghamshire CC (1976) *County Structure Plan: Report of Survey*.

Buckinghamshire CC (1980) *County Structure Plan: Approved Written Statement*.

Buckley, W. (1967) *Sociology and Modern Systems Theory*, Englewood Cliffs, NJ, Prentice-Hall.

Bulpitt, J.G. (1967) *Party Politics in English Local Government*, London, Longman.

Burrell, T. (1979) 'A new approach to village planning', Paper presented to the Future for Rural Communities conference, Losehill Hall, Castleton, Derbyshire.

Burton, S.H. (1973) *Devon Villages*, London, Hale.

Butcher, H., Cole, I. and Glen, A. (1975) *Information and Action Services for Rural Areas*, University of York, Papers in Community Studies 5.

Buttel, F.H. and Flinn, W.L. (1977) 'The interdependence of rural and urban environmental problems in advanced capitalist societies: models of linkage', *Sociologia Ruralis*, 17, 255–81.

Buxton, R. (1973) *Local Government*, Harmondsworth, Penguin.

Byrne, S. (1981) 'Comment on Morley (1981)', *Town Planning Review*, 52, 306–7.

Caddy, C. (1981) 'Local planning in an area of restraint', in Fudge, C. (ed.) (1981) *Approaches to Local Planning*, Working Paper 17, University of Bristol School of Advanced Urban Studies.

Caernarvonshire CC (no date) *Structure Plan – Subject Report No 7: Structure, Policies, Commitments*.

Cambridgeshire CC (1954) *County Development Plan*.

Cambridgeshire CC (1966) 'Cambridgshire: a rural planning policy and its implementation', *Official Architecture and Planning*, 29, 1126–41.

Cambridgeshire CC (1971) *Linton Village Plan*.

Cambridgshire CC (1980) *County Structure Plan: Approved Written Statement*.

Cambridgeshire Joint Town Planning Committee (1934) *Cambridgeshire Regional Planning Report*.

Camhis, M. (1979) *Planning Theory and Philosophy*, London, Tavistock.

Cant, G. (ed.) (1980) *People and Planning in Rural Communities*, Christchurch,NZ, University of Canterbury.

Cantell, T. (1979) 'Caring for character', *Country Life*, March 22, 806–8.

Caradon DC (1980) *District Settlement Policies and Plan*.

Chadwick, G. (1971) *A Systems View of Planning*, Oxford, Pergamon.

Champion, A.G. (1981) 'Population trends in rural Britain', *Population Trends*, 26, 20–3.

Chapman, K. (1979) *People, Pattern and Process*, London, Arnold.

Cherry, G.E. (1974) 'The development of planning thought', in Bruton M.J. (ed.) (1974) *The Spirit and Purpose of Planning*, London, Hutchinson.

Cherry, G.E. (ed.) (1976) *Rural Planning Problems*, London, Leonard Hill.

Cherry, G.E. (1978) 'Rural planning: contemporary problems and future policies'. The fourth Norman Wall Memorial Lecture, Midlands New Town Society.

Cheshire CC (1977) *County Structure Plan: Report of Survey Summary*.

Cheshire CC (1979) *County Structure Plan: Approved Written Statement*.

Chisholm, M. and Oeppen, J. (1973) *The Changing Pattern of Employment*, London, Croom Helm.

Christaller, W. (trans. C.W. Baskin) (1966) *Central Places in Southern Germany*, Englewood Cliffs, NJ, Prentice Hall.

Clark, D. (1981) *Rural Housing Initiatives*, NCVO, London.

Clark, D. and Unwin, K.I. (1980) *Information Services in Rural Areas*, Norwich, GeoBooks.

Clark, D. and Unwin, K.I. (1981) 'Telecommunications and travel: potential impact in rural areas', *Regional Studies*, 15, 47–56.

Clark, G. (1981) 'Housing in the Lake District', in Bowler, I.R. (ed.) (1981) *Social Problems in Rural Communities*, Rural Geography Study Group, 18G Annual Symposium, University of Leicester.

Clark, G. (1982) 'Housing policy in the Lake District', *Transactions, IBG*, 7, 59–70.

Clarkson, S. (1980) *Jobs in the Countryside*, Wye College Department of Environmental Studies and Countryside Planning.

Clawson, M. (1966) 'Factors and forces affecting the optimum future rural settlement pattern in the United States', *Economic Geography*, 42, 283–93.

Clawson, M. (1968) *Policy Directions for US Agriculture*, Baltimore, Resources for the Future Inc.

Cleveland CC (1980) *East Cleveland County Structure Plan: Approved Written Statement*.

Cloke, P.J. (1977) 'An index of rurality for England and Wales', *Regional Studies*, 11, 31–46.

Cloke, P.J. (1977a) 'In defence of key settlement policies', *The Village*, 32, 7–11.

Cloke, P.J. (1979) *Key Settlements in Rural Areas*, London, Methuen.

Cloke, P.J. (1979a) 'New emphases for applied rural geography', *Progress in Human Geography*, 4, 181–217.

Cloke, P.J. (1980) 'The key settlement approach: the theoretical argument', *The Planner*, 66, 98–9.

Cloke, P.J. (1980a) 'Key settlements', *Town and Country Planning*, 48, 187–9.

Cloke, P.J. (1981) 'Key settlement policies at the local level', *The Village*, 35, 28–30.

Cloke, P.J. (1981a) 'Environmental planning and rural settlement policy: the case of the Kingsbridge area', *Field Studies*, 5, 469–86.

Cloke, P.J. (1982) 'Rethinking rural settlement planning', *TESG*, 73, 280–5.

Cloke, P.J. (1983) 'The economy of rural communities in national parks: a review article', *Journal of Environmental Management* (forthcoming).

Cloke, P.J. and Griffiths, M.J. (1980) 'Planning responses to urban and rural problems: a comparative study in South-west Wales', *TESG*, 71, 255–63.

Cloke, P.J. and Laycock, M. (1981) 'Social and economic co-operation in rural communities: a study of Llanaelhaearn, Wales', *Sociologia Ruralis*, 21, 81–95.

Cloke, P.J. and Park, C.C. (1983) *Resource Management in the Countryside: A Geographical Perspective*, London, Croom Helm.

Cloke, P.J. and Shaw, D.P. (forthcoming) 'Rural Settlement policies in Structure plans', *Town Planning Review*.

Cloke, P.J. and Woodward, N. (1981) Methodological problems in the economic evaluation of rural settlement planning', in Curry, N. (ed.) (1981) 'Rural settlement policy and economics', *Gloucestershire Papers in Local and Rural Planning*, 12.

Clout, H.D. (1972) *Rural Geography: An Introductory Survey*, Oxford, Pergamon.

Clout, H.D. (1975) 'Structural change in French farming: the case of the Puy-de-Dome', *TESG*, 66, 234–45.

Clwyd CC (1979) *County Structure Plan: Submitted Written Statement*.

Cohen, M.D., March, J.G. and Olsen, J.P. (1972) 'A garbage can model of organisational choice', *Administrative Science Quarterly*, March.

Coleman, A.M. (1978) 'Agricultural land losses: the evidence from maps', in Rogers, A.W, (ed.) (1978) *Urban Growth, Farmland Losses and Planning*, Rural Geography Study Group, IBG.

Commins, P. (1978) 'Socio-economic adjustments to rural depopulation', *Regional Studies*, 12, 79–94.

Commins, P. and Drudy, P.J. (1980) *Problem Rural Regions*, London, Regional Studies Association Discussion Paper II.

Connor, J. (1980) 'Rural deprivation', *County Councils Gazette*, 73, 88–92.

Coopman, S. (1981) 'Comment on Morley (1981)', *Town Planning Review*, 52, 308–9.

Cormack, P. (1978) *Heritage in Danger*, London, Quartet.

Cornish, M.S. and Cornish, S.R. (1975) 'Planners' conceptions of rural–urban characteristics: the North Yorkshire and Teeside Structure Plans', *Regional Studies*, 9, 169–80.

Cornwall CC (1956) *County Development Plan*.

Cornwall CC (1969) *County Development Plan: First Review*.

Cornwall CC (1976) *County Structure Plan: The Policy Choices*.

Cornwall CC (1976a) *County Structure Plan Topic Report: Environment*.

Cornwall CC (1980) *County Structure Plan: Submitted Written Statement*.

Cornwall CC (1980a) *County Structure Plan: Presentation to Examination in Public*.

Countryside Commission (1976) *Annual Report*, Cheltenham, Countryside Commission.

Countryside Commission (1978) *Areas of Outstanding Natural Beauty: A Discussion Paper*, Cheltenham, Countryside Commission.

Countryside Commission (1980) *Areas of Outstanding Natural Beauty: An analysis of the comments received in response to the Countryside Commission's Discussion Paper CCP 116*, Cheltenham, Countryside Commission.

Countryside Commission for Scotland (1978) *Scotlands Scenic Heritage*, Perth, Countryside Commission.

Countryside Review Committee (1976) *The Countryside – Problems and Policies*, London, HMSO.

Countryside Review Committee (1977) *Rural Communities*, London, HMSO.

Cresswell, R. (ed.) (1978) *Rural Transport and Country Planning*, Glasgow, Hill.

Cullingworth, J.B. (1979) *Town and Country Planning in Britain*, London, Allen & Unwin.

Cumberland CC (1955) *County Development Plan*.

Cumberland CC (1964) *County Development Plan: First Review*.

Cumbria CC and Lake District Special Planning Board (1976) *Choices for Cumbria: Structure Plan Report of Survey*.

Cumbria CC and Lake District Special Planning Board (1980) *Cumbria and Lake District Joint Structure Plan: Submitted Written Statement*.

Cumming, C.E. (1971) *Studies in Educational Costs*, Edinburgh, Scottish Academic Press.

Curry, N. (ed.) (1981) 'Rural settlement policy and economics', *Gloucestershire Papers in Local and Rural Planning*, 12.

Curry, N. and West C. (1981) 'Internal economies of scale in rural primary education', in Curry, N. (ed.) (1981) 'Rural settlement policy and economics', *Gloucestershire Papers in Local and Rural Planning*, 12.

Curtis, J.E. and Peters, J.W. (eds) (1970) *The Sociology of Knowledge*, London, Duckworth.

Darley, G. (1978) 'Rural settlement – rural resettlement: the future', *Built Environment*, 4, 299–310.

Dartmoor National Park Authority (1977) *Settlement Pattern: Consultative Paper*.

Dartmoor National Park Authority, Teignbridge DC and South Hams DC (1979) *Ashburton Informal Local Plan*.

Davidson, J. and Wibberley, G.P. (1977) *Planning and the Rural Environment*, Oxford, Pergamon.

Davies, B. (1978) *Universality, Selectivity and Effectiveness in Social Policy*, London, Heinemann.

Dawson, J.A. (1969) 'Some early theories of settlement location and size', *Journal, Town Planning Institute*, 55, 444–8.

Dearlove, J. (1973) *The Politics of Policy in Local Government*, Cambridge University Press.

Dennier, D.A. (1978) 'National Park Plans: a review article', *Town Planning Review*, 175–83.

Dennier, D.A. (1980) 'National Park Plans', *Countryside Planning Yearbook*, I, 49–66.

Dennis, R. and Clout, H. (1980) *A Social Geography of England and Wales*, Oxford, Pergamon.

Department of the Environment (1970) *Circular 10*, London, HMSO.

Department of the Environment (1972) *Circular 102*, London, HMSO.

Department of the Environment (1972) *Structure Plans Note 7*, London, HMSO.

Department of the Environment (1972) *Structure Plans Note 8*, London, HMSO.

Department of the Environment (1973) *Circular 122*, London, HMSO.

Department of the Environment (1973) *Advice Note 7*, London, HMSO.

Department of the Environment (1973) *Structure Plans Note 7*, London, HMSO.

Department of the Environment (1973) *Circular 142*, London, HMSO.

Department of the Environment (1973) *Widening the Choice: The Next Steps in Housing*, London, HMSO.

Department of the Environment (1974) *Circular 58(1)*, London, HMSO.

Department of the Environment (1974) *Circular 98*, London, HMSO.

Department of the Environment (1974) *Study of the Cambridge Sub-Region*, London, HMSO.

Department of the Environment (1975) *DoE and its Work*, Departmental Circular, DoE.

Department of the Environment (1976) *Circular 4*, London, HMSO.

Department of the Environment (1977) *The Causes of Rural Depopulation: Review of Research*, Working Paper CSR5, DoE.

Department of the Environment (1977) *Circular 55*, London, HMSO.

Department of the Environment (1979) *Circular 4*, London, HMSO.

Department of the Environment (1980) *Circular 9*, London, HMSO.

Department of the Environment (1980) *North Yorkshire Structure Plan: Examination in Public: Report of the Panel*.

Derbyshire CC (1977) *County Structure Plan: Report of Survey*.

Derbyshire CC (1977a) *County Structure Plan: Submitted Written Statement*.

Derbyshire CC (1980) *County Structure Plan: Approved Written Statement*.

Derounian, J. (1979) *Structure Plans and Rural Communities*, London, National Council of Social Service.

Derounian, J. (1980) 'The impact of structure plans on rural communities', *The Planner*, 66, 87.

Devon Association of Parish Councils (1976) *Town and Country Planning in Devon*.

Devon CC (1964) *County Development Plan: First Review*.

Devon CC (1977) *County Structure Plan: Report of the Survey*.

Devon CC (1981) *County Structure Plan. (1979: Submitted Written Statement.)*

Dewdney, J.C. (ed.) (1970) *Durham County and City with Teeside*. Durham, British Association for the Advancement of Science.

Dicken, P. and Lloyd, P.E. (1976) 'Geographical perspectives on United States investment in the United Kingdom', *Environment & Planning A*, 8, 685–705.

Dickinson, R.E. (1942) 'The social basis of physical planning', *Sociological Review*, 34, 51–67; 165–82.

Dobry, G. (1975) *The Development Control System*, London, HMSO.

Dorset CC (1978) *SE Dorset Structure Plan: Submitted Written Statement*.

Dorset CC (1979) *Dorset (Excluding South-east) Structure Plan: 1979 Village Facilities Survey*.

Dorset CC (1980) *Dorset (excluding South-east) Structure Plan: Draft Written Statement*.

Dower, M. (1975) 'Regional developments and the future of the British countryside', *Rural Life*, 20, 3–9.

Dower, M. (1980) 'The rural voice', *Town and Country Planning*, 49, 177–8.

Downing, P. (1979) 'Community approaches – useful models', Paper presented to the Future for Rural Communities conference, Losehill Hall, Castleton, Derbyshire.

Drudy, P.J. (ed.) (1976) *Regional and Rural Development*, Chalfont St Giles, Alpha Academic.

Drudy, P.J. (1978) 'Depopulation in a prosperous agricultural sub-region', *Regional Studies*, 12, 149–60.

Dungate, M. (1980) 'Rural self-help', *Voluntary Action*, 2, 17–21.

Dunn, M.C. (1976) 'Population change and the settlement pattern', in Cherry, G.E. (ed.) (1976) *Rural Planning Problems*, London, Leonard Hill.

Dunn, M., Rawson, M. and Rogers, A. (1981) *Rural Housing: Competition and Choice*, London, Allen & Unwin.

Dunsire, A. (1978) *Implementation in a Bureaucracy*, Oxford, Martin Robertson.

Durham CC (1932) *North-East Durham Joint Town Planning Scheme*.

Durham CC (1954) *County Development Plan*.

Durham CC (1964) *County Development Plan: Amendment*.

Durham CC (1978) *County Structure Plan: Report of Survey (Volume 3) Choosing the Policies*.

Durham CC (1978a) *County Structure Plan: Submitted Written Statement*.

Dyfed CC (1978) *County Structure Plan: Draft Written Statement*.

East Hertfordshire DC (1980) *East Hertfordshire District Plan: Written Statement*.

East Hertfordshire DC (1981) *East Hertfordshire District Plan: Written Statement Modifications*.

East Lindsey DC (1977) *Draft Wragby District Plan*.

East Suffolk CC (1965) *Policy for the Classification of Settlements*.

East Sussex CC (1953) *County Development Plan*.

East Sussex CC (1978) *County Structure Plan: Approved Written Statement*.

Economic Commission for Europe (1978) 'The impact of energy considerations on the planning and development of human settlements', *Ekistics*, 45, 193–200.

Eden DC (1979) *Penrith District Plan: Written Statement*.

Eden DC (1980) *Appleby Advisory Plan: Written Statement*.

Ekhaugen, K., Gronmo, S. and Kirby, D. (1980) 'State support to small stores: a Nordic form of consumer policy', *Journal of Consumer Policy*, 4, 195–211.

Elgin, D.S. and Mitchell, A. (1977) 'Voluntary simplicity', *The Futurist*, August, 200–9; 254–61.

Elgin, D.S. and Mitchell, A. (1978) 'Voluntary simplicity: life-style of the future?', *Ekistics*, 45, 207–212.

Elkins, S. (1974) *Politics and Land Use Planning*, Cambridge University Press.

Elkins, S. (1975) 'Comparative urban politics and interorganizational behaviour', in Young, K. (ed.) (1975) *Essays on the Study of Urban Politics*, London, Macmillan.

Ellis, W.N. (1975) 'The new ruralism: the post-industrial age is upon us', *The Futurist*, August, 202–4.

Elson, M.J. (1979) *Perspectives on Green Belt Local Plans*, Working Paper 38, Oxford Polytechnic Department of Town Planning.

Elson, M.J. (1981) 'Structure plan policies for pressured rural areas', *Countryside Planning Yearbook*, 2, 49–70.

Emerson, A.E. and Compton, R. (1968) *Some Social Trends*, Report to the Suffolk Rural Community Council.

Essex CC (1965) *County Development Plan: First Review*.

Essex CC (1978) *County Structure Plan: Draft Report of Survey*.

Essex CC (1979) *County Structure Plan: Submitted Written Statement*.

Eversley, D. (1973) *The Planner in Society*, London, Faber & Faber.

Eversley, D. (1974) 'Conservation for the minority?', *Built Environment*, January, 14–15.

Exmoor National Park Committee (1977) *Exmoor National Park Plan*.

Faludi, A. (1970) 'The planning environment and the meaning of planning', *Regional Studies*, 4, 1–9.

Fay, B. (1975) *Social Theory and Political Practice*, London, Allen & Unwin.

Fladmark, J.M. (1980) 'Scottish countryside: planning in changing circumstances', *The Planner*, 66, 70–2.

Fookes, T.W. (1974) 'Bracey revived: a study of settlement service areas', *New Zealand Journal of Geography*, 57, 14–19.

Friedmann, J. (1966) 'Planning as a vocation', *Plan Canada*, 6, 99–124.

Friedmann, J. and Hudson, B. (1974) 'Knowledge and action: a guide to planning theory', *Journal of the American Institute of Planners*, 40, 2–16.

Friend, J. (1980) 'Planning in a multi-organizational context', *Town Planning Review*, 51, 261–9.

Fudge, C. (1981) 'Self-help and social policy', *The Planner*, 67, 60–1.

Fudge, C. (ed.) (1981) *Approaches to Local Planning*, Working Paper 17, University of Bristol School for Advanced Urban Studies.

Gasson, R. (1973) 'Industry and migration of farmworkers', *Oxford Agrarian Studies*, 2, 141–60.

Gault, I. (1981) *Green Belt Policies in Development Plans*. Working Paper 41, Oxford Polytechnic Department of Town Planning.

Giggs, J.A. (1970) 'Fringe expansion and suburbanization around Nottingham: a metropolitan area approach', *East Midland Geographer*, 5, 9–18.

Gilder, I.M. (1979) 'Rural planning policies: an economic appraisal', *Progress in Planning*, 11, 213–271.

Gilder. I.M. (1980) 'Do we need key settlement policies?' *The Planner*, 66, 99–112.

Gilder, I.M. and McLaughlin, B.P. (1978) *Rural Communities in West Suffolk*, Chelmsford, Chelmer Institute of Higher Education.

Gilg, A.W. (1978) *Countryside Planning: The First Three Decades 1945–76*, Newton Abbot, David & Charles.

Gilg, A.W. (1978a) 'Needed: a new "Scott" Inquiry', *Town Planning Review*, 49, 353–61.

Gillon, S. (1981) 'Selling rural council houses', *Town and Country Planning*, 50, 115–17.

Glass, R. (1959) 'The evaluation of planning: some sociological considerations', *International Social Science Journal*, 2, 393–409.

Glasson, J. (1979) 'The nature and teaching of implementation in regional development and planning', in Minay, C. (ed.) (1979) *Implementation-Views from an Ivory Tower*, Department of Town Planning, Oxford Polytechnic.

Gloucestershire CC (1955) *County Development Plan*.

Gloucestershire CC (1979) *County Structure Plan: Submitted Written Statement*.

Glyn-Jones, A. (1979) *Rural Recovery: Has it Begun?*, Devon CC and University of Exeter.

Goodall, B. and Kirby, A. (eds) (1979) *Resources and Planning*, Oxford, Pergamon.

Grabow, S.J. and Haskin, A. (1973) 'Foundations for a radical concept of planning', *Journal of the American Institute of Planners*, 39, 106–7.

Grafton, D. (1980) *Planning for Remote Rural Areas: The Swiss Experience*, Discussion Paper 5, University of Southampton Department of Geography.

Green, D. (1977) 'Planners must recognize differences between town and country', *The Times*, 17 May.

Green, R.J. (1966) 'The remote countryside – a plan for contraction', *Planning Outlook*, 1, 17–37.

Green, R.J. (1971) *Country Planning: the Future of the Rural Regions*, Manchester University Press.

Green, R.J. (1980) 'Planning the rural sub-regions: a personal view', *Countryside Planning Yearbook*, 1, 67–85.

Green, R.J. and Ayton, J.B. (1967) 'Changes in the pattern of rural settlement', Paper presented to the Town Planning Institute Research Conference.

Gregory, D.G. (1970) *Green Belts and Development Control*, University of Birmingham, Centre for Urban and Regional Studies.

Gregory, D. (1973) 'Green belt policy and the conurbation', in Joyce, F.E. (ed.) (1973) *Metropolitan Development and Change: The West Midlands – A Policy Review*, London, Teakfield.

Gupta, S.P. and Hutton, J.P. (1968) *Economies of Scale in Local Government Services*, London, HMSO.

Gwent CC (1978) *County Structure Plan: Report of Survey*.

Gwent CC (1978) *County Structure Plan: Submitted Written Statement*.

Gwynedd CC (1980) *Merionnydd Structure Plan: Approved Written Statement.*
Gwynedd CC (1980a) *Dyffryn Conwy Structure Plan: Approved Written Statement.*
Gwynedd CC (1980b) *Caernarvonshire Structure Plan: Approved Written Statement.*
Gwynedd CC (1980c) *Anglesey Structure Plan: Approved Written Statement.*
Gyford, J. (1976) *Local Politics in Britain*, London, Croom Helm.
Hahn, A.J. (1970) 'Planning in rural areas', *Journal, American Institute of Planners*, 34, 44–9.
Haines, G.H. (1973) *Whose Countryside?* London, Dent.
Hall, P. (1974) *Urban and Regional Planning*, Harmondsworth, Penguin.
Hall, P. (1979) 'Whatever happened to planning?', *New Society*, 17 May, 384–5.
Hall, P., Thomas, R., Gracey, H. and Drewett, R. (1973) *The Containment of Urban England*, London, Allen & Unwin.
Halpern, J.M. (1967) *The Changing Village Community*, Englewood Cliffs, NJ, Prentice-Hall.
Hambleton, R. (1981) 'Policy planning systems and implementation: some implications for planning theory', Paper presented to the Planning Theory in the 1980s conference, Oxford Polytechnic, April.
Hamnett, C. and Williams, P. (1979) *Gentrification in London 1961–71: An Empirical and Theoretical Analysis of Social Change*, Centre for Urban and Regional Studies, University of Birmingham.
Hamnett, C. and Williams, P. (1980) 'Social change in London: a study of gentrification', *London Journal*, 6, 51–6.
Hampshire CC (1955) *County Development Plan.*
Hampshire CC (1977) *South Hampshire Structure Plan: Approved Written Statement.*
Hampshire CC (1979) *Coast and Conservation Policy.*
Hampshire CC (1980) *Mid Hampshire Structure Plan: Approved Written Statement.*
Hampshire CC (1980a) *NE Hampshire Structure Plan: Approved Written Statement.*
Hampshire CC and Mass Observations Ltd (1966) *Village Life in Hampshire*, Winchester, Hampshire CC.
Hancock, T. (1976) 'Planning in rural settlements', *Town and Country Planning*, 44, 520–23.
Hancock, T. (1976a) 'Planning and community clusters', *Town and Country Planning*, 44, 264–8.
Hancock, T. (1978) 'A benign future for planning', *Built Environment*, 4, 315–21.
Hancock, T. and McCormack, R. (1976) 'Cluster housing at Broom Park, Dartington, Devon', *Architects Journal*, 164, 299–305.
Harman, R.G. (1978) 'Retailing in rural areas: a case study in Norfolk', *Geoforum*, 9, 107–26.
Haynes, R.M., Bentham, C.G., Spencer, M.B. and Spratley, J.M. (1978) *Community Hospital Planning Study: Summary Report*, Norwich, University of East Anglia.
Healey, P. (1979) 'On implementation: some thoughts on the issues raised by planners' current interest in implementation', in Minay, C. (ed.) (1979) *Implementation – Views from an Ivory Tower*, Oxford Polytechnic Department of Town Planning.
Healey, P. (1980) *The Implementation of Selective Restraint Policies*, Working Paper 45, Oxford Polytechnic Department of Town Planning.
Healey, P., Evans, S. and Terry, S. (1980) *The Implementation of Selective Restraint Policy: Approaches to Land Release for Local Needs*, Oxford Polytechnic Department of Town Planning.
Hereford and Worcester CC (1975) *Worcestershire Structure Plan: Approved Written Statement.*
Hereford and Worcester CC (1976) *Herefordshire Structure Plan: Approved Written Statement.*

Hereford and Worcester CC (1978) *Rural Community Development Project Report*.

Hereford and Worcester Rural Community Development Project (1978) *Report of the Working Party*, Hereford and Worcester CC.

Hereford and Worcester Rural Community Development Project (1980) *Schools Study 1977-9*, Hereford and Worcester CC.

Hereford and Worcester Rural Community Development Project (1981) *Wyeside Community Project 1978-80*, Hereford and Worcester CC.

Hereford and Worcester Rural Community Development Project (1981a) *Publicity Leaflet for Wyeside Community Project, 1978-80*.

Herington, J. and Evans, D. (1979) *The Spatial Pattern of Movement in 'Key' and 'Non-key' Settlements*, University of Loughborough Department of Geography.

Hertfordshire CC (1958) *County Development Plan*.

Hertfordshire CC (1971) *County Development Plan: First Review*.

Hertfordshire CC (1976) *County Structure Plan: Written Statement*.

Hertfordshire CC (1979) *County Structure Plan: Approved Written Statement*.

Hertfordshire CC (1979) *Countywide Rural Settlements Study*.

Hertfordshire CC (1979a) *Countywide Housing Study*.

Hertfordshire CC (1980) *County Structure Plan: Alterations 1980*.

Hibbs, J. (1975) *The Bus and Coach Industry: Its Economics and Organization*, Oxford Pergamon.

Hindess, B. (1971) *The Decline of Working Class Politics*, London, McGibbon & Kee.

Hirschmann, A.O. (1958) *The Strategy of Economic Development*, Newhaven, Yale University Press.

HM Treasury (1976) 'Rural depopulation', Report of the Inter-departmental Working Group, London.

Hoath, D. (1978) *Council Housing*, London, Sweet & Maxwell.

Hobbs, F.D. and Doling, J.F. (1981) *Planning for Engineers and Surveyors*, Oxford, Pergamon.

Hodge, G. (1966) 'Do villages grow? – some perspectives and predictions', *Rural Sociology*, 31, 183-96.

Hodge, I. and Whitby, M. (1981) *Rural Employment: Trends, Options, Choices*, London, Methuen.

Hood, N. and Young, S. (1976) US investment in Scotland – aspects of the branch factory syndrome', *Scottish Journal of Political Economy*, 23, 279-94.

Hookway, R. and Garvie, A. (1978) 'National Park plans' *The Planner*, 64, 20-3.

Horsham DC (1978) *Steyning, Bramber and Upper Beeding Local Plan 1978-88*.

Horsham DC (1979) *Horsham Area District Plan: Possible Strategies Policy Option Report*.

Horsham DC (1980) *Horsham Area District Plan: Public Participation Report*.

Horsham DC (1980a) *Horsham Area District Plan: Implementation and Monitoring Report*.

Horsham DC (1980b) *Horsham Area Interim District Plan*.

Horton, J. (1970) 'Order and conflict theories of social problems as competing ideologies', in Curtis, J.E. and Peters, J.W. (eds) (1970) *The Sociology of Knowledge*, London, Duckworth.

House, J.W. (1965) *Rural North East England 1951-61*, University of Newcastle upon Tyne Department of Geography.

Hughes, C.G. (1980) 'Key settlements in rural areas', *Landscape Planning*, 7(4), 394-6.

Humberside CC (1979) *County Structure Plan: Approved Written Statement*.

Huntingdon DC (1976) *Sawtry Village Plan*.

Huntingdonshire CC (1959) *County Development Plan: First Review*.

Jackson, M. and Nolan, M. (1971) 'Threshold analysis: concept, criticisms and current usage', *Chartered Surveyor*, 104, 288-93.

Jackson, M. and Nolan, M. (1973) 'Threshold analysis II: urban growth and programming', *Chartered Surveyor*, 105, 308–15.

Jenkins, W.I. (1978) *Policy Analysis: A Political and Organisational Perspective*, Oxford, Martin Robertson.

Johnston, R.J. (1966) 'Central places and the settlement pattern', *AAAG*, 56, 541–9.

Jones, P. and Oliphant, R. (eds) (1976) *Local Shops: Problems and Prospects*, Reading Unit for Retail Planning Information.

Joyce, F.E. (ed.) (1973) *Metropolitan Development and Change: The West Midlands – A Policy Review*, London, Teakfield.

JURUE (1974) *Land Availability and the Residential Land Conversion Process*, Joint Unit for Research into the Urban Environment, University of Aston.

JURUE (1977) *Planning and Land Availability*, Joint Unit for Research into the Urban Environment, University of Aston.

Keeble, L. (ed.) (1969) *Principles and Practice of Town and Country Planning*, London, Estates Gazette.

Kent CC (1958) *County Development Plan*.

Kent CC (1972) *County Development Plan: First Review*.

Kent CC (1976) *County Structure Plan: Report of Survey*.

Kent CC (1980) *County Structure Plan: Approved Written Statement*.

Kingham, M. (1981) 'Create your own housing', *The Planner*, 67, 68–9.

Kirby, D., Olsen, J.A., Sjoholt, P. and Stolen, J. (1981) *The Norwegian Aid Programme to Shops in Sparsely Populated Areas*, Oslo, Norwegian Fund for Market and Distribution Research.

Kirkoswald and Lazonby Parish Councils (1981) *Kirkoswald and Lazonby Parishes: Past, Present, Future*.

Klein, R. and Lewis, J. (1977) 'Advice and dissent in British Government : the case of the special advisers', *Policy and Politics*, September, 1–25.

Knox, P. and Cottam, B. (1981) 'Rural deprivation in Scotland: a preliminary assessment', *TESG*, 72, 162–75.

Knox, P. and Cullen, J. (1981) 'Town planning and the internal survival mechanisms of urbanised capitalism', *Area*, 13, 183–8.

Kotter, H. (1962) 'Economic and social implications of rural industrialization', *International Labour Review*, 86, 1–14.

Kovalev, S.A. (1968) 'Problems in the Soviet geography of rural settlement', *Soviet Geography*, 9, 641–51.

Kovalev, S.A. (1972) 'Transformation of rural settlements in the Soviet Union', *Geoforum*, 9, 33–45.

Kyllingstad, R. (1975) 'Tanker om landsbygdsplanlegging', *Plan og Arbeid*, 6, 222–6.

Labour Party National Executive Committee (1979) *Rural Areas: An Interim Statement*.

Lake District Special Planning Board (1979) *Draft Settlement Policy Statement: Eden*.

Lancashire CC (1962) *County Development Plan: First Review*.

Lancashire CC (1980) *North-east Lancashire Structure Plan: Approved Written Statement*.

Lancashire CC (1980a) *Central and North Lancashire Structure Plan: Submitted Written Statement*.

Lassey, W.R. (1977) *Planning in Rural Environments*, New York, McGraw-Hill.

Leach, S. (1980) 'Organizational interests and inter-organizational behaviour in town planning', *Town Planning Review*, 51, 286–99.

Leach, S. and Moore, N. (1979) 'County/district relations in Shire and Metropolitan counties in the field of town and country planning: a comparison', *Policy and Politics*, 7, 165–79.

Lee, J.M. (1963) *Social Leaders and Public Persons, A Study of Country Government* in Cheshire Since 1888, Oxford, Clarendon.

Lefaver, S. (1978) 'A new framework for rural planning', *Urban Land*, 37, 7–14.

Lefebvre, H. (1978) 'Reflections on the politics of space', in Peet, R. (ed.) (1978) *Radical Geography: Alternative Viewpoints on Contemporary Social Issues*, London, Methuen.

Leicestershire CC (1974) *County Structure Plan: Report of Survey*.

Leicestershire CC (1976) *County Structure Plan: Approved Written Statement*.

Leominster DC (1979) *Kington District Plan: Written Statement*.

Levin, P.H. (1976) *Government and the Planning Process*, London, Allen & Unwin.

Levitt, R. (1980) *Implementing Public Policy*, London, Croom Helm.

Lewan, N. (1969) 'Hidden urbanization in Sweden', *TESG*, 60, 193–7.

Lewis, G.J. (1981) 'Changes and continuity in the rural community – a geographical perspective,' in Bowler, I.R. (ed.) (1981) *Social Problems in Rural Communities*, Rural Geography Study Group, IBG Annual Symposium, University of Leicester.

Lewis, J. and Flynn, R. (1978) *The Implementation of Urban and Regional Planning Policies*, final Report of a feasibility study for the Department of the Environment .

Lindsey, Lincolnshire CC (1955) *County Development Plan*.

Lindsey CC (1973) *Communities in Rural Lindsey*.

Lipman, V.D. (1952) 'Town and country: the study of service centres and their areas of influence', *Public Administration*, 30, 203–14.

Loew, S. (1979) *Local Planning*, London, Pembridge.

Lösch, A. (1938–9) 'The nature of economic regions', *Southern Economic Journal*, 5, 71–8.

Lowe, P. (1975) 'The environmentalist lobby', *Built Environment Quarterly*, 1, 73–6; 158–61; 235–8.

Lowe, P. (1977) 'Amenity and equity: a review of local environmental pressure groups in Britain', *Environment and Planning*, 9, 35–58.

Lowenthal, D. and Comitas, L. (1962) 'Emigration and depopulation: some neglected aspects of population geography', *Geographical Review*, 52, 195–210.

Lucey, D.I.F. and Kaldor, D. (1969) *Rural Industrialization: the Impact of Industrialization on Two Rural Communities in Western Ireland*, London, Chapman.

McAuslan, P. (1979) 'The ideologies of planning law', *Urban Law and Policy*, 2, 1–23.

McCallum, J.D. and Adams, J.G.L. (1981) 'Employment and unemployment statistics for rural areas', *Town Planning Review*, 52, 157–66.

McCleery, A. (1979) *Rural Depopulation: An Introductory Paper*, paper presented to the Population and Employment in Rural Areas conference, Inverness. Planning Exchange Forum Report 15, Glasgow.

McDougall, G. (1979) 'Social planning implementation: the need for theoretical practice', in Minay, C. (ed.) (1979) *Implementation – Views from an Ivory Tower*, Oxford Polytechnic Department of Town Planning.

MacEwen, A. and MacEwen, M. (1981) *National Parks: Conservation or Cosmetics*, London, Allen & Unwin.

MacEwen, M. (ed.) (1976) *Future Landscapes*, London, Chatto & Windus.

MacGregor, M. (1976) 'Village life: facts and myths', *Town and Country Planning*, 44, 524–7.

McLaughlin, B.P. (1976) 'Rural settlement planning: a new approach', *Town and Country Planning*, 44, 156–60.

McLaughlin, B.P. (1976a) 'The future of the village: a planner's view', *The Village*, 31, 54–7.

McLaughlin, B.P. (1979) 'A new role for rural community councils', *Town and Country Planning*, 48, 124–5.

McLaughlin, B.P. (1981) 'Rural deprivation', *The Planner*, 67, 31–3.

McLoughlin, J.B. (1969) *Urban and Regional Planning: A Systems Approach*, London, Faber & Faber.

Malisz, B. (1969) 'Implications of threshold theory for urban and regional planning', *Journal of the Town Planning Institute*, 55, 108-10.

Malvern Hills DC (1980) *Kempsey District Plan: Written Statement*.

Manson, K. (1979) 'Reasons for refusal of planning permission', *Building Trades Journal*, 177, 14.

Manson, K. (1979a) 'Preserving the planning permission to develop a site', *Building Trades Journal*, 178, 22-36.

Martin, I. (1976) 'Rural communities', in Cherry, G.E. (ed.) (1976) *Rural Planning Problems*,London, Leonard Hill.

Martin and Vorhees Associates (1981) *Review of Rural Settlement Policies, 1945-80*, London, Martin & Vorhees Associates.

Mayhew, A. (1971) 'Agrarian reform in West Germany', *Transactions IBG*, 52, 61-76.

Mid Glamorgan CC (1978) *County Structure Plan: Submitted Written Statement*.

Minay, C. (ed.) (1979) *Implementation – Views from an Ivory Tower*, Oxford Polytechnic Department of Town Planning.

Minay, C. (1979a) 'Four types of planning implementation', in Minay, C. (ed.) (1979) *Implementation-Views from an Ivory Tower*, Oxford Polytechnic Department of Town Planning.

Ministry of Agriculture, Fisheries and Food (1967) *The Changing Structure of the Agriculture Labour Force, 1945-65*, London, HMSO.

Ministry of Agriculture, Fisheries and Food (1977) *Agricultural Labour in England and Wales*, London, HMSO.

Ministry of Housing (1967) *Circular 53*, London, HMSO.

Ministry of Housing and Local Government (1955) *Circular 42*, London, HMSO.

Ministry of Housing and Local Government (1967) *Settlement in the Countryside: A Planning Method*, Planning Bulletin 8, London, HMSO.

Ministry of Housing and Local Government (1970) *Development Plans: A Manual of Form and Content*, London, HMSO.

Ministry of Town and Country Planning (1948) *Circular 40*, London, HMSO.

Ministry of Town and Country Planning (1948) *Circular 59*, London, HMSO.

Ministry of Town and Country Planning (1950) *Siting of New Houses in Country Districts*, London, HMSO.

Mitchell, C.B. (1976) *Some Social Aspects of Public Passenger Transport*, paper presented to symposium on unconventional bus services, Transport and Road Research Laboratory, Crowthorne.

Mitchell, G.D. (1950) 'Depopulation and rural social structure', *Sociological Review*, 42, 69-85.

Morley, S. (1981) 'Positive planning and direct development by local authorities', *Town Planning Review*, 52, 298-306.

Morris, H. (1925) *The Village College – Being a Memorandum on the Provision of Educational and Social Facilities for the Countryside with Special Reference to Cambridgeshire*, Cambridge University Press.

Morris, H. (1942) 'Education and the community', in D. Needham (ed,) (1942) *The Teacher of Nations*, Cambridge University Press.

Morrison, P.A. and Wheeler, J.P. (1976) 'Rural renaissance in America?', *Population Bulletin*, 31, 1-27.

Moseley, M.J. (1973) 'The impact of growth centres in rural regions: I An analysis of spatial patterns in Brittany', *Regional Studies*, 7, 57-75.

Moseley, M.J. (1973a) 'The impact of growth centres in rural regions: II An analysis of spatial flows in East Anglia', *Regional Studies*, 7, 77-94.

Moseley, M.J. (1974) *Growth Centres in Spatial Planning*, Oxford, Pergamon.

Moseley, M.J. (1977) 'A look at rural transport and accessibility', *The Village*, 23, 33–5.

Moseley, M.J. (ed.) (1978) *Social Issues in Rural Norfolk*, Norwich, University of East Anglia.

Moseley, M.J. (1979) *Accessibility: The Rural Challenge*, London, Methuen.

Moseley, M.J. (1980) 'Is rural deprivation really rural?', *The Planner*, 66, 97.

Moseley, M.J. (1980a) *'Rural Development and its Relevance to the Inner City Debate'*, SSRC Inner Cities Working Paper 9.

Moseley. M.J., Harman, R.G., Coles, O.B. and Spencer, M.B. (1977) *Rural Transport and Accessibility*, University of East Anglia Centre of East Anglian Studies.

Moseley, M.J. and Smith, P.R. (1979) 'Hungary: urban and rural planning', *Town and Country Planning*, 48, 85–7.

Moss, G. (1979) *The village – life or death*, Paper presented to the Future for Rural Communities conference, Losehill Hall, Castleton, Derbyshire.

Moss, G. (1980) *Reviving Rural Europe*, Strasbourg, Council of Europe.

Moss, G. (1981) *Britain's Wasting Acres*, London, Architectural Press.

Muir, R. and Paddison, R. (1981) *Politics, Geography and Behaviour*, London, Methuen.

Myrdal, G. (1957) *Economic Theory and Underdeveloped Regions*, London, Duckworth.

Nath, S.K. (1973) *A Perspective of Welfare Economics*, London, Macmillan.

National Association of Local Councils (1979) *Rural Life: Change or Decay*, London, NALC.

National Council for Voluntary Organizations (1981) *A Rural Strategy*, NCVO, London.

National Council for Voluntary Organizations (1980) *Towards a Rural Strategy*, London, NCVO.

National Extension College (1980) *Village Action Kit*, Cambridge, National Extension College.

Neate, S. (1981) 'Planning for change in a rural community', Paper presented to the PTRC Summer Annual Meeting, University of Warwick.

Needham, D. (1942) *The Teacher of Nations*, Cambridge University Press.

Newby, H. (1980) *Green and Pleasant Land? Social Change in Rural England*, Harmondsworth, Pelican.

Newby, H., Bell, C., Rose, D. and Saunders, P. (1978) *Property, Paternalism and Power*, London, Hutchinson.

Newton, K. (1976) *Second City Politics: Democratic Processes and Decision-Making in Birmingham*, Oxford University Press.

Norborg, K. (ed.) (1962) *IGU Symposium – Urban Geography*, Lund, IGU.

Norfolk CC (1972) *Interim Settlement Policy*.

Norfolk CC (1976) *The North Walsham Area*.

Norfolk CC (1976a) *County Structure Plan – Report of Survey*.

Norfolk CC (1977) *County Structure Plan: Draft Written Statement*.

Norfolk CC (1979) *Rural Areas in England and Wales*.

Norfolk CC (1980) *County Structure Plan: Approved Written Statement*.

North Hertfordshire DC (1980) *North Hertfordshire District Plan: Draft Written Statement*.

North York Moors National Park Committee (1979) *North York Moors Local Plan: Technical Report of Survey*.

North York Moors National Park Committee (1980) *North York Moors Interim Local plan*.

North Riding CC (1963) *County Development Plan: First Review*.

North Yorkshire CC (1980) *County Structure Plan: Approved Written Statement.*

Northamptonshire CC (1965) *A Plan for Rural Development.*

Northamptonshire CC (1977) *County Structure Plan: Report of Survey.*

Northamptonshire CC (1977a) *County Structure Plan: Submitted Written Statement.*

Northumberland CC (1966) *County Development Plan: First Review.*

Northumberland CC (1969) *Rural Northumberland Report 2: A Policy for Growth and Concentration.*

Northumberland CC (1980) *County Structure Plan: Approved Written Statement.*

Nottinghamshire CC (1959) *County Development Plan.*

Nottinghamshire CC (1966) *Plan for Rural Nottinghamshire.*

Nottinghamshire CC (1980) *County Structure Plan: Approved Written Statement.*

O'Farrell, P.N. (1970) 'A multivariate model of the spacing of urban centres in the Irish Republic', in Stephens, N. and Glassock, R.E. (eds) (1970), *Irish Geographical Studies*, Belfast, Queens University Department of Geography.

Olsson, G. (1974) 'Servitude and inequality in spatial planning: ideology and methodology in conflict', *Antipode*, 6, 16–21, reprinted in Peet, R. (ed.) (1978) *Radical Geography: Alternative Viewpoints on Contemporary Social Issues*, London, Methuen.

O'Riordan, T. (1976) *Environmentalism*, London, Pion.

Owen, S. (1980) 'Assessing the effects of local plans', *Gloucestershire Papers in Local and Rural Planning*, 9.

Oxfordshire CC (1975) *County Structure Plan: Report of Survey.*

Oxfordshire CC (1979) *County Structure Plan: Approved Written Statement.*

Pahl, R.E. (1965) *Urbs in Rure*, London School of Economics Geographical Papers, 2.

Pahl, R.E. (1965a) 'Class and community in English commuter villages', *Sociologia Ruralis*, 5, 5–23.

Pahl, R.E, (1966) 'Commuting and social change in rural areas', *Official Architecture and Planning*, July, 996–9.

Pallot, J. (1977) *Some Preliminary Thoughts on Soviet Rural Settlement Planning*, University of Leeds School of Geography.

Parsons, D.J. (1980) *Rural Gentrification: The Influence of Rural Settlement Planning Policies*, University of Sussex Department of Geography.

Parsons, T. (1966) *Societies: Evolutionary and Comparative Perspectives*, New York, McGraw-Hill.

Peak Park Joint Planning Board (1976) *Peak District National Park Structure Plan: Report of Survey.*

Peak Park Joint Planning Board (1980) *Peak Park Structure Plan: Approved Written Statement.*

Peake, H. (1916–18) 'The regrouping of rural population', *Town Planning Review*, 7, 243–50.

Peake, H. (1922) *The English Village*, London, Benn.

Pearce, J. and Hopwood, S. (1981) 'Create your own jobs – 2 Community based initiatives', *The Planner*, 67, 64–7.

Peel, J. and Sayer, M. (1973) *Towards a Rural Policy and its Application to Norfolk*, Norwich, the authors.

Peet, R. (ed.) (1978) *Radical Geography: Alternative Viewpoints on Contemporary Social Issues*, London, Methuen.

Penfold, S.F. (1974) *Housing Problems of Local People in Rural Pressure Areas*, University of Sheffield Department of Town and Country Planning.

Peregrine, T. (1979) 'The future of rural communities', Paper presented to the Future for Rural Communities conference, Losehill Hall, Castleton, Derbyshire.

Pettigrew, A. (1972) 'Information control as a power resource', *Sociology*, 6, 187–204.

Philip, A.B., Pincham, R. and Tyler, P. (1978) *A New Deal for Rural Britain*, London, Liberal Publications Department.

Phillips, A. (1976) 'Too much planning – or too little?', in MacEwen, M. (ed.) (1976) *Future Landscapes*, London, Chatto & Windus.

Phillips, D.R. and Williams, A.M. (1982) *Rural Housing and the Public Sector*, Farnborough, Gower.

Piatier, A. and Madec, J. (1977) 'Comment et pourquoi definir un espace rural?', *Economie Rurale*, 118, 3–13.

Pinker, R. (1971) *Social Theory and Social Policy*, London, Heinemann.

Pitt, P.H. (1979) 'Towards a simplified code of building control', *Royal Society of Health Journal*, 99, 3–7; 22.

The Planner (1980) 'Countryside conference report', *The Planner*, 66, 102–3.

Planning (1978) 'Problems of rural decline throughout the Continent', *Planning*, 289, 5.

Planning Advisory Group (1965) *The Future of Development Plans*, London, HMSO.

Pocock, D. and Hudson, R. (1978) *Images of the Urban Environment*, London, Macmillan.

Popper, K.R. (ed.) (1963) *Conjectures and Refutations*, London, Routledge & Kegan Paul.

Popper, K.R. (1968) *The Logic of Scientific Discovery*, London, Hutchinson.

Popper, K.R. (1969) *The Poverty of Historicism*, London, Routledge & Kegan Paul.

Popper, K.R. (1972) *Objective Knowledge: An Evolutionary Approach*, Oxford, Clarendon.

Powys CC (1977) *Structure Plan Topic Study 4: Settlement Pattern*.

Powys CC (1979) *County Structure Plan: Submitted Written Statement*.

Preece, R.A. (1981) *Patterns of Development Control in the Cotswold Area of Outstanding Natural Beauty*, Research Paper 27, University of Oxford School of Geography.

Pressman, J. and Wildavsky, A. (1973) *Implementation*, Berkeley, University of California Press.

Prochownikowa, A. (1975) 'Urbanizacja wsi czy deruraliza cja?', *Czasopismo Geogficzne*, 46, 39–40.

Radford, E. (1970) *The New Villagers*, London, Cass.

Ratcliffe, J. (1974) *An Introduction to Town and Country Planning*, London, Hutchinson.

Rawson, J. (1981) 'The impact of settlement policies of concentration and dispersal in rural Britain', Paper presented to the PTRC Summer Annual Meeting, University of Warwick.

Regional Municipality of Ottawa – Carleton (1974) *Official Plan: Ottawa – Carleton Planning Area*.

Rhodes, R.A.W. (1977) 'A rose by any other name: five books in search of policy analysis', *Local Government Studies*, 3, 71–83.

Rhodes, R.A.W. (1980) 'Somes myths in central-local relations', *Town Planning Review*, 51, 270–85.

Richmondshire DC (1981) *Redmire Village Plan*.

Riew, J. (1966) 'Economies of scale in high school operation', *Review of Economics and Statistics*, 48, 322–8.

Roberts, B.K. (1977) *Rural Settlement in Britain*, London, Hutchinson.

Roberts, M. (1974) *An Introduction to Town Planning Techniques*, London, Hutchinson.

Robertson, J. (1978) 'The politics and economics of HE and SHE', *Built Environment*, 4, 266–74.

Rodgers, A. (1970) 'Migration and industrial development: the Southern Italian experience', *Economic Geography*, 46, 111–35.

Rogers, A.W. (1976) 'Rural housing', in Cherry, G.E. (ed.) (1976) *Rural Planning Problems*, London, Leonard Hill.

Rogers, A.W. (ed.) (1978) *Urban Growth, Farmland Losses and Planning*, Rural Geography Study Group, Institute of British Geographers.

Rogers, A.W. (1981) 'Housing in the national parks', *Town and Country Planning*, 50, 193–5.

Rose, D., Saunders, P., Newby, H. and Bell, C. (1978) 'Landownership and the politics of rural areas', in Walker, A. (ed.) (1978) *Rural Poverty: Poverty, Deprivation and Planning in Rural Areas*, London, Child Poverty Action Group.

Rose, D., Saunders, P., Newby, H. and Bell, C. (1979) 'The economic and political basis of rural deprivation: a case study', in Shaw, J.M. (ed.) (1979) *Rural Deprivation and Planning*, Norwich, GeoBooks.

Rose, E. (1974) 'Philosophy and purpose of planning', in Bruton, M.J. (ed.) (1974) *The Spirit and Purpose of Planning*, London, Hutchinson.

Royal Town Planning Institute (1979) *Making Planning More Effective*, London, RTPI.

Runciman, W.G. (1972) *Relative Deprivation and Social Justice*, Harmondsworth, Penguin.

Russell, A.J. (1975) *The Village in Myth and Reality*, London, Chester House.

Salop CC (1977) *County Structure Plan: Report of Survey*.

Salop CC (1980) *County Structure Plan: Approved Written Statement*.

Saville, J. (1957) *Depopulation in England and Wales, 1851–1951*, London, Routledge & Kegan Paul.

Scott-Miller, R. (1976) *Housing in Rural Areas*, internal discussion paper, Community Council for Devon.

Self, P. and Storing, H. (1962) *The State and the Farmer*, London, Allen & Unwin.

Self, P. (1972) *Administrative Theories and Politics*, London, Allen & Unwin.

Semple, R.K. and Golledge, R.G. (1970) 'An analysis of entropy changes in a settlement pattern over time', *Economic Geography*, 46, 157–60.

Sewell, W.R.D. and Coppock, J.T. (1977) *Public Participation in Planning*, Chichester, Wiley.

Shankland, G. (1981) 'Create your own jobs – 1 The great uncounted: the role of the informal economy', *The Planner*, 67, 62–3.

Sharp, T. (1953) 'The English village', in Sharp, T. *et al.* (1953) *Design in Town and Country*, London, HMSO.

Sharp, T., Gibberd, F. and Holford, W.G. (1953) *Design in Town and Country*, London, HMSO.

Shaw, J.M. (1976) 'Can we afford villages?', *Built Environment*, 2, 135–7.

Shaw, J.M. (1976a) 'Thresholds for village foodshops', in Jones, P. and Oliphant, R. (eds) (1976) *Local Shops: Problems and Prospects*, Reading, Unit for Planning Retail Information.

Shaw, J.M. (1978) 'The social implications of village development', in Moseley, M.J. (ed.) (1978) *Social Issues in Rural Norfolk*, Norwich, University of East Anglia.

Shaw, J.M. (ed.) (1979) *Rural Deprivation and Planning*, Norwich, GeoBooks.

Shaw, M. and Stockford, R. (1979) 'The role of statutory agencies in rural areas: planning and social services', in Shaw, J.M. (ed.) (1979) *Rural Deprivation and Planning*, Norwich, GeoBooks.

Shucksmith, M. (1980) 'Local interests in a national park', *Town and Country Planning*, 49, 418–21.

Shucksmith, D.M. (1981) *No Homes for Locals?*, Farnborough, Gower.

Sigurdson, J. (1976) 'Development of rural areas in India and China', *Ambio*, 5, 98–108.

370 *An Introduction to Rural Settlement Planning*

Silverman, D. (1970) *The Theory of Organization*, London, Heinemann.

Simmie, J.M. (1971) 'Public participation: a case study from Oxfordshire', *Journal of the Royal Town Planning Institute*, 57, 161–2.

Simmie, J.M. (1974) *Citizens in Conflict: the Sociology of Town Planning*, London, Hutchinson.

Simon, H.A., Smithberg, D.W. and Thompson, V.A. (1968) *Public Administration*, New York, Knopf.

Skinner, D.N. (1976) *A Situation Report on Green Belts in Scotland*, Countryside Commission for Scotland, Edinburgh.

Smailes, A.E. (1944) 'The urban hierarchy in England and Wales', *Geography*, 29, 41–51.

Smigielski, K. (1978) *Self-Supporting Co-operative Village*, Coalville, Building and Social Housing Foundation.

Smith, D.M. (1977) *Human Geography: A Welfare Approach*, London, Arnold.

Smith, R.J. (1977) 'Planning for employment in rural areas', unpublished thesis, London School of Economics.

Social Science Research Council (1979) *Central–Local Government Relationships*, London, SSRC.

Somerset CC (1958) *County Development Plan*.

Somerset CC (1964) *County Development Plan: First Review*.

Somerset CC (1979) *County Structure Plan: Submitted Written Statement*.

South Glamorgan CC (1977) *County Structure Plan: Approved Written Statement*.

South Herefordshire DC (1980) *A District Plan for the Rural West: Draft Brief*.

South Norfolk DC (1980) *West Costessey, Wensum and York Valleys Local Plan*.

South Pembrokeshire DC (1976) *Towards a Settlement Policy*.

South Pembrokeshire District Council (1977) *St Florence Conservation Area*.

Staffordshire CC (1978) *County Structure Plan: Approved Written Statement*.

Standing Conference of Rural Community Councils (1978) *The Decline in Rural Services*, London, National Council of Social Service.

Standing Conference of Rural Community Councils (1979) *Whose Countryside?*, London, NCVO.

Stephens, N. and Glassock, R.E. (eds) (1970) *Irish Geographical Studies*, Queens University Belfast, Department of Geography.

Stewart, J. (1980) 'Inter-organizational relationships: an introduction', *Town Planning Review*, 51, 257–60.

Stockford, R. (1978) 'Social services provision in rural Norfolk', in Moseley, M.J. (ed.) (1978) *Social Issues in Rural Norfolk*, Norwich, University of East Anglia.

Stratford-on-Avon DC (1978) *Avon Valley Local (Subject Plan); Written Statement*.

Stratford-on-Avon DC (1978a) *Bishops Itchington Local (District) Plan: Written Statement*.

Stratford-on-Avon DC (1979) *Southam Local (District) Plan: Written Statement*.

Suddards, R.W. (1979) 'Section 52 agreements: a case for new legislation', *Journal of Planning and Environment Law*, October, 661–7.

Suffolk CC (1979) *County Structure Plan: Approved Written Statement*.

Surrey CC (1972) *County Development Plan – First Review*.

Surrey CC (1980) *County Structure Plan: Approved Written Statement*.

Teesdale DC (1981) *Ronaldkirk Village Plan*.

Thijsse, J.P. (1968) 'Second thoughts about a rural pattern for the future in the Netherlands', *Papers and Proceedings, Regional Science Association*, 20, 69–75.

Thomas, C. and Winyard, S. (1979) 'Rural incomes', in Shaw, J.M. (ed.) (1979) *Rural Deprivation and Planning*, Norwich, GeoBooks.

Thomas, D. (1970) *London's Green Belt*, London, Faber & Faber.

Thomas, D. (1972) 'Problems in Planning the rural-urban fringe, with special reference to London', *Geographia Polonica*, 24, 81–94.

Thorburn, A. (1971) *Planning Villages*, London, Estates Gazette.

Thorns, D.C. (1968) 'The changing system of social stratification', *Sociologia Ruralis*, 8, 161–78.

Tilling, A. (1980) 'Rural planning at district and regional level: constraints, possibilities and achievements in the 1970s', in Cant, G. (ed.) (1980) *People and Planning in Rural Communities*, Christchurch, NZ, University of Canterbury.

Torridge DC (1980) *Rural Areas Study: Preliminary Findings*.

Tourism and Recreation Research Unit (1981) *The Economy of Rural Communities in the National Parks of England and Wales*, The Tourism and Recreation Research Unit, Edinburgh.

Townend, C.B. (1960) 'The economics of waste water treatment', *Proceedings, Institute of Civil Engineers*, 15, 209–20.

Townsend, P. (1979) *Poverty in the UK*, Harmondsworth, Penguin.

Toyne, P. (1974) *Organization Location and Behaviour: Decision-Making in Economic Geography*, London, Macmillan.

Turner, R.K. and Collis, C. (1977) *The Economics of Planning*, London, Macmillan.

Van Hulten, M.H.M. (1969) 'Plan and reality in the Ijsselmeerpolders', *TESG*, 60, 67–77.

Van Meter, D.S. and Van Horn, C.E. (1975) 'The policy implementation process: a conceptual framework', *Administration and Society*, 6, 445–88.

Venner, D.G. (1976) 'The village has a future', *The Village*, 31, 39–41.

Voluntary Action Cumbria (1974) *Rural Communities Project Report*.

Voskresensky, L. (1976) 'Soviet village resettlement', *Town and Country Planning*, 44, 535–7.

Walker, A. (ed.) (1978) *Rural Poverty: Poverty, Deprivation and Planning in Rural Areas*, London, Child Poverty Action Group.

Wallace, D.B. (1981) 'Rural policy: a review article', *Town Planning Review*, 52, 215–22.

Wallace, D.B. and Drudy, P.J. (1975) *Social Problems of Rural Communities*, Agricultural Adjustment Unit, University of Newcastle upon Tyne.

Wannop, V. (1980) 'Scottish planning in practice: four distinctive characteristics', *The Planner*, 66, 64–5.

Wansdyke DC (1980) *Norton-Radstock and Environs District Plan: Draft Written Statement*.

Warford, J.J. (1969) *The South Atcham Scheme: An Economic Appraisal*, London, HMSO.

Warren, D. (1980) 'The countryside tomorrow', *Town and Country Planning*, 49, 182–4.

Warrington, R. (1978) 'Rural deprivation – out of sight, out of mind', *District Councils Review*, November, 245.

Warwick DC (1978) *Lapworth District Plan: Statement on Public Participation and Consultations Appendices*.

Warwick DC (1980) *Lapworth District Plan: Written Statement*.

Warwickshire CC (1966) *County Development Plan: An Interim Policy Statement*.

Warwickshire CC (1973) *County Structure Plan: Supplementary Report No. 5: Rural Settlements*.

Warwickshire CC (1975) *County Structure Plan: Approved Written Statement*.

Warwickshire CC (1980) *County Structure Plan: Alterations No. 3: Reviewed Policies and Proposals*.

Warwickshire Joint Planning Committee (1935) *Town and Country Planning in Warwickshire*.

Watts, P.A. (1980) 'The new block grant and controls over local authority capital payments', *Local Government Studies*, 6, 27–30.

Wear Valley DC (1981) *Countryside Management Study for the River Wear*.

Webber, R. and Craig, J. (1978) *Socio-economic Classification of Local Authority Areas*, Office of Population, Censuses and Surveys, Studies on Medical and Population Subjects 35, London, HMSO.

West Devon DC (1981) *Tavistock and District Local Plan: Issues Report*.

West Dorset DC (1976) *Charmouth Village Plan*.

West Norfolk DC (1980) *The Friars: Draft Action Area Plan*.

West Somerset DC (1979) *Stogursey: Interim Settlement Policy*.

Wheeler, P.T. (1977) 'The concept of the growth village and its application to English planning practice with special reference to the East Midlands', Paper presented to the Anglo-Hungarian Symposium, Bucharest.

Whitby, M.C. and Willis, K.G. (1978) *Rural Resource Development: An Economic Approach*, London, Methuen.

Whitehead, P.T. (1976) 'Public participation in structure planning', *Town Planning Review*, 47, 347–83.

Whitelaw, J.S. (1962) 'The measurement of urban influence in the Waikato', *New Zealand Geographer*, 18, 72–92.

Wibberley, G.P. (1978) 'A future for the countryside?', *District Councils Review*, November, 250–1.

Wibberley, G.P. (1978a) 'Mobility in the countryside', in Cresswell, R. (ed.) (1978) *Rural Transport and Country Planning*, Glasgow, Hill.

Willis, K.G. (1980) *The Economics of Town and Country Planning*, St Albans, Granada.

Wilmers, P. (1981) 'Planning, self-help and mutual aid', *The Planner*, 67, 59.

Wilson, A.G. (1969) *The Use of Analogies in Geography*, London, Centre for Environmental Studies.

Wiltshire CC (1953) *County Development Plan*.

Wiltshire CC (1959) *County Development Plan*.

Wiltshire CC (1970) *Salisbury sub-regional Study*.

Wiltshire CC (1979) *South Wiltshire Structure Plan: Submitted Written Statement*.

Wiltshire CC (1979a) *West Wiltshire Structure Plan: Submitted Written Statement*.

Wiltshire CC (1980) *North-east Wiltshire Structure Plan: Submitted Written Statement*.

Winter, H. (1980) *Homes for Locals?*, Exeter, Community Council of Devon.

Winyard, S. (1978) 'Low pay and farmworkers', in Walker, A. (ed.) (1978) *Rural Poverty: Poverty, Deprivation and Planning in Rural Areas*, London, Child Poverty Action Group.

Wolfenden Committee (1977) *The Future of Voluntary Organizations*, London, Croom Helm.

Woodruffe, B.J. (1976) *Rural Settlement Policies and Plans*, Oxford University Press.

Woollett, S. (1981) *Alternative Rural Services*, London, NCVO.

Woollett, S. (1981a) 'Providing your own community services', *The Planner*, 67, 72–3.

Wools, R. (1978) 'Conservation in the counties', *Building Design*, 424, 8–9.

Working Party on Rural Settlement Policies (1979) *A Future for the Village*, Bristol, HMSO.

Wye College, (1980) *Conflicts in the Countryside: Comments to the Countryside Review Committee*, Wye College Department of Environmental Studies and Countryside Planning.

Yeovil DC (1980) *Bruton Interim District Plan: Written Statement*.

Yorkshire and Humberside Economic Planning Board (1976) *The Pennine Uplands: Socio-Economic Interactions and Opportunities in the Yorkshire Pennines*, London, HMSO.

Yorkshire Dales National Park Committee (1979) *Local Plan Policy Framework*.

Young, K. (ed.) (1975) *Essays on the Study of Urban Politics*, London, Macmillan.

Author index

Adams, J.G.L., 325
Allison, L., 70
Ambrose, P., 35
Anderson, M.A., 307
Armstrong, J., 164
Ash, M., 213
Ashworth, W., 74
Association of County Councils, 16, 17, 22, 37, 40, 198, 216, 218, 219, 334
Association of District Councils, 16, 334, 344
Atkinson, J.R., 93–4
Austin, D., 14
Avon CC, 151, 192
Ayton, J.B., 27, 61, 64, 169, 171

Bailey, J., 13, 51
Bajan, K., 14
Banks, P., 311
Barnard, T., 286
Barnum, H.G., 60
Barr, J., 94
Barras, R., 131
Bassetlaw DC, 278–9
Batty, M., 2
Baynes, R., 87
Beale, C.L., 324
Beardmore, D., 267
Beavon, K.S.O., 56
Bedfordshire CC, 104, 127, 157
Bell, C., 36, 47, 206, 211
Bentham, C.G., 220
Beresford, P. and Beresford, S., 326
Berkshire CC, 101, 157, 190, 192–3, 305
Berry, B.J.L., 56, 60, 324
Berwickshire CC, 99
Best, R.H., 30, 31
Blacksell, M., 224–8, 290, 291, 297, 306, 307, 319, 334
Blake, J., 206
Blenkinsop, A., 296
Blondel, J., 210
Blowers, A., 94, 96, 206, 207, 210, 211, 214
Boaden, N., 232
Bonham-Carter, V., 16, 23
Bowley, M., 75

Boyle, R., 145
Bracey, H.E., 58–9
Bracken, I., 119
Braybrooke, D., 232
Breakell, M., 337
Brecon Beacons National Park Committee, 295
Broadbent, T.A., 47, 48, 59, 131
Brush, J.E., 58
Bryant, C.R., 24
Buckinghamshire CC, 131, 157, 260–3, 311
Buckley, W., 210
Bulpitt, J.G., 206
Burrell, T., 31–2
Burton, S.H., 178
Butcher, H., 338
Buttel, F.H., 13
Buxton, R., 210
Byrne, S., 347

Caddy, C., 265, 287–9
Caernarvonshire CC, 105
Cambridgeshire CC, 90, 98, 149–50, 152, 190, 270
Cambridgeshire Joint Town Planning Committee, 76
Camhis, M., 49
Cantell, T., 316, 319
Caradon DC, 271
Chadwick, G., 2
Champion, A.G., 18–19
Chapman, K., 56, 59
Cherry, G.E., 16, 47, 74, 333, 334
Cheshire CC, 129, 143, 159
Chisholm, M., 23
Christaller, W., 56
Clark, D., 329, 342, 343
Clark, G., 87, 301–2
Clarkson, S., 337
Clawson, M., 25, 60
Cleveland CC, 156
Clout, H.D., 24, 60, 311
Clwyd CC, 149, 153
Cohen, M.D., 240
Cole, I., 338
Coleman, A.M., 30

Subject index